WITHDRAWN FROM
THE LIBRARY
UNIVERSITY OF
WINCHESTER

D0266227

KINGSLEY

KINGSLEY

THE LIFE, LETTERS AND
DIARIES OF

KINGSLEY MARTIN

by

C. H. ROLPH

LONDON
VICTOR GOLLANCZ LTD
1973

ISBN 0 575 01636 1

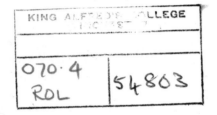

Printed in Great Britain by
The Camelot Press Ltd, London and Southampton

ACKNOWLEDGMENTS

I SUPPOSE THE first biography of any man, or *the* biography if there is never to be another, should be written (as this one is) by someone who knew him well, or thought he did. It seems that it is by no means usual. Among the multitudes who knew Kingsley Martin I found men and women who would, I am certain, present him more vividly and memorably than I, some more kindly, some less. Many of them talked about him to me for hours, and I wish to thank them all collectively for their patience while congratulating them enviously on their memories. The names of most of them appear in the text and, of course, the Index (and for that, I must not omit to thank Miss Evelyn M. Edwards). To the others I offer, as well as thanks, my apologies that they are unnamed, and the explanation that to name them all would have been to produce a huge roll-call padded out with linking paragraphs, a journalistic exercise in name-dropping. For Kingsley seems to have known nearly everyone, while the small remainder felt as if they knew him. I need also the forgiveness of the many people, both here and abroad, whom I was unable in the time available to see or to consult, though they had all offered their help. With another five years I might have written a better book; with another ten, a worse.

In particular, I must thank the following for their permission to reproduce passages from books and private letters: Mr Herbert Agar, Irene and Peggy Barclay (Kingsley's sisters, who are largely to blame for the book's being written at all), Dame Margaret Cole, Professor Donald Davie, Mrs Marguerite Dowdeswell, Granada Television Ltd, David Higham Associates Ltd, Professor Lancelot Hogben, Mr Graham Hutton, Hutchinson Publishing Group Ltd, the executors of Maynard Keynes for extracts from his letters, Professor Dan H. Laurence and the Society of Authors (for a Bernard Shaw letter), the London School of Economics (British Library of Political and Economic

Science), Mrs Sonia Orwell and Penguin Books Ltd, the Lady Stocks, Sir Francis Meynell, the University of Sussex (for access to all Kingsley's private papers and to Tom Harrisson's Mass Observation archive), the Lady Uvedale, and Professor Otakar Vočadlo.

For permission to reproduce photographs: Kingsley's sisters, Irene and Peggy Barclay, for family photographs; Mr Frank Woodman for those of his sister Dorothy; Mrs Lucille Shand for the pictures of "Mr Park" and Kingsley's cottage at Little Easton; Mr Arthur Wang for the photograph of himself playing (and, I gather, winning) a game of chess with Kingsley; Mrs Ninka Copley for the snapshot of herself with Kingsley in Venice; *The Times* for the photograph of the interior at number 1 Robert Street; and, I am proud to say, Mr Michael Ayrton for his drawing of Kingsley, so far as I know the only portrait of him in his last decade.

CONTENTS

LIST OF ILLUSTRATIONS

Chapter 1

INTRODUCTORY

IT WAS ONE of Kingsley Martin's minor sources of pride, though not always of pleasure, that he had a vivid and detailed memory of early childhood. Elaborating this in some competitive discussion he would say that he clearly remembered the moment when he was first able to walk without holding somebody's hand. And then he would recall the helpless fury with which, having once accomplished this, he felt his hand seized by a grown-up with whom he was about to cross a road. He told the tale often, as he told any tale (you might well have heard it before) from which it was possible to draw a moral. This one meant that if you held a child's hand at all while the two of you crossed the road, you must hold it so tightly that escape was impossible. Otherwise he might suddenly run loose more dangerously than if you had let him walk alone.

In a sense, it was the story of Kingsley's life; of his wish to find dependent hands and hold them, to be guide and leader to those more bewildered than he; and of his lifelong difficulty in doing so because he was never intellectually certain which road he was crossing. The destination was known and noble, the route unplanned and tentative. To some extent his father had been the same. It is astonishing how many people who knew Kingsley Martin, or thought they did, will say "His trouble was that his father" (the Reverend Basil Martin, of whom more later) "gave him no chance to quarrel with him". The surprise is but slightly diminished when you come across that precise phrase in his own autobiography.[1] What trouble was this supposed to explain? (The theme of *Father Figures* is that because his father was completely tolerant and wonderfully understanding, he remained under the paternal influence for too long. In later years people like Sir William Beveridge and C. P. Scott tried to be father figures to him, and he

[1] *Father Figures*, Hutchinson, 1966, p. 26.

quarrelled with them usefully and valuably.) Kingsley was a complex man, some said a maddening man, but any man with his intelligence, warmth, and essential simplicity is likely to exhibit his nature unintentionally. He will be, as Kingsley was, wide open to criticism and misunderstanding. It need have nothing to do with even the most dominating of fathers, and Basil Martin did no dominating at home—his children subsequently saw him as "tolerant almost to a fault—the trouble was that he set us all an impossibly high moral standard, and Kingsley identified with him in his youth and early manhood."[1] I think it will be obvious as this story of his life develops that Kingsley's legacy from his "unwitting and entirely lovable" father was a lifelong burden of irrational guilt and an ineradicable self-reproach. Everything was his fault.

It would be sad if the only "live" portrait of Kingsley were to be the one he offers in his two volumes of autobiography, where the self-denigration is as pathological as the occasional vanity; the portrait is very largely wrong. He could not, I am sure, allow himself to be fully known by anyone—though there were one or two women to whom he unburdened himself more than to any man, among these being his elder sister. Indeed, a certain aptitude in the assessment of others impeded (as it paradoxically may) any confident knowledge of himself. He gave his various inner personalities little time to observe or to reveal themselves to each other, so he remained always a number of men. "He was not an *integrated* man," Arthur Koestler told me; and coming from that contemplative student of men it is a judgment to make one thoughtful about the incomplete men who made up Kingsley Martin. Since this is a book about one of them, with glimpses of or guesses about the others, it may well be deficient by many omissions, not to say wrong attributions and uncertain pigeon-holing. Moreover, as Lord David Cecil said in presenting his biography of Melbourne,[2] "It is mainly the story of the influence exerted on his spirit by other characters and their activities. To understand him, we must understand them." So there will be discursiveness and a necessarily selective portrait gallery, for Kingsley was a man

[1] A personal communication to me from Kingsley's younger sister.

[2] *The Young Melbourne*, Constable, 1939.

with many friends, a few enemies, and a multitude of influential acquaintances. And if he tended to speak of the latter as "friends" on the slightest of grounds, it was because of his pleasure in knowing them at all: he took endless delight in meeting people, but they had to be in some way interesting.

He edited the *New Statesman*, and it was the capacity in which he was best known, for 30 years. Whether or not he "made" the paper as it is known today, a question that must figure largely in this book, it grew in those 30 years from a small, élitist, political journal (Michael Foot saw it then as "an ailing, not-very-distinguished Fabian weekly") into the liveliest and best written "journal of protest" in the English-speaking world. Accordingly, an account of his life must also be the story of that journal and the times it mirrored; and in its preparation I have had the help of many writers and politicians. To these (with, I hope, few omissions) I have recorded my acknowledgments on page 5; and although their recollections were as confusing and contradictory as the man himself—there was no unanimity, for example, on his capacity as an editor, some critics seeing him as a lucky one and some as a near-genius—I met none who dissented from my own verdict that he was a brilliant journalist, a man of fundamental kindness, and one with a sort of happy genius for vicarious suffering. The miseries of the world appalled him, though he might have been even less happy without them. And his lifelong, sometimes obsessive misery was an unfounded fear that he had hurt the deepest feelings of a succession of women.

He had other ambitions, and in private conversation would reveal, as to some of them, that their non-realisation was a humiliation to him. He wanted to be a history professor, and believed himself to have been cheated of that career by a trick of fate. To some of his friends he seems to have had a conception of himself as a much-loved teaching philosopher, in the tradition of G. E. Moore and the great Cambridge philosophy school in whose "marvellous afterglow" he spent his undergraduate days, walking and talking with that lovable pedagogue Lowes Dickinson. (It is typical of his many-sidedness that he would often, nevertheless, assert that philosophy was a closed book to him. More than once he reminded me gleefully of H. L.

Mencken's discovery that there is no record in human history of a happy philosopher.) He wanted, at one time, to edit a great newspaper like *The Guardian*, a job for which he was really unfitted. In early life he wanted to be a preacher, which may explain why he used the front page of the *New Statesman*, and much of the London Diary, as a pulpit. He had also wanted to be an actor. But to some of these preoccupations I will return later. He never wanted to be a public servant, a lawyer, or a career politician. In his final years he had passionately wanted to be a "television personality"—he told me that it amounted to a wretched longing, and the confession (for that was how I saw it) left me speechless. What an odd ambition in such a man! He was not even a particularly good broadcaster, did not read well from a prepared script (you could always tell he was reading), and fell over his words when unscripted: defects which the television cameras and technicians will always accentuate.[1] Envy contributed much to what he would privately describe as this "terrible humiliation"; envy of his friends' success as television performers—John Freeman, A. J. P. Taylor, Malcolm Muggeridge, Lord Boothby, Norman MacKenzie. Television's attraction for him was its scope for actor and teacher combined, rather (I think) than the limelight and the likelihood of more people nudging each other in the street when they saw him.

If didacticism were the test, he was a born teacher and it was this that had drawn him to the academic life, on which he turned his back for ever when he left the London School of Economics to join the *Manchester Guardian* in 1927; though he made at least two attempts, in 1934 and 1950, to return to it. Indistinct and diffuse as a lecturer, he was nevertheless an infectious and kindly mentor in a small seminar or tutorial: he genuinely loved stimulating a young mind to enquiry. And in propitious after-dinner company he was a scintillating talker—rather than a listener. (Lady Wootton once said that there are

[1] T. C. Worsley, one of the best dramatic critics the *New Statesman* has had and later its literary editor, wrote a play which was produced at the Bristol Old Vic and was not successful. He was bitterly disappointed. Kingsley knew he was and tried to comfort him with the story of his (own) "humiliation" as a television reject.

two kinds of conversation. One is like tennis, in which you return your opponent's ball as regularly and often as you can, and the other like golf, in which you keep on playing your own and just leave a space for your opponent to use. Kingsley's, she said, was more like golf.)

But those who came under his tutelage, whether captive or not, remembered him vividly as a teacher. It began when he was nine years old and nourished itself on his sister Peggy, who was three. At that age he taught her patiently and successfully how to set up a chess-board; and at five she had learned from him the whole of the Greek alphabet. Neither of these accomplishments she ever forgot. He used to set her examination papers in a variety of subjects, which she completed because she enjoyed learning, admired her brother, wanted him to think well of her, was interested in being clever rather than "good", and was nevertheless overawed by him (though, she once said, he would probably have been very surprised to know all this). He was almost, you might say, in the tradition recalled by Dr Arnold of Rugby, whose father presented him at the age of three with the 24 volumes of Smollett's *History of England* "as a reward for proficiency in his studies".[1]

Later he taught enthusiastically at WEA lectures and at summer schools. It was the experience of some writers that, as an editor, he was teaching, teaching all the time, at least in dealing with non-staff contributors. (If you were on the *New Statesman* editorial staff you were supposed to know how to write an article.) Having glanced quickly through a proffered piece, he would stand in his office looking out over Lincoln's Inn Fields and ask what it meant. Not unkindly or derisively, but in a tone of slightly squeaky and worried perplexity. Each attempt to explain would provoke further questions, many of them of the kind that you would hear only from a judge sitting with a specially simian-looking jury, or from a child listening unwillingly to a difficult story. And then suddenly he would wheel round and say: "Now, why on earth don't you go away and write all that before you forget it?" The author would pick up his battered baby and make for the door, which, if he was at all sensitive, he would have closed before the discussion

[1] Quoted in Lytton Strachey's *Queen Victoria*, Penguin, p. 163.

began (it usually stood open). But if he looked back as he left, he would probably see Kingsley smiling and nodding in a way that could make him seem the very embodiment of benevolence. And this in many ways he was.

But it was not entirely benevolence, although he was a great encourager of young writers—nor was it entirely the simulated ignorance of a teacher playing the role of fat-headed listener: the range of Kingsley's genuine ignorance about worldly and scientific things was a source of constant amazement to the lesser men about him. (He once asked his colleagues what a turf accountant was. What was difficult about turfs?) It was also, and this I hope will become increasingly plain as this book proceeds, the source of his strength as a journalist. It made him ask all the right questions, the simplest questions, and he asked them with an unselfconsciousness that many of us could envy. "I have always admired your tactlessness as a questioner," V. S. Pritchett wrote to him in an open *New Statesman* letter on his 70th birthday, "and have marvelled at what you get out of people." Often the most elementary of statements, as that sherry contains brandy, or that modern cars have a differential back axle, or that prostitutes don't usually *want* to be "rescued" (I think of three genuine instances), would be greeted with the familiar semi-falsetto "Oh *really*?" Once in his fifties he came across the word menopause, and asked a number of women on the staff if that was what they called it? At the same time if he knew some such thing and discovered that you didn't, his pitying surprise could be withering. "He could be *very* damaging with his superiority," his sister Peggy told me, "and he spoke to people as if they were always his intellectual equals, reacting badly when he found they were not, and losing patience with them inexcusably."

Add to all this that he was a hereditary puritan, an agnostic of the kind that must whistle loudly when the dark comes down (in his last few years he was terrified of death), a man of the Enlightenment, a pacifist who supported war because of the Fascists, a self-styled skinflint who loved to perform acts of staggering generosity, and a man who was always powerfully (though to some of us inexplicably) attractive to women, and you have the material for a very odd kind of portrait. I hope this may nevertheless be a recognisable and convincing one. It would deserve to fail if it added up to no more than the picture of a high-powered editor and journalist, exercising a fluctuating influence on politicians and publicists throughout the world for 30 fateful years.

Kingsley Martin's editorship had a special quality which I think has never been fully realised, and has certainly not been emulated: he established and maintained an intimate contact with the intelligent poor. Among his papers I found a letter from a reader which illustrates this precisely:

> I have often wondered if you realise the great affection there is for your paper among people like us, working class people with only elementary schooling. In fact I don't think love too strong a word, when it's considered that the cost probably comes out of the food money. There are so many of us to whom "Monday flares like petrol when it sees me advancing with my prison face". Opening it is like going into a club where you have friends, where no-one is a bore and there is always something exciting going on. The world seems a more worthwhile place after reading it, however perturbing the actual news. My uncles, who are shipyard workers (I come from the North of England) consider it a wonderful achievement to have a letter printed in the correspondence columns or rate a mention in the competitions. Even in the 'dole' days we used somehow to manage to get hold of a copy and circulate it. It is so *sustaining*; and the incidental information—in the reviews for instance—can do a great deal towards widening an outlook when formal education has been meagre.[1]

Kingsley's two volumes of autobiography, and even his private diaries, are lamentably short of dates. In his later years, almost anything he wrote without the supervision of a secretary went undated. The sorting of his handwritten notes and letters involves much chronological coin-spinning. So it may be helpful if I set out here some rough indication of his life's time-schedule.[2]

[1] Letter from Mrs Joyce Sanderson of Harold Wood, Essex, dated 18 February 1954. Private collection, University of Sussex.

[2] I am against any additions to the criminal law, but I would like to see some sanction against datelessness, as, I think, would anyone who has had to sort out the posthumous papers of an unmethodical man. And I speak

He was born on 28th July 1897 and died on 17th February 1969. He lived in Hereford from his birth until 1913, then at Finchley, North London, until 1917 when he joined the Friends' Ambulance Unit for war service. In 1919 he went up to Cambridge University, he held a Princeton Fellowship from 1922 to 1923, and he returned to Cambridge as a Bye-fellow at Magdalene during 1923. From 1924 until 1927 he was lecturing at the London School of Economics and Political Science; and it was towards the end of that period, in 1926, that he married Olga Walters (see Chapter VII). From 1927 to 1930 he was a leader-writer on the *Manchester Guardian*, from 1930 to 1960 Editor of the *New Statesman*; and from 1935 onwards he was living, at first intermittently and from 1942 permanently, with Dorothy Woodman, Olga having left him in 1934. His last nine years, 1960 to 1969, he spent writing and travelling in a condition of failing health but steadfast refusal to accept a state of "retirement". Dates make for dull reading, but they are indispensable and there they are.

For the benefit of anyone who had the misfortune not to know the man or his paper, the foregoing is an outline of what Kingsley Martin was, what he did, and when. It gets a little nearer, I hope, than he did himself to the business of settling *who* he was. Writing about him in a short book of commemoration when he died,[1] Dr Anthony Storr recorded a psychiatrist's view of Kingsley's own anxious pursuit of identity, though it was the view also of a close personal friend:

> If, all one's life, one is looking for who one truly is, one has to remain open to other people, hoping to learn from them, hoping to find something new which one can incorporate into oneself, and thus strengthen and build one's identity.

It was a man thus engrossed in self-exploration who found

not only of the thousands of undated letters and lecture-notes and memoranda, but of numerous printed pamphlets, books, and propaganda sheets. Alas, even as I write, the *New Statesman* has just published its answer to the Tory Government's 1970 white paper on The Common Market. It is called "The Case Against Entry". And for the benefit of future historians and archivists, it is totally undated.

[1] *Kingsley Martin: Portrait and Self-Portrait*, edited by Mervyn Jones, Barrie and Jenkins, London, 1969.

himself editing an already unique journal of opinion at the opening of the thirties. He brought with him the loyalty of a number of good writers from Cambridge, the LSE and the *Manchester Guardian*, and editorially he inherited a further galaxy from *The Nation*, which under Hubert Henderson was then probably the best journal of its kind in the world. It had become too left-wing for its owners, the Rowntrees, who had just at that time been induced by Maynard Keynes to sell it to the *New Statesman*. It was a conjunction that was certain to excite tensions, produce explosions, and establish an author-and-public relationship as personalised as that enjoyed by Dickens himself. The long story of that relationship falls into four essential parts: the thirties, Hitler's war, the period of colonial "liberation", and the Cold War (which Kingsley considered a tragedy second only to the shooting war which it followed).

All these phases are still represented by outstanding personalities who knew and influenced him—or were influenced by him. They include, besides Olga his unhappy wife and Dorothy his subsequent companion, a number of interesting women with whom he was on terms of intimate and adventurous, but often frustrating, friendship. The publisher of his autobiography was constrained to ask him whether there were really no women in his life. There were, he replied (in effect), but they were not what he was writing about. I suppose they belonged elsewhere, perhaps in some other book. This one, it is certain, would be incomplete without them, but it gives no names where naming would give offence or hurt.

Enquiry into Kingsley's life and friendships and spheres of influence could doubtless go on for another lifetime as long as his own. I suppose that could be true of any of us if we were thought interesting enough—and even if we had not kept our diaries and our friends' letters and written millions of words in the public prints. But I recall that there hangs in a room at the Institute of Historical Research at London University a resounding exhortation from Dr Samuel Johnson, urging writers to "imitate the diligence and avoid the scrupulosity" of those learned perfectionists who "polished and polished and went to the grave with their labours unpublished".

Chapter 2

CHILDHOOD

KINGSLEY'S PARENTS WENT to live in Hereford in 1893. His father, the Rev. Basil Martin, who tells his own remarkable story in *An Impossible Parson*,[1] had been superintendent of a mission set up in Kentish Town by the Lyndhurst Road Congregational Church, Hampstead. He was finding that stronghold of dissenting respectability "a hothouse in which he could not breathe", when he received "a cordial invitation to the pastorate of Eignbrook Congregational Church, Hereford"; and this, he says, "enabled me to get married and thus commence a period of united happiness which lasted more than 41 years". He took up the ministry in January 1893 and married on 13th April. Kingsley's elder sister Irene was born just over a year later at their first Hereford house in Ingestre Street, and Kingsley himself on 28th July 1897, at number 147 Whitecross Road, Hereford (it is now number 210). This house was then, as he says in *Father Figures*,[2] "on the edge of the country", the last building as you went out of Hereford towards the White Cross. (And the White Cross, half a mile further on, has stood there since the fourteenth century, when it marked the place where people could leave their market produce for collection instead of bringing it into the plague-ridden city.) An agreeable house, he calls it, from which the family, to the vociferous disgust of Kingsley as a six-year-old, had to move because its owner had sold it "over their heads" to a Hereford publican who wanted immediate possession.

It is a square-built, semi-detached house on three floors, surrounded and darkened now by a straggling and neglected shrubbery which was once a fine orchard. It still has many a counterpart in suburban London, with peeling walls, rising

[1] Allen & Unwin, London, 1935.
[2] Hutchinson, London, 1966.

damp, and tattily improvised nameplates under rusting bell-pushes which evoke no response. You can see that it was once the "last house", for the building line was set back when the road was extended, imparting to it now a rather cruel conspicuousness. Kingsley, who had heard the grown-ups discussing the misfortune that had befallen them and deploring the necessity to move, was prejudiced from the outset against the home to which he was being taken; but he is justified in describing this as "a poky, ill-favoured place in a terrace".[1] It is half a mile further citywards along the Whitecross Road, and is the double-fronted central section of a six-house terrace, built in red brick, and three storeys high. It now calls itself a guest-house, bed and breakfast only; and its paved front garden has been covered with toy windmills, little bridges over goldfish-pools, plastic penguins looking disoriented and the inevitable angling gnomes.

But those gnomes, and the featureless modern turmoil of Whitecross Road, are within a few hundred yards of one of the quietest and most beautiful cathedral precincts in England. The Cathedral School, where Kingsley learned, eclipsed his classmates, played, pondered, suffered and swanked, is as timeless and inviolate as an Oxbridge college. There are people living in its shade who remember the Martin family, though that family left the city as long ago as 1913; and I have talked to present-day members of the Eignbrook Congregational Church who were friends of the Martins from 1900 onwards. The Rev. Basil Martin and his wife, loved and cherished there for 20 years, have left in that church community—and outside it—a reputation for goodness of a kind that seems rarer today.

Basil Martin's ministry, nonetheless, had failed to endear him to those of his congregation to whom chapel-going was no more than the social conformity of the time. The sad circumstances of his departure in 1913 could never have been foreseen by William Collins, the historian of his church and a much respected Hereford tradesman, or those others of the Church Meeting which had invited him to take up the ministry on 29th December 1893. "We trust you will not find us stereotyped

[1] *Father Figures*, p. 18.

in any of our modes of thought," said the invitation,[1] "nor yet wedded to particular methods of action. Convince us of a more excellent way of doing good, and widening our sphere of influence, and we will cheerfully walk in it." Having recorded which, Mr Collins adds:

> The moment the pulpit ceases to voice the terrible social and economic evils that are eating out the vitals of the nation, out of deference to the man in the square pew[2] it is prostituting its high calling. Preaching is not the narration of facts. It is the discovery of ideas behind the facts. Mr Martin has few compeers in the sphere of ideas. He is a philosopher by nature and by training, capable of high effort and self-sacrifice, but incapable of selling his conscience for a mess of pottage or saying in the pulpit what he does not believe in his heart.

Yet "many times he had been misunderstood, misrepresented and misjudged by his fellow Christians, mainly because the atmosphere he breathed was different". His "transparency of thought, sincerity of conviction, and purity of motive have brought him many difficulties and disappointments. The fact is, he has fed his people at times with the strong meat of the Word when they were fit only to be fed on milk, and the result was theological dyspepsia. The critics outside and inside his church did not try to understand his point of view, which, of course, is in advance of Nonconformist opinion; and some of his own people failed to see how closely politics and theology were allied."

Basil Martin preached socialism and pacifism to a congregation upon whose conventional burgesses and prosperous farmers he depended for his income. These loved him less than the poorer members did, and in the end they made his ministry untenable. But Kingsley may be less fair to them in his autobiography than the history of nonconformity will excuse.[3] The reactionary Cavalier Parliament of 1661 had been, as Macaulay said, "more zealous for Royalty than the King, more zealous

[1] William Collins, *The Congregational Church, Hereford*, C. E. Brumwell, 10 Broad Street, Hereford, 1913, pp. 63–5.

[2] i.e. the well-to-do church member who rented a pew with its own "stable door".

[3] *Father Figures*, p. 42.

for episcopacy than the Bishops". It had been the theory of every English government that religious nonconformity was tantamount to civil disobedience, and to be punished accordingly. The Conventicle Act of 1664 made attendance at religious meetings other than those of the Established Church punishable by fines, later by transportation for a third offence, and then by death for those who returned from transportation. This was why the original "manse" of the Eignbrook Congregational Church, still to be seen in Hereford, had been built without ground-floor windows: thus were the King's bailiffs prevented from spying upon the members at their unlawful assemblies for worship. The house also has an underground escape route, recently discovered by excavation next door. Dissenters went in fear for their liberty and their lives. It was a long time ago, but it was an unforgettable heritage. Such hard-won "rights" are held dear, to the point of fanaticism, by men who *want* to believe in something.

And the Congregationalists were known as Dissenters and Heretics, even in Kingsley's childhood, by the Anglican clergy at the Cathedral, among whom he perforce spent much of his time as a schoolboy. Both words were terms of opprobrium. The Rev. Basil Martin's position was certainly the more difficult for being in a cathedral city, and it so happened that he had himself been the son of a dissenting minister, attending a Cathedral School (in the City of Oxford). He had become more widely known than any respectable minister would have been by reason of his condemnation of the Boer War and his advocacy of social reforms and pacifism. He should perhaps have known, from his experience as assistant to the Rev. Dr Horton at Lyndhurst Road Congregational Church, Hampstead, that these are not the cornerstones of the Congregational faith. He told Kingsley in later years that the distinguished Dr Horton (whose name is still revered in Congregational circles) "spoke as if God was his intimate counsellor and as if no-one with any sense ought to have any doubts or be troubled by the miseries of the poor". That has been said, cruelly and often, of many a good parson and many a sectarian faith; and it was sometimes said of the "Dissenters" in Hereford that they considered themselves privileged to know the seating plan for the

Kingdom of Heaven, where they had all the front seats, though there might be standing room for those few Anglicans who had been good enough to send parcels to nonconformist jumble sales.

It seems likely that Basil Martin, who had decided at the age of eighteen that he would follow his father into the Christian ministry, never seriously thought of leaving the Church in a lifetime of theological perplexity. In 1893, at the age of thirty-five, when he found that he couldn't get on with Dr Horton at Hampstead ("his intellectual and spiritual power alike so humiliated me that I never could be myself in his presence, or say a word to him that did not sound trivial"),[1] he was able to take his pick from a number of jobs open to him. Apart from the invitation to Hereford, there was the offer of a social-work appointment at Middlesbrough and another from Quintin Hogg at the Polytechnic, both of which, it is true, had the disadvantage of vagueness and uncertainty of tenure. But there may be wishful hindsight in Kingsley's reference to this period in his own autobiography:[2]

> It is quite clear to me that . . . Basil Martin would have left the ministry altogether at this point of his career if he had had anything to live on. . . . As it was, he had no alternative but to accept an invitation from a Congregational Church in the Cathedral town of Hereford. He desperately wanted to get married. . . .

It is clear that, on the contrary, there was no lack of alternatives, and equally clear in the recollection of Kingsley's sister Irene that their father wanted to stay in the ministry, to which he felt a genuine call. And twelve years afterwards at Hereford, Basil Martin made the following declaration of belief to a meeting of church members who had expressed concern about the radicalism of his preaching: "I believe in the atonement of Christ with all my heart. I believe in the inspiration of the Bible, but not in the sense that each word is indited by the Spirit of God. I believe in salvation through faith in Jesus Christ. I believe in a future life of rewards and punishments. I believe Jesus Christ is the Saviour of the World, and the

[1] *An Impossible Parson*, p. 85. [2] *Father Figures*, p. 37.

central truth of the New Testament teaching." He was not a man who could have brought himself, in whatever extremity, to make that declaration without meaning every word of it at the time. And the church deacons tactfully recorded in 1913, when he was leaving Eignbrook, that

> We have no need to recall the circumstances of 1905 which wrung from Mr Martin this declaration of belief, except to remark that it was made in the interests of truth and in defence of his ministerial character, as a teacher of religion.[1]

But Basil Martin had known what it was to be execrated in the streets and followed by jeering youths. If he was seen sitting in one of the horse-buses on his way to or from his church, stones were thrown at the bus windows. When he left the Church Hall on a week-night after "Christian Endeavour" classes, members of the class had to form a bodyguard and escort him home.

Among his enemies in that predominantly Anglican town were those who favoured the new Church of England Schools, and who knew that Basil Martin so heartily disapproved of them that he always deducted the education apportionment on his demand note for rates before settling up. Bailiffs thereupon called and took away some of his furniture, which friends bought back at the subsequent auctions and restored to him. This kind of charade was commonplace in the nonconformist world of Edwardian days, and played some part in the development of simpler and more lawful facilities for the exercise of the dissident conscience.

But his interest in education also took positive forms. He was a great believer in the contemporary "Adult School" movement and established the Men's Adult School attached to his church. It was a method of "teaching men how to live", by lectures and open discussion about history, literature, economics and citizenship; all of which, however, were considered subordinate to the "free study of the Scriptures". His wife was president of a similar school for women, which added hygiene, biology and domestic economy to its scripture study.

[1] William Collins, *The Congregational Church, Hereford*, p. 67.

Between them they "cheered many grey lives, and filled a niche in the temple of the common life of the people."[1] There was a National Adult School Union, and Basil was on its panel of lecturers for many years. When he retired from the ministry its week-end schools were his main preoccupation.

It was in this atmosphere that Kingsley spent his boyhood. In such circumstances you need to be absolutely certain that your father is right, for otherwise your existence and your father's, and the affronts that he suffers in the name of the family credo, become quite meaningless. To discuss all this with the few present-day members of the Eignbrook Congregational Church at Hereford who were members in Basil Martin's time is to realise that his stature, at least among the poorer members, was little short of heroic. He probably got the adulation given today to the politician, the pop-star, the TV personality, the "Any Questions" pundit, the football idol. There was no radio, and there was little money to buy newspapers. The dominant paper in Kingsley's circle was A. G. Gardiner's *Daily News*, which the Rev. Basil Martin read aloud to the family at breakfast time. (A. G. Gardiner's *Prophets, Priests and Kings* was read, at one time or another, by the entire family.) But most of the nonconformists in the neighbourhood would be split between the *South Wales Daily News* printed at Cardiff (it died in 1929), and the *Daily Chronicle* under Lloyd George. A friend of Basil Martin's, Robertson Nicoll, who was then the leading journalist in nonconformist affairs, was editing the *British Weekly*; and Basil Martin wrote occasional articles for him, though he profoundly disapproved of the paper and it was not often in the house. And there was the *Christian Herald*, in which the converted working-man would "give his testimony". Kingsley's boyhood acquaintance with periodical literature was largely of this kind; a detached acquaintanceship, on the whole, for his main interest was in books.

He was always a delicate child, in days when child funerals were depressingly frequent and had to be cheaply arranged: his parents were constantly worried about him. At the age of three, when in conformity with the current medical supersti-

[1] William Collins, *The Congregational Church, Hereford.*

tion he had his tonsils out, he went to stay in Birmingham with a wealthy relative (who, years later, was to stand him a convalescent trip to South Africa). He never forgot the tonsils operation, which was probably revived and then fixed in his memory by the death in 1915 of a seven-year-old brother, under a similar operation. This child, Hugh, had a congenital thyroid deficiency; he was a strangely intelligent little boy with an uncannily good memory, but late in talking and unable to learn like other children. Mrs Martin told friends at the time of his death that she would "rather he went than that he should not grow up like other children". But for a long time she was inconsolable.

Kingsley's illnesses as a boy were frequent, facilitating much reading in bed but also involving—in a way typical of the family and the period—his mother and his elder sister in long sessions of reading to him: Henry Seton Merriman, Stanley Weyman, Dickens, Rider Haggard, Baroness Orczy—and *Ivanhoe* (in a mercifully abridged edition) many times over. The whole family were great readers-aloud; which in those days was common among literate families with little or no money to spend on places of entertainment. Visitors to the house were assured of a welcome by the children if they would read a story. Speakers down from London for Basil Martin's Sunday afternoon "conferences" (which, truth to tell, were usually Socialist seminars) would often stay at his house—and read to his children. Among these was Mrs Despard, the suffragette leader, who read them *Alice in Wonderland* and was canonized from that day.

Some of Kingsley's illnesses he seems to have taken lightly enough, for his sister Irene recalls that when he was eight years old his mother, going to his bedroom one evening to resume an *Ivanhoe* reading, found him jumping up and down on the bed as if on a trampoline and shouting: "By the Beard of my Father Abraham I shall die of monotony!" He thought in later years that his father's "extraordinary tolerance" in relation to his children's reading was perhaps a mistake, and that they would have benefited much from more guidance at the hands of so well-read and thoughtful a man. It couldn't be said that Kingsley was in general a precocious reader, but at the age of ten he was enjoying the adventures of Baron Münchausen, unaware (he once told me) that like *Gulliver's Travels* the book was a satire, and convinced that the author was a liar. When Kingsley was editing the *New Statesman* he would defensively underline his dislike of special "travel supplements" and their supporting travel-agency advertisements by declaring that the author of Münchausen was the first man to produce one.

Perhaps because of his delicate health he was not an even-tempered boy. He was always pale, with prominent and over-bright eyes, constant colds and a chronic respiratory infection. He was lively and moody by turns, small, clever, cocky and cheeky. He was a day-boy at the Cathedral School whose first headmaster had been the Bishop of Hereford, appointed in 1381 to govern the boys "with birch and rod". If you were to judge from Kingsley's own account of the school (in *Father Figures*, page 51) the tradition might be thought to have persisted through six centuries; flogging and classical languages, in that order, being its main preoccupations. And here, having started with the undoubted handicap of a professionally dissenting father, he was unpopular, unhappy and bullied. Unforgivably, he had much to be cocky about, for he was not only habitually top of his form, or near it, but quite good at games as well, a combination as rare as it is intolerable. He hated school but was immensely eager to learn. Daily he set off willingly enough, though it would be carrying the thing too far to say that he did it with shining morning face. He was an unlikely boy to stand up to the school bullies, the memory of whom came in later life to engage an almost clinical interest in his mind. He was puzzled about bullies. He once showed Frank Hardie, a close friend of his in the thirties, the exact spot in Hereford where the school bully had made him buy an ice cream and watch until the bully had finished eating it. Kingsley always declared that his schooling was no doubt intended to be sound, imaginative and thorough, and that the headmaster in his time, Dr Wragge, was lucky in his staff. In particular, whenever he ruefully mentioned his lack of any deep musical appreciation, he would say that if the musical director of that school, Dr G. R. Sinclair, had failed to awaken him musically no one would ever do it. No one ever did: though he differed in this from other members of the family—and his paternal grandfather had the rare gift of "perfect pitch". Dr Sinclair, by the way, was a close friend of Elgar (who at the age of twenty-one was a violinist in the 1878 Three Choirs Festival at Hereford); and he is the subject of the eleventh Enigma Variation.

Kingsley as a boy seems in fact to have had few friends, belonging neither to the starchy Anglican world nor among the street-playing boys of the Whitecross Road area. The staunchest of these, with whom he maintained some contact throughout his life, though they drifted apart at the University stage, was T. J. F. York, a schoolmaster who died at Hastings in 1970 and who thought Kingsley's schoolday memories (like many of his unhappy recollections, not always of childhood) were highly selective. These two boys evolved a form of two-man cricket, to be played in convenient alley-ways. Each picked a team of his own favourite county players from a collection of cigarette-card portraits, impersonating them all in turn both at bowling and batting. Mrs York told me in 1971 how she had lately found that Kingsley had completely forgotten it. Inevitably he spent much of his time with his father or with grown-ups from among the tradespeople like "Shirty" Collins, the Hereford men's outfitter and a prolific local writer, who played chess with his father and taught him to do the same. Collins liked Kingsley because he took the trouble to get to know him. To some of these grown-ups he was an interesting boy. Dawdling home from school in his Eton collar and school cap, he would fall into step beside some total stranger in the street and engage him in conversation. In Edwardian Hereford this was precocious and incomprehensible in a child. To some he was badly brought up and ill-mannered to an extent that was thought shocking in a minister's son. Certainly he was disobedient at home and certainly he was duly spanked by his father. When, as editor and journalist, he came to campaign against corporal punishment, he was always quick to disown "any belief that you can't make children do what you want by hitting them". He knew that, for short periods, you could. But he raged against social injustice, as he saw it, and against cruelty to animals—no one remembers seeing him treat any animal other than gently, and there are relatively few boys of whom that could be said? The bellowings and the screams of animals being slaughtered in Hereford's famous cattle market were a constant nightmare to him, sending him home sometimes in tears.

From about 1905 to 1912 the Rev. Basil Martin's income varied between £200 and £250 a year. By contemporary standards this was not poverty in any absolute sense, but the duties of a minister's wife meant that Mrs Martin had to pay for domestic help, while the unofficial calls on the family purse would have kept them poor on double the income. That they got their three children to universities suggests something in the nature of a fiscal miracle. Travel and other treats were rare, holidays were cycling and walking tours—sometimes an "exchange" with another Congregationalist minister, which of course was no holiday for the parents. And the social round, to judge from the family letters, consisted mainly of church meetings and outings, bazaars, lectures and visits to relatives. They gained enormously, it must be said, by living in a country town. They had a summer season boat on the River Wye, an early love of wild life, holidays in the lush Welsh valleys where they stayed in farmhouses and went to bed by candle-light. They were all passionately fond of the countryside from their earliest years; and subsequent attempts, prompted by I know not what kind of jealous instinct, to present Kingsley as a townsman trying to be a countryman at his week-end cottage, could hardly be further from the truth.

Basil Martin and his wife taught their children (and Kingsley never forgot) the need for total honesty in affairs of money and property, leavened with the recognition that social injustice was widespread. But Kingsley also inherited much of his father's aptitude for honest thinking, and an acceptance that the perfect moral life was not merely unattainable but illusory. Basil Martin's essential credo is, perhaps, best summarised in his book *An Impossible Parson* (p. 79):

> Would it be possible to live a perfect life in a perfect world? Could there be any courage, generosity, patience or sympathy, where there was no sin or suffering? If there were no difficulties there would be no heroism. If there were no weakness there

> could be no compassion. If we had no enemies we could not be forgiving. Love itself would be a poor thing if it involved no self denial. . . . If we lived in perpetual sunshine we should never see the stars.

The story of a 1906 train journey to Ilfracombe, which illustrates some of this rather neatly, survives in the family memory because train-journey holidays were unusual. A full rail ticket was necessary for anyone over twelve and a half ticket for anyone over three. The two daughters, Irene and Peggy, were respectively just twelve and three. Basil Martin bought a full ticket for Irene and a half ticket for Peggy; and "rather for fun", Irene recalls, "when the man came along the train for tickets, father kept mine in his pocket. Nothing was said—the Inspector took it that I was under twelve, that Peggy was under three, and that Peggy's ticket was mine. It impressed us enormously. Father regarded cheating the railway as 'quite as bad as stealing a pair of boots'." And it is significant, perhaps, that he chose the pair of boots for his comparison, since a man who steals only one pair (as distinct from a shop-full or a truck-load) is likely to be stealing in need and in desperation. This non-Proudhonian view of theft, the more striking in a Christian socialist, can be illustrated by another incident of Kingsley's childhood.

A prominent member of the Eignbrook congregation, a "gentleman farmer" and a Liberal—in those days an unusual combination—had a fine farmhouse overlooking the Welsh valleys, and the Martin children often went there to see the daughters. One warm summer's evening the farmer's wife, who was much loved in the neighbourhood, was standing with the ten-year-old Kingsley at the huge farmhouse window looking across the meadows. Towards them, silhouetted against the setting sun, came a young man and a girl with their arms round each other, farmworkers returning after a day in the fields. "We wonder what's going to happen about them," said the farmer's wife to Kingsley. "Those two, you see, are very much in love but they can't afford to marry." And, as Kingsley used to recall, she clearly thought of it as something she might have read in a novel. She was objectively interested. It never entered her mind that if her husband paid them a living wage instead of the current twelve shillings a week they could have married. It was a picture that would be likely to remain in Kingsley's mind. (But it was from his mother, who was uncommitted politically, and not from his socialist father, that he got an explanation at that time: "You see, if a labourer on that farm fell ill, the farmer and his wife would be very kind to him. They would go round and take food to the man and his wife and see that the family didn't starve. But they would still not pay him a living wage.") That farmer, incidentally, was one of the church members whose disapproval of the Rev. Basil Martin, which was both profound and reciprocated, eventually brought his ministry to an end.

Kingsley had an even more political boyhood than the children of many a trade union leader. Most middle-class children of the period knew what it was, anyway, to spend hours in the boring company of talkative grown-ups, who seemed to have so many unoccupied hours to fill. Hereford grown-ups were always going on about the Tories and the Progressives, Free Trade, the Big Loaf and the Small Loaf, Chinese slavery, and Joseph Chamberlain with his monocle. And people who were children then will have no difficulty in recalling the never-ending street-corner conversations between neighbours and friends, conducted two or three feet above the heads of children waiting, with varying patience, for the adjournment that seemed as though it would never come. It was thus that Kingsley imbibed the milk of politics and found it, on the whole, less indigestible than did his contemporaries—or his sisters.

His parents had named him after Charles Kingsley, whom Basil Martin revered as a great Liberal, a Christian Socialist, a Chartist supporter and a champion of the poor. Kingsley himself said in later years that his own reverence for the author of *Hereward the Wake*, *Westward Ho!* and *The Water Babies* (none of which he had enjoyed reading anyway) was modified by the great man's anti-intellectualism. Charles Kingsley, he recalled, was contemptuous about George Eliot and Goethe, and got his Cambridge Professorship of Modern History on the strength of his having written three historical novels, none of them "modern"—and on the patronage of Queen Victoria, in which he had basked like any sycophantic Balmoral ghillie.

Politics were discussed interminably at family meal times. The younger sister, Peggy, found it all so boring that for the rest of her life she was unable to read a newspaper with interest or enjoyment, and even when she read history the political side of it repelled her. But the family involvement may be judged by this extract from a letter written by Mrs Martin to her elder daughter Irene on 12th January 1906, the year of the great Liberal revival:

> We are full of the election here—it grows more exciting every day, and now it is close at hand and no-one knows who will win. Father has gone to speak at a meeting at Westfields tonight, and they will be crowded out and perhaps have a lot of roughs to shout them down. Mr Aitken preached a sermon last Sunday *against* the Liberals, and last night a meeting was held in the White Cross Inn Room, and Mr Witts[1] called on him to repeat what had been said on Sunday. There was great excitement, and cries of "Shame" against Mr Aitken. Father comes home so delighted from all our good meetings he can't go to sleep. . . . Kingsley has a green and yellow Liberal favour pinned on his coat.

The election over and Campbell-Bannerman (the anti-imperialist) installed, the household resumed its more even tenor; but its tenor was always political because Basil Martin saw political action, in a society such as ours, as the means by which men with a regard for social justice could approach the achievement of the will of God. There was a fortnightly Hereford City Parliament, in effect a political debating society. Basil Martin was the leader of its Independent Labour Party. This is how the record of its first meeting began:

> THE OPENING OF PARLIAMENT
>
> *November 21st 1908*
>
> Only the initiated know the immense amount of thought and labour involved in the opening of a new Parliament. Some of its glory was shorn by the absence of the King and Queen, which only gave emphasis to the decreasing powers of the Monarchy.

[1] The principal draper in town. He became an Alderman and Mayor of Hereford and was still, in his eighties, active as a leading Liberal when Frank Owen won the sensational Liberal victory at Hereford in the 1929 By-Election.

> The country is Republican in everything save name. Monarchy owes its existence and perpetuation not to politics, but to religion. The hard facts of history prove this. A republic is the ideal form of self-government in which supreme power is vested in the people and is directly exercised by them. The trend of public thought, nay of world thought, is in this direction. The aristocracy is a patent nobility, a closed phalanx, the creation and plaything of Monarchy. It is not a guarantee either of character or intellect. We are not fools enough to think that a king by scribbling a man's name upon a bit of parchment is making a nobler superior creature out of a common human being. It is a huge mistake to think we are governed by King and Parliament. As a plain matter of fact we are governed by successive cabinets which ignore the King and often the House of Commons too. The moment guidance ceases to come from the people, that moment Parliament loses the motive power of her existence. God save the people![1]

A prominent member was Laurence Housman, whom the same record describes as "one of the ablest exponents of jingoism on the Unionist benches", and who had not then written his famous plays but was art critic on the *Manchester Guardian.* Kingsley, who greatly admired him, was to see him in the course of his long life become a pacifist, a feminist, a socialist and finally a Quaker. Housman and Basil Martin were the best of friends; and the same book records Housman as saying that "the Rev. Basil Martin, the leader of the ILP, sees good in everything and believes the world is moving in the direction of a collective social system".

By the end of October the Rev. Basil, away from home at a conference, was writing to his ten-year-old son:

> I sent you my fourth move on Saturday: I don't know why you failed to receive it. So now I am doing what is very rash—I am sending you three more moves all at once:
>
> Pawn to Queen's Bishop 3
> Pawn to Queen's Rook's 3
> Rook to King's square.

Politics, ill-health, reading, chess, religion—Cathedral School all the week and Congregationalism all the weekend—cycling,

[1] *All Round the City*, Wm Collins, 14 High Street, Hereford, 1909.

visiting relatives, bird's-nesting (and a huge collection of birds' eggs), stamp-collecting, boating on the River Wye, and books, books, books: these were the threads in Kingsley's boyhood. But not writing. He was not one of those precociously compulsive scribblers of whom everyone will say confidently (and, as a rule, wrongly): "He's sure to be a writer." Until he was about fourteen it was difficult to get him to write the simplest letter (as may be guessed from the chess letter above). The man who did as much as anyone to introduce him to the world of books was Mr C. E. Brumwell, the bookseller whose pretty shop still stands at number 10 Broad Street, Hereford, and who presented a collection of Chinese pieces to the Hereford City Library where they are still exhibited. (A man well known to the Martin family was master of the City workhouses and the father of Gilbert Harding, who was born on those premises and became, in his last years, what Kingsley would have loved to be—a television personality. It is a sobering reflection, and might have surprised Kingsley today, that there can be few people under 30 to whom Gilbert Harding's name means anything whatsoever.)

Towards the end of 1912 it had become plain to everyone that Basil Martin's ministry at Eignbrook Congregational Church was coming to an end. The really unmistakable sign that his radicalism had finally lost favour with the prosperous business men who formed the finance committee—and who therefore ran the church and paid him—was the steady fall in the amount of money they were willing to let him have. "I wish you were at home tonight," wrote Mrs Martin on 14th November 1912 to their daughter Irene, now aged eighteen and staying with an aunt in London. "It is seven o'clock and father has just gone round to the Meeting." It was a meeting of the Finance Committee at which a "vote of confidence in the Minister" was to be contested. "I feel very sick about it now the time has actually come. . . . In my heart I know we can't have a home in Hereford much longer." And when the result of the meeting was known—a vote of 50 in favour and 11 against—Basil Martin knew nevertheless that he must go. One member had stood up, said he was ashamed of the debt to the Minister, and offered to give £5 at once towards wiping it off. But, he added, he always felt that Eignbrook was a cold place, and often wished that the Minister could put a little more warmth into his manner. It was an observation that no doubt did much to qualify such comfort as was to be drawn from the vote of confidence. It may have derived from the generally accepted fact that the Minister had little "small talk" and spoke, even in gossipy surroundings, pithily or not at all. He didn't know how to chat to a neighbour, and his wife always felt that he suffered from this as a Minister.

Basil Martin applied for admission to the Unitarian Ministry, although, he wrote later, "I was told by one of the most progressive ministers in Congregationalism that they were so cold that I should be frozen to death in a week."[1] He was in fact warmly welcomed. His theology had reached a curious stage, the culmination of years of "agonising reappraisal". The knowledge of Jesus, he found, was limited by the age in which he lived, and Jesus was "evidently mistaken on many subjects". There was "no proof that he had been born of a virgin, or that he was without sin."

> The Christ of traditional theology as expressed in the Catholic creed was incredible. It meant that a child, nursed by his mother, learning lessons at school, growing into manhood, often weary and weak, confessing the limitation of his knowledge, crying to his Father in heaven for help and surrendering himself to His will, at last dying upon the cross, was himself the creator of the Universe, upholding all things by the word of his power. Whether he was supposed to have stripped himself of power and knowledge for thirty years (supposing such a thing to be conceivable) or to have possessed it all the time, and kept it in subjection, the belief was equally incredible and meaningless. It meant that God, the Creator, Himself died and rose again, not in a poetic and mythical sense like Osiris, but literally and actually. Nor could I see what reality there would be in such a sacrifice. I should not be impressed by the sacrifice of a millionaire who should condescend to live in a London slum for a few days and then return to his former magnificence.
>
> Not only so, but scholars of repute had thrown doubt upon the whole narrative; some maintained that it was a mythical

[1] *An Impossible Parson*, p. 139.

representation of a great spiritual movement. If I had accepted this view it would have been a personal loss, but it would not have shaken my faith, for I had long since ceased to depend on the record of past events. This would put one at the mercy of experts in historical criticism who, to say the least, are not infallible.

Thinking of Jesus as a supreme though imperfect expression of the divine nature and purpose, I thought of the worship of Christ not as the worship of a man but the worship of God in the aspect of redeemer. I regarded the discussion about the Trinity as futile.[1]

In August 1913 the Martins left Hereford and went to live at 23 Chislehurst Avenue, Finchley. Basil had been appointed Minister at the Finchley Unitarian Church, which was known as Granville Hall. (It still is, but its worshippers are now Christadelphians.) He found the Finchley house himself and bought it at once for £600. From outside it looks a fairly typical suburban "semi-detached", but it is unexpectedly spacious. And the very large front room, which Basil Martin lined with books and used as a study, became the temple of Kingsley's father-worship and, for many years after he had left home, the focus of a recurring and acute nostalgia. For those who like following up the threads of causation in the lives of families, it is of interest to note that the move to Finchley was the first step on Kingsley's road to an ill-starred and tragic marriage, for it brought him into contact with Olga Walters.

Just before the move it was decided that Kingsley, who was small in stature, moody, frequently ill with chest and throat complaints, and not responsive to the known medical treatments, must go to South Africa for the "change of air" which in those days, and especially in the eyes of those who could not afford it, seemed to possess magical properties. Pulmonary consumption was an illness of which people were then very frightened. Few families did not know the grief of having lost at least one member, or a close friend, to this killer disease; and one needs to have lived in those days to believe that it could have caused such obsessive anxiety, and indeed panic. "Fresh air" and the wide-open bedroom window were thought

[1] *An Impossible Parson*, pp. 133–4.

to be the sovereign preventives (it's only in recent years that the doctors have been telling us that wide open bedroom windows can give our children bronchitis). Printed notices in trams and buses concerned themselves with "the interests of health and the prevention of consumption". A friend of Irene's had recently died of consumption, and the youth she was eventually to marry had just been sent, at the age of sixteen, to work on a poultry farm near Tenterden, in Kent, because the open-air life was thought likely to benefit a condition then known euphemistically as "overgrowing one's strength". An artist brother of Mrs Martin's, Frank Turberville, had gone some years before to South Africa because he too was threatened with consumption. He had established a farm near Grahamstown and had become a strong and healthy man. It was decided that Kingsley should join him for six months. Since the Martins had absolutely no money for such a project, the fare was provided by "Cousin Emily", a wealthy cousin of Mrs Martin's father living at Edgbaston. She was the widow of a prosperous Birmingham business man; she was also a pillar of the Methodist Church and a well-known Birmingham character who probably deserves a book all to herself.

From Teneriffe, on his way to Cape Town in the SS *Bulawayo*, Kingsley sent home an enormous letter. It was a three weeks' diary, undated as usual and filling 21 un-numbered pages. It goes some way to redeem his past as a lazy scribe, and is the earliest document among his papers—he was now sixteen—to suggest his flair and journalistic promise. Strangely, but I think characteristically, it is repeated word for word in an exercise-book diary of the voyage. And for the rest of his life he kept this naïve habit—verbatim repetition of what he felt was well said, so long as the two documents were unlikely to meet the same eyes. He had plenty to write about. The ship went "straight through the middle" of a vast school of porpoises, it was followed by albatrosses, its engines failed in the Bay of Biscay and it rolled helplessly for a whole day in heavy seas, Kingsley joining the rest of the passengers to hang white-faced over the rails. (A great shout from the crew stirred him sufficiently and in time to see a whale leap half out of the water.)

A prominent feature of all his letters home, from this point until he reaches his mid-twenties, is that whatever questionings may have been exercising his mind about the faith he had been brought up in, he gives much space to the religious episodes he judges likely to interest his parents as Dissenters. And one hears in them echoes of the conflict he must have felt between his compulsory school-time Cathedral services and his week-ends of Congregationalism at home:

> Sunday: We had service this morning conducted by the Chaplain and Chief Officer. Both read badly; but the hymns went quite well and it was a nice service altogether. Of course we had to pray for each of the Royal Family in turn, and say credos etc., but I could join in most of it all right. We are very quiet today, as befitteth the Sabbath Day, and only a very few are playing any cards. All the others read and go to sleep, eat and go to bed.

To fill the long idle days he was reading Jeffery Farnol's *The Amateur Gentleman* and *The Money Moon* ("by the same author as *The Broad Highway* and consequently with the same defects") and making a beginning with J. R. Green's *Short History of the English People*, a book which he came to love. On the following Sunday he reported that

> as usual we were "moved in sundry places" by the Scriptures; although the only part of *me* which felt moved was my digestive functions, and this, I think, was due more to the motion of the boat than to any readings of the Gospel (in which the Chief Officer lost all his aitches) or of the Epistles (in which he picked them all up again twice over).

Christianity still seemed to him at that time the only formalised recognition of goodness and social justice; but not Anglicanism. His diary records a deck-chair conversation with an elderly passenger, a Mr Cheffins, who thought that if the Bishop of Hereford (meaning Dr Percival, who happened to be a friend of Basil Martin's) really believed in Welsh disestablishment he ought not to pocket his stipend while holding views contrary to the interests of the Church which paid him. Kingsley retorted that most of the clergy were in the same boat, since they "represented" the 39 Articles of Religion which they didn't believe in. "I said I was sure he didn't either, and therefore he ought not to call himself a member of the Anglican Church. He answered that he didn't know whether he believed them or not, as it was so long ago since he had read them, but he wasn't going to enter into a discussion with me on such a topic. He still affirmed that the Bishop ought to resign, said he didn't know about the other clergy, and finally told me I was too young to study such a difficult subject as theology." Attached to another of his letters from South Africa is a note, obviously written many years later, which says:

> One conviction from my childhood remained deep down inside me. I was convinced that the minority, the under-dog, was right and also that he could never win. Nevertheless I felt compelled to be an outspoken member of this minority. I was always afraid, but most of all I was afraid of what I should think of myself if I ran away.

It was in South Africa that, with much time on his hands, he began to write, and wrote prolifically, both in diaries and letters, with the happy fecundity to be expected of someone who is to write for a living. He travelled about with his big cousin, learning much about cattle farming and fruit growing and the divine right by which the English settlers enjoyed the servitude of the Bantu population. He returned from South Africa in January 1914 after an absence of six and a half months and rejoined his parents at their new Finchley home. One short essay from among his miscellaneous South African scribblings is worth quoting as illustrative of his developing narrative style, his natural interests and, I suppose, his sentimentality. He had found a pair of woodpeckers digging a nest in a rotten oak tree a few yards away from the door of the hut where he slept. For many days he watched the progress of their work, noticing how one kept a look-out while the other pecked. To keep off predatory cats and other animals, Kingsley piled thorn bushes round the tree. "I was pleased to find that the woodpeckers seemed to understand my kind intent, and that they would fearlessly allow me to stand close by to watch them at their work." He continued:

> Their industry was marvellous, for the wood though dead was still hard; and after about a fortnight's energetic work the pair

seemed to decide to give up this hole and begin another higher in the tree, where the wood was softer. It seemed a truly shameful waste of so much tireless activity. This second attempt, however, proved more successful; and at length when I saw the mother's head appearing sometimes at the mouth of the hole, I knew an egg was being hatched.

Some weeks later I noticed a change. The mother was to be seen again outside, and the pair were continually entering the hole with grubs in their beaks. . . . A few nights later as I passed that way I found to my extreme sorrow that something—whether cat, wind or Kaffir I never knew—had wrenched away the bark and rotten wood behind the nest, leaving the single woodpecker chick almost exposed. We could hear the anxiety of the father and mother when they saw that their carefully built home was no longer capable of protecting their chick. We tenderly carried the shivering and half-naked little bird to the incubator where ostrich chicks were being hatched, and there we tried to feed him on grasshoppers. Hour by hour we could see that our little charge grew weaker. His grasshopper diet was not agreeing with him, and on the next day he died. Why, I kept asking myself, was Nature so cruel? Could so much loving toil, so much ceaseless energy, all be thrown away without leaving any trace in the world? . . . Somehow, somewhere, if our dim understanding could discern and interpret it, some good must be the outcome. No love or honest work can be spent in vain.

He cherished this illusion all his life. And all his life he pursued two independent lines of thought about the animal world, parallel and irreconcilable. He came to recognise that he, like most of us, was more disturbed about (for example) vivisection or biological research when the animals concerned were cuddly and toylike than when they were rats or snakes. And when it came to meat-eating he was less guilt-ridden about fillet steak or oysters than about hares and larks. I remember his being horrified on seeing, in a private zoo, a live toad waiting patiently to be eaten by a snake. Yet he would have been able at any time, I think, to feed those grasshoppers to the woodpecker. His love of animals was unconsciously delineated by sizes and appearances. But he knew it was, and often wrote amusingly about his own dilemma.

Chapter 3

ADOLESCENCE

"I FINISHED MY education," wrote Kingsley in his autobiography, "as a day boy at Mill Hill, a non-conformist school then presided over by Sir John McClure."[1] It seems more likely that that was where his education effectively began, where "for six hours a day, five days a week, the classical Sixth sat around the long oak table in the library" and the classics master prepared him for a scholarship—of which he was cheated by the outbreak of war. For here he first tasted the political philosophy of Aeschylus, Homer, Plato, Socrates, the Stoics and Marcus Aurelius. Secretly, for the classics master would not have approved, he read Gilbert Murray's translations and found in them poetry. And he formed a brief and happy friendship with a Mill Hill boy named Tom Applebee, whom he mentions only passingly in his book but who, I believe, had a profound influence on him throughout his life.

Tom Applebee became well known to the Martin family. He was Kingsley's one compensation for the unhappiness of school life—for at Mill Hill, as at the Hereford Cathedral School, he was (he always insisted) intensely miserable. Tom was "a big, genial boy," says Kingsley's sister, "with an open, honest face and a great love of the Greek poets". In the two years they knew each other the two boys went for long walks sustained by long discussions, Greek poetry being the main bond between them. The association played, it may safely be said, a larger part than that of any schoolmaster in Kingsley's development as a philologian—and as the champion of clear writing that he became. His love of English poetry can't be said to have developed, in later years, beyond the enjoyment of the romantics and the narrative poets, and even these served largely to sharpen his nostalgia for the Greek reading which he never really resumed once the 1914 war had engulfed him.

[1] *Father Figures*, p. 57.

When he came to edit the *New Statesman* he figured in many a droll encounter with poets and literary editors (and we shall return to them) who saw meaning in modern poems where he saw none. "Ah well," he would say at length, "if it means something to you there must be others like you"; but he clearly felt that the others were an odd fringe.

Sir John McClure, the Mill Hill headmaster, was "persistently good to him" and tolerant of his "eccentric attitude to the war"; and the same was true of Tom Applebee, who belonged to the School Officers' Training Corps and never upbraided him for his refusal to join. Tom and he reached a good understanding about this:

> We agreed that it was no good calling yourself a Christian, promising to return good for evil and love your enemies, if you took part in a vast horror of lies, hatred and slaughter. It seemed to us that you had to betray one or other of two allegiances. I could not fight for my country because I had already enlisted in the army of the pacifists. Just as the son of an Indian Army Officer might be moved to romantic endeavour by his father's sword hanging on the wall, so did my mother's stories of how nearly my father was killed by the crowd in the Boer War move me to believe in the splendour of non-resistance. . . . So Tom, who was a year older than I, put on khaki.[1]

During Tom's pre-draft training they continued their exploration of the Greek poets when they could. Tom would "turn up unexpectedly with a volume of Greek poetry in his pocket and demand a walk". When he was drafted to France he was killed within his first few days. "No-one else's death mattered to me so much—I imagined him 'hanging on the old barbed wire'"; in so few words Kingsley disposes of this early tragedy in his intellectual life. But when the news of Tom's death came, in August 1916, the Martin family were on holiday at Tenterden in Kent, Basil Martin having "exchanged" for a fortnight with the Unitarian minister there. They stayed in an old farmhouse. "Kingsley was in the next room to mine," says his sister Irene, "and I can remember hearing him sobbing and sobbing

[1] *Father Figures*, p. 65.

half the night". To my own knowledge it was a grief that Kingsley carried with him always.

At the age of eighteen, while still at school, he had to go before a Conscientious Objectors Tribunal. His father addressed the Tribunal on his behalf, and the commanding officer of the School OTC supplied a letter testifying to his sincerity. On the strength of that and of his father's well-known position as a pacifist, he was "exempted absolutely" from military service. At school he was then turned out of his study and subjected by the boys to considerable persecution, though some of the older boys were reluctantly impressed by the pacifist arguments which he was no doubt able to deploy with convincing skill. He decided to join the Friends' Ambulance Unit and try to get to France.

He was now regarding himself as an "ethical Christian". The move over to Unitarianism had coincided happily with his growing adolescent scepticism about the mystical aspects of Christianity, and the muddled thinking of the church about war and peace. During a family holiday at Peaslake in Surrey he went with his mother to an Anglican service in the village church. "A more extraordinary performance I never assisted at," he wrote in a small paper notebook. "A Communion Service followed the other, so that we got through—in 1½ hours—three hymns, three psalms, more prayers than I could count, a Gospel, an Old Testament reading, then in the Communion Service one from the Epistles and another from Luke, a sermon and other things which I couldn't give a name to. An aged missionary came to preach, and did so sitting, from the litany stool. He gave us the strangest discourse I've ever heard. His text was 'How beautiful are the feet of them who preach the gospel of *peace*'. This made me hope for a little common sense, but Oh! how pitiful it was! First he talked about the work he had done in New Zealand—he was one who had beautiful feet. (I was sorry I couldn't see them more clearly, but they seemed to be rather large for the stool). . . . He told us how great a work missionaries did, how little *we* did, and how much we should give to atone for our misdeeds. As proof of the wonderful power of the gospel of peace he told us that many Maoris had become Christians and were consequently serving with us in the present war. Which, I suppose, is the crowning sign of the efficacy of the gospel of peace. I could have wept when I thought of how small a number were listening to Father's logical and beautiful teaching, and how none of this congregation except us had the intelligence (or perhaps the cynicism?) to see the terrible incongruity of mixing the gospel of the Prince of Peace, the appeal for endless money and the present war into one heterogeneous mass. But the church has no message for today, I think, unless it is to tell us that we must still believe and worship just exactly as our great-great-grandfathers did before us."

His father had come to accept that if all men were divine the difference between the nature of Jesus and other good men, however great, was a difference not of kind but of degree. And God was immanent: his "dwelling was the light of setting suns", Wordsworth's phrase in the *Lines Composed a Few Miles Above Tintern Abbey*, which Tennyson thought "almost the grandest in the English language":

> I have felt
> A presence that disturbs me with the joy
> Of elevated thoughts; a sense sublime
> Of something far more deeply interfused,
> Whose dwelling is the light of setting suns,
> And the round ocean, and the living air,
> And the blue sky, and in the mind of man.

Thus for the time being Unitarianism suited Kingsley, who was relieved to find a church as old as the Reformation which rejected the doctrines of the Trinity and the divinity of Christ in favour of a one-person God. Reason and conscience were its criteria of belief. Since Unitarians believed in the abiding goodness of human nature, they were critical of the doctrines of the Fall, the Atonement, and the eternal punishment. For the rest of his life Kingsley was asking why men did not abandon their search for the origins of evil and look for the origins of good.

In his letters home, from France and elsewhere, he never omitted to enquire about the progress of his father's ministry at Finchley. After an admittedly late start, he became the kind of correspondent to gladden any parent's heart: assiduous, conscientious, highly literate and affectionate, knowing just what would interest each member of the family, totally undemanding himself. Nor was he doing this merely as a dutiful son out to please his father: one of the first things he did when, in 1919, he was up at Cambridge was to seek out the Unitarian Church.

Eventually at Princeton, where he found Unitarianism much in evidence, he had time to read Emerson's lecture *On The Defects of Historical Christianity*. He then concluded (not having yet decided that he had no soul) that Emerson's transcendentalism, the doctrine that "the highest revelation is that God is in every man", must be right, and that even redemption was to be sought within the soul. Finally, Emerson lost favour with him when he found him to have for so long opposed the abolition of slavery and to have given way, with great reluctance, only in 1856. There is some evidence in Kingsley's Princeton diaries in 1922 that Emerson was a fallen idol and that Unitarianism fell with him. Nevertheless Frank Hardie, who did not meet him until the early thirties, recalls that Kingsley asked him in 1934 to accompany him to a Unitarian church service.

But at the age of seventeen and eighteen Kingsley was already striking the attitude of an anti-mystic of exceptional intolerance. Both his sisters dabbled for a time in occultism. Though they dismiss it now, they believed themselves (at different periods) to have the gift of spirit writing. Peggy, who was only twelve, was doing "automatic writing" soon after their little brother died.

"I used to get messages that were supposed to come from him," she told me. "I never went into a trance or anything like that. But then I gave it up because I felt, even at that age, that my conscious mind was entering into it and I thought I might be cheating, so to speak. I genuinely believed that I was influenced. But Kingsley tested everything by the intellect—we all did in time, and all had the same terrific inward conflict. . . . But it was impossible for me to discuss it with him, or indeed discuss anything, because I always had this terrible inferiority with him. I was tongue-tied with him, and it lasted all our lives. He could be *very* damaging, with his superiority. He loved arguing, and was insensitive of the hurtful effect he might have on some less articulate person with equally deep convictions. To me the supernatural was a reality, and religion a mystical experience. To him it was an exercise in dialectics.

"Admiring him as I did," wrote Peggy,[1] "I found myself in conflict—almost ashamed of what I believed intuitively because it appeared to have no rational basis. I'm sure he would have welcomed discussion but I knew I could not stand up to him. I think many sensitive people felt as I did—you needed to be pretty tough and sure of yourself to counter such arrogant self-assurance as he could display on occasion. I was neither tough nor confident, as children we were seldom happy together and sometimes I hated him. He was bullied at school, and as is so often the case he took it out on me when he came home. He could easily make me cry, and when he taunted me I would fly at him in impotent rage, knowing that he would always get the better of me. I feel sad that we never achieved a comfortable, companionable relationship.

"My mother said when we quarrelled that it was 'six to one and half a dozen to the other', but it wasn't. I felt the dice were loaded against me!" She later became a child psychotherapist, and exceptionally able to assess with objectivity the effect upon her of a brilliant brother who preceded her through university at Cambridge. (He was a don at Magdalene while she was an undergraduate at Newnham, and he helped to pay her university fees himself. She felt that he overshadowed her until she escaped into marriage.)

Irene, Peggy's senior by nine years and Kingsley's by three, enjoyed a quiet ascendancy which he seldom challenged, a relationship which, because it was calmer, is less easy to record, presents fewer graphic opportunities. Her own temporary interest in Spiritualism came just after their little brother died in 1915, and was stimulated by a friendship with a Celtic mystic. When it began to wane Kingsley said to her: "Well, I've given up any idea of a belief in a future life, but I don't see any reason why you should. I've done it largely as a matter of fashion—to be like other people." Irene never found

[1] In a personal letter to the author.

him intolerant or hurtful, as Peggy did. Both sisters were extremely alert, though he often seemed intellectually cocksure; but Irene had the great advantage of being three years older instead of six years younger. You will never effectively diminish a gap like that, even in the longest life.

You would suppose, perhaps, that the growth of unbelief in the present century would by corollary entail the death of superstition. Exactly the opposite seems to be taking place. There is a proliferation of cults that no previous century has exceeded, astrology being of course prominent among them because of its relatively harmless sooth-saying and its auxiliary value in selling newspapers.

Even in much later life, Kingsley's self-consciously unscientific reaction to the "frightening silences between the stars" seemed sometimes to blunt his scepticism about astrology: but in his teens he was certainly more credulous. Among the family's friends at Finchley was a Mrs Stewart King who lived exactly opposite Mill Hill School. She was very fond of Kingsley and encouraged him to go across to her house in the afternoons and read. She was an astrologist; and he was never heard to deride her beliefs or practices. This may have had something to do with a horoscope she provided, which not only constructed a picture of him that was highly flattering in parts, but foretold a rosy future of the kind he most wished to have. It is undated, but it was certainly in 1916, and he was eighteen years old:

> "According to the position of the planets at your birth . . . your personal magnetism makes you popular." (At this stage in his life this seems to have been an overstatement.) "You are refined, artistic, and musical." (He candidly and always disclaimed all three.) "You have a feeling of pity and protection for the weak and oppressed, and a love for animals. There is a liability to go to extremes and to be changeable in mood, now buoyant and happy, now sad and depressed. You are rather critical and satirical, inclined to court opposition and so make some enemies—and you should specially avoid religious and legal disputes" (the former he always loved and the latter he found boring and stupid). "You know your own mind and are seldom at a loss to know what to do or say" (an unrecognisable Kingsley). "Although

you are rational, logical and scientific, there is a mystical tendency in your mental make-up and you will always be interested in occult subjects." (Well, he never quite got over it.) "A great deal of travel is shown, and much pleasure should come of it. . . . You will be attractive to women and should be guarded in your relations with them, as some difficulty is caused by rashness, jealousy, having two love affairs at the same time. . . . You will however marry and become a devoted husband and your wife will be an enthusiast like yourself. . . . Your power of mediumistic sympathy would enable you to be a writer, especially of poetry, plays and novels, although you could write equally well on philosophical and scientific subjects however abstruse and recondite. . . . You will always have enough money and you will be well off in the latter part of your life. . . . You have a real sense of the brotherhood of man, and communal and co-operative schemes for its realisation appeal strongly to you. The prevalent middle-class type of mind, which says 'Myself and my wife, my son John and his wife and none but us' is anathema to you. The planets are all setting in your horoscope, and this may cause you to have a fatalistic feeling at times."

He was never without it. But he proceeded at once to fulfil one of the less reckless of Mrs Stewart King's prophecies by discovering himself as a writer.

By way of a beginning, he won the 1916 Old Millhillians' Literary Prize with an essay on "The Quest for Success". "The unknown is fraught with no terrors for the resolute," wrote Kingsley, now nineteen. "The youthful idealist, far different from Christian, is sure that the lions lying in the path to the celestial city will always be chained. . . . This is the testing time of life: the valley of humiliation through which the idealist must pass, and from which he must come forth much changed in outlook." Kingsley at this time was fascinated by the effect of war-danger as a social leveller. "It seems that folk could not realise the dignity of drudgery until the catastrophe of a great war showed it them. Now it is clear that their safety and happiness depends on the so-called working man. . . . Yet it does seem strange that the ladies who would take a taxi, but a few months ago, rather than sit on the next seat in a train to a man in corduroys, now go out of their way to be near him because he is in khaki. . . . Those who despise the planters of the world's cabbages rather resemble the first-class passengers in an ocean liner who shudder at the sight of the grimy stoker who keeps the vessel moving. . . . There must be someone at the bottom of the social pyramid, and if his work is bad the whole will fall."

Meanwhile, though the war spread its huge and sombre backcloth to his life, it gets relatively small attention in his diaries. A typical Mill Hill entry—for 5th April 1916—reads:

> Chapel service for those killed in war. Impressive in its way although it makes one feel how mistaken it all is. Climbed in through the library window and took a volume of Landor's *Imaginary Conversations*. Ran a very hard heat of the mile against Lister, who just gained the better of me at the last sprint. Was inwardly more piqued over this trifle than a philosopher should be. Tired in the evening. Holidays begin—my last.

On the following Sunday, 9th April 1916:

> Go to the morning service and hear Mr Spedding, who is unutterably tiring. Bible reading, prayers, and sermon all alike in a muddle.

And at last on Tuesday, 5th June 1917:

> Received my marching orders to go to France—one more week at home would have been so pleasant! I am glad to go though sorry that all my (other) arrangements now come to nothing. . . . Irene dashed into town to get my Red Cross buttons; Mother buys me a very nice valise, so much more useful and serviceable than a kitbag. Useful after the war! A new chapter in my life opening.

Thereafter he wrote countless long letters and detailed diaries in all the uncomfortable places to which his war service took him. It was as though he needed discomfort as an inspiration. Some of his private references to the Tribunal system for examining conscientious objection to war are rather less than fair. The Tribunals were not all "local big-wigs and sycophantic shopkeepers" who saw the exemption system as sentimental folly. Most of them had sons or relatives in the armed forces, and they were confronted by some pretty tiresome individualists. But there was plenty of scope for amusement in the confused passions represented by the ladies who handed white feathers to young men not in uniform.[1] (This custom reappeared for a short time in 1941: "it caused at least two suicides and forced the government to develop a badge to identify men exempted from service on medical grounds".)[2] On 19th June 1917 Kingsley was to record in his diary:

> Kingston (one of his F.A.U. companions) today shows me a most amusing newspaper cutting. An extract:
> *Mr Harold Smith* said he would exclude from the franchise every C.O. who had not taken up arms for his country in this time of emergency.
> *Mr Snowden* asked the Hon. Member why he was not serving, as he was of military age?
> *Mr H. Smith* said that that was a matter for his conscience (loud and ironical cheers).

Another man, Russell (who, incidentally, beat Kingsley in many games of chess), suggested that Mr Harold Smith M.P. meant no more than that his conscience bade him decide whether he could serve his country better in Parliament than in the trenches. Kingsley would have none of it. "I don't think anything beats this," he wrote. "Mr H. Smith must have been very nearly converted, I think, by his own involuntary answer. How could a man contrive to make so great a fool of himself?"

He went first to Jordans Village, near Chalfont St Peter, for a month's camp training. His letter-writing began at once with a delighted description of the old Mayflower Barn and the 1688 Quaker Meeting House. From Buckinghamshire to the Thames-side Star and Garter Hospital at Richmond—of which he gives a gloomily graphic description in *Father Figures*: it was one of the most harrowing of all the military hospitals, the injuries and the physical condition of the patients were frightful, "nursing" was bereft of all possible romance and excitements. There is no doubt that he was bewildered and enraged by the

[1] I was handed a white feather by a quite elderly woman when I was thirteen. [CHR.]

[2] Angus Calder, *The People's War*, Panther Books, 1969, p. 269.

pointless suffering around him. Every mutilated arrival, every death, seemed to him a separate political outrage. Hardly less outrageous, in his parents' view, was the hospital's decision to send him home one day in the care of a Sergeant because it was believed he had contracted diphtheria! It wasn't diphtheria, but thereafter for the rest of his life he suffered from an intermittent throat infection which he always called "a Star and Garter".

He went from there for a few weeks, in January 1917, to Uffculme Hospital, Moor Green, Birmingham, where he was working as an orderly when he was granted conditional exemption by the Finchley Tribunal on 1st February 1917. This was his second appearance before them. The first time, while he was still at school, they had exempted him "absolutely".[1] But he had joined the Friends' Ambulance Unit because he wanted to get to France; and on his second appearance, now a trained orderly, his exemption was made conditional on his so continuing.

It was a period of his life which he would never discuss; and it came as a surprise to some of his friends that he was able to give it a few pages in his autobiography. It grimly filled the interval in his career between school and university.

[1] See p. 44.

Chapter 4

WAR AND THE FRIENDS' AMBULANCE UNIT

"I, BASIL KINGSLEY MARTIN, of 23 Chislehurst Avenue, N. Finchley, in undertaking service with the Friends' Ambulance Unit, hereby agree to comply with the conditions which entitle me to protection under the Geneva Convention, and to observe the rules, regulations and orders issued by the Officer Commanding or by the Committee, provided that I am not called upon to enlist; and that my conscientious objection to military service is respected." Thus began his form of Declaration and Agreement. It bound him to "conform to all proper military etiquette when wearing uniform"; to obey the postal censorship regulations; to serve for the duration of the war (with the right to leave after six months, which would usually mean going into the armed forces after all—as many members did); to do no writing for the press and take no photographs whatever; and not only to serve without pay but to buy his own uniform and kit, though he was to get his food, lodging and travelling expenses plus 75 French centimes a week to pay his laundry bills, if any.

He now found himself in a variety of French hotels, huts, camps and old railway carriages, with plenty of time to develop his growing habit of letter writing and desultory diary-keeping. And from a huge collection of tattered penny exercise books I take the following extracts, self-selected on grounds of legibility. They will be sufficient, I hope, to suggest the range of his war experience:

Sunday June 10th 1917. Dunkirk

There have been almost continual air raids, but the moon has gone now, so there is a possibility of a rest. . . . Graveson and I go for a walk on the shore. I find him interesting (which usually means that he is a good listener). This is the "Continental Tour" continued. In the afternoon we sit and peel, or rather scrub, potatoes.

Graveson was a botanist, a science graduate of King's College, Cambridge, who (Kingsley wrote in a further letter) "knows, I do believe, all there is to know about botany". He told Kingsley he had found 285 varieties of wild flowers in one July day in Hertfordshire. "Do you know that there is a greater variety of wild flowers to be found in October than in April? . . . We go out together frequently: I take a book, and read when he comes to a spot where he wishes to botanise. . . . Every time the ambulance train stops for a minute, he jumps off and walks up and down the siding with a curious jerky step hunting for specimens."

Another man friendly with Kingsley was Corporal Gill, who was Curator of the Newcastle-upon-Tyne Natural History Museum—"an expert naturalist and a most delightful person. . . . I have got to know him by asking his help in German." (Kingsley announces in a letter dated 11th October 1917 that he is going to teach himself German.)

Monday June 11th 1917 I am up to my eyes in chloride of lime [he had been on latrine duties]. It's all right while dry, but it gets damp in the afternoon, skins my arms and hands and leaves me very sore and wretched.

Tuesday June 12th 1917 Last night I had two hours—from 11 p.m. till 1 a.m.—on night guard. For the Fourth Army have arrived here, and we are expecting our goods to be purloined and our quarters taken. . . . Tonight also we expect an air raid: the Germans know of their presence, and as they are very near us we expect a very lively time.

Thursday June 14th 1917 I get some talk with some of the [Fourth Army] men in one of the buses. They know they are fools to have joined, but believe now in reprisals if they will hasten the end of the war. They admitted that I was right about hitting the wrong man in war. It is astonishing how this new, burning desire for peace, and hatred of the "doormat behaviour" of officers towards the men, grows.

Wednesday June 20th 1917 Fed up with everybody and everything. Get down very late for breakfast, because I did not hear the bell, and get run down by the Kitchen Orderly. I get into a fluster and make a fool of myself generally. I always act the goat like this, everywhere. I wonder if other people are such hopeless asses as I am?

Thursday June 26th 1917 Since my last doleful entry I have recovered some of my self-respect, largely because of a little excursion I made through the glass roof above the wash-and-brush-up establishment. Took a step backward and was found (all my past life having come up before me) hanging on to the woodwork. A slight cut and unlimited amusement. The people working in the room below seemed surprised to see my legs. . . . I've done something to cheer up the establishment a little, and that's worth doing.

But the following night the Germans bombarded Dunkirk from Dixmude, 30 miles away, with the long-range guns they were later to train across the English Channel. They blew up a row of ammunition wagons at the sea-plane base; and they demolished the Casino, in which some Fourth Army men were billeted:

Wednesday June 27th 1917 Men passed me in the road carrying a man, or the remains of one. . . . He was red from face to foot, and grey on the top. I very soon found some work carrying stretchers. I don't think I can ever forget seeing the long rope ladder that came from the top storey—for the stairs were blown to atoms. At the top window we saw some men, and were told there were three wounded up there. One man carried another down on his back; the other two, almost naked, climbed down by themselves with their wounds open and bleeding. I carried a few to the cars, and then we went and got breakfast to the tune of the bombardment. The shot on the Casino killed some nine or ten, I believe, and mutilated many more. It was the first Red Cross work I've done.

Sunday July 1st 1917 Bird (the deputy C.O.) remarked to me the other day that he was sorry I was going on an ambulance train—it was a pity all the good men got lost that way! [Graveson too had just been posted to an ambulance train; this was the ambition of most F.A.U. men, but exposed them to greatly increased danger.] I could not get any very definite understanding of his meaning. On Wednesday night, Graveson's last night here, we went out together to the study circle. Ernest Jones was very good, I thought. We took the Beatitudes as a starting point, and the discussion turned largely on the "poor in spirit". I asked them whether they really thought this meant that the gentle people have the greatest influence in the world, and Jones looked grateful to me for taking the subject away from the usual platitudes. He asks me to open, but I don't like to, being by far the youngest there.

From July 1917 until the Armistice he was almost continually on ambulance trains, between the Somme fronts, Ypres, Amiens, Rouen, le Havre, Abbeville, Etaples, Etretat and the many other towns of Northern France whose names will long recall that ghastly campaign to so many minds. It enabled him to talk and listen to the wounded:

> This job of looking after wounded men [he wrote in one of his innumerable exercise books] is a peculiarly good vantage point for following the changes in the outlook and psychology of soldiers during the war. A wounded man, lying with nothing but his pain to think about for perhaps ten hours in an intolerably slow and jolting train, is apt to be grateful for the chance to speak his mind freely. And here I will admit that I have never met with anything but friendship—or envy or amused tolerance—from soldiers. The people who give you white feathers and twit you with cowardice are not soldiers, but elderly females who have already "given" their nephews to the service of their country in France. Soldiers are apt to take a different view. "Oh," they say, "so you're a conscientious objector? Well, good luck to you. Wish I'd thought of that dodge myself." . . . But such discussions took place only in England and before one had settled down to the job. In France we are all in the same mess together, all under shell fire, and only interested in rations and wondering when the war will be over and if you have a cushier job than most. For the moment you are the man who can get an extra tin of bully beef, or scrounge a tin of Ideal milk; and tomorrow can look after itself.

At about this time he wrote (and failed to date) what was probably intended as an article for the *Fourgon* (the magazine of No. 11 ambulance train). It stated more clearly than, I think, he ever did subsequently his own position at that time on the subject of conscientious objection, a position which he was to abandon completely almost 25 years later. "The pacifist is told that he is not only unpatriotic but pro-German. The true pacifist, however, believing in universal brotherhood and hating militarism wherever it is, is far from being a friend to 'Germany', the very fountain-head of militarism. He opposes war, indeed, partly because he is a patriot and considers that war is detrimental to the highest interests of his country. He believes that the nation is greatest which bases its power on peace and spends its millions on the uplifting of its citizens and not on the piling up of armaments. *Dulce et decorum est pro patria mori*: The C.O. agrees: but while he is ready to die he believes it to be wrong to kill."

And on the charge of cowardice: "The men who have stood the ordeal of a hostile tribunal with all the stigma attached to the name of C.O. today, the brutal treatment which has been their lot in barracks in various parts of England and France, the trial before Courts Martial and sentence to penal servitude—even if hopelessly misguided, these are not cowards. Even those in the army itself admit this. It is not long since one soldier who had witnessed the cruelty with which a C.O. in his barracks had been treated wrote home that 'they are the fighters, not we'. It requires more courage to suffer in obscure dishonour among a handful of enthusiasts than to march in a popular uniform applauded by thousands.

"Of the other charges brought against him the most specious is that of inconsistency. His stand, it is said, is illogical because, while refusing to fight, he enjoys the safety ensured by the armed forces and aids in the war by paying his taxes. But the fallacy in this argument is clear. A man's property is his, in keeping for the State. He has gained it from the State and by the help of the State. If the nation demands its money back in taxes, the individual is not responsible for the way in which it is used. But the battle for liberty of conscience has long been fought and, before the war, we believed that it was won. If the individual must not think for himself, has the State then an absolute right to command obedience in everything? Were the Germans right in invading Belgium when the State ordered? Were the soldiers justified in adopting their government's policy of 'frightfulness'? Were the Turks to be commended when they annihilated the Armenian people at the State's direction? We believe that British soldiers would not have committed such atrocities as did the Germans in Belgium, even if they were ordered by their superiors. The German then is the better soldier, because the more implicitly obedient in carrying out even the most infamous of commands?

"The martyrs of history have all been those who have refused to execute the commands of the State which seemed to them, as individuals, to be wrong. They were conscientious objectors who disobeyed the legally constituted authority of the State. If we do not admit this, then Antigone should have left her brother unburied, Peter and John should have left off preaching at the command of the Sanhedrin, Sir Thomas More should have obeyed Henry VIII, and all the mighty host of martyrs from Christ onwards have been wrong.

"Finally the C.O. is charged with fanaticism. This charge argues a certain respect from those who make it. The pacifist is a fanatic who believes that his principles must hold in difficult times as well as in easy ones, if they are to have any value. Before the war, all the world talked of peace and goodwill. The C.O. asks, not unnaturally, what is the use of talking about loving your enemies in time of peace when you have no enemies to love? The practical application of the principle comes in war time. Thus his fanaticism lies in his consistency. . . . The C.O. then is one who, in spite of fierce opposition and persecution, abides by the principles he held before the war, obeying as he believes a command higher than that of the State.

"A young man before a Tribunal a few weeks ago was asked the usual question as to what he should do if his mother and sister were attacked? Would he not defend them? He asked if he might in return put a question to the military representative. Permission was granted and he said: 'If I were a dispatch rider, and German soldiers attacked my mother and sisters at the moment when a superior officer gave me an important and urgent dispatch to take, what would be my duty?' The military representative said that, although he thought it would be a hard case, it would be his duty to take the dispatches. The young man answered: 'Sir, I have my dispatches'. That is the true Quaker attitude."

In another paper written at about the same period, Kingsley set down his own classification of "conchies":

"First there is the Quaker, whom nobody doubts. Second, the funk: his motives are *very* mixed—a chance to escape, a feeling that war is stupid, and an idea of doing something with less danger and less mischief. Third—the Plymouth Brethren, who rely on verbal inspiration—'Thou shalt not kill'. Fourth, the intelligent funk like myself, who analyses his motives: no real fear of being killed, no fear in air raids, enjoyment in seeing shell-fire: yet this is a temperament which would have lost its head promptly in an engagement, got shell-shock, and been shot for cowardice. Fifth, the political objector who knows and understands he is fighting a different war. Sixth, the out-and-out ethical Christian, which I'm not really. Of course dislike and even hatred of all these types will be likely to fetter the observer. But let sympathy and love be married to insight—then the world and mankind will lie open before him."

And from his hundreds of long letters home, the following few extracts will complement the diaries:

> *August 1st 1917* [to his father] . . . I can see I shall have to leave this letter very shortly and go out somewhere—some kind individual is lending our coach a gramophone this afternoon, and I think I dislike gramophones as much as you do.

I record this sadly but dutifully as one whose musical education was advancing rapidly, in 1917, by way of this epoch-making invention. Many years later Kingsley was to show me, proudly and in his own drawing room, one of those EMG hand-made gramophones with vast "exponential" horns which dignified all the best apartments; *never* knowing (I believe) that the improved reproduction was due mainly to electrical recording, a discovery which brought mankind over the brow of a hill.

> *October 11th 1917* [to his father] Mother says I am safer here than in London. That's too true, I fear. [Actually it was far from true, but he consistently underplayed the danger of ambulance train work, to the point of refusing to admit any danger at all.] I'm getting quite nervous about your being in Finchley.[1] It would be rotten to get my first leave and find you all in little

[1] The famous destruction of a Zeppelin at Cuffley (its descent in flames was visible for 50 miles around) had made the whole of London seem suddenly one small target.

pieces and No. 23 burnt to the ground. As to the moon—that's always the way: they come over HQ every single night that there's a moon. . . . I'm awfully glad Granville Hall[1] is sticking it so pluckily. . . . I do like your sermon subjects again. What do you mean by "Life's Present Tenses"? I could do with a few more sermons here sometimes. I don't want, if I can help it, to acquire the objectionable habit of swearing [in fact he never did] but it's extraordinarily difficult to avoid it. No. 11 is not quite as bad in this and other respects as some other trains. . . . Now one of the things I have always said to myself is: "When you get some time to yourself, Kingsley Martin, you're to learn German on your own." Now you will find somewhere I *know* that we have a German Bible in the house—I think on the nursery shelves. Please at once take it to Weymouth Street[2] for me and it will be in time to come with the next F.A.U. parcels.

8th November 1917 [to his mother] I don't want you to send me any more parcels. From all I hear about food in England, and prices and so forth, I think you are more in need of parcels from me than I from you.

11th November 1917 [to his father] . . . It's time you preached another batch of unpatriotic sermons, and took your chance of people leaving the church! But I believe people would begin to listen, if you got up some pacifist lectures now. They are getting fed up with the war. Of course I don't know that they'll like hearing about the origins of the present war, but they'll stand a lot of peace talk now, I believe.

20th January 1918 [to his father] . . . I wish you were only about ten years older than me, father dear. When I come home on leave we will have some good walks together, and just think of sitting round the study fire chatting! . . . There is talk of a football match this afternoon. There are people on the train who won't play because it's Sunday. They have my sympathy but not my support. It's true I never played football on Sunday in England, but that was not on principle. . . . I'm glad you are reading *The Old Wives' Tale*. It's a powerful book and the style strikes me as his very best. . . . Life is sad, I know, but I think Arnold Bennett might be a little less depressing. . . . I always like to picture you going to church on the Sunday mornings. And I like to write on Sunday, too, as my share in the Sunday worship.

[1] The Finchley Unitarian Church.
[2] The Friends' Ambulance Unit Headquarters.

12th March 1918 [to his mother] We are now on the run again. . . . No longer can I talk of sunshine, novels, magazines, games—men have been fighting, killing each other. I do not ask God to stop this hideous, awful warfare: I ask men to. . . . I do not know whether it's cowardice that makes me shrink from fighting: if so I am proud of being a coward. I do not think I'm afraid of being killed—I am terribly afraid of killing. Whether I should be just a common coward on the battlefield of course I do not know. No-one can who has not faced it.

19th March 1918 [a Diary entry] A sudden great rush of gas cases. Germans have fired gas shells continuously for 48 hours. Probably prelude to a big push.

21st March 1918 [Diary] Hindenburg offensive has started. . . . We carry on with all-day fatigues every day till the 28th when the train leaves for base. Things at the front sound worse and worse. Apparently an utter rout of the Fifth Army. Albert captured and cavalry at Edgehill of all places. Hope it will finish the war.

29th March 1918 [Diary] Several stations *this* side of Amiens, a strange and awful sight. On the ground, hundreds of stretcher cases lying, and hundreds of "walking wounded" sitting about. They have been constantly loading trains for eleven days now. We get a load of 25 stretchers, some of them serious, and six sitters. We leave about 6.0 and reach Rouen at 4.30 next morning! Completely fagged out with watching cases all night, sleep all morning of 30th.

21st April 1918 [to his mother] I have just finished *The Soul of a Bishop*. . . . I think it's rather feeble—it has none of the lasting qualities which, I believe, will make *Mr Britling Sees It Through* a classical war document. . . . I am writing articles for *The Fourgon* in the intervals between carrying patients. The intervals may disappear again shortly. . . . I do wish Father could mind less about Granville Hall and his lack of obvious success. It's the one thing I did get all wrong when I was home on leave.

28th July 1918. [Written on his 21st birthday to the family] Funnily enough I feel just the same age as I did yesterday and that is about 2½. . . . I shouldn't like to live my seventeenth year again. I find it very interesting to think over school again. I realise how much of my troubles was my own fault. . . . In America there are trees which, when hollow, contract in the wet and expand in the sun. A certain traveller went inside one of these hollows to get shade from the sun, and fell asleep. Meanwhile there was a thunderstorm, and the opening nearly closed up. When he awoke and found himself held tight, he saw that he was destined to die of starvation—the wet weather season had set in. He began, as people always do in stories, to think over his past life. He could only remember bad things he'd done, and no good ones. The best thing he could remember having done was giving a penny to a beggar. This made him feel so small that he found he could squeeze through the crack in the tree and escape. . . .

Now as to a happy birthday, or as Father says "Happier returns". Believe me I am happy and I intend to be happy. It is the first article of my creed. . . . Maybe it will be tested some day. It will be interesting to see if it stands the strain.[1] As it is I consider my present life a sort of Arcadia. I realise too that my happiness is not really independent of circumstances. It is to some extent independent of place and food and so forth; but take away books and friendship and I'd soon give out, I fear. . . .

It was wicked of you to name me Basil Kingsley. How can a bloke live up to Basil Martin *and* Charles Kingsley, especially when his own people have such a high opinion of him and them? My love to you all, my own dear folk: your entirely and completely grown up—Kingsley Martin.[2]

August 25th 1918 [to the family] This Sunday evening is sunny and beautiful, but the world is so horrible, so inconceivably horrible, so near me. I seem to mind the war, and feel its suffering, more and more. It's all so stale and sordid and overpowering. Everyone is more cheerful now we are advancing again; but is all the good that could ever come out of it worth *one* of the characters that are ruined by it or one of these lives or even limbs that are lost?

By the time of the Armistice he was editing the *Fourgon*, and at the end of 1918 he was preparing a Souvenir Edition. He had spent Armistice Day in Boulogne, on leave for England,[3] with

[1] It must be said that it did, though Kingsley became much less happy as the years went on.

[2] Letters from overseas had to be signed with the full name, for the information of the Censoring Officer.

[3] He says in *Father Figures* (p. 88): "I happened to get leave on Armistice Day and crossed to London", but his diaries written at the time show that his later memory was at fault.

leisure for a long entry beginning "Alas, my poor diary, how I have neglected you." And he went on:

> *11th November 1918* Tonight is a great occasion—I may never know so great a one in my life again. Boulogne, and I have no doubt at all France and England, are in a fever of rejoicing. I am reminded of Carlyle's diary: "I noticed this morning that the men at the corner of the street were more than usually drunk, and then I remembered that it was the birthday of our Redeemer"... It's a good time to be going on leave.

and then:

> *London 16.11.18* We have a good crossing... Victoria all alight was a joy, crowds and crowds of folk against the railings cheering like mad. "See the Conquering Hero Comes!"—and the first they cheered were four F.A.U. conchies! A dear old lady in the train had called me Tommy, and thought my Red Cross meant Grenadier Guards.... Home as delicious as ever.

Back in France again (at Etaples):

> *28th December 1918* A belated Christmas dinner. Make menu cards and other preparations in the morning. An excellent dinner—and a fearful wash-up afterwards.

He had hoped for demobilisation before Christmas, but he was to spend Christmas Day on the Belgian–German frontier, starting at Herbesthal, near Aix-la-Chapelle, where "there was work to be done among German prisoners". But he also managed to do a lot of writing and editing. "It seems a strange thing," he wrote on 23rd December, "for us to be swanking around with the German officials saluting us. At night we move. I wake up at Düren and in the morning we are near Cologne. There is snow on the ground and one has hopes of seeing the famous Cathedral and bridge, and enjoying a view of the Rhine. No such luck. Xmas, for which we have made such joyful preparations, dies for us."

However, another entry in his diary, this time bearing no place-name, suggests a lack of reverence and enthusiasm in the available Christmas feeling:

Xmas Diary 1918

7.0 Wakened by waits singing "Christians Awake". A grim jest.
7.15 Go to sleep again.
7.30 Breakfast bell.
7.31 Think about getting up.
7.32 Wake up my ward partner.
7.35 Thinking seriously of getting up.
7.40 Get up.
8.0 Breakfast.
8.30 Wonder whether one should do any work on Xmas Day.
9.30 Continue wondering, but light the stove, since wondering is a cold job.
10.30 Read a book, as I have not yet decided.
11.30 Decide that one should work, but that it is now too late to begin.
12.0 Wonder what dinner will be like.
12.30 Still wondering.
1.30 Find out.
3 to 4.30 Walk about to regain appetite for tea.
4.30 Appease appetite.

On 29th December he wrote home from Etaples to say that "the 25th found work for me (and others) up in the Fatherland, but although we saw the Cologne spires in the distance we got no nearer"—and then a PS: "Have just heard I am demobilised and to return tout de suite."

1st January 1919 Rather unpleasant passage, although might be worse. Not sick at all. Violent snub from Red Cross girl.

3rd January 1919 Go over to Letchworth and see Evelyn. . . . Broken ends don't join very easily. . . .

Evelyn was a cousin of his mother's, to whom, though she was twice his age, he had completely lost his heart; and the affection was mutual. There is little doubt that throughout her life she retained an interest in him which went a long way beyond cousinship.

But the references to the non-negotiable Red Cross girl and the failure to resume with Evelyn are the very first acknowledgments, throughout Kingsley's voluminous diaries and letters from 1912 to 1919, that any girls existed other than his sisters. On the 13th January there was a party in the Finchley house to celebrate his homecoming, at which, before an audience of 60 or 70 people, "the Misses Sykes did a sketch". It was through the Misses Sykes (Edith and Ethel) who were members of the Unitarian Church, that Kingsley was to meet the girl he married: they were the aunts of Olga Walters.

But meanwhile:

> I go to Cambridge on Tuesday. Feel no excitement about it, scarcely interest. Have picked up broken ends with Mrs Stewart King on second visit. Not so when I saw Evelyn.

He had been doubtful about his Cambridge prospects for that year. He wrote from Calais on 15th December to tell his father that he had had a not very optimistic letter from Sir John McClure, the headmaster at Mill Hill School. But:

> I thought Dr McClure's letter satisfactory—I know the difficulty of course. You see there is only so much money going, and I suppose each of the men who hold scholarships at the Varsity now expects a leaving scholarship from school at the same time. In the ordinary run of things, some men would be finishing with their scholarships now, and their money would be vacant. Is £75 a year—which apparently I can safely rely on—enough for me to go to Cambridge without any undue strain on the family cash-box? I shall write to Ramsey, I think, and see what he says.

Frank Ramsey, then about seventeen, was the son of the President of Magdalene and was then himself at Trinity College. Kingsley refers to him affectionately in *Father Figures* as "a wonderful human being, utterly simple, unselfseeking and candid"; and he was Kingsley's mentor in many ways. He died at 26, but three of the short essays he had written are now regarded as seminal papers. In 1970, when Harvard decided to found a chair of "Probability Theory with Regard to Economics", they called it the Frank Ramsey Professorship. A paper he wrote on Mathematical Logic is now known as "Ramsey's Theorem". Another on "Projections for a Planning Scheme" is known as The Ramsey Model. "The cleverest Englishman of his generation," was how he was described to me by R. B. Braithwaite, now Emeritus Professor of Moral Philosophy at Cambridge, who was a contemporary of his (and Kingsley's) at the University—and who had known, in that generation, both Maynard Keynes and Lytton Strachey. "He shone in the world of applied and pure mathematics, in what might be called the philosophy of probability, and in economics." (He was probably the youngest member of "The Apostles".) There is no record of what he told Kingsley about the cost of Cambridge; but a Mrs Edwards, a friend of the family and a wealthy member of the Finchley Unitarian Church, was so determined that he should go to Cambridge that she presented Kingsley's father with a cheque for £100. Without it he might well have been unable to take up his exhibition, which soon in fact became a scholarship. As it was, he lived frugally, ate scrappily, cycled everywhere to save train fares, and always (and unconcernedly) looked shabby in a sports jacket and flannel trousers in which, it was unkindly rumoured, he used to sleep at nights. "It's quite fair to say that he had a pretty odd appearance," says J. B. Priestley, "because that's why I remember him at Cambridge—I was at Trinity Hall while he was at Magdalene. We hardly knew each other, and I should have no recollection of him there but for his odd appearance."

Chapter 5

CAMBRIDGE AS STUDENT

WHEN THE FIRST elation of his arrival at Magdalene College had subsided, that rare elation "like falling in love without the anxiety", it was not long before the anxiety began to insinuate itself. Then he felt, on occasion, almost as though he were treading the ashes of a departed civilisation. "It is hard to imagine", he wrote 45 years later, "what the outbreak of war" (in 1914) "meant to that generation of liberals", who had trusted so unwisely in human reason. His own generation had "grown accustomed to the idea of civilisation breaking down. We knew long before 1939 that war was upon us." But to the Edwardian Cambridge philosophers "the war with Germany was the violent end to what they had believed was a more or less civilising process".[1]

Two people whose advice he valued had said he should read history at Cambridge—Sir John McClure at Mill Hill School and Frank Ramsey. It was thought by his family that he might turn eventually to journalism—and indeed as early as 1922, when the thought had never entered his head, Graham Wallas was asking him whether he hoped to become one day the editor of the *New Statesman*. Long after that event he remarked to me, when I had ventured to speak in praise of G. M. Trevelyan's *History of England*, that I should commit to memory Dean Inge's remark that "events in the past may be roughly divided into those which probably never happened and those which do not matter—that is what makes the trade of historian so attractive". He affected to laugh at historians and was as disrespectful about them as they have traditionally been about each other (and as a number of contemporary ones certainly were about him). But history was his first love, whether you called it history, biographical study or political science. The Cambridge history tripos was, he thought, "a preparation for

[1] *Father Figures*, p. 123.

the profession of journalism", and he came to believe that the journalist who lacked it might too easily become a commercial hack or an advertising copy-writer. Even if it was too narrow a view of journalism, his own career could certainly be cited in its support.

Those who knew him at Cambridge agree that he worked hard, discriminatingly turned up at lectures, and read with a voracity in which discrimination played a smaller part. His letters home reveal a first year reading programme which took in Shaw, Arnold Bennett, Wells, George Eliot, J. M. Synge, Barrie, Peacock, and *The Young Visiters* as well as the required constitutional and social historians and the nineteenth-century utilitarians.

His first appearance in print, which was in *The Cambridge Magazine*, was not until 24th January 1920—an article about Shaw's *Arms and the Man*, signed B.K.M. It was probably inspired by his having just acted in a Cambridge performance of the play, but was not a review of any production. It was a polemic against war and all its bogus heroics, using the play as a "peg". Raina's heroics, he said, "produce a spontaneous laugh today among those who know that Bluntschli is right in saying that 'all soldiers are afraid to die'". ("Those who know" was a coterie phrase which was to become one of Kingsley's gossip-writing characteristics.) "It was a Prime Minister and not a soldier," he went on, "who said that the war was being fought to establish the principles of the Christian religion. Soldiers . . . know that no war is really a crusade; they know that those who fight always believe in their cause, though they seldom know what it is." (Had he forgotten how, in France in 1917, the wounded soldiers on Ambulance Train No. 11 had cursed the war and derided its trumpeted motives?) Shaw's war satire was enjoying a revived popularity, said Kingsley in the *Cambridge Magazine*, because it was "exactly appreciated by those who are but lately relieved to find they are only amateurs and not, as they half feared, professional soldiers. The net result is that Shaw is popular almost for the first time."

And Shaw, who had in fact been popular since *Candida* in 1897, received a copy of this article from Mrs Edwards, the

Unitarian Church member who had already helped with his University expenses.[1] "Very good stuff," wrote GBS to Mrs Edwards. "He has talent enough to make six ordinary theatre critics and leave a good deal to spare." On the strength of the *Cambridge Magazine* piece, this was an essay in hyperbole, or perhaps clairvoyance, rather than a judgment, for GBS knew who BKM was and clearly wished him well.

It was at Cambridge that Kingsley's reluctance to join movements and societies was put to its first and biggest test. He was never a great joiner. Rather surprisingly he would join literary, historical, debating and chess societies rather than political ones (he played chess for the university). There was a Labour Club whose president was Euan Montagu: it met in rooms at Magdalene and, although Kingsley would often be there, he did not become a member. There was a Communist enclave known as "The Spillikins" which was, in fact, a ginger group in the Labour Club; and upon this he turned a disapproving eye. "I always found him eager to understand what was involved," one of its members told me, "never unsympathetic, but then at the last moment drawing back or hesitating—a congenital liberal, and I use that phrase pejoratively. His attitude always was 'will it do more harm than good?'"

In December 1921 he delivered an address on the subject of Guild Socialism to a meeting organised by the Cambridge Trades Council and Labour Party; and saw himself fully reported in the local paper.[2] At that time he was much excited by Guild Socialism, to which he had been introduced by Margaret and G. D. H. Cole at a 1919 Socialist summer school in the Lake District. This occasion was organised and largely financed by A. K. Bulley, a rich Lancashire textile merchant, who was an active Fabian and whom Kingsley came to know well; and among the party was Kenneth Grahame, author of *The Wind in the Willows*. Guild Socialism was the British version of syndicalism—control, but not ownership, of industry by the workers, that is to say by the trade unions reorganised as guilds. The National Guilds League, founded in 1915, had only two or three years to live when Kingsley discovered it; but he liked

[1] See p. 66.

[2] *Cambridge Press and News*, 2 December 1921.

the idea of railwaymen running but not owning the railways, miners running but not owning the mines, leaders instead of "bosses"—he saw it as a new "motive for work". The capitalists, of course, would oppose this and "there would be some rough play, but no revolution" because the British army and navy would not be induced to become revolutionary, and too many of the workers were supporters of capitalism. "I want to see the capitalist deprived of his power," he declared, "like a stranded starfish."

And then as a further illustration of his political hopes, consider this passage from a review he contributed to *Youth* in February 1921, the book being *Economic Liberty*, by Harold Cox:[1]

> Mr Cox attacks the socialism of 30 years ago and likes best hitting the "Webbism" of the Fabian essays, irrespective of any advance made in socialist theory since their publication. Under those circumstances it was interesting to see in the *New Statesman* a review of "Economic Liberty" by the arch collectivist himself. Mr Webb has altered his position very greatly since 1889: and now, so far from wishing to centralise all administration, proposes two Parliaments and a great system of regional self-government. It is, however, still true that Mr Webb is apt to speak as if liberty were equivalent to a minimum wage and a maximum day, good insurance schemes and efficient hospitals and schools. The first problem before Socialists today is that of the relation of Trade Unions and other associative bodies to the greatest of associations—the State. They are not concerned with discussing whether competition was a good thing, but whether there is any other way than that of violent revolution for destroying the vast trust system which has been substituted for it.

Although in 1921 he was thus writing of competition as a thing which had died, he came to believe in it as worthy of resuscitation (especially among weekly periodicals). But in 1921 he was very much feeling his way and was confident only about Guild Socialism. "Just as a lark is contented in a six-inch nest and equally at home in the expanse of the sky," he wrote in *Youth* for March 1921, "so is man adapted to the

[1] Longmans Green, 1921.

intense consciousness of the small group and to the more vague absorption in the world of humanity. But the lark cannot survive in a ten-foot room nor perhaps the man in the nation state. . . . Our principle [*sic*] instincts were evolved during the period in which men lived in small herds; and our present effort to combine on the huge national scale is highly artificial, and can only be done successfully by a most difficult process of adaptation. One way in which this may be made easier is perhaps that suggested by Guild Socialism."

Later he came to see that Guild Socialism would die because it allowed no room for the *consumer* to have any say. If you had this kind of monopoly it became a syndicalism: if the producer had all the say, the consumer went to the wall, the Guilds would fix everything including the prices, and in the end Guild Socialism would be as oppressive as any other kind of State system.

He now became more interested in the diplomatic origins of the war and the torrent of books denouncing its futility, savagery and dreariness: among them John Dos Passos' *Three Soldiers* and Spengler's *Prussianism and Socialism*. But much more important to him, then and for the next 25 years, was the Union of Democratic Control. It was just then reviving its Cambridge branch and inspiring one of Kingsley's rare group allegiances. The formal revival on 1st March 1920 was the occasion of a student uproar which the local newspapers, though not unused to student uproar, described as a riot. The influence of the UDC on Kingsley's life from that point was such as to merit here a digression.

The Union of Democratic Control was a kind of shadow Foreign Office, unofficial, non-party, non-aligned, never seeking office, and founded by private citizens upon distrust of secret diplomacy. One of the most powerful protest movements this country has seen, it was born the day after Britain entered the war against Germany in 1914. The birth took place in an atmosphere wherein it was treason to speak the truth about war and impracticable to organise against it. From the beginning, the function of the UDC was "to inform public opinion about international affairs in order to kill for ever the pernicious effects of secret diplomacy". But it was also to become an important research organisation and a centre of activity against all militaristic tendencies; an organisation, to quote one of its leaflets, "for the discovery and publication of the hard facts in a world dazed by accidentally or deliberately propagated fantasy". Fifteen of its leading figures became members of the 1924 Labour Government. And Kingsley Martin was to become its Chairman.

Essentially, its founder was E. D. Morel, a crusading journalist who in 1904 had founded and led a successful campaign to liberate the Congo Free State from oppression by the Belgians under Leopold II. Morel had found that his campaign was being secretly obstructed at every step by the British Foreign Office, which shared the fear of the French that Belgium might, because of it, be "pushed into the arms of Germany". In other words, Anglo-German ill-feeling was making Anglo-French cordiality indispensable to British Foreign policy; and accordingly, if the French wanted the Belgian Congo left alone, the Belgian Congo would be officially left alone, and anyone unofficially interfering with it would have as unhappy a time as could be diplomatically arranged for him. E. D. Morel's campaign succeeded in the face of this, and an extraordinary story it is.[1] He was appalled and embittered by the duplicity of the Foreign Office, a state of mind that was intensified during the Agadir crisis of 1911, and led him to publish a vehemently pro-German account of that.[2]

From the beginning of the century Morel had a powerful ally in Arthur Ponsonby, the son of Queen Victoria's private secretary. Ponsonby, who had served in the Diplomatic Corps as well as the Foreign Office before taking up a political career, became the leading critic of both those skilfully devious institutions and spent his life advocating parliamentary control of their activities. In 1914, when he was chairman of the Liberal Party's Foreign Affairs Group, he strenuously tried to keep Britain out of the war, urging (as Kingsley was to do, *mutatis mutandis*, in the case of Czechoslovakia 35 years later) that the violation of Belgian neutrality could not be an adequate reason, even if anything could, for the misery and degradation of war.

[1] See Louis and Stenger's *E. D. Morel's History of the Congo Reform Association*, Oxford, 1968. [2] *Morocco in Diplomacy*, London, 1912.

In the patriotic fever of 1914 the name of Ponsonby became almost an obscenity among the millions. People spat when they used it, in those circles where spitting was a conventional form of rhetoric. At this point he was introduced to E. D. Morel by Charles Trevelyan, who was Parliamentary Secretary to the Board of Education but was as disturbed as both of them about British secret diplomacy and its dangers for the peace of the world. The moment war was declared on Germany in 1914, Trevelyan resigned from the Government.

It was these three men who founded the Union of Democratic Control as a wartime dissenting organisation. They were soon joined by Ramsay MacDonald, Norman Angell, Bertrand Russell, Graham Wallas, Lowes Dickinson, and other progressives concerned to put an end to secret diplomacy. By November that year the UDC had seven branches and by the end of 1917 there were more than 100, the total membership being about 10,000 and largely identical with that of the Independent Labour Party. Its ideal of "open covenants openly arrived at", which became in due course the watchword of the League of Nations, was never in fact achieved or likely to be. Nevertheless, to quote A. J. P. Taylor's *English History, 1914–1945*,[1] "in the end the ghost of E. D. Morel determined British Foreign Policy after the war"; though Mr Taylor showed what he thought of the UDC in a characteristic letter to Kingsley on 3rd October 1948 accepting an invitation to address it. "Its record on Germany is, I suppose, the worst in the country," he said. "It was even founded as a pro-German institution."

UDC meetings were broken up by soldiers on leave, Morel and Bertrand Russell were imprisoned, Special Branch men shadowed and reported on leading members throughout the war and for some years after it. The movement closed down in December 1966, its archives going to Hull University. But it could be revived. The Special Branch still casts an occasional eye in its direction, as one might if an extinct volcano were suddenly thought to have emitted a thin wisp of smoke.

This Cambridge revival in 1921 began with a meeting in St Andrew's Hall addressed by Norman Angell and attended by

[1] O.U.P., 1965, pp. 52 and 199.

Kingsley, as an excited organiser. He was in the company of Lowes Dickinson, then a don at King's and a man destined to influence Kingsley's life profoundly. Among other well-known names on the list of organisers were those of Norman Bentwich, Maurice Dobb, Arthur Eddington, G. E. Moore, Eileen Power and R. H. Thouless. Feeling against the UDC ran high, the meeting was broken up by students and an attempt was made to carry off Norman Angell and duck him in the river Cam. From King's College Lowes Dickinson wrote a letter to *The New Cambridge*,[1] condemning the use of "ragging" for the suppression of free speech; and an ensuing correspondence, in which Kingsley joined, showed that free speech in university towns was a plant as tender then as it had always been before and has conspicuously been since. Kingsley wrote an editorial for *Youth* about another UDC meeting at which the audience shouted down the man who was to become Minister for Air as Lord Thomson (he died in the crash of the great airship R101 at Beauvais in 1930):

> It is because General Thomson is so much opposed to the methods of Bolshevism, the methods of force and impatience, that he is a Socialist. He is convinced that nothing but a sane Labour policy can prevent the hot-heads in each party "fighting it out to a finish". If they are allowed to do that there will soon be no world left for them to divide. He told us that his platform is very frequently "ragged" in other parts of the country by Communists, for whom he is much too moderate. In Cambridge a crowd of undergraduates turn out to meet probably the best-informed and one of the most able opponents of violent methods in this country, and their only contribution to the social problem is to shout "Bolshie". Popular Bolshevism and traditional public school Toryism both ban the use of reason and hard thinking. . . . *Youth* will endeavour to find out what a case is before it shouts for or against it.

Bolshie, Kingsley announced for the first of many times, was a term "used simply to denote all opinions of which the Northcliffe Press does not approve", and a product of the post-war blockade of Russia by her former allies. This, he wrote in *Youth* for November 1920, reviewing a book of Raymond

[1] 13 March, 1920.

Postgate's,[1] was "forcing industrial autocracy upon Russia" in a manner exactly reminiscent of the betrayal of the French Revolution. "However much the present rulers of Russia may wish to free her, they are forced from without, and from within, to employ the methods of Tsardom. . . . There are times in the world's history when mere reformist measures seem the course of despair. Revolution by violence, on the other hand, appears to be suicide."

This (he said) was "Mr Postgate's dilemma". But it was also his own, then and in later years. His oscillations between reformist despair and the denunciation of suicidal violence informed, perhaps one should say bedevilled, his political writing for the next half century.

He was already finding that the written word was a more comfortable and reliable weapon than the spoken. In his undergraduate days, at least, he seems not to have gone down well in Union debates. *The New Cambridge* of 13th November 1920 reported a resolution "that this House desires to associate itself with the sentiments expressed in the Oxford letter to the German professors". (The House decided that it did, by 214 to 157.) A group of professors at Oxford had written to a similar group in Germany suggesting, in effect, that at least among academics the 1914–1918 hatchet should now be buried. Mr Walter Runciman of Trinity (now Lord Runciman), the proposer, said that the victor must surely offer his hand to the loser, hostility could not go on for ever, friendship must take its place, and it should begin now. And *The New Cambridge*, reporting the debate in terms that no one would call impartial, thus presented Kingsley as one of Runciman's supporters:

> Mr B. K. Martin (Magdalene) tried to be very funny and merely succeeded in being excessively cheap. The member from Magdalene ought to know that a series of superior sneers form no answer to the arguments of opponents. When Mr Martin is not supercilious he is very good.

When *The New Cambridge* was not supercilious, it was not supercilious. A fortnight earlier the member from Magdalene had

[1] *The Bolshevik Theory*, Grant Richards, 1920.

spoken in the Union in favour of home rule and dominion status for Ireland, earning himself this notice in *The New Cambridge*,[1] whose reporter must have been waiting for him:

> Mr B. K. Martin (Magdalene) succeeded at length, after three weary weeks of waiting, in addressing the House. This apparently overcame him, for his voice showed unmistakable signs of wear and tear. The Irish, he said, have no loyalty to England, so why persist in acting as if they have?

But to say that Kingsley was not, in the view of his contemporaries, a striking success in University debates is a judgment arrived at in contemplation of his brilliant career as a journalist. Thereafter he never lacked for invitations to lecture and debate. Indeed once a political writer is established he will constantly be invited to address meetings, as if good writing and good speaking were synonymous; and it is astonishing what those meetings will put up with. But what undergraduate Cambridge said about Kingsley in 1920 should, in all fairness, be set against what *Isis* said on 30th October 1935 when he talked to the Oxford University Labour Club on international affairs:

> The standard of discussion by Labour Club visitors has been amazingly high. Following on Messrs Cole and Crossman last week, Kingsley Martin, New Statesman oracle, gave a lucid and fair review of the international situation. He was gloriously witty and managed to suspend judgment on sanctions[2] without being inconclusive. Like Mr Cole he crosses his bridges when he comes to them. His survey of party differences on both sides was masterly.

At Cambridge he was only just emerging as a powerful left wing writer, not yet fully committed in revolutionary fervour to "a classless society without bloodshed", not yet willing to turn his back on the church, not yet disenchanted with the "uses of history".

In May 1922 the Rev. Conrad Noel, then vicar of Thaxted, in Essex, ended a long battle with the ecclesiastical authorities

[1] 30 October 1920.
[2] Italy had invaded Abyssinia three weeks earlier.

over his habit of displaying the Red Flag, as well as the Sinn Fein Flag, in his 15th century church. There had also been numerous battles with students from Cambridge, who had found that Thaxted was within reasonable cycling and ragging distance and that these two flags, representing Communism and Irish independence, were an invitation to undergraduate brawling in the church. Father Noel wrote a pamphlet about it all,[1] which Kingsley reviewed in *Granta* for 19th May 1922. "The Vicar of Thaxted," he wrote, "tells us that violent revolution in this country is likely to come, not from the workers, but from those whose only notion of refuting an argument is to shoot those who use it; and that such a spirit of cheerful imbecility was shown by those gentlemen who made raids upon his parish church because the people of Thaxted chose to decorate it with unorthodox flags. . . . He has the courage to point out that the Kingdom of Heaven, as taught by Christ, referred to a social order to be built sooner or later by us, and that if the Church is to have any hand in bringing this about it must concern itself with the revolutionary doctrines of Christ and apply them to our present society."

But he thought Father Noel was guilty of "a false idealisation of the middle ages" and of entering upon an unfortunate and "elaborate explanation of certain obscure passages in the apostolic reports of Christ's remarks". It was not profitable, said Kingsley, "to justify one's policy and conduct" (e.g. the Red Flag in the church) "by quoting authorities, even if the authorities are as distinguished as Jesus Christ and Mr G. K. Chesterton." Later, when he had a week-end cottage at Dunmow, he was to have many discussions with Father Noel, whose church services he sometimes attended (as a kind of nostalgic indulgence) while Dorothy Woodman, on some special occasion, detachedly played the organ. But at Cambridge his inherited attachment to the Christian faith was weakening, despite the influence of a distinguished Congregational minister whom he much admired—Dr H. C. Carter of Emanuel Church, Cambridge, who had been a leading pacifist figure during the war. Carter used to hold tea-parties every

[1] Conrad Noel, *The Battle of the Flags*, Labour Publicity Co. Ltd, London, 1922.

Sunday in term-time, at which all undergraduates were specially welcome. Kingsley went to many of these with his cousin Geoffrey Turberville, then reading Classics at Trinity. Usually they went on to the evening service at Emanuel Church afterwards; and Kingsley, after hearing the first of Dr Carter's sermons, remarked to his cousin that it was the first sermon that had ever made him listen throughout. (He may have meant the first sermon not delivered by his father; but it has to be remembered, even so, that as a boy he planned cricket teams during the long services in the Hereford Congregational Church.)[1]

In his Cambridge days, both as undergraduate and as don, he was totally fascinated by "The Apostles", the "secret society of intellectuals" which was founded in the 1820's by F. D. Maurice, the great moral theologian who became Professor of English Literature at King's College, London. Its early members included Tennyson and Arthur Henry Hallam; and its story is told by R. F. Harrod in his *Life of John Maynard Keynes*, and more fully by the fabulous Henry Sidgwick in A. S. and E. M. Sidgwick's *Memoir*, published in 1906. In his autobiography, Kingsley speaks of the jealousy he was spared by not knowing that "several of his intimate friends" were members of The Apostles, whose bond was "the pursuit of truth with a duty of absolute candour and the right to challenge *any* proposition so long as it was done sincerely and not from a love of paradox". Membership in Kingsley's time, he records ruefully, meant that you would acquire for life the companionship of "men like Bertrand Russell, G. E. Moore, J. M. Keynes, Lytton Strachey, Desmond MacCarthy, Goldsworthy Lowes Dickinson, E. M. Forster, Leonard Woolf and Roger Fry". Well, of all those men the only two he never came to know personally were G. E. Moore and Lytton Strachey; and some of them were later his intimate friends. The trouble was, he suffered acutely from any feeling of exclusion, from being consciously ineligible for some hallowed enclave in which there was good conversation, wit, and enquiry; and his private diaries show how he nourished that consciousness of it on a diet of self-depreciation. But "he ought not to have known about The Apostles", one of them told me rather frostily. "He might have

[1] *Father Figures*, p. 98.

known that it existed in the last century, but he shouldn't have known it still existed when he was at Cambridge. It was the continued existence that was *really* secret. Of course people have referred to The Apostles so much in memoirs since then that it doesn't matter any more. He was certainly considered for membership, but it wasn't really for historians, it was for philosophers." One of its members was Guy Burgess.

Many years later Kingsley wrote an account, which he may have intended to publish but never did, of the conversations in students' rooms, in "those first days in Cambridge after the war; the happiest in all my life"; and of an odd friendship which ended very sadly. The friendship he refers to briefly in *Father Figures* (page 97); but the surrounding circumstances are described in what amounts to a revealing passage of Cambridge autobiography—in which, I think, all the names are fictitious, all the characters are real, yet each is made to carry one or more of Kingsley's own characteristics. It is in a crumpled typewritten document among his papers.

"We all arrived so unexpectedly; the war had seemed likely to go on for ever, and then suddenly there was the Armistice and we were demobbed and there we were, each in his own college room, with no-one to stop us reading all day and talking all night. It seemed too good to be true. Whitworth, I remember, was still wearing his naval officer's uniform. Simon had been a private, and still wore khaki trousers with a sports jacket because his scholarship didn't run to flannels. I had been in the Friends Ambulance Unit; Jenkins had been a 'ranker' officer; and Harding, a more whole-hogging conchie than I, had been in gaol. We were all members of the Labour Party and saw a lot of each other in one way or another. Jenkins had rooms in Jesus Lane, and asked everyone he met to have tea there. He preferred members of the Labour Party because, in his simple-hearted way, he thought Labour stood for making good all the fine promises of the war, and that naturally all decent people would be in the Party. He was delighted when he got us up to his rather poky little room, with the cracked piano, and saw our astonishment at seeing on the table, not the usual tea and burnt toast but all kinds of tinned stuff and several sorts of jam and a whole loaf of bread, and the pink cakes and sugar buns you get at a children's Sunday School outing. We found the Sunday School atmosphere hard to bear. Most of us came from Chapel stock and had left tea fights behind us with *Onward Christian Soldiers* and *Pull for the Shore*.

"We weren't snobs in the usual sense. We were never less rude to Chivers because his father was a peer; and no-one suffered so much from our contempt as Jacobson, who inherited half a million pounds while he was up there. We weren't interested in money, or clothes, or rank, or even success. I never had a suit of clothes all the time I was in Cambridge. I saved my fares by sending forward a bag by train and cycling between home and Cambridge. I managed to scrape ten pounds, so that I could go abroad in the vacs, by always having bread and cheese and marmalade for lunch and cooking porridge for myself at breakfast. . . . We didn't mind Jenkins having a Suffolk brogue that sounded like a foreign language, and we might have decided to display him as a genuine member of the working class if he had eaten peas with a knife. What worried us was his mental conventionality, not his rough manners. We had no fashions in clothes, but we were terrible sticklers for the latest thing in ideas. We could have put up with Jenkins believing strange evangelical doctrines if only he had been able to give reasons. The first article of our creed was to examine everything and reject what couldn't be supported with good evidence or at least good argument. The boisterous platitudes which made up most of Jenkins's conversations were a bit trying when we were interested in Marx and Freud, and whether God existed, and whether you ought to sleep with a woman without being married—an entirely abstract question for most of us in those days, because we were all working too hard to worry about any woman.

"Whitworth thought Jenkins was a bore, who really supposed the world would suddenly become good and happy if Ramsay MacDonald became Prime Minister. 'I have a high opinion of Jenkins in a way,' said Whitworth to me once. 'He began the war as a private and ended as a captain, which wasn't bad. He says he is going to educate himself and then go into politics and serve the Labour movement. He says it is up to everyone to do their bit for Labour in peace, as they have for the country in war. He can never resist a cliché. I think that's why I find excuses for not going to his parties and not asking him to mine.' 'He wouldn't come to your rooms if you asked him,' I said. 'I've tried to get him to mine but he will never come. I think somewhere at the back of his mind is the feeling that he doesn't belong. . . . But if we were real Socialists he would feel at home with us in our own rooms.' Socialism was the fashion. . . . We had our livings to earn and Socialism didn't interfere: those who were going into politics found Socialism fitted all right. Most of the others allowed their interest in Socialism to lapse: it was just so much intellectual wild oats. I remember the jar I got one day after I had made a Socialist speech, and someone told me I reminded him of an architect who built a house, and said in answer to a complaint about the architecture that he was going to add that on afterwards. He said my Socialism was just a decoration.

"Harding had had a different experience from the rest of us. He said Cambridge life was 'too damned comfortable' to produce anyone who would want to change the world. 'I'd have been the same,' he said, 'if I'd not had the experience of fighting with partisans who were desperate and dying every day for their Socialism. All the people who called themselves Socialists in your sense had long ago given up and accepted the Germans as inevitable. The only people who held on were simple men and women rather like Jenkins. They didn't understand doctrine, but they thought people ought to be equal, to be allowed to live in their own way, and sing songs together without a lot of upper-class snobbery and foreign interference. Many of them stuck it out because they were Socialists in practice, structural not decorative Socialists. It's because I've known a few people like Jenkins in tough spots that I agree we're all snobs up at Cambridge, damned snobs.'

"One day I got a note from Jenkins asking me to have breakfast with him. When I got there I found Brown and Granger and several other Labour Club lads there already. We were still eating eggs and bacon when Jenkins drew out of his pocket an enormous document which, he said, he'd sat up writing until three in the morning—it was an analysis of our characters and qualifications to edit a weekly magazine.

He insisted on reading it all through, aloud. He explained that he had been personally financing, out of his gratuity money, an extremely callow undergraduate weekly called *The Young Socialist*. It wasn't doing well, but he believed it could make a profit if one of us would edit it. He clearly thought this would be a great honour for one of us, but none of us would have dreamed of doing it in the year before our Finals. Brown, he said, was the cleverest of us, but perhaps not the best Socialist. Maybe Granger was more sincere; someone else wrote better; but on consideration he'd decided to ask me because I had such a fine character! I was terribly embarrassed. We all slipped away to non-existent appointments. Nothing came of it except that I wrote one or two editorials for him, not to hurt his feelings. It was practice for me because I already thought of being a journalist. After that, I got my degree and went off to America.

"Well, there was a girl called Sybil who was a member of the Labour Club for a time. I think her Socialism had something to do with Bob Stephen. She married an Earl or something later on, and lived happily ever afterward, or at least until her divorce. She was extremely easy on the eye and much run after. One day Hugh Dalton came to speak at the café where we used to meet, on King's Parade. Jenkins gave me a nudge. 'You see that girl over there,' he said, pointing at Sybil. 'It's a funny thing, but I keep on looking at her and wanting to speak to her, though I don't even know her name. The other day she was coming out of a lecture and I noticed she had her shoelace undone. I went up to her and said: "Do you mind, Miss, if I do up your shoe?," and I did. Funny, wasn't it, when I didn't even know what to call her?'

"Now comes the part I don't much like telling. I thought this story so funny at the time that when Jenkins had gone I told it to a group of men and Newnhamites on the way home. It went down well as a story, but back in my rooms I felt mean, and wrote to several of them to say I hoped they and the others wouldn't repeat what I had told them.

"Then a good bit later I ran into him at the railway station—it was after I had gone down. He was looking less gay than usual, he wasn't quite so full of that awful bonhomie of his.

He told me he'd been in Cambridge winding up the affairs of his paper. He'd spent every penny of his gratuity and a good bit over. He had thought more people were keen about Socialism. The printer had let him down. It was bad, really, because he'd given all his time to politics and his paper and failed to get his degree. . . . He'd promised all sorts of things to his father and mother—his father was a small retired shop-keeper; I expect he had to use all his savings to get Jenkins out of his financial mess. . . . And I expect the girl came into it; probably he fell for her pretty hard. After all, he was no child. I'm sure he had never looked at a woman before, and he must have been about 26 when he left Cambridge. I expect she let him make a fool of himself and then told him he was an under-bred little twerp, or something like that. . . . I think he had always assumed people were as simple and affectionate as himself, that Socialists would want to share everything; and when he began to find out that the movement wasn't like that, it knocked the wind clean out of him.

"Just before the train came in he said one thing that rather took my breath away, coming from him. He said: 'I suppose I made a mistake coming to Cambridge. It's better to stick to your own class, isn't it?' I said none of us were class-conscious, most of the Cambridge scholarships went to members of the proletariat; but it didn't sound very convincing. When I got into the carriage he was looking at me in that puzzled, dog-like way he had when he was listening to something difficult that he thought must be important. A year later he threw himself off a railway bridge—I read about the inquest in a local paper."

Anyone who knew Kingsley could extract from this story, containing as it does many facts of obvious authenticity, a composite and rather poignant, and of course totally lopsided self-portrait (of all things, Kingsley was no snob). He told me once that he had never seen suicide as a possible solution to his own dilemmas, but he had immense sympathy for those who felt drawn or driven to it by disillusionment or despair, or even by the all-too-universal feeling of being misunderstood or under-rated. But at Cambridge he was probably further from it than at any subsequent period of his life.

No one person affected his life, at Cambridge and for years

after, so deeply as Goldsworthy Lowes Dickinson, historian, philosopher, don, and Fellow of King's College from 1887 until he died in 1932. There is no doubt that Kingsley had an exquisite romantic affection for "Goldie"; not in the least homosexual as that word is commonly understood (or even misunderstood), but ennobling and irradiating, and to be described only as love. Goldie was one of a handful of men (Shaw was another) to whom in succession Kingsley sought to transfer his feelings about his father. And Goldie's reaction was that of a father, his letters to Kingsley showing a delightful concern which, again, amounted to love. (Either you loved Kingsley, or you found him insupportable—until he was old: once he was an old man, which he achieved rather suddenly and prematurely, I think he excited a protective affection in almost everyone.)[1] "[Goldie] was nearly 40 years older than I," writes Kingsley,[2] "and I remain astonished that he had so much time for me. We went away on holidays together and had a great deal of fun, in spite of the fact that I was obsessed with misery about the muddle I was making of my personal life" (this, I think, relates rather to his post-graduate life—he returned to Magdalene as a don in 1923), "and that he was in a mood of the deepest gloom about the world. One can be very unhappy and at the same time enjoy life."

Goldie was undoubtedly one of those men who, without effort and often in spite of themselves, bring out the best in others. He was accordingly, said Kingsley, "uniquely capable of friendship". He has been described as one of those rather ugly people you can't help feeling drawn to; a little swarthy man with large ears, a long thin nose, almost invisible eyes, a very long upper lip, a compressed mouth, a scholar's stoop and a strange shambling walk. His students thought he looked like the Carpenter in *Alice in Wonderland*. And, in common (it seems) with almost everyone who knew him, his students loved him. His absorption was humanity and how it might be saved from its follies; and his only enemies were inanimate things, which were ranged malevolently against him. Letters inserted themselves in the wrong envelopes, keys hid in unthinkable places, bath-

[1] See the letter from Verity's daughter, pp. 395–6.

[2] *Father Figures*, p. 117.

room geysers which were longing to blow up waited until it was he who was in the bath before letting themselves go. He had worked all his life until the 1914 war (Kingsley used to say) on the preposterous assumption that men were reasonable. In the end he came to the conclusion that at the root of human nature there lay only madness; and because he never found a bridge between these two extremes he was always detached from current affairs, except during the short period when the League of Nations looked like being a practical alternative to world lunacy. Before 1914 he was a kind of Conservative—he even thought of fighting in the Boer War. He became a kind of socialist concerned to do good to his fellow men without the remotest idea what they were like.

I was talking to Kingsley one day over lunch about writers by whom we had both been consciously influenced. I mentioned Hazlitt, Stevenson and Macaulay. "Don't you try writing like Macaulay for me," he said. (It was during the seemingly endless post-war period of paper rationing.) Had I read Lowes Dickinson's *Modern Symposium*? I knew that Kingsley as a young man used to read this aloud to anyone he could induce to listen to him. I said that if I could have written that I would be very proud. "You would not," he replied, "because a man who can write like that is a man to whom pride is unknown. I wasn't expecting you to *write* like it. I commend it to you, though, as the equal of your three heroes all rolled into one." I remember saying that if I gave him an article written in the style of the *Modern Symposium* he would turn that down as smartly as the Macaulay one. "I'm not talking about style and manner," he said, "I don't want a pastiche of any kind. I'm talking about cogency and logic in dialectics, and clear thinking, and verbal economy, and the way they inevitably lead to clear writing."

And when I re-examined the *Modern Symposium* and *The Greek View of Life* I could see, suddenly and excitingly, that Kingsley's writing was in some ways an echo of them. I could, I am sure, compile a comparative anthology of the two men's work in which many passages set side by side would prove the truth of what I say. I am equally sure that if Kingsley had written an elegy on the death of Goldie, an *Adonais* such as Shelley wrote of Keats, he would have loved to be able to say:

Life, like a dome of many coloured glass,
Stains the white radiance of Eternity,
Until Death tramples it to fragments.

It was also Lowes Dickinson who predisposed Kingsley to believe, rather later in life, that India was the one truly religious country in the world, mystical and melancholy and uniquely perceptive of the ideal; that China was irreligious, commonsense, materialistic, and able to laugh at life; and that man had no need of God. Perhaps the most important thing one can say of Lowes Dickinson is that he and Leonard Woolf had more to do with the conception of a League of Nations than any other two men of their time.

In February 1922, while still at Cambridge, Kingsley spent a profitable week-end at a Socialist conference at Dunsford, near Midhurst. The company included Bertrand Russell, the Webbs and their niece Mrs Barbara Drake (an expert on women in the trade union movement), W. H. Rivers, the anthropologist, George Orwell, Hugh Dalton, and (as she then was) Mrs Barbara Wootton. "Mrs Drake," wrote Kingsley in a paper-covered diary, "opened a discussion on a proposal for a joint professional council, which Sidney took hold of very gently, bit through, masticated and finally delivered up as chewed pulp. . . . Beatrice lost her temper, bullied Blair,[1] and wouldn't let Russell get a word in edgeways. I was sitting on the hearth-rug with Russell and urging him to 'go on', which he at last did, beginning: 'But Mrs Webb, I *will* say something I've been trying to get out for the last half hour.' Claws shown by Mrs Webb very badly. Laski, as W. H. Rivers noticed, was snubbed and not treated very seriously. Mrs Webb talked much too much, Mrs Wootton always up to her part. I said little, though I came in over Guilds and challenged Mrs Webb when she spoke of some representative party she didn't like as 'creatures'! . . . General impressions *re* individuals:

> Laski is getting a reputation as a charlatan. Mrs Webb is detested by most, especially by women, and tolerated or respected by others. Sidney—a great brain and a kind and lovable person. Mrs Wootton—really able. Miss Power a specialist, with chiefly

[1] George Orwell.

good looks as a recommendation in other things—v. attractive. (I've no doubt either of these two could make me fall in love with them if they wanted to, which they would not be likely to do.) Russell one of the most witty, charming and lovable people, very like a more kindly reincarnation of Voltaire."

The seeds of a lifelong Dutch-barometer relationship with Freudian theory were at this time implanted in his mind by Dr John Rickman, the psychologist, whom he came to know at Cambridge:

August 17th 1922 I have got from him more than I ever had before, an idea of what Freudianism means. Most illuminating of all his observations is his analysis of factors no-one else would take into account concerning nations. For example—France's exaggerated nervous fear of Germany is partly due to the sexual institution in France of "coitus interruptus", which produces excitement and nervous fear and therefore aggression for the individual. Explainable by the fact that connection of this sort satisfies only the physical craving and not the psychological. As for Russia, she has found a fixation in the oral stage, when the dominant characteristic seems to be the "identification" seen in kissing, reaching agreement by the general will, i.e., complete identification of opinion in the total absence of any self . . . Rickman was interesting, too, on the psychology of individual C.O.s and pacifists—the reasons are all sexual. I'm not sure whether "love of humanity" is always homosexuality, but certainly usually. Another interesting example is the man who thinks the army is a bad thing because [he is] unconsciously afraid to live only with men . . . or again refuses to identify Germany with the Devil because to recognise the Devil would be to recognise God and he has a desire to suppress "Father domination". Astounding stuff! But I'm not inclined to scoff. [And then, written later or with a different pen]: Yes, I am!

This is a curious first entry into my diary! But I feel a definite need of a Diary now. It will help me in many ways, I believe—possibly sexually by allowing me to work things off.

And then on his last day at Magdalene:

Sunday 20th August 1922 My last day in Cambridge . . . I'm not at all sure just now whether I'm sorry to be leaving. I'm sorry to be leaving the Fellows' garden here, the Varsity library, this kind of life with its apparent leisure and good society. Also to be leaving certain individuals, though the number I mind about is rather small and Goldie is far the most important. But I like seeing Richard often,[1] and Frank[2] is better than anyone I know; and yet their minds work so differently, really, that I doubt if I should find enough permanent satisfaction in them. I feel so very much older in many ways. [He was three years older than both of them.] Rivers,[3] after all, was the person who mattered really most (except for Goldie). I think I remember our lunches together, our weekend at Dunsford, our casual good relationship, with as much pleasure as anything up here. That fellowship, the food to eat by the fire, the cheese, the nuts and oranges, the discussions on his motives in standing for Parliament—which no-one understood [Rivers had facetiously said that he wanted the opportunity to psychoanalyse Lloyd George]—his astonishing boyishness, immense capacity for work. I like to think of him last, lying out all the afternoon in the Fellows' Garden with me and RBB,[4] clearly rather tired and overdone, the feel of the grass on his back and the sun in his face. Amongst other things that day he weighed the advantages of Princeton against Harvard [Kingsley had really hoped to go to Harvard], telling me I should have spent a busy, interesting year at Harvard, but that anyway it was now my job to write something worth having.

[1] Richard Braithwaite, now Emeritus Professor of Moral Philosophy at Cambridge.

[2] Frank Ramsey.

[3] W. H. R. Rivers, the psychologist, who died suddenly while preparing to fight a Parliamentary election.

[4] Richard Braithwaite.

Chapter 6

PRINCETON

IT WAS 1922. Having got his History "first" at Magdalene, he was rewarded by his college by being appointed "Donaldson Bye-Fellow". He could have had a full fellowship if he had been willing (and able) to teach economics; but he was inclined to believe, even in those days, that if all the economists in the world were laid end to end they would not reach a conclusion. I always suspected that he had adventitiously "picked up" more economics than he pretended to have, but he saw it as little more than the anatomy of greed; so that when economists argued in his company (and he held that wherever there are two economists there are two doctrines) he would be an impatient listener until he saw a chance to inject a new topic. Economics bored him, and he evaded the dismal science by allowing it to be known that he was what the statisticians call a "non-numerate". His love was history. He had been a representative of an age in which men made more history than they could consume. His third year "special subject" had been the Period of the Enlightenment, and in the course of it he was asked to lecture and examine the second year students who were following him. He was at this time getting less than £250 a year (including the bye-fellowship) and would shortly be helping to pay for his sister Peggy at Newnham.

In that year, King's College offered an open fellowship, and although he was determined to compete for it he saw no way of acquiring the leisure to produce the necessary thesis. Then, most opportunely, he was awarded a twelve-months "Jane Eliza Procter" fellowship at Princeton University. It was one of those hospitable arrangements under which that beautiful seat of learning (and "football") enables a man to study and write undisturbed for a whole year except on Saturdays. What Kingsley was then already writing became his first—and probably his best—book, *The Triumph of Lord Palmerston*;

and it arose from his desire to find out why ordinary people, to whom war is such an unmerited and unspeakable tragedy, wave their hats and cheer to the echo as each war begins, and how far war is really "inevitable" in conditions of international anarchy. Dr A. S. Ramsey, the President of Magdalene College, Cambridge, wrote on 2nd December 1922 to tell him that he was commending him to the Provost of King's—"I am glad that the dissertation is near its end [it was in fact by this time completed and dispatched]; it means I hope that you will have a little leisure."

The book is concerned with the Crimean War, which in 1922 was the most recent campaign about which you could have access to Foreign Office papers. It is an examination of the psychological mechanism of war fever. One of its central assumptions is that there is no such thing as "public opinion"—there is only public emotion, which is manipulated by the newspapers so skilfully that in the excitement of a great crisis it can be mistaken for the *vox populi*: Kingsley knew about this, but he was not prepared to find that Governments, Foreign Secretaries, and (once they were invented) Ministers of Propaganda actually wrote leading articles for sympathetic newspapers. Having established that they did—he found for example that Palmerston, as Home Secretary, dictated leaders for the *Morning Post*—he was less surprised to discover that they used the opportunity to tell lies. The experience of E. D. Morel with the Foreign Office in 1904[1] over the Belgian Congo atrocities had prepared him for that. He concluded that there is a "public opinion" ready for war in each generation; that is to say it takes a generation (usually computed, according to the OED, at 30 years) to get over the disillusion of the last.

When this thesis was published he had a much-prized letter from G. M. Trevelyan saying that if Britain had not fought in the Crimea she would have gone to war for the Southern States against the North in the American Civil War less than ten years later. Kingsley's book had been completed with surprising speed, and must have been nearly written before he left England, for he arrived at Princeton on 18th September 1922 and by 23rd November was writing home—

[1] See p. 72.

> Delivered of a fine child, after lengthy birth-pangs. Weight 231 pages, wrapped in swaddling clothes, registered and labelled. . . . I wish I could come home with him! I shall start another in a week or two; but first I shall sleep. . . . For the first time I understand a mother's love.

And a month later (17th December) his diary says: "I can't help believing that the child of my heart is good. . . . Nothing I can think of would mean happiness equal to a Fellowship at King's, with possibly a real opportunity to develop Political Science at Cambridge. But I do doubt my powers. I'm sure I should wear myself out. My innocence (in thought and word), my constant forgetfulness and haste, my general irregularity, and at times, to my surprise, my lassitude—what can such a weak and poor creature accomplish? Perhaps above all my inability to believe anything, my constant vague understanding of the other side, my real *ex parte* attitude. . . . I'm *so* broad-minded! I wish I believed in something. The thing which disturbs me most is the impossibility of knowing right from wrong. Then one must judge by results—and I know nothing of results. I'm not sure whether I could not have been happier (but I must define 'happier'?) if the Persians had won at Marathon or if the Huns and barbarian invaders had been kept back another century from Rome."

Thereafter he had time to look round. On 22nd September a diary entry records his surprise that America was "not English or American primarily—English stock is merely the ruling stock over an area about the size of Europe, in which are included as many different races, languages and newspapers as in Europe. Complete districts in New York are Yiddish, with only Yiddish papers; others Italian, Chinese, German etc., where English is scarcely understood; and all over the States there are towns which are almost purely German or Italian, Polish or Czech, etc. . . . In New York I visited various Labour centres, colleges and bureaux and found some of the folk delightful. The strikes which have been represented as defeats for the men here seem to be victorious. They have at any rate made impossible a wholesale cutting down of wages. The Labour movement is a fight undisguised here, a fight for power on questions of wages and hours. Socialism is not a practical issue, and does not appear in discussion at all. The sort of thing that appears is that 15 men have just been arrested in Michigan for holding a meeting, and that an injunction has been issued restraining all strike action by forbidding the 'damage to property' caused by keeping men from work. This is now being fought out and the Attorney-General, Dougherty, a fraudulent ex-business crook, is now being 'impeached' for this injunction. This country lies somewhere back about 1820 in its politics and about 2020 in its machinery and comforts."

Nothing about Princeton stirred him to such shocked eloquence as its football. Saturday, he found, was given over to it. Reading and thinking were impossible. He wrote home on 4th October 1922:

> In an immense area holding 50,000 people, built up in concrete on the pattern of the colosseum, gladiatorial combats, known euphemistically as football matches, then take place. The heroes from some visiting university, accompanied by many admirers, sit one side while Princetonians sit opposite. Their chief function is to shout, not with the undisciplined variegated shouting of spontaneous enthusiasm, but in orderly, trained chorus, led by trainers who dance grotesquely before them, signalling with heads, arms, legs and bodies in a manner hideous and wonderful to behold. The method is both competitive and antiphonal. . . . Each side brings some 20 heroes. Eleven of these do battle at a time: the rest are reserves who fill up the ranks directly one of the original cohort is destroyed or shows signs of doing an insufficient share of the fighting. In the match I saw, against Johns Hopkins, Princeton used two whole teams in order to practice as many men as possible for the more serious matches to come. Princeton of course is too strong for Johns Hopkins. . . . No-one was killed—it was after all only the first match of the season—and only half a dozen were seriously disabled. When an accident occurs the combatants draw breath a moment, talking unconcernedly in groups, the wounded hero is carried off, a fresh man in armour takes his place and the charge is renewed. . . . As in the mild pastime which the decadent English youth calls Rugby, the object is to put a leather oval ball behind a line or kick it over a bar. But here six or more men on each side meet each other in a compact mass, and with indescribable fury attempt to throw the opposition back. The stronger team may after a prolonged battle

> have broken the ranks opposite them, trampled on their remains and succeeded in advancing 10 yards. . . . To watch their struggles, 50,000 people pay three dollars each; and many thousands more turn disconsolate away through lack of space.

And then, to end the same letter, the inevitable reference to the Unitarian Church at Finchley:

> What a day it will be when the *gallery* at Granville Hall is fitted! May I be there to see!

Princeton delighted him, to judge by his diary entries ("an idyllic setting", "perfectly planned", etc.) but he muted his enthusiasm in letters home. "Better than I had expected, and really perfect in its way for me," he wrote to his sister Peggy, who was about to go up to Cambridge as an exhibitioner. ("Wish I was there to share it with you, but I'm inclined to think there are quite a lot of advantages in my not being there this year." Peggy thought there were, too.) "The Graduate College is a wonderful piece of architecture. If you must build modern Gothic at all—and of course it's grossly unsuitable and expensive—you couldn't do it better. Einstein when he was here said it was like an unsmoked pipe. . . . The Graduate School is at the top of a hill and the view from my window is lovely. Immediately in front is a golf course, which gives the place rather the aspect of a huge pavilion where people take baths and leave their coats. For many, that's just about what it is. . . . The library contains half a million books. . . . Imagine me in charming rooms with a fine view, getting up something after 8 o'clock, going down to the breakfast room, eating grapefruit, cereal, eggs and toast. Then returning to my charming rooms and vainly trying to find something useful to say about Public Opinion till about 12 noon. I give it up in despair, read the paper, talk to some graduates or professors over another pleasant meal: visit the library, play tennis, change, put on a gown, feed in an immense Gothic dining hall, talk in someone's rooms for a time, return to my own and write letters and work. . . . But especially I want to let you know that though Princeton is about as reactionary as any place could be, many Southerners, no pacifists, no "radicals", and only a small percentage of intelligence, I'm going to have a good time here and should, with luck, get my book done."

On Christmas Day, 1922, he was staying with friends at the New York School of Social Research, and wrote home to the family:

> Never so lazy or so contented. Yesterday I paid a visit to Judge Hand, really an admirable person, and Mrs Hand asked me to dinner on Saturday next. On Wednesday I go to New Haven (i.e. Yale) and stay with a friend of Laski's while the meetings of the Historical Association are on foot. On my return I go to stay for a couple of days with Graham Wallas's friend Mrs Bacon, and then return to Princeton. . . . The Dunhams at Baltimore[1] are not at all strongly Unitarian. Dr Dunham is obviously merely "ethical" and Mrs D. is very anxious to explain that she's non-sectarian. I went to call on Miss Ramshead with her. Miss R. is a much more robust person and a strenuous Unitarian with a capital U. . . . I must tell you of an amazing remark she made at Washington. While discussing the smallness of the Unitarian body in England, she said she could never understand it. There were so many people who had really been Unitarians. For instance, "why hadn't Browning, Huxley and Tennyson ever joined the Unitarian Church?" I think the Recording Angel will make an entry on the credit side for me that I didn't laugh at this wonderful piece of sectarian naïvete.
>
> I may very likely get a job offered me to lecture at a Summer School in California in July; in which case I should get a good view of the States and come home at the end of August *rich*—i.e. with a few hundred pounds.[2] . . . The East, where I am now, is only a transplanted and debauched England. I shall be a much more valuable person if I've seen the Middle and the Far West.

He had been dissatisfied with the amount of work he was doing since the completion of his thesis—which, to judge from his diary of social engagements, can't have been much at this stage. "At each week-end dinner party I go to, someone asks me to another party—it's like a snowball. . . . I am sick at heart about Europe. How long will it be before England and France are fighting?" And he concludes this Christmas letter by

[1] Friends of his father. Dr Dunham was a medical research fellow at Johns Hopkins University.

[2] This did not materialise.

invoking Tennyson's *Maud* for a final note of gloomy foreboding:

I feel a little inclined to repeat with Tennyson tonight:

> Ah, what shall I be at fifty
> Should Nature keep me alive,
> If I find the world so bitter
> When I am but twenty five?

For "about half the day is spent in violent and unprofitable argument over the newspapers", he wrote on 2nd February 1923. "Mr Balfour would be a dangerous radical in this place."

At about the same time (though the letter is undated) he says "fortunately I am altogether supported on foreign affairs by the Oxford Procter Fellow[1]—son of Sir Charles Harris who runs the War Office, a very brilliant person and a Fellow of All Souls, aged 27—in most ways a high Tory: and together we argue against the whole graduate college, which, I'm told, never argued publicly about anything until my arrival!"

> I'm afraid many of the students here just hate me, and this troubles me because I like almost everyone here. They are some of them stupid, almost all ignorant about European things, astoundingly Gladstonian—or is there some Presbyterian shadow of Gladstone to be found?—in their belief in the eternal laws of right and wrong, in progress, in the perfect sincerity of their own motives and those of their country. But they nearly all mean well and are friendly, even if one is a Bolshevik and a pro-German. On several occasions I've heard of people who, being asked if they've met me, say "no, but they've heard of my pro-Germanism and don't want to". I am probably believed to be a Jew—I've no proof of this—and if you knew what that means in this country!
>
> This probably gives a false impression.[2] I've made some

[1] Dr Reginald Harris, who became the editor of *The Nineteenth Century and After*, and a leader-writer for *The Times* and *The Economist*. In 1923 he was the "Jane Eliza Procter Visiting Fellow" from Oxford, Kingsley being the one from Cambridge—they arrived from England together.

[2] It is certainly not the recollection of those who knew him at Princeton. Herbert Agar, for example, says he was well liked and his company sought by everyone. "He had this awful self-criticism," Agar told me, "self-reproach and anxiety about having offended people."

friends who will remain as long as I live; and I've done some poor, overruled, meek, thinking people a real service by expressing their point of view.[1] For in Princeton there are a lot of liberal people, but (contrary to the normal habit of "radicals") they are all quiet, and the floor is occupied by gramophones—with exclusively 1918 English and French records. Now this, owing to the presence of Harris and myself, is no longer so. Then there are some nice, quiet folk, with a great love for harmony and good form, who go away when an argument begins. I don't blame them. I've got so tired of it myself lately that I go away myself!

In fact, at 3.30 a.m. that Christmas night, he was scribbling a long diary entry about a bitter quarrel with his Christmas host, Harry Dana, Professor of English in Columbia University (Dana was a grandson of Henry Wadsworth Longfellow):

Xmas Night 1922. 3.30 a.m. I had a most extraordinary conversation with Harry Dana tonight. I will try for the sake of my own mental honesty—and sleep at present is out of the question—to go through a few points in an extraordinary and rambling series of arguments. I knew that Harry hated England and loathed the British Empire. I don't especially love the political entity called England, and only defend the Empire—if at all—on grounds of possible utility; i.e. that worse might befall if it collapsed—a poor position at best but an honest one. We began on the subject of corruptibility. I said, and I may be wrong here, that English administration was less corrupt than that of other nations. He leaped on me as if I had touched a raw spot, and denounced me as "exactly like all the other Britishers, a hypocrite, dealing with abstractions, the only thing he hated was hypocrisy" etc. It was only with great patience that I got him to see I was talking of a certain individual freedom from *financial* corruption—bribes and nepotism—which I am inclined to think is characteristic of the English public servant. [There ensued a long argument about British "domination" of the USA and Canada.] It was impossible for me to explain what I was getting at. And when he was most excited and taunting me with hypocrisy, I said I should like to hit him. Now this delighted him. It was, he said, the Bolshie's only argument—when defeated he would want to hit. He knew well enough that I wanted to hit

[1] He clearly saw this at his function when he was editor of the *New Statesman*, and discharged it faithfully.

The Martin family in Hereford, Kingsley on right

Kingsley with his sister Irene

Mrs Basil Martin

Kingsley with his sisters
Irene (*l*) and Peggy (*r*) in 1916

> him not because I couldn't answer his arguments but because he didn't give me an opportunity. I sincerely believe H.D. is insane on this question. I said so. He found in this another proof of the Britisher's intolerance—when anyone disagrees with him he is insane. . . . Every time I am mentioned now he will say "Oh yes, BKM, quite radical in some things, mind you I like him but he's got this awful British hypocrisy about the British Empire. . . ." Well, I may defend things the British Empire have done and are doing—it would be strange if any country *never* did a defensible action—but I know that would open the floodgates of HD's wrath. Just now I feel as if he had publicly made a fool of himself and I was blushing for him. Why does a good intellect go so extravagantly astray? He could only shout and bawl irrelevancies; he showed that a scholar and a critic can behave like the Northcliffe Press. Oh, when shall I get to sleep again? It's 4.30.

And it was, after all, Christmas night. Dana apologised the next day. "He was terribly overdone and neurasthenic," recorded Kingsley; "I ought not to have stayed with him."

Kingsley, it must be said, could row unrestrainedly on rare occasions. One of these had been a few nights earlier after playing chess for Princeton against Penn University. He had gone to bed tired in the Princeton Club in Philadelphia. The bedrooms happened to be full, and he was given a bed behind a screen in a sitting-room. In the small hours he was awakened by a group of merrymaking students who had just returned from a late night binge. Noticing him in bed, they began to pelt him with pillows until the screen collapsed and completed the process of rousing him. He leapt from his bed in fury and dashed at his persecutors. They dispersed in all directions; one of them, having no time to take the lift, ran up the stairs with Kingsley in hot pursuit, got into a bedroom and tried to slam the door. When the janitor finally pulled Kingsley off him, the man was lying nearly strangled on the bed. Thirty years later (22nd October 1951) Kingsley recalled this episode in his London Diary in the *New Statesman*, and got a letter from a lawyer in Buffalo who identified himself as the nearly-strangled man. "I never to this day pass the portals of the Club without a shudder at my near escape from death that night," said the writer. "I did it by biting you . . . I can still feel about my throat your long searching fingers." Kingsley replied delightedly, denied that he had long searching fingers, and hoped they would meet the following year when he was visiting the States. They met by appointment in New York in 1952 and became firm friends.

On 22nd March he was writing to his father that he was nearly 26 and felt very old,

> as if I had developed a philosophy which would save me from suffering quite as much as you have in the world, and which is permanent. This may be only delusion: but I am unable to expect much from life, or, what is the serious thing, much from myself. I am not really an able person in any important way, and yet I'm never content to be second. I wish I could cease to be jealous and ambitious and yet, if I did, I should cease to do any work at all.

In fact what he was doing (he wrote on 16th March) was "thinking out a few things which matter—and I'm grateful for the quiet opportunity here". He was also reading a vast quantity of assorted literature, of which Jane Austen's *Love and Freindship*, Frazer's *Passages from the Old Testament Selected for their Literary Beauty*, and Lytton Strachey's *Books and Characters* may be selected as representing an eclecticism which nothing ever brought under control. Essentially, he was thinking his way towards an acceptable rationalism (which he was rather concerned to conceal from his parents). "I'm quite sure that when I knew him at Princeton," Herbert Agar told me, "he was totally agnostic, but still very much enquiring. He was always in and out of the library. One of the things that *may* have given him grounds for thinking himself to be unpopular—and it was in his nature to seize on it—was the *way* he discovered that Fellows in the Graduate College were not members of the Faculty. When he went first to the library and was asked what he was, he said 'I'm a member of the Faculty' and he was given the run of all the books." (He wrote to his younger sister: "Imagine my delight—I can take out as many books as I want".) "Later he discovered that he *wasn't* a member of the Faculty and couldn't be given these facilities. A Fellow at Princeton is only a member of the Graduate College who is lucky enough to have been given an endowment; whereas at Cambridge if you are a Fellow you are a member of the Faculty."

It was a distinction that already irked him at Cambridge, where his Magdalene Bye-Fellowship meant that he was not a member of the governing body there either. (At that time bye-fellowships were unique to Magdalene and rather disapproved of by the other colleges, who thought the post ought to be that of a research student or something of that kind.)

He formed a close friendship with Herbert Agar and Adeline, his first wife; and for Adeline, who mothered him and sewed buttons on his clothes, he developed—in fact he rather fostered—a romantic attachment which she was wise enough to recognise as a belated attack of calf love. Agar, then tutoring at Princeton for three years, was to become literary editor of *The English Review* and then editor of the *Louisville Courier-Journal*. He was Counsellor to the American Ambassador in London during the war, and wrote, among many other books, that seminal work *A Time for Greatness*.[1] The Agars were hospitable Americans *par excellence*. "Harris and I continue to find hidden Liberals, like modest violets," wrote Kingsley to his family on 1st March 1923, "and our friendship with the Agars increases. I think it's a good thing that Herbert has already married Adeline, or Harris and I would be engaged to her by this time." The phrase heralded a growing and absorbing infatuation for a married woman years older than he. On 1st February 1923 he confided to his diary:

> Sex again worries me frightfully. Mrs Agar says her sister will just suit me as a remedy, but is doubtful if she will come here before I go back. I would just go for the first attractive girl now, I think—I'm as dangerous as anyone can be just now. What would happen if I became a don again and fell in love with every girl who came to see me? I devise a theory that since great thoughts commonly occur in the bathtub (witness Archimedes and Mrs Agar), the reason for the lack of ideas in the Graduate College is the presence of shower baths instead.

And on 23rd February he is writing "Harris and I both in

[1] Eyre & Spottiswoode, London, 1943.

love with Herbert and Adeline: Went there to dinner last night, talked about everything under the sun till five this morning, then had breakfast at the Baltimore,[1] came home and went to bed at six! They are a joyous oasis in the desert—it's worth having come to USA to know them. . . . When do I tell Adeline I'm in love with her?" What he did, characteristically, was to tell Herbert Agar first; but he was disclosing, with agonised and shamefaced honesty, what the Agars had both sympathetically known for some time. Neither of them minded. "After all," Herbert Agar told me, "it's nice to be loved, and it was transparently innocent."

> *25th March 1923* As to work I do incredibly little. At present my difficulties are increased by having really fallen in love for the first time. What is the good of loving a married woman of 35? I guess I'll get over it soon, but at present I'm rather like a callow youth in Shakespeare—melancholy and fiery and useless... she is large, heavy and rather bony in places, has a large mouth and not awfully good other features. She has glorious—my God, yes—glorious hair and a wonderful complexion and just the most lovely expression. She likes me but has no hint of passion for me. Why should she seem the most desirable thing in the world? Something one would do all the conventional things for—beginning with dying and possibly even ending up with living for her? I'll get over it I guess, and that will make friendship again seem all that is necessary and good. I see her every day just now almost, and hope to get her to teach me some German—beginning with Heine, who is lovely and simple.

Herbert Agar remembers all this very well. "He was undoubtedly attractive to women, and he was always surprised about it. He was also guilty—for no reason whatsoever. He was riddled with guilt about my first wife, which both she and I tried to dispel. He couldn't stop talking about it, to me as well as to her, and telling us how miserable it made him. It was unfortunate that such a guilt-ridden man should fall into this extra opportunity to feel guilt about nothing—absolutely nothing. It was the most innocent relationship. Adeline was impressed by him, as I was—by his mind and his abilities, and as anyone in the world would be she was pleased at having

[1] A restaurant in Princeton.

someone so fond of her. . . . He was a very highly sexed man, and about this for some weird reason he always felt guilty. But I just can't imagine him being consciously unkind to anybody, and that's a big thing to say about anyone."

His diary records long talks with a succession of distinguished Americans: Professor Roscoe Pound of the Harvard Law School, who told him that A. L. Lowell, the historian and educationalist, was "if not exactly cowardly, inclined to put things off instead of facing them, and to go on hoping things will blow over"; Paul More, who had been editor of *The Nation*, with whom he had many conversations—and with whom also he went to see a Mary Pickford film:

> Tonight (March 24th) saw a deplorable show. Bad sentiment and morals—just devastatingly bad for the intellect altogether. Mary Pickford is pretty, but nothing too bad can be said about this continual debauching of the mind. Rather like alcohol or any other kind of drug. Neither art, beauty nor intellect wanted. . . . What is to be said for a university whose undergraduates continually go to such a place—every night?[1]

Justice Oliver Wendell Holmes—"one of the very best men I've ever come across; a touching faith in Laski's word, a wide knowledge and quick intelligence, delicious scepticism and adorable vanity, works off his old jokes on me and, I think, likes me. Mrs H. a caustic old dear, bald and ugly—she keeps him a good deal in order and chaffs him in a valuable way." From Holmes he learned that we know nothing of good and evil, and that the only solution is to be a "betabilitarian". Dean Acheson (then in practice as a lawyer) talked to him about German reparations and American financial aid for Europe, endorsing his belief that to "squeeze Germany until the pips squeak' would lead to disaster. Justice Brandeis ("immensely impressive") expounded an earnest belief that one day there would come a massive reaction against advertising. "I asked him whether we were to picture people going into a shop for 'any kind of soap not advertised'? But what he means is that people will object to anything widely advertised on the ground that the waste in overhead charges involved *must* mean

[1] I have been unable to identify this Mary Pickford orgy. [CHR.]

higher prices, just as the people at election times suddenly refuse to obey the papers."

In March 1923 he was still waiting anxiously for news from King's. "Let me know at once if you hear about the King's Fellowship," he wrote to his parents—"after me I hope Blackett gets it." It was in fact awarded to P. M. S. Blackett (now Professor Lord Blackett, O.M., C.H., ex-President of the Royal Society). The blow was softened on 18th March by a letter from Lowes Dickinson, the language of which may help to show why "Goldie" was so greatly loved:

> My dear Martin, I am very sorry we did not elect you today. I feel sure you will be as disappointed as I am. But I want now not to dwell upon that, but to say one or two things for which I hope you will be feeling ready by the time you get this. In the first place your non-election is no reflection upon your work. It was well reported on and well up to our fellowship standard. What really happened was that you came in competition with Blackett, also a very good man, and we had to perform the difficult feat of choosing between you.

Also, Kingsley was apprised from less urbane sources, Cambridge was "bulging with historians" whereas a scientist of Blackett's distinction was a rarity.

> The other thing I shall now say (went on Lowes Dickinson) is this. I should very much have liked you as a fellow of King's and I know you wanted to come. But I am not sure that it would really have been the best thing for you, with your interests. I mean that it is difficult, at Cambridge, to get the kind of contacts and inspirations which are needed for good work on political science, bearing on the contemporary world, which is what I look forward to your doing. And it is, I think, more likely than not that a year or two hence you will be rather glad you were not tempted to stay with us. Which means that the loss is rather ours than yours. . . . I can hardly advise but I think you would have not a bad chance of getting something at the LSE (with Wallas's support). Of course it is I suppose possible that Magdalene may keep you on? I can hardly advise—except this: not to take what has happened too much to heart, and above all not to let it disturb your belief in yourself.

Kingsley's scribbled diary for 27th March records: "I knew it already, and I had never expected success; but I mind to a foolish degree. So much so that I don't want to write about it. . . . Life is an experimental science in which you cannot fix the conditions but must accept the results. Pessimists therefore call it an art." But in a letter to his mother a month later, he said: "I'm not unhappy about it, although I felt bad at having been so very close. Goldie makes it clear that it lay between the two of us. His letter is wonderful, and it did a great deal to cheer me up. He really is the dearest person, to try to comfort me like that, and take so much trouble and thought about it . . . I hear from Salter[1] (who is going to be married, marvel of marvels!) that Laski is pulling some strings for me at the London School of Economics, so that is my most probable fate. Also I've received a letter this morning from H. W. V. Temperley[2] asking if he shall propose my name as a lecturer in Political Science next year in place of John Butler, who is now in Parliament. I have accepted his offer (it would bring in something up to £150 in the year only). The ideal thing will be to make some arrangement between the two, but I guess that's likely to prove impossible; and if London objects to my doing work at Cambridge I may have to chuck Cambridge. . . . But it's nice to find that folk haven't forgotten me."

He also had on 8th May "a still more remarkable letter from Maynard Keynes, which overwhelmed me". (It said that Kingsley's thesis was "interesting, subtle and learned".) "He has never shown any interest in me before. I have always thought he disliked me. But he suggests my writing for *The Nation*, and his commendation of my thesis couldn't be higher."

And on 6th June 1923 he sailed for home in the *Berengaria*, after a "wonderful last evening with Herbert and Adeline—who may, I think, find me likeable again in time. I realise that she has taken many things which are sincere in me as being dramatisations, as well as the ones which really are. I fear that, being rather strung up when she said goodbye last

[1] Frank Salter, Kingsley's history tutor at Magdalene College, Cambridge.

[2] Cambridge Professor of Modern History.

night, I may have again seemed dramatic. But she is wonderfully good to me." He had had a cable from the President of Magdalene, suggesting that he should now return to England and explore the possibility of a history fellowship at some other College.

Back at Magdalene, with his bye-fellowship renewed for a further year, he did some lecturing, some research for the book which later appeared as *French Liberal Thought in the Eighteenth Century*, and some WEA lecturing at Rugby; and (with growing frequency) he lectured at the London School of Economics. He also wrote many book reviews; and it is interesting to find from these that in 1924 his style was already firmly established. In the New York *Literary Review* for 3rd May 1925 there is a Kingsley Martin piece which could well have been written 45 years later. The book was Volume III of the *Cambridge History of British Foreign Policy*, edited by Sir Adolphus Ward and Dr G. P. Gooch; and though the review was written while Kingsley was still regarding modern war as having only economic (i.e. capitalistic) causes, the set and style and above all the *readability* of it is the Kingsley Martin of the *New Statesman* from 1930 to 1960.

One evening in 1924 he went to one of Harold Laski's lectures in Cambridge and found himself sitting next to an attractive science research student. It was not necessarily a disloyalty to his friend Laski that he discovered her to be the more interesting subject. After the lecture he was deep in conversation with her when Laski approached them and said: "I see that you know each other?" Well, they said, they were beginning; and Kingsley asked her if she was doing anything that evening. She was not. At the end of the evening he asked her if she was doing anything the following day? No. By the end of the following day they had discovered that they were in love. It was at the close of a term; and they both decided, since Kingsley had very comfortable rooms in Magdalene, that the vacation, or as much of it as they could arrange, would be best spent in Cambridge.

These were idyllic weeks for Kingsley, who now perceived—at the age of 27—that he had met the real thing at last, obsessive, total and transfiguring. His diaries, which refer to her as

Verity, for a time refer to little else: "Spring has come—a wonderful walk in the Botanical Gardens and along the Backs with V.—bulbs and trees shouting and singing for joy" is a typical entry. It was a time in his life, perhaps the only time, when he did not feel excluded from total happiness. They walked about in Cambridge and in the countryside, Verity introducing him to places he had never visited in his undergraduate days—the Cavendish Laboratory, the Strangeways, the Biochemical where J. B. S. Haldane worked. It was the first time Kingsley had been made aware, in any significant or practical way, of what was happening in science—these were the great Cambridge days of J. J. Thomson, Rutherford, Gowland Hopkins, Bateson, Jane Harrison, Rivers. Their exciting work was often the subject of his talk with Verity; and yet, once the idyll was broken, it wasn't until the late thirties that he returned to them, with some idea of opening up the *New Statesman* to science and its social implications.

Towards the end of the summer he went on a previously planned holiday to Paris, with some old friends—Laski, Kingsley Smellie,[1] Ginsberg[2] and Finer.[3] On his return he found Verity had decided after all to marry the man to whom she was already committed and that life, for him, had suddenly lost its savour.

At the same time he found that his book was being extremely well reviewed:

> I am unhappy to have so many projects floating and none really maturing; much idle reading and little real work (e.g. Forster's *Passage to India*—a gift from V. and a work that only the Gods can understand). My book has had the advantage of really making me a recognised historian and even a literary figure in a small way! Anyway I am to be Margaret Irwin's[4] guest at the Pen Club on July 1st! Much of this is pleasant; but I've no grip on life, and except for the hope that I may get one some day, would willingly leave it.

[1] A Cambridge contemporary, later Professor of Political Science at the LSE.

[2] Professor of Sociology at the LSE.

[3] Then Reader in Public Administration at the LSE.

[4] The historical novelist, author of *Royal Flush*, etc.

A few years later, Margaret Irwin came to mean more to him than recognition as a historian; but the evening at the Pen Club brought him the first of many contacts with Lady Gregory,[1] Rebecca West, Amber Reeves, Galsworthy and Henry W. Nevinson. By this time (July 1925) he had taken up his lectureship at the London School of Economics and left his parents' Finchley home to live in a tiny flat at number 5 Guilford Street, Bloomsbury, opposite the Foundling Hospital. And he renewed contact with Olga Walters, with whom, after a couple of years of agonised indecision, he was to make his disastrous marriage.

But at many times during those two years he would have married Verity at the merest word from her. Throughout 1924 and 1925 he was torn almost apart by Verity and Olga. At a message from Verity he would cycle non-stop from London to Cambridge—this he did many times—and make "one more last effort to sort things out". His elder sister Irene, with whom he always had the closest possible ties, used every resource of an exceptionally understanding nature to help and advise him. He turned to psycho-analysis, driven to it by desperation rather than attracted to it by intelligent enquiry or simple credulity. His dreams, he had been told while he was at Princeton, were dramatisations of his unconscious wishes, and since he had been *consciously* searching for reasons why he should not marry Olga he was easily induced to believe that that was the consummation which his true mind desired. This was muddled in his thoughts with a new belief, as strong but equally reluctant, that his love for his father was really a repressed hatred and jealousy, and that his unwillingness hitherto to recognise this as the source of his troubles was due to his active banishment of the system of feeling from the conscious mind into the region of the unconscious.

"I wonder why you think you want psycho-analysis?" Lowes Dickinson wrote to him on 10th August 1925. "I don't know whether it is aged stupidity which makes me so suspicious of its effects, but I am. . . . I shall certainly come to see you and make acquaintance with your wife when I get a chance. When are you to be married?" Kingsley at that time did not know whether he was to marry Verity or Olga. He had been obsessed

[1] The Irish playwright.

for months with a sense of sexual malaise which he clearly could not understand. "I think I am really better," he put in his diary, "but in spite of Olga, who has changed—very sure of herself, not as attractive as when she was full of shyness and admiration (here is the swank devil!). I think I shall do the analysis. I fear I can never get things right with women unless I do. I'm getting—like Ellis—furtive in meeting anyone's gaze. Oh God, I want full life and strength and work—and I *will* have them."

Chapter 7

OLGA

KINGSLEY HAD MET Olga Walters before he went to Princeton. She was the youngest of the three handsome daughters of Dr F. R. Walters, who was Medical Officer of Health for part of Surrey and ran (at a loss) a private sanatorium in the pinewoods at Tongham, near Farnham. . . . Kingsley was invited there for a week-end in 1922, an arrangement which, not to put too fine a point upon it, was probably a piece of experimental match-making inspired by the Misses Sykes, Olga's two aunts who lived in Finchley and went to the Unitarian Church. Olga sometimes came to stay with them, and on such occasions had already once or twice met Kingsley, in other company. Dr Walters was a much-loved man, a devoted medico with the same kind of dedication to the service of humanity as Kingsley found in the more celebrated and eccentric Harry Roberts.[1] His wife was, by contrast, the very prototype of the Victorian octopus; Victorian, too, in the way she set about marrying off one of her daughters to Kingsley. She is remembered as an extremely dominant woman, with the supposedly weak heart that is so powerful an aid to domination; a talented artist, a great organiser, a firm presider over the little domestic ceremonies. Irene was also invited for that first week-end with Kingsley as his elder sister and chaperone, no doubt (she thought herself) by way of giving the invitation the "balance" of respectability. She recalls an episode that might have come straight from the pages of Mrs Gaskell:

> Mrs Walters sat in a chair with her three beautiful daughters grouped around her. Someone put a footstool under her feet. It was evening. The little maid came in to have the alarm clock wound for the morning. She advanced and handed Mrs Walters the clock; and then she backed away as if in the presence of royalty. Mrs Walters wound the clock, permitting herself some

[1] See *Editor*, pp. 139–48.

little pleasantry as she did so. The maid then advanced to receive the clock, curtseyed, and withdrew.

Mrs Walters had her eye on Kingsley as a suitable mate for the oldest daughter, Margaret, but Kingsley's eye fell, at least speculatively, upon Olga, the youngest. The middle daughter, Gwenda, made her own marriage arrangements and Margaret remained unmarried. Olga went up to Cambridge to read anthropology ("I was made to nurse until I ran away"). She was at Newnham with Kingsley's sister Peggy, they became close friends, and it is probable that Peggy got closer than anyone to understanding Olga's complex, fey and self-analytical nature. Olga is remembered as an original and entertaining girl with a love of fantasy, some skill as an artist, a painstakingly ornamental and stylised way of writing, and a habit of speech which owed much to the emerging popularity of A. A. Milne and the Christopher Robin syndrome. She was slender and rather tall, with regular features, a lean and well-modelled head, and a hair-style which in those days was known as an Eton crop. She fluttered her eyelids as she talked. Some of her contemporaries recall her as an undeveloped version of Virginia Woolf—to whom, in her twenties, she bore a striking resemblance which, in all likelihood, she would have been at some pains to cultivate. She certainly had the spirit to rebel against all her mother's views except the eligibility of Kingsley as a possible husband; and to anyone as susceptible as Kingsley she would probably have no ultimate difficulty in making herself irresistible.

But the process did not begin at once. During his absence at Princeton he had made no references to her in his letters and diaries. On his return to Cambridge he was quickly involved with Verity. The two women hardly met at Cambridge, or indeed afterwards, although in 1932 Olga was writing of Verity as "a person who caught the imagination—I admired her beyond reason". But Verity was, after all, about to marry, and this played some part in Kingsley's vulnerability to other girls, Olga particularly. During a family holiday at Lower Beeding in Sussex he allowed himself to fall in love with Olga, or perhaps to fall in love with the idea of being in love with someone so attractive, unusual, original—and so much in love with him. (Olga was there, during the Cambridge vacation, as the friend of Kingsley's sister Peggy.) But during the same period—throughout 1924 and part of 1925—he contrived to be much in the company of Verity; and when he was seen with her he was always gratified to be taken aside and told (as he commonly was) how lucky he was to have the affection of someone so beautiful, so clever, so personally charming. And on Sunday 10th November 1924, still at his parents' home in Finchley:

> Home, and very jolly this evening. Olga much in love with me, I fear. And I? Weak as ever.

By May 1925, the situation still unresolved and his mind still cowering from its own accusations of weakmindedness and ineptitude, he was going regularly to a psycho-analyst:

> Analysis proceeding all the time—I "want to hurt Mother", apparently. It's my childish unconscious idea of love-making, and a jealousy of Father because I think he did this to Mother. I wonder why?

Not, presumably, why his father loved his mother but why it had involved so much suffering and bewilderment for a son who had reached his late twenties before knowing much about it. He analysed what he called the "dangers" still confronting him, though Verity had by this time married the other man, in a diary entry of June 1st 1926 about his desires:

> Desire to "down" analyst and get free.
> Desire to get "something settled".
> Desire not to run risk of making any kind of muddle with Olga liable to lead to precipitate acts.
> Absurd, it seems, to go on with analysis, holding up complete relations with Olga, and yet absurd to break off before end of period arranged. Shall I tomorrow tell analyst I'm not coming any more? I have decided to ask Olga to marry and this involves my surrender—not a marriage such as I had imagined in the past. But a complete giving of myself.

And on 22nd June 1926 while she was on a visit to her parents, he wrote her a letter which at the last minute he decided not to send: he put it away among his correspondence. It is perhaps the most revealing statement about her in his own diaries and papers. The diary from which these notes have been taken, running from August 1922 to July 1926, is mutilated by the rough removal of handfuls of pages, a fact which encourages the belief that the posthumous publication of what remains may have been in Kingsley's mind as a possibility and would not have been against his wishes:

> *The Moods of the Undisciplined Mind*
> *Dawn—Wednesday 22nd June 1926*
> Olga, outside my window the birds sing praises as the sun rises, and I think of you in the country, and I hope and fear. O Olga, I am so afraid—not, I think, now of a shadow only, though I am so ignorant of my nature that I never know. But I fear when I get your letters of love and longing for me—I am not cold? Why do I fear? I cannot respond as I long to do, and I am haunted by the memory of Verity's determination and her failure to respond to (her husband's) passionate but disinterested love. Need I write this to you, who understand everything? Is it not folly to hurt you? . . . I know that the world would be black without you and that I depend on you. Only I fear so much—*why* do I fear? Oh, Olga, you ask so much of me, your demand is so entire—rightly so entire—and I wonder if any amount of striving on my part can aid me in responding as I should. Am I incapable of real love? . . . I feel I must write like this. I want you, terribly, I want you to drive away my devils. The reaction I feared has come. Shall I only want you always to drive away my devils? Where is the *happiness* of love in me? Why when Irene[1] spoke to me of "the greatest happiness"—why did my heart sink and mock me? Is it that I feel I cannot live in your atmosphere? Idealism terrifies me: I thought I could do it, and now every vestige of my faith has fled from the windows of my heart. Mother talked of my being "fair to you". What is fair to you, Olga? It was not fair to you not to make every attempt to destroy the cynicism in myself. . . . God, I meant to write you such a joyous letter, full of happy plans, and looked-for sharing of work. . . . What is my fear? Something of myself which will not give? Yes, for if one loses oneself altogether there is nothing left to fear. Oh, I keep praying for faith and strength, I keep trying to drive away the haunting doubts and I cannot.

[1] His sister.

> Morning. Later
> I drove them nearly away, tho' they still haunt me. And I have faith again, for I found myself out. You see, dear, you are "the eternal womanly", in Goethe's original sense, the ideal to which I look and before which my spirit falters. But deep down I know what is permanent, and I am really permanent about you. I'm afraid for you with me—afraid you may have so terrible a disappointment, because second-bests are not any good to you. You will make no compromise adjustments. But I *do* believe we can succeed, I do want your happiness; and to climb utterly out of this old skin and waken afresh to life.

On 29th December 1925, on a solitary walking tour by means of which he hoped to find diversion and briefly forget about Verity's marriage, he was staying at Monk's House, Rodmell, the cottage which Leonard and Virginia Woolf had recently converted into an ideal "writers' retreat". "The great lesson I've learned," he wrote, "and it's taken so long to learn it, is that life is a *whole*. Has Olga taught it me or have I learnt it myself? I never knew till lately what it meant—'to thine own self be true'. It means so much to me now. And so with this coarse sex struggle it will go—because I shall cease to desire and struggle, and it will not matter because I shall have found a principle of living. Oh, my God, whoever thou art, help me to be *whole*. I know now what that means. Perhaps the Bible would mean something now. . . . Father has always known this. I must talk with him, and tell him what I feel about Puritanism."

I think he never did. And this was within about six months of his own marriage. On New Year's Day 1926, sitting in the guest's bedroom at Monk's House in the small hours, he wrote:

> I know tonight how people feel when they write great poetry. But I cannot write poems or find words which will express the emotions which drove me, laughing, crying, shouting and singing, up to the Downs, overwhelmed me as I lay in the rough grass and drank of the beauty above me. Only once has a night ever before been to me so wonderful—and then I was not alone. But since we are separated it is well to be alone.

He had already come to believe, with hopelessly mixed feelings, that Verity's own marriage had not in fact brought her happiness. He must have confided his distress about all this to Lowes

Dickinson, who wrote to him from King's College on August 2nd 1926:

> What a business that marriage seems to be! I must say that I like you all the better for not taking advantage of the husband. I have always thought this the really weak point in adultery, rather than the so-to-speak religious or moral one. I have my insincere relations. But I fancy that both young and old are mostly cynical or indifferent about that. The great thing about you is that you can work, and observe some proportion: this latter a very hard thing to do when one is in love. And in my old age I feel it to be true that the only thing that matters is one's actual legacy of work, after all these struggles and confusions.

On another occasion Lowes Dickinson, who understood the anguish and poetry of love in a way that has sometimes been said to be most accessible to the deeply thoughtful homosexual, sent Kingsley his own "apostrophe to Plato" on what love meant to the Platonist: "I mean the kind of love you knew when you were young, when the soul seemed to be the body, and body soul; when poetry and philosophy are born together like twins, and the mother and father of both is love. That was the moment you seized and set in heaven like a star, for generous youths from that day to this to worship." Kingsley wanted almost desperately to believe that there was a sensuous universe of ecstatic love, both heterosexual and homosexual, which most people never so much as glimpsed; and he had known from adolescence that he was not homosexual. His long sessions of psychoanalysis had, I believe, bewildered rather than helped him, convincing him for life that he was "different". A medical friend of mine once told him in my presence (and he was at that time 63) that he was far too worried about his interest in sex and would have more reason to worry if it were absent. Commending the Elizabethan approach to sex, the doctor quoted to him Eric Partridge's book *Shakespeare's Bawdy*, which presents Shakespeare as a man who not only enjoyed sex but took a curious interest in it. (Partridge says that Shakespeare "was no instinctive sensualist, he was an intellectual voluptuary, and a thinker keenly and shrewdly probing into sex, its mysteries, its mechanism, its exercise and expertise, and its influence on life and character".) Kingsley's awareness of its influence on life and character, however, got in the way of any effort to come to terms with it; so that he remained one of those men condemned by the modern prurience to be spoken of behind the hand as a voyeur. It was, and it was sometimes intended to be, a cruel and dismissive epithet, and was not the less cruel because he had come to accept it as accurate.

Nevertheless, and though he had married Olga,[1] he remained devoted to Verity for the rest of his life. In 1934, indeed, he came once more very near to marrying her. He was, I believe, mistaken in supposing that, when it came to a final decision, she would have married him; but she was nothing if not human, and his devotion was precious to her. He married Olga at the Finchley Unitarian Church, his father conducting the simplest of ceremonies with no one present but the closest members of the two families. The couple had been living for some months in his two little ground-floor rooms at number 5 Guilford Street, but they stayed there now for only a few weeks before moving to number 47 Great Ormond Street. And even so early in the marriage its probable course might have been foretold by anyone who could have considered together the two following diary entries, written less than three weeks after the wedding:

> *Olga, 25th July 1926* It seems there is some treachery at the root of our relations. When I came to Great Ormond Street I put my heart into an idea of a house we could work and live in, a Russian fairy-tale house. Kingsley pulled me to Barker's and made me buy ugly furniture in a great rampageous hurry. Kingsley understood for a moment: he said "A child is dead". No other child came to take its place, because Kingsley could not share in my heart's dreams. I don't believe we shall ever find a new place again. I feel heart-broken. . . . Perhaps poverty, or a change to a different place and job for Kingsley, will bring us together in a way that may mean real creation. . . .
>
> *Kingsley, 26th July 1926* Steadily fitting in more with Olga, but she is difficult with folk. Success with Goldie, who came alone. Shocking failure tonight with Burns[2] and the Browns[3]—ought never to have had people like the Browns, whom I did not know much. With the others, I talked and showed off in the old style—

[1] On 7 July 1926. [2] C. Delisle Burns, a lecturer at the LSE.
[3] Isobel Brown of the LSE and her husband.

> I think partly or largely due to the feeling that no-one would say anything at all if I left off talking. Oh, miserable! No contacts at all. What I ought to be worrying about, and probably am, is failure about Olga and the others. I could have helped in drawing out Burns and Brown if I had really tried, instead of attempting to dominate and spread myself. I really wanted to, and forgot again—also I feared no-one would talk if I left off; which is true—having started wrong. Began "excited"—always fatal.

The Bloomsbury they now lived in had already acquired its legendary and seemingly imperishable aura of intellectualism; but as Kingsley says in *Father Figures* (page 149) they were "on the edge of Bloomsbury but not of it". Demographically, he used to say, it was a place where the couples were triangles who lived in squares. "Bloomsbury Square is dead," wrote Olga in one of her massive diaries: "dirty unhappy trees, stupid blank offices, unfinished respectability cut across by crude Americanism." A "fixed and considerable proportion of each day," she complained, "is spent in the laborious and inefficient pursuit of housework, which leads to no end and is associated in my mind with years of futile misery." The proportion of housework seems likely to have been fixed rather than considerable, and she sought expression for her creative urges by designing book jackets and typing some of Kingsley's manuscripts—for example his hard-hitting little book on *The British Public and the General Strike*[1] which, in effect, lost him his job at the LSE because Sir William Beveridge had been a member of the guilty Coal Commission. Kingsley bought her a gramophone and she began to acquire a library of "miraculous and exquisite" ballet recordings. She began the writing of numerous stories and poems which she never finished; an autobiography; and a book called *Through The Ark*—which eventually she did finish and published in Paris years later, with the Obelisk Press (in the distinguished and variegated company of Cyril Connolly's *Rock Pool* and Henry Miller's *Tropic of Cancer*).

Through The Ark is "an allegory of the modern world". It likens the world she knew to the Ark in which Noah had cared for the world's animals; but the part of Noah is played by

[1] Hogarth Press, 1926.

"Longinus", who is a giraffe and can therefore see farther than anyone else. The giraffe is probably Maynard Keynes, whose range of vision amazed her and who, she thought, looked like a giraffe. And the rest of the animals almost certainly include a number of other people she had met through Kingsley. They can hardly have been gratified. Among them, to judge from her written notes, are Kingsley, the Webbs, Professor Andrade, Bertrand Russell, R. H. Tawney, and members of her family. "The whole story," she wrote, "is influenced mainly by Dante and by the illustrations of W. H. Hudson's *Green Mansions*." To anyone else it might more probably suggest an amusing pastiche of Aesop, la Fontaine, Lewis Carroll, George Orwell and Winnie-the-Pooh. It is undeniably witty and almost certainly defamatory, though the libelled intelligentsia, if they sought redress, would face the usual difficulty about the cap fitting. And it was commended (by its publisher) for the "suave ferocity of its satire".

Living in London, and especially Bloomsbury, gave Olga the literary and artistic contacts she thought she needed. And when Kingsley was appointed to the *Manchester Guardian* in 1927 (see Chapter 8) she was more dismayed than at first she allowed him to know. Within a few months of their marriage they were living at number 20 Kingston Road, Didsbury, Manchester. She hated it, and began to develop a kind of poetic solitude from which she never again emerged. "The only thing I liked about life in Didsbury," she recorded some years later, "was the corner by the Cock Inn, which was lit up at night. The river was a sad, wretched, evil river and it stank." But there was one other thing she liked about it—a big black mongrel Labrador-type dog called Benjy, which Kingsley, to mitigate her self-imposed loneliness, had bought her in response to many entreaties. Benjy seems not to have been a popular dog, but Olga was devoted to him, crooned to him and read him stories. She also did much painting (which she called "William Blake-ish") using an empty top storey as a studio-cum-storeroom; and had a violent row with an eminent art critic, when he touched up one of her paintings while she was out of the room.

In general she was ill-at-ease there, and it became a stormily theatrical setting in which Kingsley was cast in two roles—as the author of all her misfortunes and as the object of her intensely feminine and tortuously articulate romanticism. In a letter he had from C. P. Scott, editor of the *Manchester Guardian* (he quotes another passage from it in *Father Figures*, page 166), she was made welcome enough: "Your visit was a great pleasure, as also was that of your wife. It was a happy stroke to bring her, and if she accepts our Manchester I need not be afraid of you. Please give her my best remembrances." She did not accept our Manchester, and Manchester's readiness to accept her was gradually reduced to that of a small and static circle of friends which included Professor Clay of Manchester University and his wife (and both she and Kingsley found him friendly and her intolerable); C. P. Scott, the Editor—"a sly old fox," noted Olga; "quick, piercing, quite unscrupulous, with fair domed forehead and white locks"; and "Ted Scott I loved. He had considering, very steadfast grey eyes; was not quick, but was very independent, although he found it difficult to come to conclusions. Independent, yes; but much afraid of his father and could not argue with him." There was also A. P. Wadsworth, Labour Correspondent of the *Guardian*, "rotund, sits on fences and chuckles a trifle savagely at everybody, enormously able, really knows his subject"; Professor and Mary Stocks (now Lady Stocks), whom she loved; and Malcolm and Kitty Muggeridge, the former being at that time a *Guardian* colleague of Kingsley's and the latter having been with Olga at the London School of Economics. ("I love Kit Muggeridge," wrote Olga to her temporarily absent husband in October 1929; "she has such a nice deprecating please-share-my-point-of-view grin. She asked me to go and see her on Tuesday, so I will if not sick.")

Olga's very odd personality, which to some people presented itself as no more than an irritating affectation of speech and manner, can only be judged today from her letters and diaries. Kingsley's papers, with those lent to me by his sister Irene, include an immense number of Olga's letters, diaries and drawings. The letters begin from the time when Kingsley had left the London School of Economics, in May 1927, to become a leader-writer with the *Manchester Guardian*. During his absences in London she took occasional short holidays with friends. From Coxwold in Yorkshire, in an undated letter probably written in 1928, she wrote to Kingsley in London. (He had accepted the *Manchester Guardian* job on condition that he could have three months of each year in London "to maintain necessary contacts"):

My dearest loved-one,

Separation stretching out its arms staggers across the mute dark. I've walked miles today and am correspondingly tired. Missed a silly train by five minutes and had to remain 1½ hours at a cheerless spot. True, they gave me tea but it was of poor quality. On the station were innumerable fowls in packing cases. They eyed you through the slits with serious, almost argumentative attention. Finally the station master courteously toasted me before his private fire. There is but one line here and the arrival and departure of a train is a great event. Frequently the York train and the Pickering train stand side by side at a station offering each other the next turn on the single line. . . . Mine host and family have been out to a shooting party and have come home very full of themselves. I went today to Mrs Wadsworth's[1] three villages, and of the three I named for yours Hutton-le-Hole. Both itself—green and up-and-downish, on both sides of a stream with Heath Robinson bridges, close to the moors but with trees and pastures near also—and its postmistress who acts as landlady, are most pleasing. . . . Darling, I'm sad you feel so little confident, but that may mend. For myself I feel crooked and blind with tears and sentimentality, apt to lavish affection on stray lugworms and centipedes. . . . Oh darling don't let me cry my affection out to shivering ghosts and the empty air: I don't expect much, but the emptiness breaks my heart all the same. . . . Beauty abides in the waving trees and in the magic growth of daylight and in the stars at night. I shall learn, if you will be patient. O Kingsley, dear Kingsley, when I look for you I see a thousand unrecognisable shapes and it is only in the cathedral or in the glimmering, blurred peace of a walk at night to a strange place, when the earth is untroubled, that love perches on my shoulder and I feel the true *you* present—or perhaps only the you I am capable of loving. Have patience, dear, or I may dissolve away in tears and be barren again, and I have waited so long for inspiration. Anger and fear and deceit still walk the earth.

[1] Wife of the *Manchester Guardian* man who later became editor.

But when they were at home in Didsbury together she seemed to him more and more remote, uncommunicative, chronically untidy (Kingsley's tidy mother was "appalled at the hugger-mugger they lived in"), and constantly suffering from some *maladie imaginaire*. On 25th February 1928 his sister Irene (who was genuinely fond of Olga) wrote to commiserate with him—"very bad that she should feel so run down and have to be in bed when the Editor comes to lunch, and to miss concerts. On Friday I was at an At Home where I saw Goldie,[1] who of course began to talk about you and Olga at once. He said 'I liked Kingsley's wife so much. She seemed to me to have extraordinary perception. I should think their marriage is very happy'." Goldie's own perception was sadly at fault. Olga's, on the other hand, is apparent in a brief diary entry at that time about Irene: "rich, concrete personality; competent standing in the world; independent, sincere, tragically deep in feeling, intelligent, humorous, scornfully direct, sensible by force of circumstances rather than by nature".

Already Olga had committed to her diary a belief that Kingsley's "functions" in life were "fighting, truth-hunting, intense interest in personality, and in current ideas and battles; everything which is alive. Intellectual arrogance, blind and hungry senses, sometimes insistent, cruel, devouring, sometimes humiliated and ashamed. Easy to hurt, difficult to defeat because his fighting methods are unconsciously crooked. A chameleon—but a sincere and courageous chameleon. . . . Kingsley's function is to be absorbed into personalities and ideas and to battle for a clear idea of good. My function to Kingsley is to be a place into which he can withdraw himself and become free from desire, and recreated with armour and vision and continual 'touch' and understanding. . . . He who is afraid to lose his way will not find it." In another entry she describes him as "sensitive, profound, impressionable, reflective, versatile, humorous, kindly, a passion for truth, real modesty; superimposed cult of the intellectual, unemotional life which is cutting to the root of the real life in him. Meant to be profound and happy rather than brilliant and successful.

[1] Lowes Dickinson.

Evidently has taken a wrong turning somewhere. . . . He has a multitude of viewpoints but no goal."

"What have I done?" (she went on). "What did I learn at school? A little physiology, something about English composition, French language and conversation. I acquired an interest in German literature, learned to listen to music, acquired a veneration for 'research'. In between school and college what did I learn? Something about housework and fowls;[1] enough Anglo-Saxon, Caesar, and Geometry to get through an exam. I read and enjoyed Chaucer, Spenser, Milton, Keats. At College —I learned a little about the Middle Ages, about the origins of tragedy. I read Burke and Sir Thomas Browne with great labour and little understanding; enjoyed Traherne, Coleridge, Shelley, Swinburne, Blake, William Morris, *The Ring and the Book*, translations of Greek tragedy, Conrad, Shakespeare, Landor, *The Crock of Gold*, Elizabethan plays. I began to make a few tentative friendships, explored Cambridge countryside, learned something of physical anthropology, about psychology, about the customs of savages. Helped arrange a museum. Since then—I've read Hardy, Wells, Chesterton, Shaw, Ibsen, Tolstoy, Tchehov, Dostoievsky, Turgenev. Learned a little English history, begun to be interested in politics, tried to teach, escaped from home, learned shorthand[2] and typewriting, helped Kingsley write a book, started a book of my own, began to learn to draw, listened to Beethoven, looked at Japanese prints, Flemish Dutch and Spanish painters, Cezanne, Van Gogh, Rodin, Epstein. Worked in a publishing office and in a museum. Tried to do book-jackets. Joined the New Fabian group. Fallen in love, and made some friends."

Throughout her diaries there is an almost childlike awareness of her own passive bi-sexuality and the intense attachments that bound her, for greatly differing periods, to various women. And these highly romanticised episodes usually had a theme of poetic dreaming, metaphysics, or ecstatic artistic enjoyment. This was well enough known to Kingsley, long before they married; though he was in no doubt, nor need he have doubted,

[1] A reference to her teenage domesticity at her father's sanatorium.

[2] Parts of her diaries are written in perfectly-formed, elementary Pitman's shorthand.

that she genuinely and tenderly loved him as a woman loves a man. But he was passionate as well as compassionate, and for him the situation was therefore loaded with difficulties which he was likely to find deeply distressing and quite insoluble.

On 14th November 1927, now in Manchester, she is recording the beginnings of her estrangement from him; though there is one cause of it which comes in for scant reference—her determination to postpone "having his children". In one rare mention of it she says: "I do still think that I have got to acquire a public function before putting my energies into children—I think that is essential to our mutual happiness".

"I find the result of marriage to be aesthetic starvation," she wrote in a diary on 14th December 1927. "... The difficulty is that I don't know where Kingsley is heading to. I am perplexed and afraid and have no-one to talk to. . . . Kingsley won't understand anything that isn't spoken plainly. Well? I think there is no-one here to whom it is possible to talk except—perhaps—Ted Scott and Professor Stocks. Both of these are trustworthy, intelligent and sympathetic. Ted is interested in life more or less philosophically—as I am—and Stocks is interested in thought and its expression quite disinterestedly. There is a feeling that Kingsley may want me at any moment—that I must stand by to help. . . . Kingsley wants again to experiment, to have dinner parties and people to stay here, to get his toes into Manchester—as an onlooker anyway. The *Guardian* is not sufficing him, does not ask enough or allow enough room. . . . Perhaps he is abandoning the onlooker attitude? Does he think of himself as a possible revolutionary spokesman? I think so. Like Shaw, he is a devourer, but both are capable of creating and do create. The *Guardian* is not a sufficient stimulus to him." (The sad truth was that the *Guardian* did not like him, and had begun the cruelly unnerving process of dropping his articles at the last minute. As senior leader-writer he was having to watch his work being superseded.)

"Why has this house ceased to live?" she wrote on 25th November. "I don't want to live in it. There is not a room in it where I feel at home and free. I am so sick of the emptiness of life, so tired of these analytical habits. Bodily languor and habits of doubt and self-contempt weaken my frantic and feeble efforts to lead a creative life. A life of marriage and sex is utterly disintegrative of creative purpose and the atmosphere of freedom. My life is shut in, there is no longer any particular meaning in it."

She learned to play chess, as "a form of contact with Kingsley and a deliverance from the past". But she felt that they both approached it as a self-conscious form of contact-making, calling for mutual tolerance of a nature which is specially difficult at the chess-board. She knew he was putting up with her inexpertness; while what she was putting up with, and it may well have been the more difficult, was his habit of approaching each rapid victory by way of a kind of psychological warfare, saying almost to himself, "If you do that, of course, there's only one thing I *can* do and that really settles the thing," or "If you do that, then I've got to do this and you might as well give up."

She spent much time apostrophising John Barclay, the man who married Kingsley's sister Irene and to whom she liked to confide her troubles. John Barclay had been a member of the Finchley Unitarian Church. In the first World War he was an infantry officer, and was wounded and badly gassed. Throughout the thirties he was a determined pacifist, at a time when Kingsley's own feelings were changing in the opposite direction. John Barclay worked closely with the Rev. Dick Sheppard in the Peace Pledge Union, about which Kingsley was never more than lukewarm; and the two men found little in common though they retained a mutual respect and even admiration. They were never really at ease together despite the repeated efforts of both Olga and Irene to bridge the gap between them.

"Now Kingsley wants a mistress and I feel soured," wrote Olga in her diary on 24th February 1928. "And I am jealous of his having the *Guardian* to go to. Do I want to get stronger simply in order to be used up having children? It's no use talking to Kingsley about this. I wouldn't yield to the fascination of Kingsley when I first knew him. Fascination's no use. I am so sick of this empty passion which cannot be satisfied. I am sick of it, I am sick of myself. Why can't my love be innocent? I wanted Kingsley's children when I felt free, but I don't feel free any more. Kingsley is an extremely destructive person. But he can't help that; it's the goblin soul in him, with the force of a man and the passions of a sensual type of genius. . . . He won't let our union be a spiritual one. His life is a violent life of the nerves and the senses, punctuated by sleep. Often this violence is senseless, other times it jerks cruelly through to its objective, leaving half the stages bungled. Then to do it again bores him, and he shows off like a monkey.

"I can't help a great deal of introversion. It's a lifelong habit; and I don't get on with people, don't find their small-talk or their preoccupations interesting. Can't help that. I am now almost spiritually bankrupt, living on Kingsley's charity. . . . I will go on trying."

And she recalled her childhood inhibitions about sex. "I was awfully frightened of physical sensations, and shocked if people talked about bodies—also frightened and disgusted. And I hated having to learn Physiology, my first term at Lingholt. Probably I've repressed a good deal of curiosity about bodily matters. I puzzled over them when I was small, always with a feeling of guilt, awe and shame. But I never asked questions about them—that would have been too shameful."

By the middle of 1928, still in Manchester, Kingsley's own diary was recording his special dilemma (was it not extraordinary and pathetic, such a breakdown of conjugal communication resulting in all this simultaneous and ultra-private scribbling?)

> *May 7th 1928* It's no use going back to Verity, or expecting anything to work, until I've got something to say to her beyond what I had some years ago. And that must be worked out with Olga. I must win some "plus" before I'm any good. I must get through things to my own solution—or to our solution. I must kill regret, control desire, and stick to my job. . . . I shall have to fight this battle every day. When Mrs K.[1] told me the worst thing I could do would be to marry a young girl,[2] and that I should be tired of her in two years and would fall back on work, both prophesies were right, things being as they were, my being and continuing to be the sort of person I seemed to be, and Olga being

[1] Probably Mrs Stewart King (see p. 48).
[2] Olga was twenty-five when they married.

an ordinary person. But I can change, with Olga's help. I can learn the value of "plenty of work for the faculties, plenty of rest for the nerves, control for desire and atrophy for conceit". Opening myself to new things and to all the "plus" I can find, and resolutely turning my back on fascination. It's only possible if I change myself, and that *is* possible.

May 18th 1928 Fight *fascination*—which makes the search for what matters most impossible. Verity is fascination. With Olga I've seen farther—she is there, open and with vision, and if I can be open to what I've seen, and not fascinated with the easiest and most stimulating, I'm sure we'll all three succeed yet. Work and Olga are not really incompatible: Verity and Olga are. They are the three pulls. . . . Olga has seen and has the capacity to see more "plus" than anyone I know—and it's that I want; a positive religion to give this world.

Verity stands for a *life*—natural companionship as well as excitement and working, with the faculties which are obviously mine. Olga for a more strenuous and athletic effort, a combined spiritual striving, which may become the *real* fascination when one has worked at it. Olga means doing things for *our* sake far more.

When they had left Manchester, and Kingsley had begun his long editorship of the *New Statesman*, they lived in a flat at number 8 Ormonde Terrace, Primrose Hill. Here they formed a new circle of friends, and renewed contact with some old ones. They included V. S. Pritchett and his first wife, Dr Joan Malleson and Miles Malleson, Cecil Lewis, Ellen Wilkinson (whom Olga described jealously as "a shrunken little hunchback with red eyes"), Herbert and Adeline Agar, Hugh Gaitskell, W. N. ("Trilby") Ewer of the *Daily News*, Graham Hutton of *The Economist*, and a well-known Bloomsbury habitué called Charles Skepper—of whom more later.

Within two years of their resumed London life she was in love with a man who was one of Kingsley's closest friends and colleagues. For some reason she referred to him privately as Rimini (which was not his name). "I love him," she wrote on New Year's Day of 1934, "with happiness, with some pity and much appreciation, and with a desire to be honest with him, not to deceive nor to conceal. . . . What am I to do [about] the hell of desire unsatisfied? I want to justify my loves by increasing the beauty of the world and developing new powers and new understanding in myself. Writing does not help: it passes the time and one can get interested in the technique of it, but it releases nothing, it is a mere disciplined employment, not an action of any importance." (She had done some book-reviewing for the *Manchester Guardian* and—after Kingsley's arrival—for the *New Statesman*, in her own name of Olga Martin: but her stories and poems were not being accepted.) "I desire to be open and honest with Rimini. This desire has a violent sexual emotion belonging with it." But two days later: "I find no great reason to fuss about Rimini. I have written no more poems to him, and find myself contentedly loving the two of them—Kingsley on the romantic side rather, and Rimini with affectionate rivalry. If Rimini were to make love to me I should fall for him; although not to an extraordinary depth. But of course he won't . . . I am grateful to him for the extraordinary freedom of his house and his company."

The gratitude, and the fancied intimacy with Rimini, induced in her a new objectivity about Kingsley: "Has Kingsley got through his mother complex or not?" she wrote on 21st February 1934. "If his willingness to have children by me be physically effective, yes; but I think it is not—deeper layers of his mind prevent this. How am I to produce in him the willingness? By giving him ease of mind."

The theme was now incessant and repetitive; but Rimini was beginning to dominate her mind and her desires, and the process was being consciously abetted by Kingsley. He had by this time (1934) acquired his cottage at Little Easton, near Dunmow, his London address now being 16 Great James Street, Bloomsbury. He was pushing her into the arms of Rimini.

Olga and he were now living almost separate lives. In the four years between coming back to London and moving from Primrose Hill to number 16 Great James Street, the susceptible Kingsley was vanquished (I choose the word with deliberation) by a succession of young women—four at least—whose names need no mention; while Olga pursued, in her world of fantasy, a largely imaginary affair with Rimini which was predominantly unhappy. She and Kingsley were trying to escape from each other. She confided much in Charles Skepper, her friend and Kingsley's—indeed he was everyone's friend, a self-proclaimed homosexual whom everyone accepted and understood and who took a detached view of what Kingsley called the triangles in the Bloomsbury squares. "Why not sex only," he suggested to her unexpectedly, "since love has become so hurtful to you?" She then realised "how profoundly I as a woman have been humiliated, and therefore in what an agony of miserable shame I should be if I were to sleep with someone I didn't love. . . . If Rimini had run away with me and been tender and boisterous, it might have come right. . . . Now what does he mean to me? A person who enjoys conquering endless pretty, artificial girls in fashionable clothes. A poet who has never realised himself and perhaps now never will. A blunt, brusque creature with engaging ways which make people forgive him his lack of consideration for them. A fiendishly proud, white-hot lover who never lets himself go because he is afraid. . . ."

And from this point, as if with that final descriptive paradox, her diary becomes progressively less logical and coherent, the "stream of consciousness" method becomes dominant and her story can be learned only from other sources. Rimini, however, had forsaken her. He may well have realised, a little late perhaps, that both Kingsley and Olga were, so to speak, benevolently exploiting him. By 1st August 1934 she was living alone at 109 Charlotte Street, Tottenham Court Road, the house of a music teacher who took paying guests. Kingsley too was living alone at 16 Great James Street; and from there he wrote to his sister Irene: "Poor Olga—it was too bad of him to leave her like that, so *terribly* humiliating."

Although they had separated thus, they still sometimes went about together. (On 27th August 1934 Kingsley was writing to Maynard Keynes, then living at West Firle in Sussex: "Would it be all right for Olga and me to come down on Saturday? I think we would probably come by train, though if it is a very nice day I might be tempted to motor.") And for a year or two she still appeared at Kingsley's parties at Great James Street, abstractedly playing the part of hostess or sometimes sitting glumly in corners. She knew everyone who came to the parties, and they knew her, there were no pretences about her situation.

Her staunchest friend, the man who consoled her while condemning no one else, was the popular, cheerful, extrovert, homosexual, wealthy *bon vivant* Charles Skepper. In the Charlotte Street house where she now lodged there was a young girl studying music and ballet, and Olga found solace in her company and enthusiasm. The girl was to go to France for further tuition. Olga longed to go to France, perhaps to Paris, to have a left bank studio and do some painting and teaching. In the end she was invited to go there and stay with the wealthy Skepper family while she looked round for accommodation; and by 1936 she was living and working in a small studio flat in the Rue Broca, near the prison of La Santé. Her immediate neighbour was Alexander Werth, at that time Paris correspondent of the *Sunday Times*: and it was he who, at Kingsley's urgent request, had secured the flat for her. There ensued an "arranged" divorce which was made absolute on 14th October 1940. She had a maintenance allowance of £350 a year from Kingsley, and was hoping to sell pictures. There is no record that she ever did, but she breakfasted late every day and spent much time at a café in the Boulevarde Montparnasse, a noisy Polish place called Chez Wadja, much frequented by artists and students. She loved it and while she was there she became animated for short periods. Her life was largely aimless and her mind too distracted for sustained effort of any kind.

Alexander Werth's flat was a link in an escape chain from Nazi Germany and later from Nazi-occupied France. Olga became to some extent involved in this work, and since Kingsley was a frequent visitor of Werth's, he saw her from time to time during these immediate pre-war years. He was constantly worried about her welfare, and his enquiries about her from England (Werth used to say) were never-ending—he was "like an old hen disturbed about a difficult chick". Charles Skepper had meanwhile been travelling in the Far East, doing some dilettante trading in oriental carpets. When the war came he began to work for the British broadcasting station in Shanghai. Shanghai fell to the Japanese and he joined a guerrilla group to harass the Japanese forces and was captured. His release was secured on some rather mysterious diplomatic grounds; but after his return to England, emaciated and ill, he was soon back in France as a member of the French underground movement, acting for the British. He called one day at his father's factory near Paris to get some money, and one of the factory employees promptly betrayed him to the Gestapo. He was arrested and was never seen or heard of again. He had not indeed expected to return from this mission, for which he had been parachuted into France. Olga's grief about this was thought to have added greatly to the stresses that finally unhinged her mind. In a farewell letter to his father he had asked that £20,000 of his money be given to the LSE for the development of sociological research; and the bequest led to the establishment of Skepper House, in Endsleigh Street, which the LSE today uses for that purpose. He was a man with a multitude of friends, and Olga's diaries show that his kindness to her was selfless and inexhaustible.

When the war began she stored all her belongings in a friend's garage in Paris (where they miraculously survived for her to collect in 1945), and came back to England. Kingsley prevailed upon Harold Nicolson, who knew her and was at that time Parliamentary Secretary to the Ministry of Information, to find her a job in the Ministry; and thus for a time she contrived to live quietly and, she hoped, usefully (but kept no diaries).

She had, however, by this time developed an acute condition of persecution mania, partly because of the political atmosphere she had lived through in France in the late thirties, partly because she was that kind of eccentric anyway; and this, because it resulted in some noticeably odd behaviour, began to make it difficult for her to live as quietly as she now wished. She believed herself to be watched, followed, and spied upon everywhere. Of course her visible reaction to this belief made her conspicuous and talked-about, the delusion that she was "watched" became a reality because oddity does attract public curiosity, and her mental deterioration followed a pattern sadly familiar to anyone who has had to listen to present-day stories of paranoia. During the air-raids on London she was completely fearless and seemed not to know what it was all about. She occasionally went for holidays to a hotel in Cornwall

In Friends' Ambulance Unit uniform, 1917

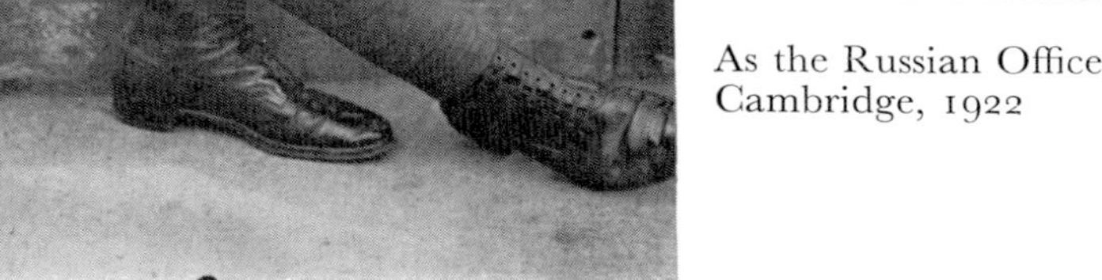

As the Russian Officer in *Arms and the Man* at Cambridge, 1922

Olga in about 1926

which was run by V. S. Pritchett's former wife, with whom in Bloomsbury days she had formed a very close friendship. And it was there that, in 1952, her oddity became so pronounced and such an embarrassment to other hotel guests that "something had to be done about it". She was got into the county mental hospital at Bodmin under what was then called a "three-day detention order", and Kingsley learned by telephone, in the middle of a Monday morning editorial conference, that that was where she was.

He was appalled. There is no doubt that today she would be treated as an outpatient. Indeed her case seems to have been exactly suitable for "day hospital" treatment. As it was, there is little room for doubt that the stark conditions in the Bodmin institution did irreparable further damage to her personality, filled her with a lifelong horror of what she called "the bin", and got firmly in the way of any chance that she would ever benefit from psychiatric treatment (though she was twice more, in later years, persuaded to attempt it, as a voluntary patient for very short periods). Kingsley got her out of Bodmin with the aid of a solicitor after a few weeks, and she returned to the flat where she lived alone in Crossfield Road, Hampstead.

And there she remained until 1955, managing her life more or less adequately, discreetly watched over by a few friends—particularly by Kingsley's sister Irene—and acquiring a growing retinue of cats. Then she bought a cottage at Clandon, near Newlands Corner, Guildford, which was divided into two flats, had a walled garden, and became for her something like a fortress. Over the next seven or eight years her mental condition deteriorated steadily. Her growing eccentricity, and the cats, encouraged the occupants of the upstairs flat to move out; and thereafter she steadfastly refused ever to let it again. "Anyone coming in there," she said, "would immediately set about having me put in a bin." She would allow no one inside the house—even her favourite sister Gwenda was turned away at the door. She lived the life of a total recluse, with all the blinds and curtains drawn across the windows day and night. The number of cats grew to about 20; there were piles of earth in each room for them to use. The bath was always full of cat-food tins, not all of them empty; and as may be imagined the

E

stench in the house was appalling. The whole plumbing system was out of order, the walls and ceilings sodden; but she would allow no plumber to come near in case the general state of the house led him to "tell the authorities"—who would have her put away. She habitually carried two paper carrier-bags, one containing food and coal and the other clothing. And on the night of 17th December 1964, in the road near her cottage, she was knocked down by a car and killed outright, still holding her two carrier-bags.

In contrast with the chaos and disorder in her household, the chronic disrepair of the building and the once fine garden that had become a wilderness, her housekeeping accounts and her general money affairs were found to be in perfect order—she had always known that unpaid bills would lead to enquiries about her capacity to manage her affairs. And to the utter astonishment of Kingsley, who had paid her £350 a year for 24 years, she died worth £24,000.

That is the story of Olga Martin, which it has seemed best to tell in one chapter, though her influence must be understood as present through the rest of this book. I should think it likely that a closer study of her diaries and letters, wildly convoluted and inconsequential as they are, would be rewarding to anyone interested in the gradual deterioration of a sensitive and creative mind under the erosive influence of sex-guilt imaginings and word-conscious poetic fantasy. Kingsley never ceased to blame himself for her unhappiness, her failure, and her madness; and no one ever succeeded in dislodging this *idée fixe*, not the closest of his friends, not one of the women who subsequently befriended, understood, and comforted him, not one of the psychiatrists to whom he took the troubles that burdened him. I know of only one beneficent outcome of those 43 years of vicarious suffering and tortured guilt. As many a man and woman would attest, they made Kingsley Martin an endearingly sympathetic listener to anyone with marriage or other emotional problems and a desire to talk to someone about them.

Chapter 8

TEACHER TURNED WRITER

SIDNEY AND BEATRICE WEBB had believed that if only you could bring people to the serious study of economics you could turn them into Socialists. In 1884 they had joined forces with Graham Wallas and Bernard Shaw to found the Fabian Society "for the advancement of Socialism by democratic means".

Shaw himself gave an interesting account of its origin, in a letter to Kingsley on 14th October 1947—Kingsley had just been giving an account of it on the radio. "I heard your broadcast," wrote G.B.S. "Webb was not the founder of the Fabian Society. It was founded by a Rosminian philosopher named Davidson and was excessively unfabian, dreaming of colonies of Perfect Lifers in Brazil, and discussing the abolition of money and the substitution of pass-books, and constitutional anarchism and all sorts of nonsense, in each others' lodgings. It split into a political section led by Hubert Bland, calling itself the Fabian Society, and a Fellowship of the New Life, with Perfectionist views. The Fabian section had one working man member named Phillips; and it managed to get out a tract entitled *Why are the Many Poor?* This tract came my way. I, being a newly converted Marxist looking for a political shop, saw that the title Fabian, obviously educated, was an inspiration. I joined it and found it a handful of hopeless amateurs needing above all things Webb, whom I had picked out as a political genius, and on whom I had forced my very uncongenial acquaintance, I being all artist and an incorrigible actor, and he the simplest soul and ablest youth in the world. I roped him into the Fabian; and his knowledge, ability, and administrative experience as an upper division civil servant at once swept all the nonsense and Bohemian anarchism out of it, and made it what it finally became."

It put itself on the map with the publication in 1889 of the celebrated *Fabian Essays* under Shaw's editorship. Then the Webbs came to believe that the "serious study" they sought to foster needed two further stimuli, the one academic, the other literary. In 1898, in two rented offices in the Adelphi district near the Strand, they established "a modest institute devoted to economic research and teaching" which became the London School of Economics and Political Science, and, in due course, a school of the University of London. And in 1913 they established the *New Statesman*. Both, since birth, have been storm-centres of political controversy.

Apparently with some misgiving Sir William Beveridge, the Director of the LSE, appointed Kingsley in October 1924 (at first part-time) as an assistant lecturer under Professor Harold Laski in the Department of Political Science. In June 1923 he had applied for a Fellowship, but Beveridge, who gave him an interview, reminded him that he had already held two research fellowships and ought now to be looking for a good lectureship. However, said Beveridge, the School at that time unfortunately had no lectureship to offer. Beveridge, wrote Kingsley to his parents, was "most kind, and seemed really concerned about me; and of course was perfectly right". He then made a similar application to Christ's College, Cambridge, without success; and among several letters of condolence from Cambridge dons was one from Lowes Dickinson saying, "I am sorry to hear this news and I think it very foolish of Christ's. Also I expect, for the moment, it is rather a blow to you, especially as you want some money just now. Somehow, though, I feel sure you will make your way all right, and I daresay be glad later that you did not come here." And this time Goldie was right. A Cambridge college, says Kingsley in his autobiography,[1] is "controlled by a small group of learned men who must somehow get on with one another and are naturally reluctant to import a brash, undisciplined, left-wing person, always inclined to insist on his own views, suitable or not". In the same year he had missed at least the chance of being a history tutor at Peterhouse: failing to recognise the significance of an invitation to dine at high table, he had decided he was too late, too hot and too tired after a day's cycling, had stayed in his rooms at

[1] *Father Figures*, p. 146.

Magdalene and thought up an explanation for the morrow. A day or two later he met his intended host, H. W. V. Temperley (who later became Master of Peterhouse and Cambridge Professor of Modern History). "What happened to you?" said Temperley. "All the Fellows were assembled and we waited till nearly eight o'clock, because we're considering electing a new history tutor." Whatever the effect of Kingsley's explanation, they elected another man; and Kingsley was far more upset about this episode, and his own seeming discourtesy, than you would gather from the light-hearted reference to it in his autobiography. It is obvious that he believed he would have got the job.

It turned out that Beveridge had actually disliked him almost from the moment he saw him; and anyway Beveridge may not have felt, as a rather proper right-wing Liberal who had written many leaders for the *Morning Post*, that this rather shabbily turned-out young man, who questioned everything on principle and seemed to believe in nothing except the doom of capitalism, was likely to improve the School's already dubious reputation among the rich people to whom it was constantly turning for money. But "it seemed my natural home," Kingsley records. "It was then, as it had always been, a wonderful home of free discussion, happily mixed race, and genuine learning." Believing that capitalism was evil and doomed, and that there could be no liberty without a large measure of social equality, he was prepared to settle in and enjoy himself.

On the whole, he did not. The LSE seems to have presented a striking contrast to his picture of a Cambridge college, where "a small group of learned men must somehow get on with one another". To many people, both inside it and outside it, the academic world has always seemed conspicuous for its malicious gossip and jealousy, the ample but precious talking-time being, all too often, ill-spent. And although the staff of the LSE "contained more distinguished persons than you could have got together anywhere in Oxford or Cambridge, every meeting of the professorial council was a more or less open dog-fight".[1] Whether because of this or in spite of it, the LSE is still probably what H. G. Wells called it—"the most vigorous and

[1] *Father Figures*, p. 154.

efficient centre of modern social, political and economic thought in the world."

Kingsley found it, rather to his surprise, a place where he was "not compelled to think things out". Perhaps there was so much strident thinking going on that a seat on the fence was attractive if not, for so percipient a man, inevitable. His interest in the LSE had been kindled at Cambridge by Dr Frank Salter, his history tutor, who had made a practice of inviting LSE political science men—Laski, Graham Wallas and others—to tell the students at Magdalene how the application of historical inference to contemporary social conditions welded history and economics into what they called political science. Instead of discussing Rousseau's social contract they talked about the best way to fight an election. Instead of talking about Aristotle they lectured on Bentham and how a municipal authority could secure the greatest happiness of the greatest number. And yet they were not so severely practical as to forget the mild excitement of following up historical Ifs, especially when the process brought some lesson painlessly home.

Although Graham Wallas took a liking to Kingsley and urged him to get a job "in touch with reality" at the LSE, it was Laski, more than anyone, who lured him there, eased his entry, and befriended him through the three years of his lectureship.

Nevertheless it was Laski who, unwittingly, convinced him step by step that his future lay in journalism rather than in the universities. (Even more ironically, it was the Professorship of Political Science in the University of London that Kingsley wanted when Laski died in 1950. He had then to be gently told that his candidature would be even less acceptable to the Senate than Laski's tenure of office had been for the major part of its 25 years.) Graham Wallas had encouraged him to believe, years before, that his future probably lay in journalism, though Wallas had been among his warmest sponsors when he was hoping for a fellowship at King's. "I've just sent off to the Provost of King's," he wrote to Kingsley on 11th November 1922, "a little essay on the present state of political science, and your relation to it, whose combined pathos and dignity nearly moved me to tears. I hope that you will succeed."

Graham Wallas's *Human Nature in Politics*, his outstanding book on sociology, was not written until he was over 50 and was the product of many years of vigorous participation in left-wing causes. It had the effect of a revelation on Kingsley as an undergraduate, who never missed a Graham Wallas lecture at Cambridge. He always said (and he repeated it in *Father Figures*, p. 93) that Wallas resigned from the Highgate School where he was teaching because he disapproved of religion in schools. The truth was, as his daughter told Kingsley after *Father Figures* was published, that he was dismissed because he refused to comply with a sudden decision by the headmaster that all the assistant masters must take Holy Communion.

In 1953 Kingsley published an affectionate "biographical memoir" of Laski,[1] most of which was in fact written by Norman MacKenzie, then an assistant editor at the *New Statesman* (who, moreover, did all the American research). For a variety of reasons, mainly the demands of editorial work at the *New Statesman* but partly the need (as he saw it) to rationalise some of Laski's better-known shortcomings, Kingsley had great difficulty with this book. In fact he got bored and, at one time, disposed to shelve it. It is probable that without the insistence of Norman MacKenzie (and the valuable research assistance of Pat Llewelyn-Davies,[2] whom he had met through John Strachey), it would not have been completed until ten years later, when Kingsley had retired and could write it himself. It might then, incidentally, have had a better reception from the reviewers; for Laski in his later years was not popular with the Press and in 1953 the reasons were too fresh in their memory for quick judgments to be impartial. (As it was, Kingsley was always uneasy that Norman MacKenzie got so small a share of the credit and an even less equitable part of the financial rewards.)

Kingsley recorded that his first meeting with Laski left him "stunned, as most young men were, by this man who seemed to know everything about all the subjects that interested me, by his library of all the books I thought I wanted to read, and by his endless stream of anecdotes about all the famous men of our

[1] Kingsley Martin, *Harold Laski*, Gollancz, London.
[2] Now Lady Llewelyn-Davies, a life peer.

day".[1] He looked about seventeen years old, and his domed forehead and big round spectacles lent him the classic appearance of the too-clever boy whose intellect, being too large for its clothing, is indecently exposed. Kingsley recalls graphically that Laski when lecturing "stood at attention, for all the world like a schoolboy about to recite. His face was expressionless; he made no gestures. . . . His voice was monotonous, his eloquence was polished, his fluency staggering, his sentences labyrinthine".[2] It is an exact picture of Laski in the lecture theatre. He shared with C. E. M. Joad the highly unusual characteristic that his vocabulary did not include the words "er" or "um". With those two words to use, either man might have been condemned by the unattractiveness of his personality to small audiences. As it was, everyone crowded in to listen because they knew they would hear someone thinking brilliantly and lucidly aloud, that the punctuation would all come along in the right places, that there would be no opening clauses left to sicken and die, and that there would be none of that journalese which, as J. A. Spender once said,

> results from the efforts of the non-literary mind to discover alternatives for the obvious where none are necessary; journalese is best avoided by the frank acceptance of even a hard-worn phrase when it expresses what you want to say.

As Kingsley's friendship with Laski grew, so did the antipathy with which Beveridge contemplated them both. They personified the left wing politics of social change and student controversy, which throughout the history of the LSE have presented a yawning gulf to the trusts and bankers to whom it looked for funds (and who would probably have seen the gulf as a smoking pit). Laski wrote much for the *Daily Herald*; and Beveridge, who deprecated "political activities" on the part of the staff but might with difficulty have been persuaded to condone *Daily Herald* articles, would have found it impossible to see nothing political in Laski's chairmanship of the Labour Party. Once in 1934 Beveridge issued a statement to the Press about "certain reported utterances in Moscow" by the *enfant terrible* of his Political Science Department. "We feel it our

[1] *Harold Laski*, p. 48. [2] *Op cit.*, p. 59.

duty to make plain," said this statement regally, "that if Professor Laski's statements have been correctly reported, the University can accept no responsibility for personal expressions of opinion by any of its professors." No one actually took this to mean that the University *would* back its professors if the report about Laski turned out to be inaccurate. But Laski was furious, and Maynard Keynes wrote to the *New Statesman* (which Kingsley was now editing) on 15th July 1934 to ask whether it was usual for the University of London to express opinions on the views of its professors? "What's the appropriate body for this purpose?" he wanted to know. "One had assumed it to be well established in England, as distinguished from Moscow or Berlin, that a professor is entitled to the unfettered expression of his opinions and that no one but himself has any responsibility in the matter. What are we coming to? . . Fortunately the Founders of the London School of Economics, with a wise foresight, expressly provided in its Charter for the complete freedom of its teachers in the expression of their political opinions."

Laski survived this kind of thing for sixteen years, until Beveridge was succeeded by Sir Alexander Carr-Saunders in 1937 and the whole atmosphere of the LSE was transformed. Due tribute has been paid elsewhere to the incredible Laski record of lecturing, writing, supervising, holding seminars and giving private help and tuition to legions of students—to say nothing of helping some of them financially. Laski knew, and so did everyone else, that there would have been no objection from the Senate or Beveridge (though there might have been trouble with the students) if he had publicly supported the Primrose League. He slipped out of every ambush by the dextrous use of a fable, a story, a recollection, an apt authority that made the enemy lower their guns just long enough. His prodigious memory was thought by many to be a snare: essays (it was said) were found to have been "lifted" complete, but it may well have been done from memory. It was also known that he would adapt or adorn any recollection to suit an immediate purpose; and because of this "slickness" he was, in general, not trusted by his colleagues. A habit which failed to endear him to his artistic friends (and he took a great interest in modern art) was that of trying to get them to commit themselves about the pictures hanging in his rooms, which were unidentifiable pieces cut from steamship posters and framed for the occasion.

It was, however, the secretary of the LSE, Mrs Mair, who really worried Kingsley; and he rather worried her. He says she was "a handsome middle-aged woman, administratively efficient but snobbish beyond belief".[1] It is conceded by those who staffed the LSE during the Beveridge reign that Mrs Mair's most considerable achievement was to bring about total agreement in the senior common room on one subject: detestation of Mrs Mair. "She was like a Sultana in a palace," one of the professors told me: "she was a consummate snob; she had her favourites on the staff and they had to be well-connected people, which of course some of them were; she could manipulate Beveridge like clay—you could hardly ever get to see him without her being present; he had a mother fixation which had fastened itself on her. It was well known that the price of getting Beveridge to go anywhere was that you had to have her too. She guarded him like a Gorgon, he had no direct contact with us. We all complained to the Webbs, but they couldn't do anything. A deputation of the senior professors went to see the chairman of the Governors, Sir Josiah Stamp, and said 'we *must* ask you to dismiss this woman the moment she arrives at the minimum age for retirement; she has made the place intolerable'. And in due course the Governors did. Beveridge was so enraged that he left with her, and went to University College, Oxford, as Master—that was in 1937; but University College had to take her too. So did the Ministry of Labour when the war came. Eventually she married him."

"Behind the trouble at the LSE," Laski wrote to Beatrice Webb on 13th March 1934, "is a long history in which Beveridge and Mrs Mair have a serious responsibility. To run a place like the School on a policy of favouritism and benevolent autocracy always must result in an explosion somewhere. . . . And a good deal is the outcome of our bitterly sectarian economics. If our teachers will not discuss the living issues of today reasonably, the students will discuss them among them-

[1] *Father Figures*, p. 154.

selves; and in the absence of official guidance in lecture and class, extremists invariably get the upper hand." To Laski's many critics, the spectacle of Laski deploring extremists was like Satan rebuking sin. "In innumerable letters, lectures, articles and books," wrote Kingsley in the *Dictionary of National Biography* when Laski died, "which had wide influence in many countries, he argued that a social revolution in some form was inevitable, but that whether it came peacefully or violently depended on the readiness of the ruling class to yield its power and privilege." Which, said the Laski-haters, was precisely the morality of the footpad. But it was, after all, Sidney and Beatrice Webb whose belief in the necessity for a "trained and responsible" ruling class, to supersede the inefficient capitalist bosses, had led them to set up the LSE in 1898.

Kingsley's three years there, 1924–1927, were politically exciting years in which he made many friends in the Labour Party, as well as among political activists, at both extremes, whose views he totally rejected. In the very month in which he took up his new lectureship, Ramsay MacDonald's government was forced into resignation by the absurd affair of the *Workers' Weekly* prosecution.[1] J. R. Campbell, acting editor, had published an article urging soldiers never again to fire on their "fellow workers". The Director of Public Prosecutions decided that Campbell must be tried for "incitement to mutiny". The Attorney-General (Sir Patrick Hastings) overruled the D.P.P. and the case was dropped. Kingsley wrote at the time that this turned the decision into a "political" one, according to "an ancient and fictional humbug which still flourishes". Parliament had interfered with the Courts. The resulting uproar was deafening. You would have thought no one had ever heard of cabinet discussions about the expediency of prosecuting somebody or leaving him alone. The Labour Government, which was a tired and ineffectual one outnumbered in Parliament, took the opportunity to scuttle to the country and a Tory administration came in with Stanley Baldwin as premier. Kingsley was intensely interested in all this, and his LSE

[1] *R. v. Campbell 1924*. For a succinct and characteristically robust note of this case, see A. J. P. Taylor, *English History, 1914–1945*, O.U.P., London, 1965, page 225.

diaries are full of contemporary notes scribbled at such speed that not even he, probably, would have been able to read them in later years. (He was always asking people what they made of something he had scribbled. And it must have been some gift of divination through which one man, Norman MacKenzie, could unfailingly tell him. Or perhaps Norman could always bluff him.)

It was however a period in which his rather sombre state of mind was occasionally tinged with optimism, though this, again, he confined to his diaries. He rather liked Baldwin, thought the Locarno Peace Treaty might be the beginning of a settled era (the Government thought this sufficiently probable to give the schoolchildren a day's holiday), and held that Germany's request for admission to the League of Nations should be granted. He read and marginally annotated (a lifelong habit of his) a number of outstanding new books, among them Keynes's *The End of Laissez-Faire*, Beatrice Webb's *My Apprenticeship*, G. M. Trevelyan's *History of England*, R. H. Tawney's *Religion and the Rise of Capitalism*, and even that vast, gloomy, ill-written, and unforgettable novel of Theodore Dreiser's, *An American Tragedy*. A literary event which he seems not to have noticed at the time was the appearance, among all these significant works, of Hitler's *Mein Kampf*.

By the beginning of 1927 he was noticing that the *New Statesman* under Clifford Sharp, to which he was an occasional contributor, had developed (or regressed) into a weekly symposium of tabloid articles unable to discuss progressive ideas at adequate length. He welcomed the change from the enormous masses of worthy but barely readable print with which Sidney and Beatrice Webb had formerly filled it, but he wanted to establish a quarterly magazine in which the discussion could be at the same time thorough and digestible. A colleague at the LSE, another junior member of the teaching staff, was W. A. Robson (now Professor Emeritus of Public Administration in the University of London); and they discovered that the same idea had occurred to them both. Every government since 1918, they agreed, had been unconstructive. The General Strike, perhaps more than anything, had shown the futility of looking to "elected" governments until you had an educated democracy to elect them. This was to be achieved by small coterie publications for the painless education of the educators. Unemployment, education, public health, the position of women, relations with Russia, the economic subjection of (and the failure to disarm) Germany, the vacillation about disarmament at home, the inertia of the Fabian Society, convinced these two men that there was scope for a quarterly review which, circulating among the political intelligentsia, would do for *practical* political science at home what *The Round Table* once did for imperialism. They got together a publishing committee and launched the *Political Quarterly*. Harold Macmillan was its unlikely publisher. The committee comprised Leonard Woolf, Professor A. M. Carr-Saunders (then in charge of social science studies at Liverpool University), Harold Laski, Maynard Keynes, Professor Theodore Gregory, W. A. Robson and Kingsley. The two last-named were its joint editors, it was an instant success, and Kingsley was launched as a press man.

The behaviour of the press in the *Workers' Weekly* case, and the affair of the "Zinoviev letter" a few months later, had revived his interest in the way popular "opinion" is formed and manipulated. He had chosen this as the subject of his first book,[1] and it was now the subject of his second—*The British Public and the General Strike*. This brilliant little polemic contained some tart comments about the report of the 1925 Samuel Commission on the coal-mining industry; and the major author of that report was Sir William Beveridge. This time the marginal annotating had been done by Beveridge, and the book was *The British Public and the General Strike*. He summoned Kingsley to his room. "He lectured me about it as if I were a student who had shown him a bad essay," wrote Kingsley.[2] "The fact that I had written it in the summer vacation and that it was irrelevant to my academic work did not deter him." (Did he not mean "relevant? What is more relevant to political science than a general strike?)

It would be wrong, however, to say that he lost his LSE job as the *direct* result of writing this book. It was a culmination.

[1] *The Triumph of Lord Palmerston.*
[2] *Father Figures*, p. 163.

Promotion from assistant lecturer to full status would have increased his salary from £250 to £360 a year, and when the time came Beveridge passed him over. A month later, still fuming, he had a totally unexpected letter from C. P. Scott, editor of the *Manchester Guardian*, who was looking for a leader writer:

15th March 1927

Dear Mr Kingsley Martin,

Mitrany,[1] whom I think you know and who also knows we are in need of a recruit for the staff, mentioned to me the other day that he thought you might be inclined to look to journalism as a profession. I should be glad to know if this is at all the case. I have read and liked your little book on the general strike, and your larger book on Palmerston has, of course, been very well received.

Yours sincerely,
C. P. Scott.

It is worth pausing here to note the possible consequences of writing a "well received" book. It may earn you and your heirs and successors a great deal of money, if you have invented a fictional character who is equally adroit with revolvers and women. Or it may earn you £8.4.2., as Kingsley's Palmerston book did, and lodge your name significantly in the memories of people like C. P. Scott. Kingsley wrote at once to say that Mitrany had been quite right, and on 18th March Scott replied that "the post is virtually that of successor to Montague,[2] with a corresponding salary. . . . I did not suppose", Scott said, "that you would commit yourself further than to come to Manchester for a few weeks to test the work, and so that we might both become acquainted. Could you run down for a night soon and stay with me?"

He took Olga, and C. P. Scott seems to have approved of her.[3] It turned out that Beveridge was going to require a

[1] Professor David Mitrany, of the Institute for Advanced Study at Princeton, had been a member of the *Guardian*'s editorial staff and was well known to Kingsley.

[2] C. E. Montague, author of *Disenchantment*, perhaps the most powerful anti-war book to be published in the 1920's. ("War hath no fury like the non-combatant" was his message.)

[3] See p. 117.

term's notice, but relented when, perhaps, he fully realised that he was going to be rid of Kingsley Martin; and he agreed to accept notice in April that Kingsley would merely complete the current term. "So far as we are concerned," wrote Scott on 29th April 1927, "we require no further experiment":

> I have seen enough of your work to be assured of its quality. And as to the nine-months' year, we gladly accept that as a necessary condition, which I can see that it is. You suggested a proportionate difference in salary, and I would propose therefore £800 as a commencing salary instead of the £1,000 I had offered for the full year. There is no difficulty whatever from Crozier.[1] He feels about the whole thing just as Ted[2] and I feel. Need I say, my dear fellow, how glad we shall all be if you feel able, on reflection, to accept this arrangement, and how considerable a gain I feel it would be to the character and resources of the MG.

However, the full correspondence shows that Kingsley had not won his "nine months' year" without a struggle. Ted Scott had held out little hope of his getting such a concession out of the old man (C.P.S. was over 80 when Kingsley joined the paper, and in all he was editor for 59 years—a record in British journalism beaten only by Sir Bruce Ingram, who edited the *Illustrated London News* for 63). "So far as I am personally concerned," wrote Ted Scott on 12th May, "I agree entirely with all you say about the desirability of occasional visits to London. But . . .

> the editor likes to be in personal contact, and to have all his resources available for what the night may bring forth, so that any suggested absence requires specific justification. That is the present position. I think it's wrong, but it persists. If you alter it I shall regard it as your first substantial service to the paper. So you see you have after all drawn from me an opinion of which the editor would disapprove. But as you say, we have been very frank with one another."

Which indicates that when you were offered a job by C. P. Scott you did not make conditions. To accept such a precedent,

[1] W. P. Crozier was then Scott's right-hand man, and edited the paper from 1932 until his death in 1944.

[2] E. T. Scott ("Ted"), Scott's son, was editor from 1929 to 1932.

the old man must have wanted Kingsley very much. (J. L. Hammond wrote to him on 18th May: "I wish you every happiness. For the M.G. I am unfeignedly glad. It is a great stroke for them. For you, I think you have made the right decision and you have done the most important thing in making what you want and expect quite clear.") One thing he can hardly have expected was that the *Guardian* went so far as to buy the house at Didsbury for him to live in. There is a long and perceptive portrait of Scott in *Father Figures*, with an account of how the old man revised his opinion of Kingsley, came to dislike him, and sought to get rid of him. Among his distinguished colleagues on the paper were Neville Cardus, Howard Spring, F. A. Voigt, Hugh Massingham (whose father, H. W. Massingham, was editor of *The Nation*), Ivor Brown and (in Kingsley's last few months there) Malcolm Muggeridge, who told me that C. P. Scott used to grumble to him about Kingsley.

"C.P. was a fastidious old man himself," said Malcolm Muggeridge, "very elegant and pernickety; and I know that he rather shrank from Kingsley, as a rather shabby-looking man, the first day he got him there. It was impossible not to feel rather sorry for Kingsley—his period with the paper was an absolute flop. . . . He and I used to set off to the *Guardian* Office together in his extraordinary old car, and he would tell me he was having a bad time there. He was being side-tracked in the way you can be on a paper—a very stiff test of morale, to go to editorial conferences and *not write*. He was ostensibly first leader-writer. Wadsworth and the others spoke irritably about him."

It is a difficult thing today, reading the leaders that Kingsley had been writing, to understand what it was that the paper expected of him. They are not, it is true, written with quite the same liveliness, drollery and perception as one came to expect in the *New Statesman*, nor had they the same economy. But there was an awful lot of space to fill in those spacious days, when people spent much of their lives reading newspapers. If a man can be told he has no more than 200 words in which to deliver the message, it concentrates his mind and tautens his style significantly. As it was, Kingsley was turning out what he himself ruefully considered to be non-committal articles of 1,200 or 1,500 words, of the kind which have to end "It is greatly to be hoped that . . .". or "whether this can be done remains to be seen"; phrases which seem rarer today everywhere, and rarer perhaps in the *Guardian* even among the "quality" newspapers. The subject matter of these articles was as various as Bechuanaland and Blasphemy, Child Labour and the Channel Tunnel, Education and The Empire, Films and Flogging, Honours and Housing, Patriotism and Prohibition, Russia and Rates, Slavery and Smoke Abatement. But if it is sometimes apparent, looking at these old *Guardian* leaders, that he was writing on matters he didn't much enjoy writing about, some of the surrounding leaders by his colleagues reflect a similar control of passion. Those, you are driven to conclude, were the days. And he seems to have made surprisingly little impact. In David Ayerst's carefully documented book *Guardian: Biography of a Newspaper*,[1] a packed and absorbing volume of more than 600 pages, Kingsley is dismissed in these few words:

> Kingsley Martin had been appointed in 1927 as a political leader-writer. He stayed three years, but neither he nor the Scotts were happy together. Both his politics and his writing proved unacceptable. The editorship of the *New Statesman* fortunately became vacant at the moment when Martin's arrangement with the M.G. finally proved unworkable. He was offered the appointment to the immediate satisfaction of the M.G. and the lasting advantage of the *New Statesman*.

And that, quite gracefully, is all. Yet Kingsley was frequently writing then, as he always wrote thereafter, in a way that took you through to the end of any article whether you wanted to read it or not. Malcolm Muggeridge (of whom the same has always been true) says "one ground one's teeth and went on compulsively reading a Kingsley Martin piece, even if one thought it was all wrong". Perhaps this can be dangerous in a solidly liberal newspaper. "The Scotts had decided," wrote Kingsley in *Father Figures* (p. 185), "that I was both incompetent and dangerously left-wing. They had no faculty of teaching. In many ways I was, no doubt, unteachable, but about writing

[1] Collins, London, 1971.

I should have been quick to learn. In fact I have kept many of my articles in a scrap book, and re-reading my later efforts I have discovered that some of them were not half bad." There is in fact nothing in any of them to justify such modesty. Kingsley himself, however, believed that C. P. Scott "possessed a quick sense of what [*Guardian*] readers would stand and what they would not stand. . . . Even those who do not have the sense to read it are saner, more tolerant and more intelligent because its sanity, tolerance and intelligence have become part of our national inheritance"—this was Kingsley writing in the *New Statesman* on 9th January 1932, and the occasion was Scott's death. The qualities he thus attributed to Scott and the *Guardian* are precisely those he brought to the *New Statesman*.

It is impossible, though, to refrain from quoting one of his *Guardian* pieces for quite another reason, namely his chronic and, it must be said, rather endearing aptitude for getting a funny story all wrong unless there was someone to take him through it carefully a number of times. Almost the last thing he wrote for the *Guardian* was a short leader on 1st September 1930 about the Rev. W. A. Spooner, warden of New College, Oxford, who had just died at the age of 86. It lamented that this distinguished scholar should be popularly renowned because once, reading out in chapel the first line of the hymn "Conquering Kings Their Titles Take", he said "Kingering Kongs Their Tatles Tike". For some reason, wrote Kingsley, "it set the wits and quidnuncs off on their task of invention. They saddled him with the responsibility for calling pink jelly 'stink puff' and saying 'pigs fleas' when he meant 'figs, please'." Kingsley's article went on to throw doubt on the legend that Dr Spooner had urged his flock to come more often to church because it was "ill work talking to beery wenches", and that when he found his own pew occupied by strangers he said to the verger: "These people are occupewing my pie: sew them into another sheet".

Fine so far. But in recalling the famous (if no doubt invented) story of Dr Spooner's quest for "an inn called the Green Man at Dulwich", Kingsley reported the inversion as "the Dull Man at Woolwich". It would be unkind and untrue to say that this was exactly typical, and yet it invokes with affection the image of a colleague who, whatever else he may have been, was never dull even at the rare moments when he was green.

He had filled in many hours of the time that would otherwise have hung heavily on his hands in finishing a book begun five years before during his bye-Fellowship at Cambridge. This was *French Liberal Thought in the Eighteenth Century*;[1] a historian's attempt to step back into that period, take his modern reading with him, and consider the views of the encyclopaedists and revolutionaries with what might be called the twentieth-century Cambridge critical apparatus. It is carefully comparative and non-opinionated; and has a fascinating chapter on Montesquieu's visit to England in 1730 (half-way through the production of his monumental *L'Esprit de Lois*). Kingsley and Olga worked on this book together at intervals from 1926 onwards, and in his preface he acknowledges her "collaboration both in writing and revising". He was also reviewing books for journals as various as the *Cambridge Review*, the *Quarterly*, *Time and Tide* and *The Spectator*. He was a magnificent book-reviewer, and as good reviewers do he amassed an impressive library of review copies. He had a way of acquiring multi-volume works in this manner. They ranged from the fourteen volumes of the Barchester Novels in the Shakespeare Head edition published in 1930 by the Oxford University Press, to the 35-volume facsimile edition of Diderot's *Encyclopédie*, which he reviewed for the *Times Literary Supplement* in the very last month of his life. The Trollope review was in *Time and Tide* for 28th February 1930, and not only have I always regarded it as a reviewer's model, deserving of inclusion in any anthology of literary criticism, but also I recall it with grateful affection because it started me on Trollope.

By 1929 his editorial work on the *Political Quarterly* was giving him a further interest (Olga would read and correct the proofs of it as they arrived from the printer, and he records somewhere that she was "a proof reader in a thousand"). He did a little "guest lecturing" at Manchester University and elsewhere—before leaving London he had asked Professor Clay whether Manchester could offer him a part time lectureship, but there was none available. And he did some acting in local

[1] Benn, 1929; republished by Hutchinson, London, 1955.

dramatic societies. Lady Stocks recalls in her autobiography[1] that he took part in some of the drama productions of the Manchester University Settlement, which was then functioning at the Round House—newly equipped with an unexpected bequest. He played the part of de Stogumber, Chaplain to the Cardinal of Winchester, in Shaw's *St Joan*; and Professor John Stocks (Lady Stocks's husband) was the Inquisitor.

The tenor of his domestic life in Didsbury may be judged by the extracts from Olga's diaries in the last chapter. The house in Kingston Road was large and sparsely furnished and rather cheerless. Essentially it lacked a chatelaine, for Olga was not interested in it, in Manchester, in her neighbours (with a very few exceptions), or in Kingsley's office colleagues. Or, he once complained, in anything other than Benjy, the big black dog. After a few months he began inviting two or three friends home to dinner, but all too often Olga, having got a meal ready, would awkwardly excuse herself and retire to bed. The dinner parties soon stopped. Then Kingsley, who was being much better paid than other members of the editorial staff, and knew that they knew he was, took to asking a few colleagues to an occasional hotel meal. Olga never went to these, and after a time the others began to excuse themselves too—not, it may well be, from any dislike of their host but because they found the situation embarrassing. The cumulative effect of all this upon Kingsley, a company-loving man, must be imagined.

He still wrote often to Verity, and contrived to see her from time to time. He was fond of Olga still, but his fondness took the form of a loyal, sentimental and guilt-ridden concern; and in a man of Kingsley's compassion this was strong enough to overcome the irritation he now increasingly felt about her poetic abstraction, her role of frustrated artist and her attitudinising. They had married because they were sorry for each other and genuinely believed, in a rather bewildered way, that they could be mutually helpful. And though this may be the classic formula for an eventually unhappy marriage it is not necessarily the road to divorce or separation. Kingsley was capable of enduring such a marriage for life, but not, I believe, of achieving much that would be worthwhile in the whole course of it. The

[1] Mary Stocks, *My Commonplace Book*, Peter Davies, 1970, p. 154.

break-up, which almost coincided with his arrival at the *New Statesman*, left them both unattached and rather desolate; but it left Kingsley, at all events, with the capacity to recover, enjoy some freedom again and address his mind more vigorously to the stupendous problems which confronted the editor of a journal of opinion in the thirties.

"You have done your level best for the *Guardian*," Ted Scott had written to him in January 1930, "and I could not wish for a more loyal colleague. But I fear that with us you would always feel yourself a little too much under restraint to do yourself justice, and I hope (and believe) that you will be able to find an opening into which you will be able to throw yourself more freely. You are a little wasting yourself here, and that is good neither for you nor for us. Of course there is no hurry." Ted Scott had been editor since July 1929—though his father had become Governing Director, the classic role for editors who have retired but are unable to believe it or behave like it. "The circulation was low," wrote Kingsley in *Father Figures*:[1] "it seemed likely to revive when C.P. retired and Ted Scott became editor. But then C.P. didn't properly retire." The extraordinary thing is that when Kingsley was writing those words in 1965, he had himself been "retired" for five years and was still barely able to behave like it—a subject to which I must return. Yet he used to sweep aside as a shallow wisecrack the aphorism that the only thing men learn from history is that they do not learn from history. "The light which experience gives," said Coleridge, "is a lantern on the stern, which shines only on the waves behind us."

Kingsley remained genuinely fond of Ted Scott, who had understood the problem about Olga—he and his wife had befriended and entertained her during Kingsley's long absences in London and (on one or two occasions) abroad; and she trusted them. Ted survived his indomitable father by only three months—he was drowned while sailing on Lake Windermere in April 1932; and Kingsley, in his private scribbled diaries, recorded a grief the intensity of which would, I believe, have been a surprise to many.

Professor Stocks wrote to him (13th August 1930) to suggest

[1] P. 185.

that he should "seek re-entry to University work". But "the History of Political Theory," said Stocks, "is unfortunately a subject in which there are not many posts going. It falls on the borderline between Philosophy and Public Administration. Still, the political field generally is an expanding one from the academic point of view, and there are not too many qualified persons. We shall miss you at the Settlement" (where Kingsley was an active member of the drama group) "but I will take no action until I hear definitely from you that you must resign. I hope you will leave this to the last."

He took his leave of the *Manchester Guardian* at the end of 1930. He had already arranged, on a recent visit to London, the lease of the flat at Primrose Hill; and, having settled in, the first thing he did was to go and see Leonard Woolf, who was literary editor of *The Nation* and a firm friend. "I was both sorry and glad at your news," Woolf told him, "but you are certainly wise to leave the *Guardian*. You should easily get a job in London. We must talk to Keynes."

Chapter 9

THE NEW EDITOR

"TAKE IT FOR seven years," said Leonard Woolf when he heard about Keynes's *New Statesman* suggestion. "Not for longer, because journalism rots the brain." So Kingsley took it and stayed 30 years, without manifest brain damage. Woolf always knew he *would* remain, and that the excitement and immediacy of it, the being at the centre of things, meeting important people in political life, would always overcome the attraction (which never weakened) of a return to academic life.

He told so often the story of the Savoy lunch party at which he was vetted for the editorship that it has acquired a number of versions. Of them all, the two that most resemble each other are the one in *Father Figures* (page 190) and the one he used in a broadcast on the 25th anniversary of the *New Statesman*'s birth—which Edward Hyams reproduced in his book *The New Statesman, 1913–1963* (page 118). In June 1957 Kingsley was supplied with a third variant by Lady Uvedale, the widow of H. B. Lees-Smith, who was Liberal MP for Northampton (and Postmaster-General in the 1931 "National" Government), was then a director of the paper, and was present at the Savoy lunch. The others present were Edward Whitley, Chairman of the Board, and Arnold Bennett, who had written to Ted Scott of the *Manchester Guardian* to ask whether Kingsley could be recommended. (There was already a confident assurance that he could from Maynard Keynes of *The Nation*, who was still hoping to combine the two papers.) "I can add a few more details about your luncheon," wrote Lady Uvedale:

> Perhaps you never knew that the cost was borrowed by Arnold Bennett from Gordon Robbins, our next-door neighbour? Arnold Bennett first borrowed £1 from my husband, but as he paid for Bertie's[1] luncheon, Bertie did not mind much that he never saw

[1] i.e. Lees-Smith's.

> the £1 back again! Gordon Robbins was the Editor of *The Times*.[1] Naturally he was a little perturbed when he heard that Bertie had already supplied £1, as he felt quite rightly that he would never see his £5 back again. . . . You are quite right that Arnold Bennett was a Director of the Savoy, but I believe the Board had hinted to him that a directorship of the Hotel did not include his habit of having innumerable meals there, *and* entertaining guests, at the Hotel's expense. Do you remember a dish of tasteless fish that day? The waiter murmured to Bertie "specially flown over from Geneva today". Arnold Bennett liked that sort of magnificence, as you know. It was that very tasteless fresh water carp—a Dover sole would have been far nicer.

Kingsley's recollection was that it was he who guessed it came by air that morning ("for once I was quick"). He may even have persuaded himself that Bennett had thus in some way been impressed and that the fate of the *New Statesman* had been poised upon so small an incident—an account which, says Edward Hyams, "is more entertaining than convincing".

But he was appointed. (He used to say quizzically that it was always best that an aspiring editor should be approved by an established editor—and Arnold Bennett had once edited *Woman*.) Keynes was pleased, though he would have been happier if Kingsley's arrival had coincided with an amalgamation of *Nation* and *New Statesman*, which was what he wanted, rather than a briefly postponed gobbling-up of the one by the other, which was what he got. (The *Nation*'s Board and shareholders still form a separate entity.) For a few months Kingsley edited the two papers as separate entities, until it became obvious that they were harming each other at a time when the survival of both was in question, and Kingsley was like a circus performer standing on two horses going at different speeds. *The Nation*, which had itself gobbled up *The Athenaeum* ten years earlier, had been losing money fast. In three years under Massingham the combined *Nation and Athenaeum* had lost what was left of its Liberal readership and the support of the long-suffering Rowntrees who were its principal owners. Massingham was told he could have the paper for himself if he could raise the funds to buy it, and for a time he tried in

[1] Robbins was at that time "day editor".

vain to interest Lord Haldane's group of left-wing liberals in putting up the money. In the end it was bought, in the autumn of 1923, by Maynard Keynes, Walter Layton, the Cadbury family and the Rowntree Trust. Beatrice Webb described these men in her diary (December 1922) as

> a group of Liberals whose bond of union is their belief in the possibility of finding a progressive policy in national affairs which is not based upon a collectivist dogma.

And this group proposed complete amalgamation with the *New Statesman* "in order to avoid commercial loss by the competition of two journals whose policy and public are to a very large extent the same, and to produce a greatly improved journal". But the "group of Liberals" never succeeded in bringing off an amalgamation. For nine more years the *Nation and Athenaeum* carried on; and so did the *New Statesman* despite constant rows between its Directors and its Editor, Clifford Sharp—who always felt that he had the Webbs behind him. There was nearly a final breach in 1924, when C. M. Lloyd and G. D. H. Cole, the two distinguished academics who were doing most of the work, nearly resigned over a Clifford Sharp "leader" attacking Ramsay MacDonald. "I cannot go on," wrote Lloyd to Mrs Webb, "if such articles continue. This week [20th October 1924] there has been a change. His leader is again one with which I don't agree BUT it is altogether different in tone. It is also followed by articles by Cole and Huddlestone which are entirely pro-labour Party and pro-MacDonald."

It is tempting to compare this with a *Preliminary Memorandum Descriptive of Proposed New Weekly Journal* which had heralded the birth of the *New Statesman* in October 1912. The new paper's comments and articles, according to this, were to reflect

> a complete independence of those exigencies of party politics which necessarily arise from time to time to limit the freedom of party organs of all kinds.

Indeed, on 24th October 1924 Sharp wrote to Sidney Webb:

> The Board met this afternoon and demanded my instant resignation (Bennett alone dissenting).... Personally I do not care. The

> Company will have to pay me a couple of thousand pounds, and apart from that I can easily double my income at once. Also I have long wanted to be free to travel, before I am *quite* middle-aged. . . . When they asked for my resignation I immediately offered to buy them all out at par. I can do that of course very easily ten times over.[1] I would get a cheque tomorrow morning.... I wish I could blow the whole show up so that the paper could never appear again. . . . Don't bother to answer this before polling day,[2] though I don't imagine the thought of polling day bothers *you* much. But MacDonald! What an ass he has made of himself! His vanity has jeopardised the whole future of Europe, and why shouldn't I say so?

He was supported by MacCarthy, Lloyd, Robert Lynd and John Roberts—and above all by Bernard Shaw. The Board "reversed their decision *sans phrase*", wrote Sharp to Webb a week later (3rd November), "and what is more they did it very charmingly. So the question of buying them out," he concluded magnanimously, "does not arise."

Meanwhile the *Nation and Athenaeum* was being edited by H. D. Henderson, whom Kingsley called "an argumentative Scottish economist" and who vigorously preached Keynesian doctrines—until he left the paper in January 1930 to become secretary of the Economic Advisory Council. Then the cold douche of practicality led to some disenchantment with the principles he had for so long imbibed from men like Keynes and Norman Angell; and as a Fellow of All Souls, Oxford, Henderson launched a fierce attack on Keynes's *General Theory of Employment, Interest and Money*, which seems to have survived the onslaught. Kingsley was in frequent touch with Henderson until the latter's death in 1952. Another economist, Harold Wright,[3] had taken over the editorship of the *Nation and Athenaeum* in 1930, but after a few months the new owners decided that it could not survive and authorised Keynes, as chairman, to reopen negotiations with John Roberts, the *New*

[1] So far as anyone knew, Sharp had no money.

[2] Webb was then MP for Seaham Harbour, where Ramsay MacDonald succeeded him in 1929.

[3] In 1931, as Kingsley took up the editorship, Wright and Norman Angell published their controversial book *Can Governments Cure Unemployment?*

Statesman's managing director. Roberts was determined, as Hyams records in his book,[1]

> that the New Statesman should acquire the *Nation and Athenaeum* and be in complete control of the new weekly; that the *New Statesman* staff, not the *Nation* staff, should keep their jobs; and that the new joint paper should be as *New Statesman*ly as ever. He foresaw a very bright future for the paper if he could get his own way, and he was not in the least intimidated by the tremendous standing of his opposite number.

Roberts got his way, as he did in most matters and for a long time. The Statesman and Nation Publishing Company Ltd was formed with a capital of £32,000, and Kingsley Martin became the first editor of the *New Statesman and Nation*. Within a year or two it was widely and irreverently known, with a mixture of constant affection and weekend rage, as the *New Staggers and Naggers*.

But in setting the scene for his arrival, one must conclude the story of the first editor, Clifford Sharp; who, as Beatrice Webb said in a letter to Kingsley on 3rd April 1934, "*made* the paper and ought to have the credit of it." Sharp was the Webbs' own discovery and protégé, and of his brilliance as journalist and editor there can be no doubt. But several times he brought the paper within sight of ruin by what seems now a lunatic recklessness about the defamation laws (even more draconian then than they are now); and as early as 20th February 1922 Beatrice Webb was confiding to her diary, in an entry not hitherto made public:[2]

> Clifford Sharp, alas, looks as if the rumour that he is a heavy drinker was true. He has the unmistakable lines about the mouth which one can recognise as the result of alcoholic self-indulgence. . . . The strength of his constitution is itself a danger, as it enables him to go on with his work. The Asquith set has deteriorated him in a way I could not have believed possible. But while there is youth there is hope: some event may yet turn the current of his life. What little influence Sidney and I have on him is gone—we cannot help. All we can do for him is to be

[1] *The New Statesman, 1913–1963*, p. 120.

[2] Beatrice Webb's Diaries, Passfield Collection, LSE Library.

silent. When St John Ervine the other day called him a drunkard I flatly denied it. "He may drink too much for his health," I said, "but most of the war generation do that. They'll grow out of it."

Mrs Webb was not fond of the Asquiths, and among them, she was probably least fond of Margot. Clifford Sharp had been rather taken up by Margot, and Mrs Webb had watched with disapproval his gradual absorption into the Asquith circle. On 10th December 1922 she wrote in her diary:[1]

> Clifford Sharp had a natural affinity for the Asquiths and their set, and where the door was opened wide to this delectable social abode, and Margot, with her wit, flattery, and caressing familiarities beckoned to him, he was doomed to enter in and have the door sharply closed behind him. The liking was spontaneous on his side. Sharp has the same political temperament as Asquith; the same coarse-grained character and strong commonplace intelligence; the same conventionality of culture and outlook; the same contempt for enthusiasm and idealism; the same liking for heavy drinking, smoking and card playing; the same taste for ornamental and parasitic women.

But by the autumn of 1928 Mrs Webb had accepted what Shaw called the inevitability of a change of editor. "After an interval of six years," she wrote on 12th August,[2]

> Clifford Sharp came here for a weekend—he had intimated that he would like to see us again, and we had wished to close the episode of unfriendliness due to his anti-Labour policy during the three General Elections. He has not changed except that he looked more physically shattered by drink; but he was sane, cynically able, and frank—he was contemptuous of the Labour Party: its leaders had no courage, it was based on the interests of one class, its only chance was coalition with the Liberals, and that would mean an inward split. Politics were deadly dull, there were no issues of interest to the general public, there was a dearth of talent in public life and literature. . . . He told us a good deal about Beaverbrook, who had made him various offers of highly paid employment. He was tired of the *New Statesman* but hated the idea of anyone else controlling it. He dislikes J.R.M., despises

[1] Beatrice Webb's Diaries, Passfield Collection, LSE Library.
[2] Ibid.

Clynes, respects [Arthur] Henderson but regards him as a dullard. . . . I should not be surprised if Clifford Sharp ended by drinking himself past recovery.

Even if Sharp's departure had seemed to the Webbs inevitable since 1928, it was the inevitability of gradualness. As Edward Hyams observes in his story of the *New Statesman and Nation*,[1] while it was possible to regard Sharp as editor and get the work done by G. D. H. Cole, C. M. Lloyd and Desmond MacCarthy, no one might have thought of making a change: Sharp would get better. "It is not, thank God, in the English character to face the fact that a man is a dismal failure and kick him out—some other way has to be found to make room for a better man. Only death or total collapse could remove Sharp from office as editor of a paper he was felt to have created and brought to life." But the directors decided in the end to give him the sack quietly and without fuss, softening the blow by way of a sabbatical year in America. It is not clear whether they supposed that, because America was then in the hard-drinking throes of "Prohibition", he would find it harder to get whisky, but off to America he went, and his downfall was quickly completed. In due course S. K. Ratcliffe and Alfred Orage, who had known him for years and were then lecturing and writing in America, discovered his plight and arranged for him to return to England. But not to the *New Statesman*.

There were many who supposed that Sharp's successor would be G. D. H. Cole, who in effect had been sharing with C. M. Lloyd the editorship of the "front half" through the long and worrying period of Sharp's decline. Cole, who for nearly 20 years had been one of the most prolific British writers on socialism, was what his wife Margaret called "a strong Tory in everything but politics", but in politics he was always a convinced and convincing socialist; though a natural teacher rather than a natural journalist. The weekly discussion circle which grew up around him at Oxford in 1925 (the Cole Group, as it came to be known) and which he enjoyed until his death 35 years later, is still a legendary institution and attracted such men as Colin Clark, Sir John Betjeman, W. H. Auden, Hugh

[1] *Op. cit.*, p. 116.

Gaitskell, John Parker (the one who became an MP), Evan Durbin and Michael Stewart. In 1913, the year when the *New Statesman* was founded, he had written an influential book (the first of a torrent) called *The World of Labour*, and from 1918 he had been writing both for the *New Statesman* and for *The Nation*. At the end of 1918 *The Nation* rejected an article which the *New Statesman* then accepted; from which point he was mainly a *New Statesman* man. (His story is told in one of the best of recent biographies, *The Life of G. D. H. Cole*, by Dame Margaret Cole.)[1]

It was his lifelong habit to write his articles in minute longhand, seldom hesitating for a word, and with never an alteration. He knew exactly what he was going to say, and what he then said seemed to him so self-evident that he was always taken aback if it was challenged before going to the printer. (He was accustomed to dealing with challenge once he was in print, for that came from the uninstructed whom it was one's duty to instruct.) He was to become a Director of the *New Statesman and Nation* in 1947 and in 1956 he was chairman of its board—for a difficult and testing period to which I will return.

C. M. Lloyd ("Mostyn" Lloyd to all his contemporaries) was an economist teaching political science at the LSE and, in effect for years, filling the all-too-familiar role of the assistant editor who never gets the job, the recognition, or the pay. He came to the *New Statesman* in its very earliest days—indeed he was involved with the Webbs and Bernard Shaw in the planning of it. A quietly busy and conscientious man, a gentle person of great charm, he was second favourite for the editorship when Sharp left.

Neither of these two men, who had been next-door neighbours in Hampstead as well as already co-operating colleagues at the office, had ever envisaged that a new man could possibly be appointed editor. Only one question, they thought, presented itself: which of them was it to be? And they had often and openly discussed each other's qualifications and shortcomings, each pretending to prefer the chances of the other. But while Lloyd was surprised rather than hurt, Cole was outraged at the Board's ingratitude. He announced that he would not of

[1] Macmillan, London, 1971.

course be writing any more for the paper. "You have no right," Kingsley wrote to him, "to penalise the paper or me because the Directors have chosen to make me editor." Cole then relented and "wrote one of his best articles for the second issue". Nevertheless on 1st March 1931 Maynard Keynes was writing to Kingsley: "What is this I read in *The Observer* about G. D. H. Cole trying to raise £25,000 to run a new socialist weekly?" (The New Fabian Research Bureau was thinking of starting a paper, but it was never a serious project.) Of Kingsley's appointment, Dame Margaret says in her *Life of G. D. H. Cole* (p. 181) that

> at the time it looked very much of a leap in the dark. . . . Their choice turned out brilliantly and resulted in a journal that was unique for so long as [Kingsley] remained its editor. Douglas came to realise this without rancour, and also, I think, that he himself could never have done what Martin did. . . . His first flash of resentment had been quickly put aside at the mere suggestion that he was indulging in personal pique.

And yet Mostyn Lloyd, at any rate, had known that Kingsley regarded himself as eligible for the job, and must have been strangely obtuse in privately ruling him out. As early as 3rd July 1930 he had a letter from Kingsley (still in Manchester) saying that "in view of our conversation of a few months back" he wanted to mention a change in his position:

> I told you I had decided on my wife's account that I could not remain here very much longer, and also that my job was not offering enough scope and freedom. . . . The three years contract I had with the MG is nearly at an end and I have had a long talk with the Editor about my position. We agree that I am not quite enough in sympathy with his policy to enable me to write without restraint, or for him to be able to leave the main policy stuff in my hands, without a good deal of discussion and difficulty. . . . So I must find another job. . . . At present, apart from the Directors of the MG and Hammond, no-one knows of this decision except you. . . . Without my mentioning it, E. T. Scott asked me if I thought there was a possibility of my getting the *New Statesman* job, and remarked that he thought my politics were just about right for it and that it was a job I should do well. So if a letter from the editor of the MG would in any way help

> my prospects I am sure he would be ready to write one. . . . I have not now anything definite in mind except the possibility of the NS. As you know I'd rather work with you on the NS than anything else. So if you are in a position to give me any kind of hint as to how things stand it would help very much.

If Mostyn Lloyd was regarding himself as Editor Elect, he must have concealed the fact very skilfully from Kingsley, who would be neither so ingenuous nor so purblind as to seek the help of a known rival.

A source of strain between Kingsley and Douglas Cole was that Kingsley thought Cole's writing "lacking in colour and emphasis", while Cole thought Kingsley's achieved colour and emphasis (as it often did) at the expense of syntax and, what was worse, of dignity. But Cole was not only measurelessly well-informed on his subjects, he was "as reliable as the sun and moon" (Leonard Woolf's words) with his copy. The fact that there is usually one such person among an editor's entourage is what prevents editors from going out of their minds.

Re-reading today the editorials of those years, one has the sensation of sitting through a tutorial at which (though it may require some effort) those who contrive to keep awake are likely to hear something they would never otherwise have thought of. The over-long articles of the first few years were soon discontinued, probably under the genial influence of the looming prospect of profit; and by 1930 they had become small-type 5,000-word supplements about democracy, dictators, drains and disaster. To judge from the columns of the paper itself, Kingsley seems to have been "tapered" in, very much as Sharp was faded out. There is no announcement of his appointment, nor is there any mention of the marriage of the two papers other than the words "New Statesman and Nation, Vol. 1, No. 1." Looked at today it seems a fat, leisurely paper, solid and scholarly; healthily crammed with advertisements (full pages—at £16—devoted to tobacco, beer, banks and, far above all, books—Thornton Butterworth advertising Churchill's *World Crisis*, "Four Volumes in One, 832 pages," for 21s.); its contributors including Laurence Binyon, Augustine Birrell, Edmund Blunden, E. M. Forster, J. L. Hammond, J. M. Keynes, Harold Laski, Desmond MacCarthy, Bronislaw

Malinowski, Raymond Mortimer, H. W. Nevinson, V. S. Pritchett, H. F. M. Prescott, Bertrand Russell, Dame Ethel Smyth, Lytton Strachey, Graham Wallas, Leonard and Virginia Woolf. Many of its letters were signed "Your Reviewer", while others began "Sir, My attention has been called . . .", which always seems to mean "Sir, Nothing could induce me in the ordinary way to read your stinking publication . . ." Vol. 1, No. 1 contained a delectable essay from Virginia Woolf in the form of a letter *All About Books*, and on a back page dismissed Sellars' and Yeatman's *1066 and All That* in ten lines of rather tight-lipped pedagogy. And it is impossible to forgo the chance to notice, however cruelly, that the Editorial Notes in Kingsley's first number concluded thus:

> Two events have just emphasised the rapid decline of the power of the Nazis in Germany. On Sunday the Reichsbanner, or Republican Defence Organisation, held manifestations throughout the Reich. They were attended by large numbers of people, and revealed the strength of Republican sentiment in Germany and its determination to resist any Putsch attempts on the part of Hitlerites. . . . Even the notorious Commander Ehrhardt has been constrained to admit that Hitler has achieved nothing, and that by his political escapades he has committed a political Hari-Kari [*sic*]. It would seem that Hitler's success at the last election has been a blessing in disguise, in that it came before he and his followers were ripe for it.

Kingsley was of course beginning his editorship at the opening of a decade which was probably the most fateful in the history of man. The Sino-Japanese War, the rise of Hitler, Mussolini's seizure of Abyssinia, the collapse of the League of Nations, the Spanish Civil War, the Munich crisis and the long-foreseen outbreak of World War II were the giant peaks of these ten years. But in 1931 alone there was the formation by Oswald Mosley of his quasi-fascist "New Party"; the collapse of the Credit-Anstalt in Austria, and then of the German currency; the beginning of the huge exodus of persecuted Jews from central Europe; the report of the "May" Committee urging, because of an estimated budget deficit of £100 million—we spend that today on two aircraft!—that there must be economies so drastic that the cabinet was fatally divided, the Government resigned, and Ramsay MacDonald formed his "National" Government with a majority of 502; the Invergordon naval mutiny; the panic behaviour of the foreign holders of sterling; the odd anti-climax of Britain's departure from the gold standard—"nobody told us," cried Sidney Webb, now Lord Passfield, "that we *could* do this", although we had been using paper money quite happily for seventeen years; and the beginning of Brazil's official destruction of its vast stocks of surplus coffee. The title of Thomas Middleton's seventeenth-century play epitomised the popular feeling: *A Mad World, My Masters.*

New Statesman readers had their first opportunity to judge their new editor's socialism from a review of R. H. Tawney's book *Equality*:[1]

> It is even argued that since men vary in talents and since some must make decisions and others accept them, the goal of social equality is unattainable. And because the present national income would not, if it were shared out equally, make us all rich, some pretend that we should not aim at a more equitable distribution of what wealth we have. . . . On board ship someone must give orders, some do dirty work and others clean, but that does not make the captain an object of resentment.[2] . . . The 18th Century humanists who made equality a battle cry of revolution were aiming, not at a communist Utopia but at the destruction of a caste system. . . . It is the corrosion of this inequality—a corrosion which affects the poor, who learn to worship wealth, as well as the rich, whose energies are wasted in guarding their preserves—against which Mr Tawney directs his eloquence and wit.

At home in Primrose Hill, Kingsley was cultivating and enlarging a circle of political and literary friends. He was always a gregarious man, he loved talking and listening and marshalling; and this he could do to the best advantage in his own rooms because there he could be, if not the chairman (and he was always a good chairman) then the *primus inter pares*. When he was not surrounded by arguing friends he was talking

[1] *New Statesman and Nation*, 7 February 1931.

[2] An analogy that seems to have lodged in his mind since the day when he wrote his winning essay at Mill Hill School, fifteen years before, on "The Quest for Success." (See p. 49.)

to one of them on the telephone: he spent more time on the telephone than any man (or even woman) I have known. Some of his friends and colleagues thought he wasted too much time talking and listening to those he judged to be well-informed, and that he should have spent more time reading Hansard, blue-books, current literature and the foreign press. Those who believed him to be, accordingly, "the prey of the last speaker" would jockey for position round his editorial ear on a Tuesday night; among these in the thirties being Konni Zilliacus[1] and Elizabeth Wiskemann,[2] who were concerned not so much to feed him with ideas as to stop him saying something about Central and Eastern Europe that they would think harmful. A more likely assessment of his last-minute malleability is that he listened to half a dozen experts when he got the chance, and then largely adopted the views of the one who seemed closest to what he himself had been thinking already.

He now had no inhibition about mixing his home and office life. Olga was, for a time, more conformable in London than she had been in Manchester, partaking more easily of his success than she had of his failure. In the large drawing room at Primrose Hill she played hostess more happily to the casual though almost daily gatherings for political and literary gossip. The time she now spent alone with Kingsley was reduced to a minimum by these occasions and by weekend schools and conferences. The tenor of their life together may be judged by the extracts from their diaries given in Chapter 7; but they were materially comfortable. Their home at number 8 Ormonde Terrace was a first-floor balcony flat on the corner of St Edmund's Terrace; and not even a house agent could overstate the charm of its position or the view down the green slopes of Primrose Hill, which started at the very door. Primrose Hill is a small and well-tended park which adjoins the Zoological Gardens in Regent's Park; a green and pleasant spot which now, although you have to look hard for primroses, totally belies its description by Edmund Gosse in *Father and Son*—

[1] Labour MP for the Gorton Division of Manchester, an extreme left-winger, and a man who exerted great influence on Kingsley.

[2] Historian, and Central European Correspondent of the *New Statesman* for many years; a friend of Kingsley's from his Cambridge days.

> I expected to see a mountain absolutely carpeted with primroses, a terrestrial galaxy like that which covered the hill that led up to Montgomery Castle in Donne's poem. But at length, as we walked from the Chalk Farm direction, a miserable acclivity stole into view—surrounded, even in those days, on most sides by houses, with its grass worn to the buff by millions of boots, and resembling what I meant by "the country" about as much as Poplar resembles Paradise.

Incidentally both Ormonde Terrace and St Edmund's Terrace now proclaim themselves as being in the City of Westminster, a fact which might well surprise even the most knowing of Londoners.

Kingsley also presided every week at a Monday *New Statesman* lunch, where the food was less important than the talk, and the talk was seldom related, unless by accident, to the contents of the week's forthcoming paper. The party assembled in an assortment of places, including the Red Lion Restaurant in Red Lion Square and a basement café in Great Queen Street close to the *New Statesman*'s offices at number 10. It was usually a distinguished company, and its guests would include high-up civil servants who were as skilled in the art of "planting" information of the kind they wanted to publicise as the surrounding journalists were in extracting more interesting information as a quid pro quo. In Great Queen Street a woman in a white apron supplied them with potatoes roasted in their jackets and a plate of cold meat winter or summer, accompanied by what one or two of the regulars regarded as a minimal quantity of alcohol. Graham Hutton, the financial writer, who was at that time foreign correspondent as well as assistant editor of *The Economist*, recalls that it was at one of these lunches that Maynard Keynes, on "the famous 21st September 1931", arrived late from the Treasury rubbing his hands and chuckling like a boy who has just exploded a firework underneath someone he doesn't like. "There were a dozen of us there," says Hutton, "including Nicholas Davenport, who was then writing a City page for Kingsley. We all said 'what's the matter—what's happened?' And Keynes said, 'At one stroke, Britain has resumed the financial hegemony of the world!' And we all sat down and started talking about it."

Britain had abandoned the gold standard. Keynes was chairman of the newly-formed Statesman and Nation Publishing Company and he took his chairmanship very seriously, as Kingsley was increasingly to learn with a mixture of gratitude and irritation.

Having inherited an outstanding team of contributors who had been working for an absentee editor, and who now saw some evidence of stability in a newly organised paper, Kingsley was soon in trouble over the fees that he was proposing to pay them. It was a kind of trouble from which he never escaped. At the *Manchester Guardian*, with a salary which had reached £950 by the time he left, he had little to do with the notoriously small fees it paid to its writers, but supposed that contributors made up in gratification and prestige for what they lacked in cash. He felt that you should be no less proud to write for the *New Statesman* and that money was purely secondary. Even if you weren't proud, it gave you a cachet that attracted other work—broadcasting and lecturing, reviewing and advising. This, of course, was all very well if you were writing signed pieces, but at first that was the privilege of the few. It was Raymond Mortimer who successfully urged that everything should be signed except "shorter notices" about books and, of course, the editorials; and it was he who prevailed upon Kingsley to pay for every contribution accepted, whether it was published or not. Kingsley was fortified in his parsimony by Keynes, who used to say that he could write the whole of a *New Statesman* issue himself in three hours and thoroughly enjoy the process, and that it was absurd to pay large fees for a pleasant exercise that was also a privilege. The trouble was, everyone knew that Keynes could have done precisely what he boasted (the only page that *might* have been a little below par, Raymond Mortimer told me, was the music page). For 30 years Kingsley battled with his contributors' demands, beginning inauspiciously with Desmond MacCarthy. There is no record of the fee he offered but MacCarthy's letter (dated 1st July 1931) survives:

> You have upset my temper, and awoken in me an old grievance. Really! At my age to be asked to "write short", and then paid

> by the inch! You make me feel I'm writing for a niggardly paper. A poor paper I don't mind writing for, but a niggardly one—well I'm damned if I will. The NS has got a fine circulation now. I want £5. 5. 0 an article and £4 a month retainer. I never got a rise all the years I worked for it, and never asked for one because I knew the paper was poor—and although I knew that Lynd had got one. But when I discovered that the paper could afford to pay my successor exactly double what it had paid me,[1] I confess I felt aggrieved. Now the NS has added to its own circulation that of *The Nation* I have no scruple in asking for what is my due considering the value of my contributions to the paper. I hope you will see this in the light I do.

Kingsley saw the light, and MacCarthy got what he demanded.

In the second volume of his memoirs, *Editor*, page 15, Kingsley records the episode as seen from the other side of the desk. Having reflected that "if the pound sterling was worth four times as much in the thirties as it is today, our payments were not particularly stingy", he goes on to say:

> I certainly did my best to save money in the days before we were prosperous, and I expect I was too slow in adjusting salaries and payments per thousand words when we began to be able to afford more. Anyway Robert Lynd ("Y.Y.") never complained about seven guineas for his weekly essay, nor did Desmond MacCarthy ask for more than six guineas for his famous dramatic criticisms.

The same situation arose in 1939 when V. S. Pritchett was writing the weekly *Books in General* article. Each of these took him a long time, and for each one he was paid £6. Accordingly he "had to go and earn some money to be able to afford to write for the *New Statesman*". One day Raymond Mortimer, who was literary editor, said to him: "Why do you work so hard?" Pritchett told him he had to keep his family. "How much are you paid for a *Books in General*?" asked Mortimer, and

[1] Desmond MacCarthy had been literary editor until 1928, when he succeeded Sir Edmund Gosse as senior literary critic on the *Sunday Times*. He was succeeded as literary editor of the *New Statesman* by R. Ellis Roberts, of whom Kingsley said in *Father Figures* (p. 199) that he was "the only writer on the NS whose contributions I could not stomach—I found his writing intolerable." He could hardly have been worth twice as much as Desmond MacCarthy.

Pritchett told him. "Good God!" said Mortimer, and went in at once to remonstrate with Kingsley. Later Pritchett was summoned. "You must be living very extravagantly?" said Kingsley. "What do you want all this money for?" Pritchett mentioned the family. "But there's price control, isn't there?" Kingsley asked. "Children's clothes, for example—they're all under control? Well, all right—I'll think about it." The thinking produced a rise of £4.

There are countless stories of this kind. Throughout the 30 years of his editorship, Kingsley went on paying even some of his most distinguished contributors by the inch. On Thursday afternoons, when he was marking up the newly-printed paper with what they were all to get, he sat in his office using a foot-rule to measure their entitlement. This was why one got cheques for £11.9.6 or £3.4.8. It was the joke of the office, but it was of the kind that makes no one laugh. And there is Kingsley's own rationale in *Father Figures* (page 128), where he says he cannot remember that he "ever thought about money in a serious way" whether he was rich or poor:

> Even later on when I had money I spent the least possible on furniture and clothes, and I was preposterously and disastrously mean about all the things that add to beauty rather than efficiency. This was particularly foolish of me because I wanted everyone, especially women, to like me. I was willing to share my cash with them when I had done the things I thought important, just as I was with men. Looking back I can see that I could not afford to buy myself unpopularity by petty stinginess. . . . I can't say whether I was generous or not.

Luckily, I can. Petty stinginess there certainly was, but at a time when I myself was desperately hard up (it was about 1952) and almost too worried to write, I was working very late one night at the *New Statesman* office; trying, I remember, to finish a long radio script. I thought I was alone in the building. Suddenly I heard footsteps on the stairs, and Kingsley appeared at my door. He too was writing late. He'd heard my typewriter and had come up to investigate. What on earth was keeping me? I told him what I was doing. We gossiped for three or four minutes about other things, and then he said suddenly:

"If you find yourself in any money difficulties, I should like it if you would let me know." To a long record of lost opportunities I must add the fact that I stupidly told him "everything was perfectly all right". (No explanation of this now occurs to me.) I remember thinking, with some contrition, that he seemed slightly rebuffed as he went downstairs again. I worked on for another hour, and when I passed his door on my way out he appeared with his coat on. We walked together to Charing Cross (he was then living in Robert Street, and I at Greenwich). He briefly reminded me of his implied offer, and I, having taking up a position, idiotically sustained it. The next morning at home there was a letter from him (which he must have gone out late at night to post) saying that there was now more money in his bank account than he thought decent or could possibly use; that he had been thinking about my three children; and that he hoped I would not mind "making use of the enclosed for as long as I could possibly need it". The enclosed was a cheque for £500. Sorting his papers 20 years later for the purposes of this book I came across my own inadequate letter of startled thanks, and another from my wife. "Most of my openhandedness was rationalisation," he says in the passage I have already quoted from *Father Figures*. "It is quite clear to me that I wasn't really worrying about [people's] needs, but playing up to an image of myself as a much nicer person than I was. I couldn't bear being unpleasant or saying no. Brought up poor, I loved the swank of seeing the gratitude and surprise of people I'd helped."

Well, perhaps. But I think I knew him better than to accept that. I believe I had paid the money back within a year, but there was, and there will always remain, more than the money to pay back. I know now of many such kindnesses to other men and women; and if they enabled Kingsley to enjoy "the swank of seeing the gratitude and surprise" of their beneficiaries, they distinguish him from wealthier men who could steel themselves to forgo the swank.

I have mentioned Graham Hutton, then assistant editor of *The Economist* and for many years a regular attender at the Monday lunches. It is characteristic of Kingsley's eclectic kind of editorship that in the thirties Hutton wrote *New Statesman* editorial notes and many leading articles on foreign affairs and financial matters, for he was anything but left wing in his views. There were many contributions too from F. A. Voigt, an old *Manchester Guardian* colleague who was far to the Right, from Bob Boothby, Nicholas Davenport (who wrote the City articles—to be quoted far and wide—as "Toreador"), Lionel Fielden (head of the BBC's General Talks Department and a sparkling writer to whom socialist doctrine was anathema), Walter Elliot, and many another non-socialist writing either unsigned or under a pseudonym.

Kingsley mentions in *Editor* (page 58), as his "most important contact with different modes of thought", the weekly lunches of the influential but little-known Romney Street Group (the RSG), a luncheon club of civil servants, journalists, and politicians of all parties. This was founded in 1917 by Peter Joseph Thorpe, then drama critic of *Punch*, with the aim of trying to ensure that the post-war management of Britain's affairs should be "in the right hands". The meetings took place in the Queen Anne Street offices of Political and Economic Planning (PEP).[1] When Kingsley belonged, its chairman was that remarkable man Dr Thomas Jones, C.H., who was private secretary to three successive Prime Ministers and who, Kingsley used to say, "founded everything in this country that was worth founding, including the Arts Council, the University College of Wales at Aberystwyth, and Eirene White,[2] who was his daughter". One day in 1931 when Kingsley happened to be absent, Tom Jones, as chairman, suggested to a company of about eighteen or twenty that they should take the opportunity to discuss "what was happening to the *New Statesman*"; a topic which has sustained many an inquest, in circles both less and better informed, during the paper's 60 years of vigorous decline. The *New Statesman*, Jones suggested, was getting woolly and sentimental and imprecise, and on foreign affairs in particular you never knew where it was going. Now, with a new editor, there was a chance to formulate some proposals and

[1] The RSG now meets at 69 Great Peter Street, and is still a lively and fruitful round-the-table debate, usually on a pre-arranged topic.

[2] Now Baroness White of Rhymney.

offer them to him. Sir Wilfrid Eady of the Home Office was there, Colonel Walter Elliot, C. K. Munro the playwright (who is still a member), Henry St John Catchpole, founder of the Youth Hostels Association, Leonard Woolf, G. D. H. Cole and Graham Hutton—who at 27 was probably the youngest member present. There was an earnest discussion about the *New Statesman*; and in a letter dated 4th September 1931 Graham Hutton passed on to Kingsley the criticisms he had heard:

> The main criticisms centred on the "writing round" the main problems of the [economic] crisis which these people think they trace in the different articles. [They] thought it dangerous to substitute opposition, criticism, and appeal to the reader's vague feelings about the thing, for reasoned argument and considered counter proposals. I understood [them] to mean that the NS has a unique chance of coming out with, first of all, a criticism and then a programme which should rise above both the present Government's and also the vague TUC *ad hoc* temporisations. The *Spectator* has been, to use your word, "religious" about everything. The "Weekend" has been shrewd but careful. The more advanced thinkers naturally look to the N.S., if not for guidance, then for a clear and definite attitude backed up by factual reasons and estimated probabilities. My informants did not feel they had got either. . . . I know you will not take it amiss if I pass this information on to you, because you know I feel that the N.S. has more to offer than any other weekly.

Not quite taking it amiss, Kingsley wrote on the back of this letter: "This of course is what I do *not* have to do editorially. I must not disguise my conflicts of mind even when our editorial policy is to be firm. As a matter of personal policy, I must find a way to explain my difficulties in reaching editorial decisions. Editorially, I must throw the paper open to opinion of all kinds." And the way he chose for discussing his own difficulties, which were also those of thousands, was the London Diary. Years later, indeed, he wrote in a private memorandum assessing the policy with which he had started in 1931:

> We were a kind of bible to thousands, particularly of the student class oversea as well as to countless progressively minded people

> here. You cannot both carry weight in the City and among Dons and also speak with the voice of encouragement to the student and colonial class, which I value far more. That is our peculiar function. We were first in the field in Fabian Socialism, and so we have been in creating a non-violent socialist mind in Asia and Africa. To me it has been worth many black looks and snarky remarks at high table to know that the people of influence—including most of the Prime Ministers of Asia, Africa, and the Middle East today—are enthusiastic readers of the N.S. & N., and that they regard us as inspirers of the national and socialist revolution, the good and necessary revolution of our time.

Meanwhile he was encouraged (though he was often to be discouraged) by a letter from Keynes about his first issue and his first editorial. The editorial was headed *The Alternatives*, and it likened the political scene in England to a pantomime put on in a hospital:

> The politicians play their variety parts and the public, conscious of ailments which are not assuaged by laughter, watch the irrelevant entertainment with growing distaste. All the jolly bustle of the party conflict continues: the bargains, the close divisions and the personalities, the sudden exits and entrances, the wit, the eloquence and badinage. . . . The Labour poll drops by a third, the Liberal vote tends rapidly towards zero, and the Conservatives are split by a preposterous campaign which would never have drawn votes at all except at a time when people were beginning from very despair to welcome any display of energy, however comic and irrelevant. As for the Labour Government, it has disappointed all expectations.

John Strachey and others had resigned from the Government to support Oswald Mosley's New Party. Could the Government afford to lose them? It seemed to be afraid of planning. Dictatorships arose because democracy was slow, timid and inefficient:

> If you are lost in a wood there are three courses open to you. You may ineffectively rush about in all directions like the parties of Lord Rothermere and Lord Beaverbrook; you may sit down until your rations give out, as Mr Snowden would have us do; you may, if you are sensible, choose a likely path and follow it in

> the belief that sooner or later it will take you out of the wood. . . . The real issue is a national plan or a slow process of national stagnation.

It didn't say what the national plan should be, but it commended an accompanying article by J. L. Hammond urging capital expenditure and the resiting of industries. Keynes wrote:

> I think that the first number looked very well indeed. I liked your first leader and the whole paper had a solid, substantial air such as the *Week-End Review* is 100 miles away from.

But the two men soon began their quarrels and reconciliations. Keynes found some aspects of Kingsley's pacifism "insincere" because of his defence of Russia; and he said so in one of their interminable telephone conversations. It was the one charge that always stung Kingsley to anger, and he wrote to Keynes at once:

> Being a pacifist who wants to change the inequalities of the world as peacefully as possible, and with the maximum of consent, does not seem to me a justification for not trying to be sincere about the problem involved. (It was your accusation of insincerity which annoyed me on the phone. I have a kind of religion of sincerity. It's the one thing I am certain is valuable.) Take the question of "class justice" as one example. Surely it is plain that justice is being used as a means of suppressing dangerous opinion in most countries. When an instance which can be discussed occurs in this country, we do call attention to it in the N.S. and N. . . . In many countries now there is a technique of "frame-up" by the police in the interests of conservative opinion. Sacco and Vanzetti[1] is only the most notorious of American instances. Meerut[2] is really a terrible case. I do not know if you've followed it. . . . I do, in all sincerity, say that this Russian business [i.e. the OGPU purge of the Communist Party] is gentlemanly compared to Meerut. The prisoners had committed no illegal acts. They were three (or four was it?) years in Indian gaols waiting for the

[1] Two Italian US immigrants convicted of murder in 1920 on politically motivated (and tainted) evidence. It took the US machinery of justice seven years to put them to death.

[2] A long-drawn-out communist conspiracy case conducted by the Indian Government in 1929.

inevitable verdict. . . . Frame-ups, with the violent extortion of "confessions", are routine in America, Poland and other countries, as almost any foreign correspondent can tell you. . . . I should feel insincere if I did not call attention to these things in other countries, including the British Empire, in discussing Russian methods. Why you should think it insincere to mention this I cannot conceive. It's important for people to know that Russia is not in this matter abnormal, and I know that many people value the N.S. and N. just because it does not make the usual pretences.

In the next 20 years his defence of Communism, though it weakened progressively under the impact of the Stalin purges, the "treason trials", and the whole apparatus of terror, was to get him into much trouble of the kind that estranged him from the *Manchester Guardian*. But thus he began his editorship. By the fifties he was calling it Stalinism, which you could condemn with horror while wistfully hoping that as a system of economics communism would make headway. In this he was closer to a great number of socially respectable people who were more discreet about what they said. But it had taken only a few months to demonstrate that a new force had arrived on the scene of weekly political journalism.

Chapter 10

DOROTHY WOODMAN

EARLY IN 1934 Kingsley moved to a spacious flat on the top floor at number 16 Great James Street, Bloomsbury; and although there was a room in it for Olga, it was merely "for the sake of appearances"; she did not go with him. This pretty eighteenth-century coffee house had then been for ten years the home of Francis and Vera Meynell and their "Nonesuch Press". It is a narrow four-storey building on the corner of Northington Street, with crazily sloping ceilings and creaking stairs. If you can resist the urge to find significance in Kingsley's habit of both living and working in corner buildings, you will find it easier to discount the fact that the rear windows looked down upon Cockpit Yard.

The Nonesuch Press issued delectably designed and printed books and poetry; "every book like a caress and a compliment to its author," to quote David Garnett, a partner in the business. And Garnett might have added, in the later words of Don Marquis, that in those days publishing a volume of poetry was like dropping a rose-petal into the Grand Canyon and waiting for an echo. The Meynells lived on the second floor, the ground and first floors were their offices, and the basement contained their hand-press and type-cases. (Arnold Bennett once rather cockily challenged their right to use the word "Press" in their business title, whereupon Meynell silenced him by revealing the presence of a little typographic plant in the basement.) Among the first books published by Nonesuch was the exquisite four-volume King James Bible decorated by Stephen Gooden—30 shillings a volume then and worth a great deal more today (if you can find one); and soon afterwards came the famous *Week End Book*, a real publishing inspiration of which Virginia Woolf characteristically remarked to Francis Meynell at one of his parties: "The Hogarth Press may not make any money but at least we didn't publish the

Week End Book." Kingsley and Olga, on the other hand, had spent much time delightedly reading it to each other.

There was a great and continuous coming and going in this house, many parties both in the Meynells' rooms and in Kingsley's, and "all Bloomsbury" gathered there at various times. Sir Francis Meynell in his delightful autobiography, recalling some of the guests he entertained, inevitably names the kind of people Kingsley was then meeting in his own daily round:[1]

> We entertained a great deal in our years at 16 Great James Street. We had a wide circle of very diverse friends: "intellectuals" like Bertrand Russell, Cyril Joad, Harold Laski, Geoffrey[2] and Margaret Keynes, David Garnett; a bevy of editors, illustrators and printers; my red friends from the *Daily Herald* days, chiefly Dick[3] and Beatrice Plummer and Irene Clephane; humane politicals like the Coles and the Postgates, the Ewers and the John Stracheys; theatre people like Charles Laughton and Elsa Lanchester, the Farjeons, Colette O'Neil and Miles Malleson.[4]

Pandit Nehru was among Kingsley's occasional visitors, as also were Jomo Kenyatta, Paul Robeson, Ernst Toller, the German Socialist poet and playwright, J. D. Bernal, P. M. S. Blackett (now Professor Lord Blackett) and the people attracted by them. Dorothy Sayers rented a flat across the road, for writing rather than for living in. Ellen Wilkinson lived a few doors away, Hugh Gaitskell nearby in Great Ormond Street. Kingsley used to recall an occasion in 1934 when the news came that the Austrian Fascists had been shelling the Karl Marx Hof in Vienna; and Gaitskell, recently returned from a research appointment in Vienna, was "sitting on the floor in front of the fire with tears streaming down his face and totally unable to speak". The long and anxious discussions in Kingsley's rooms during those unforgettable years, no doubt paralleled in every

[1] Francis Meynell, *My Lives*, The Bodley Head, London, 1971, p. 189.

[2] Younger brother of Maynard Keynes; a distinguished surgeon and a prolific bibliographer.

[3] Many years later, as Sir Leslie Plummer, a Director of the *New Statesman*.

[4] Whose wife, Dr Joan Malleson, became one of Kingsley's closest friends. Her frank radio broadcasts to women made BBC history.

major city in Europe, saw the beginnings of many a plan to save the peace of the world, of many a stream of pamphlets, of many a lasting friendship, of many a trenchant "leader" in the weeklies. Another neighbour was Mervyn Horder (now Lord Horder), whose father was physician to four successive sovereigns. Mervyn was (and is) a good pianist, kept two grand pianos, and called upon guests to play duets with him at parties where Kingsley had to be discouraged from talking.

Kingsley was now living a bachelor life, seeing Olga but rarely, seeing Verity when he could, falling into some short-lived involvements with other women, and looked after by a "daily help" who knew that his wife had left him and who was maternally sympathetic. She didn't arrive in time to get him a breakfast, and the many friends who stayed for a night in this roomy and conveniently-situated flat—Aylmer Vallance, Ritchie Calder, Frank Hardie, Charles Skepper and others—came to know that breakfast, accordingly, was tea and toast. His father sometimes came over from Finchley to play chess, and on one of these occasions in 1934 he looked round and said "Where's Olga these days?" Kingsley said she was staying with friends, which in fact she was. But she never lived at Great James Street.

It was at about this time that he bought, as a week-end retreat, an "old tumble-down pub" at Little Easton, near the Essex market town of Dunmow; and this, at a total cost of less than £1,000, he restored to its external picture postcard prettiness as a thatched cottage typical of the Constable country (the inside remained fairly rough and ready). Sometimes Olga was there for a week-end, sometimes another friend; and sometimes, from 1933 onwards, Dorothy Woodman, thenceforth his wifely companion but never his wife.

He had become (as he said) "more than friends" with Dorothy Woodman in 1931. He was 35 and she was 30, and he took her to lunch (for the first of many occasions) in a rather odd basement restaurant in Chandos Street where the bamboo tables were set in stone-arched alcoves, the atmosphere was redolent of cooking-fat and cockroaches, and a leisurely service was provided by nubile waitresses. Those who knew

Dorothy at that time recall her as a big plump girl, lively, self-confident, boisterous and argumentative; attractive according to some; formidable according to others; and such a contrast to Olga that their many friends were slow to accept that she and Kingsley could possibly be in love with each other. She began to appear at Kingsley's "bachelor parties", and also to spend week-ends at the Dunmow cottage. There she was accepted uncritically by Mrs Harris, the normally conventional village woman who cleaned the cottage and had grown accustomed to the occasional appearances of Olga, known to her of course as Mrs Martin. For a short period and on rare occasions it would be Olga, and not Dorothy, who was there at the week-end; and Kingsley, to "preserve the respectabilities", would tell Mrs Harris to "make up a bed at the other end this week".

Dorothy was the daughter of a Wiltshire farmer. She was born on 14th January 1902 at Malmesbury, where her father had a smallholding. In 1913 he moved to a larger farm at Purton, six miles from Swindon. He and his wife were devout Methodists, Mrs Woodman being for many years organist to the Methodist chapel at Purton. Dorothy too became a good organist, and through contact with other musicians she developed a love of the great composers which filled much of her life. In due course she vainly tried to infect Kingsley with this enjoyment, which is so much the more intense when shared with someone else. (Kingsley was not "musical" but he was not, as I have heard it alleged, tone-deaf. He passively enjoyed Mozart, Haydn and Vivaldi; and once at a Cambridge concert with Lowes Dickinson, with whom (if with anyone) he never put on airs or pretences, he turned excitedly at the end of the Fifth Symphony of Beethoven and said it had "a greatness that was frightening".)

By 1923, when she took an honours degree in Geography and Economics at Exeter University, she had been the first girl president of the University's debating society, played hockey for the University, established herself locally as a speaker, and joined the Independent Labour Party. It was during her school and university days that she came under the cultural influence of two unusual and unforgettable men. The first was Waldemar Hoepfner, German labour captain of a Prisoners of War

Camp at Wootton Bassett, four miles from Purton, whose job it was to supply P.O.W. labour to local farmers. He was then 22, a sergeant-major in the Prussian Guard, a good linguist and a lover of books. (He became a doctor of jurisprudence and, after the second World War, a member of the Central Legal Office for the British Zone of occupation in Hamburg.) He had met the Woodman family once or twice in the course of posting and visiting his men; but after the Armistice in November 1918, when he was allowed out of camp unsupervised, he used to visit their farm more frequently and talk with the family round the kitchen table. Dorothy, who was then 16, plied him with questions about Germany, Europe, and problems of war and peace. For his part he found her, as he told me in a long letter, "by no means what you would expect when meeting a country girl; she was quick in speaking and above all in thinking, of ready wit, rather aggressive in the conversation. She already had a tendency to become an intellectual woman. . . . She told me much later (in 1931) that it was I who had broken a hole into the narrow mental horizon of a country girl and given her life a direction." They corresponded for years, though during the fifteen years of the Nazi regime he had to use addresses outside Germany. It was in no sense a love affair, its overtones were political, and it was instrumental in subjecting Dorothy, rather early, to the tremendous impact of German literature.

The other man to influence her from student days was Alfred Williams, the poet and author, who for many years was a railway worker at Swindon and who had later travelled widely in India advising on railway construction. He helped Dorothy with her degree thesis: "An Essay in Economic Development—Swindon as a Railway Centre"; but he also taught her enough Sanskrit and Indian folklore to suffuse her mind with the interest in Eastern ways and destinies which dominated the later years of her life. She also had many contacts, during her girlhood, with Stafford Cripps, who had an estate at Broadwell in Oxfordshire, about seventeen miles away, and was a frequent visitor at her parents' farmhouse.

She taught for two years at a girls' school in Chiswick and then she divided her time between two secretaryships—the one to the Women's International League, a suffragette peace movement, the other to Philip Snowden, who was at that time MP for Colne Valley and a member of the General Council of the Union of Democratic Control. It couldn't be said that Snowden was a dynamic member of the UDC. In 1915 he had refused to join it and was then surprised to find that his name had nevertheless been placed on the membership list of its General Council—"an indication of the way in which that list was often padded with nominal members", writes Marvin Swartz in his account of the UDC.[1] Snowden made a considerable but excusable fuss, demanded the removal of his name, was persuaded by the Executive Committee that the public withdrawal of it would look worse than leaving it alone, and allowed it to remain on the list for "at least a year". In the end he became an Executive Committee member himself although he seems to have given little time to it. But during this controversy Dorothy learned much about the UDC from inside; and by 1927 she was its secretary, a duty she carried out with the utmost efficiency for more than 20 years.

It must be said that in this capacity she failed to endear herself to many people. She suffered fools and novices with obvious difficulty, and was arrogant, noisy, and quick to discover base or selfish motives where she might have recognised nothing worse than slightly slower thinking. But she had emerged as a young woman of great intellectual capacity, with an outstanding aptitude for research and a way of standing with her shoulders back and talking very loudly in a high-pitched "up stage" voice.

She tried twice to get into Parliament. Her first attempt was as an ILP candidate at Wood Green in 1931, where her Liberal opponent was Edgar Wallace, who died before the election; and she lost to the Tory, the Hon. Peter Rodd, who confided to a Savile Club audience the rather hazy recollection that she was "a terribly pretty girl". The second was at Aylesbury in 1935, where she was defeated again, though this time she had been able to call upon Kingsley's growing influence for support.

It was in 1935, in fact, that she took up residence with him at

[1] *The Union of Democratic Control in British Politics during the First World War*, Clarendon Press, 1971, p. 71.

16 Great James Street, though she was frequently away at conferences, week-end political parties, UDC assignments abroad, and adventurous missions on behalf of the Committee for the Relief of Victims of German Fascism, of which more in a moment. She wrote a succession of UDC pamphlets and long reports of conferences (mainly on international affairs and the opposing prospects of disarmament and war): the common characteristics of these being that they are full of important and carefully marshalled facts (her pamphlets on Indo-China and the origins of the Vietnamese War are extremely useful today); rather flatly written; and nearly all undated. She was the prime mover in a somewhat naïve campaign of the thirties to expose the private trade in arms and war materials as a cynical and heartless racket. In a signed *New Statesman* article on 30th January 1932 ("The Manufacture of Armaments") she had argued that "if armaments manufacturers were under State control, the non-social interests of this class would be largely removed and the future of disarmament would give more grounds for optimism". But it was to be well within her lifetime that the manufacture of arms reached, under total State control, an astronomical figure such as she had never dreamed of. And private industry would have been unlikely to produce the hydrogen bomb.

As Kingsley relates in his autobiography, she worked devotedly in the fight against Fascism and became more and more closely associated with freedom movements, first in Germany, Spain, Italy and the Balkan countries, and later in the Far East. "Dorothy was not, like me, full of fear and speculation about Fascism," wrote Kingsley in *Editor* (page 157); "she instinctively threw herself into working against it." She was frequently spoken of as a communist, but she never belonged to the Communist Party and was never, in fact, as far to the Left as contemporaries like Ellen Wilkinson. In the thirties she certainly seemed to be doing her best to attract the kind of abuse that was reserved for Communists and fellow-travellers. On 24th February 1936 the *Western Mail* reported her as telling the Swindon WEA that in Russia the workers' rents were almost negligible, that women did the same jobs for the same pay as men, that there was no unemployment, that there was complete freedom of thought—and of religious worship so long as the congregations amounted to at least 250, made their church self-supporting, and paid their minister. "If a church is made into a counter-revolutionary organisation," she said, "then I think it is perfectly right that it should be suppressed in the interests of the remaining 165,000,000 people. . . . Those who knew Russia in pre-revolutionary days knew the church to be one of the most disgraceful and corrupt organisations the world had ever known."

It was no particular wish of her own that she should become well known to the public, but shortly before she became closely acquainted with Kingsley, she was playing an exciting role in exposing what she saw as the treachery of the Reichstag Fire Trial in 1933. The Committee for the Relief of Victims of German Fascism was one of the real successes of the anti-Fascist movement in this country. Dorothy Woodman was its secretary, and among its leading members were Kingsley Martin, Victor Gollancz, Sidney (now Lord) Bernstein, Ellen Wilkinson, D. N. Pritt, and Ivor Montagu. But it was actively helped by non-members as politically aloof as F. A. Voigt, who would not join it because it was "Communist-controlled". Dorothy and Kingsley cared not a penny who was said to control it so long as it provided a machinery for combating Fascism. At one of its meetings during the Reichstag Fire Trial, F. A. Voigt, whose knowledge of Nazi Germany was unrivalled, came in with the news that there was a plot to assassinate Dimitrov[1] and his co-defendants if they were acquitted, and that only the ostentatious presence of British observers would be likely to prevent it. Dorothy volunteered to go. Harry Pollitt, then editor of the *Daily Worker*, said it was impossible that the British emissary should be a Labour Party member and not a Communist, and in the end it was arranged

[1] Georgi Dimitrov, later President of Bulgaria. At that time he was a leading official of the Comintern. He was accused with Ernst Torgler, chairman of the German Communist Party, and Martinus van der Lubbe, an ex-member of the Dutch Communist Party, of setting fire to the Reichstag; why, no one has ever discovered. There was no evidence against him or Torgler, and both of them had a complete alibi. Van der Lubbe, who had never denied his guilt, was beheaded, and Torgler and Dimitrov had to be acquitted.

that Dorothy should be accompanied by Ivor Montagu. They attended much of the trial together. After Dimitrov's acquittal, and while he was in prison awaiting Hitler's decision as to what you do with a prisoner whom you have been reluctantly obliged to acquit, the Committee organised a "Women's Watch" from this country. A group of British literary women, which included Amabel Williams-Ellis, Catherine Carswell and Dorothy Woodman, took it in turns to go to Leipzig and accompany Madam Dimitrov when she went to the prison to visit her son. They were in direct telephone contact with London in case anything happened to the prisoners, so that it could be publicised immediately in England and thus throughout the world. Dorothy and Ivor Montagu reported progress to a packed meeting in Kingsway Hall, and she wrote a long article on the whole story in the *News Chronicle* of 29th January 1934. When Hitler did eventually release Dimitrov, and whisk him away to Russia with his mother and sister, the event was reported in the London evening papers before it was even known to the German Ministry of the Interior. Dorothy's intimate involvement in such contacts with governments and minorities led to her being spoken of as a Red and a Communist, and to that she was totally indifferent.

While you could not say that this episode was representative of her political life (for it was a unique occasion), I have recalled it in some detail by way of illustrating where her interests lay and how far she was ready to go in their furtherance. The same energy sustained her in organising the India League with Krishna Menon, and the China Campaign Committee (at that time her younger sister Alice was a Methodist missionary in China, and other Chinese contacts had kept her informed of the tragic course of the Sino-Japanese War). The Union of Democratic Control involved her in every major crisis of the thirties: the Italian rape of Abyssinia, the Spanish Civil War, the various crises by which Hitler inched himself into a favourable position for a war of world conquest, the collapse of the League of Nations, the gigantic refugee problem, the inevitable war itself.

After the war, while she was still secretary of the UDC, Kingsley had become its chairman. Their colleagues included

Professor J. D. Bernal, Ashley Bramall, Ritchie Calder, and a group of Labour MPs comprising Bessie Braddock, Seymour Cocks, Tom Driberg, Maurice Edelman, John Freeman, Woodrow Wyatt and Konni Zilliacus. Dorothy became more and more interested in the reconstruction of countries now liberated from both European colonialism and Japanese war-time occupation. Her capacity for the absorption of historical and demographic detail established her as an authority on Burma, China, Thailand, India, Indonesia and (later) the United Arab Republics. She edited the magazine *Asian Horizon*, working closely with Dr Hurustiati Subandrio, wife of the Indonesian Ambassador in London. She was introduced in a press interview in 1950 as "an apple-cheeked, vegetarian intellectual who has been described as *the* key Left-wing woman".

On some of these questions, and specially the Israel–Arab problem, she and Kingsley had occasional sharp differences – he was, and I think he would still be, rather pro-Israel. He had had an unhappy episode with her as early as the time of the Munich crisis in 1938: his note in the *New Statesman* that the Czechs must not expect the world to go to war to preserve their frontiers came at a time when Dorothy was joining marches to Downing Street to chant "Stand by the Czechs". There is evidence in their correspondence of quarrels to be patched up "when we are both back home and can talk this over sensibly". (In their later years they both travelled much—and, as a rule, separately.) But there is not the smallest doubt that they were devoted to each other; or that on her side, at least, it was the unselfish nature of her devotion that made her determined not to marry.

They could have married at any time after 14th October 1940, when Kingsley's divorce was made final. Kingsley was now 43, susceptible and attractive to women—though not by any means what is usually called a womaniser. He was, to use an obsolete word, a *coquet*, and flirted with women everywhere; pleasantly, I should have thought, but in some cases with a lack of success that proves me mistaken. Dorothy was 38 and losing what physical charm she had. Whether or not it was caused by her strictly vegetarian diet, she certainly was growing very fat and seemed at times strangely unaware of it. She favoured flamboyant clothes of a kind that drew attention to her size. Kingsley used to say that she could have been a peeress three times over; by which he meant that three men who had proposed to her had later become life peers (so far as I know he didn't name them). He was always justly proud of her scholarship and industry and he comported himself as if he were her impresario. It was he who would have married and she who declined. He was certain that he had at last found the woman who could be his life-partner. She was not so sure. She knew that women liked him, yet far from being jealous she disapproved of those who did not. It seemed to her that the time might well come when he would want to live with somebody else. If it came she would not want him to feel tied to her by some quasi-mystical bond which lawyers would have to undo. Above all they could both, if unmarried, have experimental or short-lived liaisons without the sense of unwished finality; and they both did. They came to agree that if a couple wanted children, then society being what it was they ought to marry, but if not there was no purpose in marrying. Women who came to know Dorothy well contended that, in spite of all this, she was a mother *manqué*, who would in one mood speak impatiently of "other people's brats" and at other times lavish extravagant affection on children who were brought to see her. Kingsley himself was always interested in children and was constantly enquiring about the well-being of those he knew. Once when I took my own children to see him at his Rodmell cottage my three-year-old son, who had a highly developed gift for falling into ponds, fell into a tatty little newt-pond of which Kingsley was strangely proud. Howling with indignation he was fished out by Kingsley, who sat him on his knee and took his wet clothes off, trying at the same time to tell him a story that might pacify him while he was being dried. The story failed, and so did all other blandishments until Kingsley suddenly roared "SHUT UP!" The noise stopped as if by a master switch and the drying was completed in startled silence, Kingsley grinning like a genial Mr Punch.

Once when Kingsley was in Australia and had been too busy for some time to write to Dorothy, she sent him a frantic letter asking if all was well. He responded with a contrite cablegram from Sydney. In her reply (8th November 1950) she said:

> It was so thoughtful of you to send me the cable. But please, my dear, why the remorse? You know that, contrary to most people's ideas about me, I have an appalling anxiety complex about people I love. I was so worried I couldn't think of anything else, and every time the telephone went I was afraid it was bad news about you. This is *silly*. But I am made that way. When I speak about my inability to be a mother, I have this very much in mind. I do NOT know the psychological basis of this neurosis. Perhaps it is a kind of transferred possessiveness? It's certainly not a conscious possessiveness.

Their non-marriage was certainly a source of minor difficulties in the social and domestic world. How were they to be invited to parties, announced by a stentorian master-of-ceremonies, described by secretaries making travel arrangements? To some people Dorothy declared emphatically that she did NOT wish to be called Mrs Kingsley Martin. Others bitterly offended her by not doing so. Kingsley refers to her often in his letters as "my wife"; she never called him "my husband". She held oddly aloof from Kingsley's family (except that in the later years she confided much in some matters to Irene), even though they were willing to welcome her.

In 1940, at about the time of the divorce, the flat at Great James Street was severely damaged in an air raid. Kingsley and Dorothy went to live for a time in an ultra-modern, empty house in Highgate, where a variety of friends took refuge with them at nights, though they would have been better off in the street—the house was virtually made of glass. The glass was duly blown in by a land mine and they moved again, this time to share a house with C. E. M. Joad in East Heath Road, Hampstead. This suited Kingsley, who not only thoroughly enjoyed Joad's witty conversation, his gift for epigram, and his attitudinising, but was able to beat him nightly at chess. But for Dorothy it was too literal an adoption of "any port in a storm"—she detested Joad, and when Dorothy detested anyone she went in for it thoroughly. The atmosphere must have tried all Joad's philosophy during the next three or four years, and he must have been a fairly trying experience for her too. He teased her about her vegetarianism, told her it was making her very fat (which something certainly was), and complained about its effect on the communal war-time meat ration. Moreover, as Kingsley records in *Editor* (page 139), Joad "made no secret of his success with women and said he was not interested in talking to any woman who wouldn't go to bed with him". The same lack of interest would extend, presumably, to women he didn't himself want to go to bed with. The two negatives would combine, in Dorothy's case, to inhibit any memorable Joad–Woodman conversations. In any event, a frequently-heard comment on Dorothy as an interlocutor was that, charming as she knew how to be, "you never quite knew what conversation you were supposed to be having"; one effect of this uncertainty being that you could find out with disconcerting suddenness that you were having the wrong one. Kingsley used to recall that he and Joad each suspected the other of stealing his butter ration, the situation coming to a head one morning in the small hours when both of them crept to the larder and, to their dismay, met there. Each had two explanations to choose from, and he had to choose quickly: (a) he was investigating the theft; (b) he was going to replenish his own butter dish. They rejected both, roared with laughter and went back to bed. It was while Kingsley was with Joad that Ritchie Calder, who sometimes stayed there too, wrote in Joad's study his notoriously influential *New Statesman* article about the horrifying muddle and corruption in London's "air raid precautions".[1]

Dorothy felt herself to have every inducement to find somewhere else to live—in London. And anyone who was proposing to live in London at that time had a wide choice and absolutely no difficulty, for London, like any other city under nightly bombardment, was widely regarded as a place to get out of. By this time—the autumn of 1944—the South of England was under regular bombardment by "flying bombs", shortly to be succeeded by V.2 rockets; and many a vacant flat or house was available at a nominal rental and sometimes for no rent at all. (If the house was still standing after the war, which seemed at

[1] "The War in East London", *New Statesman*, 21 September 1940.

times unlikely, it would be the better for having been lived in). Thus it was that they got a lease at number 14 Buckingham Street, Adelphi, another eighteenth-century picture-house which would have vanished under a "direct hit", and there they stuck it out for the rest of the war. Again, many people stayed there for a night or two, or perhaps a few weeks—it was what Ritchie Calder described as a "drop-in-place", hospitable and bohemian and untidy. Joad would come to play chess with Kingsley, and once when a game was interrupted by the arrival of a German incendiary bomb they carried the game across the street to a neighbour's house and continued it there. Later Dick Crossman and his wife had a top floor flat there, and Malcolm and Kitty Muggeridge at another time had the flat below Kingsley's—from which they retain a wry recollection of late night Oriental dancing. None of them, except perhaps Ritchie Calder, got to know Dorothy closely; and Ritchie remembered her with affection because at the time of his stay he was recovering from a cerebral haemorrhage and she mothered him attentively. In the recollection of almost everyone she was capable of extravagant kindness and motherly sympathy.

To a much greater extent than was generally believed, she also step-mothered the *New Statesman*. Her influence was underrated, by some who might otherwise have recognised it, because her articles and book reviews were rather pedestrian, and not even the most expert "subbing" will inject liveliness where it was not to be found before and cannot find surrounding nourishment. Kingsley was sensitive about this, though he knew it better than anyone. Accordingly he liked to do the subbing of Dorothy's contributions himself, and sometimes would put his foot down and altogether refuse to publish the piece. This was difficult in the case of a book review, for his practice was to leave the literary editor's department alone. A succession of literary editors formed the habit of concealing, when Kingsley looked in, any books about Burma, China and the Far East generally; not so that they might not be reviewed, but so that Dorothy might not review them. But it was tacitly understood that where Far Eastern problems and crises were to be written about editorially, or where the emerging "third world" nations were due for a few columns of encouragement or advice, Kingsley's briefing would come from Dorothy and everyone knew that it would be well-informed, sound, and vigorous. It was also known that she had some influence, and tried to assert considerably more, in the appointment of editorial staff and even (in two instances) of editors. There were some who maintained that from the mid-thirties onwards, and until she rather lost interest in the Soviet Union and turned to China and Burma, she did her best to maintain a strong crypto-communist leavening among the paper's regular contributors. But that belongs to another part of the book.

Dorothy's contribution to a British understanding of Asia's twentieth-century problems was unique. This much is apparent from her immense correspondence with Asiatic leaders and minority spokesmen; but it may be most conveniently judged from three of her books—*The Making of Burma*,[1] *The Republic of Indonesia*,[2] and, perhaps above all, *Himalayan Frontiers*,[3] the last-named being "a political review of British, Chinese, Indian and Russian rivalries". She came to accept, though in her later years she became reluctant to preach, Gandhi's devastatingly simple doctrine that "peace and a high standard of living are incompatible: if a man encumbers himself with property, then he cannot do without police". Without the property, you have nothing to lose but your chains.

[1] Cresset Press, London, 1952.
[2] Cresset Press, London, 1962.
[3] Barrie & Rockliff, The Cresset Press, London, 1969.

Chapter 11

OLDER NEW STATESMEN

IF A HISTORIAN were writing this book he would feel obliged, at this point, to put aside the man he was writing about and retell the story of the most doom-laden decade that the world has known. It would be different from all previous accounts, since we are now regaled almost daily with fresh material about the deeds and intentions of our masters in those days, about the lies officially told, the crazy chances that decided events, the blindfold, improvised strategems which we all hoped might be the product of intelligent forward planning. Even the non-historian would be tempted to present here yet another version and expect it to be taken as "the truth at last". I find this urge easy to resist. But there may be some excuse for a quick look round the social and political scene as Kingsley Martin found it when he returned to London and began his editorship, an account of some of the people who then began to shape his life, and an assessment of the part played in the thirties by his London Diary.

1931 was the year of the second National Government, when Britain went off the gold standard. Neville Chamberlain became Chancellor of the Exchequer (and "would to God", said Kingsley once, "that he had stayed there"), and John Simon Foreign Secretary; Pierre Laval became premier of France—Laval the gypsy turned politician who was to be executed as a traitor in 1945. The Japanese began their long-expected war on China, and were soon in occupation of the whole of that vast country north of the Great Wall, sympathetically watched (almost, they must have thought, cheered on) by the European powers and the League of Nations; the League failed to impose economic sanctions on Japan and thus, in effect, signed its own death warrant. The Sino-Japanese war dragged on for ten more years and then became part of the global involvement of World War II. Kingsley was in no doubt that Japan's initial successes were the start of the World War; and although he doesn't seem to have said so publicly at the time, his private diaries make it plain that it was then that he abandoned pacifism and war-resistance, as a policy certain to involve greater human suffering than the "restraint" of aggressor nations. I think that in fact, rather earlier than this, he was ready to abandon his unconditional pacifism with what remained of his religious convictions. "Pacifists," he wrote, "cannot take part usefully in international affairs. A refusal to fight may have the effect of increasing the likelihood of war."[1] At various other times he said that his mind was finally changed by the helplessness of the League of Nations in face of the Italian invasion of Abyssinia, by the receding likelihood of an alliance with the USSR against Nazi Germany, and by the bombing of Guernica during the Spanish Civil War. "The pacifists were likely, willy-nilly, to help the thugs rule the world."[2]

In 1931, Lytton Strachey had published his *Portraits in Miniature*, John Dewey his *Philosophy and Civilisation*, Mussolini his *Hundred Days*. The Soviet Union had decided that good Russians must go without Rachmaninov's music because it was decadent. The English theatre had welcomed *Cavalcade* and *Mourning Becomes Elektra*, and the cinema Charlie Chaplin in *City Lights* and René Clair's *Le Million*. And two quiet men whom the world did not notice, Cockcroft and Lawrence, had respectively developed the means of transmuting atoms and then the cyclotron by which the atom, hitherto the smallest material particle, could be smashed into smaller ones.

"In the thirties," Kingsley used to say, "we believed we could alter the world." He thought it was necessary to try. He had the same feeling of responsibility as a Prime Minister has, because he knew that what he said in the *New Statesman* mattered. He had a few critics who maintained that it mattered not at all, but a great number of political opponents (as well as supporters), some of them in high places, who knew that what the *New Statesman* said was important and influential in many parts of the world and at all levels of political literacy. He soon came to know, also, that he was editing what was at that time the best *literary* weekly in the English-speaking world; though he was not

[1] *Editor*, p. 196. [2] *Ibid.*, p. 202.

always ready, I believe, to acknowledge the extent to which the literary half secured attention for the political, notably in America. But the thirties, he used to say, were "the great age of the weeklies".

His first London Diary in the *New Statesman* was on 12th September 1931. Then and for the whole of its 30 years it was signed "Critic", and everyone knew that Critic was Kingsley Martin. And this first one was entirely political. We were in a mess; the Labour benches were mud-slinging when they should have been telling the electorate how the financial system worked; "without a change in the gold position an election will always mean a loss of confidence and so, apparently, we have before us an endless vista of Tory Government". Mr Gandhi, newly released from prison to attend the Round Table Conference on Indian Independence, would emerge as "the man who saved the Conference", which he did not; and a final paragraph about a friend of Kingsley's (multitudes of London Diary paragraphs were inspired by "a friend") who felt ashamed to be seen carrying *The Times* in his hand because its City articles were turning angry people into Communists and hastening the flight from the pound. The London Diary was a phenomenon of weekly journalism, likely to serve the social historian of the future as a quarry full of lodestone. When Kingsley published a selection from it in 1960,[1] the *Irish Times*, which enjoyed it, wondered nevertheless whether anyone "ever came round to Great Turnstile offering actual physical violence to 'Critic'."[2] Well, it happened at least once. A man arrived with a horse-whip asking loudly for Kingsley Martin. It was lunchtime and everyone was out except Aylmer Vallance, who was having sandwiches. The visitor decided to horsewhip Aylmer instead. At that moment Aylmer, to his own astonishment, recognised him as the man who had been his OTC instructor at school. "Sergeant Thompson," he roared suddenly, "stand to attention when you address me!" The man left shortly afterwards, goodwill restored, and Aylmer unwhipped. The *Irish Times*'s reviewer also thought Kingsley had a tendency to preposterous

[1] *Critic's London Diary*, Secker & Warburg, London.
[2] *Irish Times*, 14 May 1960.

pontification ("I knew Algernon Hiss well" was selected as an example, because Hiss's name was Alger); and spoke, I believe, for thousands when he said that "Mr Park, massively represented here, is a first-class horticultural bore".[1]

Kingsley used to say that the London Diary was his overflow:

> I was responsible for didactic leading articles and editorial comments, weighed down with matured judgment and serious appraisal of many-sided questions. (I wish questions had, as they say, two sides; I have always found them irregular polygons.) Such features disciplined exuberance and left no space for bubble. I wanted also to speculate about the world: sometimes to go off at half cock, without pretending that I was making an *ex cathedra* pronouncement. I was fascinated by the trivial, human things that the daily press records but, it seems to me, so often distorts. . . . I had causes at heart which were usually not news but which I thought should be supported; some jokes seemed too good to miss; there were bits of gossip that seemed significant though not stated on the highest authority.[2]

Nevertheless it was an inadequate overflow. The left-hand drawers in his office desk were always crammed with galley-proofs of his own unused material, mostly Diary. Sometimes he would search hopelessly for one that he vaguely remembered writing, pull out the wrong one, shake his head and cram it back among the rest like a used pocket handkerchief. He must have written six times as much as he ever published. One would be tempted to say that at least he thought well enough of all this "over-matter", in the first place, to have it set up in type; but the truth is that he regarded a printer as another man regards his typist—a galley proof was a rough draft on which, if it took his fancy on a second appearance, he would operate by scribbling what amounted to a revised article in its margins.

It is right to say that the London Diary was more often a symposium, the work of several hands, than Kingsley remembered it to have been when he was writing his autobiography. In *Editor* (page 11) he says "it was always my own

[1] Mr Park was Kingsley's jobbing gardener at Little Easton, a rare character; and it was no fault of his if Kingsley made him into a bore. He is referred to later.

[2] *Critic's London Diary*, Secker & Warburg, London, 1960, p. xi.

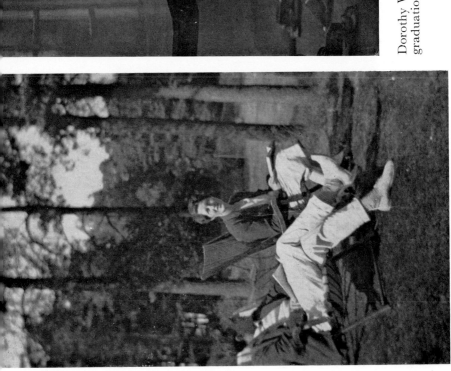

Kingsley and Olga in the garden of her father's sanatorium, Farnham, Surrey, 1930

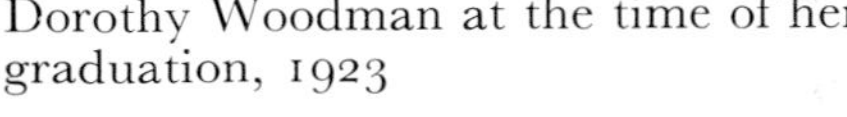

Dorothy Woodman at the time of her graduation, 1923

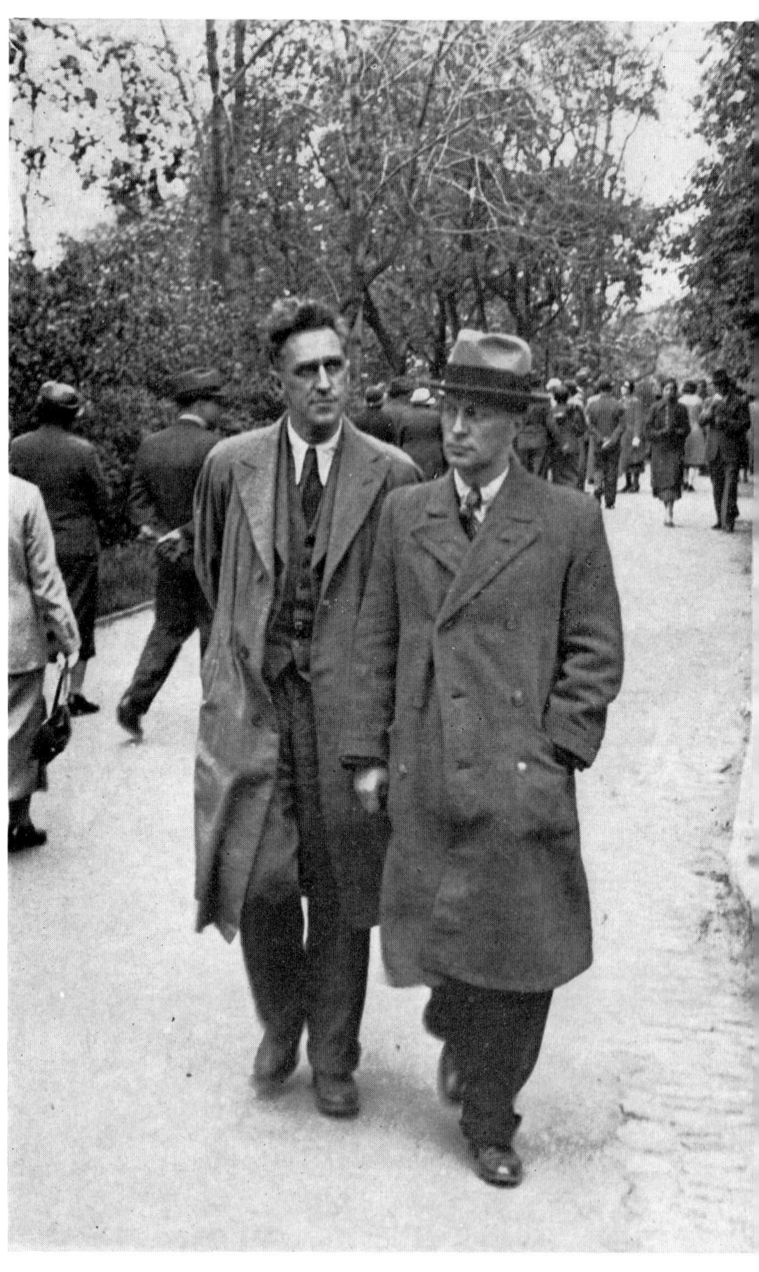

Kingsley with Professor Vočadlo in Prague, 1938

personal Diary: I wrote five-sixths of it, and re-wrote to my own liking any paragraphs submitted to me by others". In fact, more often than it seemed to him, he took paragraphs from others and used them unaltered. Dick Crossman, who joined the paper in 1937, was one of those who had the ability to write Kingsley's Diary undetectably. "I always maintained," Dick told me, "that it was because the one thing I did get out of the classics was the ability to write Lucretian and Virgilian hexameters, and if you've done Latin verse in different styles as hexameters you can do any writing in different styles in English." But there were several who wrote Kingsley-ism as "undetectably" as Dick Crossman and would hardly have known a Virgilian hexameter from a Clerihew; and there were many of those inhumanly clever winners of the Week End Competitions who could have written the whole of a London Diary indistinguishably from Kingsley at the top of his gossipy, button-holing, heart-warming best.

The five men who most influenced him at this time were Maynard Keynes, Leonard Woolf, H. N. Brailsford, C. E. M. Joad and Dr Harry Roberts. He writes of them all at some length in *Editor*, but his private correspondence with them all and especially with Keynes was voluminous. From 1932, when Germany repudiated what remained of the Treaty of Versailles, the "dragon's teeth" were seen to have matured, Keynes the prophet was enthroned, "appeasement" was accepted as wisdom and justice rather than fear and treachery. Even at that time Keynes was sometimes blamed for appeasement. He was said to have saddled the British and American peoples, and to a lesser extent the small European nations (but not the French), with such a weight of guilt by his *Economic Consequences of the Peace* that they regarded every fresh demand of Hitler's as a just claim on the past, none of these claims being any the less valid because it was usually made in a guttural scream to 100,000 supporters in steel helmets. Forty years later, in the view of many, he stood condemned. "On the economic plane," wrote Lord Balogh in *New Society* on 22nd April 1971, "and with the unjust benefit of hindsight, it can be said that Keynes's demonstration of Germany's inability to pay . . . rested on a completely static and neo-classical concept of economics; was fallacious; and did untold harm." But what was more immediate in 1931 was Keynes's hope that the reconstituted *New Statesman and Nation*, with Kingsley as its editor, could become the vehicle for a "balanced" economic policy—a policy of expansion, freer spending, and "public works"—supported by the Labour Party and based upon Keynes's own doctrines.

Unfortunately it was a bad moment for selling these ideas to the Labour Party, heavily defeated in the recent election and humbled by the defection of its leaders. This disaster was still seen as the consequence of a bankers' "ramp" and the absurdly dishonest charge that the Labour Government had been using Post Office Savings Bank money to pay the unemployed. I suppose one of the saddest aspects of the democratic scene is this cynical pretence, common to all political parties and most publicists with any hope of a hearing, that the taxpayers' money is kept in bundles labelled "P.O. Savings Bank Interest", "Road Fund", "Spitfires" and the rest. Keynes's 1931 articles and letters in the *New Statesman* unexpectedly maintained that Free Trade, after all, was one of the causes of war; and he was a perhaps unconscious progenitor of the "Buy British" campaigns (with their lapel-buttons and windscreen stickers) which waxed and waned after his death. Trade followed the flag, of course, but was itself followed by exploitation and inhumanity of many kinds; and there was no evidence that international amity necessarily thrived on these. *New Statesman* readers could swallow this without water, but some of them could not swallow even a limited form of tariff, though its object was merely to raise some money quickly (i.e. make the accounts look better). "For about two months," wrote Kingsley in *Editor* (page 44), "the Liberals and Free Traders raged in our columns. About two thousand people dropped the paper . . . but the net result was to increase the circulation." About 2,000 people were always cancelling their *New Statesman* orders and being supplanted by others who suddenly found the paper agreeable.

In many ways Keynes was the perfect foil for Kingsley, sharing, as Robert Lekachman has said in *The Age of Keynes, a Biographical Study*,[1]

[1] Penguin Books, London, 1966, p. 46. Reprinted with the permission of Penguin Books (Pelican Series), 1969.

> the intellectual's characteristic belief in the importance of ideas. The last sentence of *The General Theory of Employment, Interest and Money* is justly famous: "But, soon or late, it is ideas, not vested interest, which are dangerous for good or evil". He shared as well the intellectual's enjoyment of sheer verbal virtuosity. In Keynes the taste evidenced itself . . . as a delight in conversation upon almost any topic, whether or not he was thoroughly briefed about the merits of the opposing position. Needless to say this readiness of comment occasionally irritated the critical, especially since Keynes as frequently as not would advance his opponent's better arguments as his own the very next day.

Raymond Mortimer told me of a week-end he spent with Keynes at his Sussex home which culminated in a tremendous argument. "It was hopeless: I knew I was right because it was something I knew about. But his dialectic was so brilliant and my argument so much inferior to his that I had no *chance* of convincing him. He was the best dialectician I have ever known." I believe this to have been a common experience of Kingsley's. "Keynes *worried* him," says Lord Boothby, "much more than you would suppose from his autobiography. Keynes had a feline personality and a way of nagging. Kingsley simply never understood economics and yet he was always *trying* to understand. 'Explain it to me, then,' he would say, but his attention soon wandered."

The Keynes–Martin correspondence went on for many years, some of it trivial and domestic, most of it vital to the development of the paper, all of it leading to a probably final rupture that was prevented only by Keynes's death in 1946. Its policy-making aspects are summarised in Kingsley's autobiography (*Editor*), and will no doubt be presented more fully in the vast collected edition of Keynes's papers now being prepared by the Royal Economic Society.[1] There is not space here even to deal adequately with the long feud about H. N. Brailsford, who was Kingsley's favourite leader-writer—especially on India and Germany—and whom Keynes repeatedly accused of "drivelling irresponsibility". "The fact that you feel like that,"

[1] The first four volumes (I, II, XV and XVI) were published in 1971 by Macmillan and St Martin's Press for the Royal Economic Society. There were then understood to be twenty-four volumes in preparation.

Kingsley replied delicately, "is important and I take note of it." On another occasion (29th July 1943) when Brailsford had come in for abuse about a front page which in fact he didn't write, Kingsley told Keynes:

> The very strong language which you have taken to using, to work off feelings which I suppose are difficult to express in the Civil Service, is provocative and unjustifiable. I should not find it difficult to reply with similar phrases, but what would be the object?

However, it is impossible to resist the temptation to reveal here that Kingsley, in a letter dated 11th February 1943, told Keynes that the then Prime Minister of one of the Indian princely states, "a strict Hindu", agreed with Brailsford's (unpublished) suggestion that the USSR might be "the only solution" as to who should rule India, "since only Bolsheviks would be ruthless enough to destroy Hindu temples and Moslem mosques impartially! The hell to write about."

Nothing, perhaps, portrays their relationship more clearly than an exchange about Kingsley's written contribution to *Low's Russian Sketch Book.*[1] Keynes reviewed this in the *New Statesman:*

> . . . a little too full, perhaps, of good will. When a doubt arises, it is swallowed down if possible. Mr Martin is ready to agree on the whole that it is a grand ideal to turn peasants into machine-minders. He reflects that "these people at least have a fuller diet than Chinese coolies, and I don't think they are as poor as peasants are in India." If it is pointed out to him that the only people who really suffer from restrictions on free speech are a few educated intellectuals, he wonders doubtfully if he will find a convincing answer in Rousseau or Bentham or John Stuart Mill. When he is told that "as to fat, they rely on sunflower oil," he remembers that the whole civilisation of Greece was built up on olive oil. This is the right spirit in which to visit Russia if one wants to enjoy oneself.

Should Kingsley have taken this lying down? Many years later he was maintaining that, foolish and undignified though

[1] Gollancz, London, 1932.

it was for an author to write letters of complaint about reviews of his books, an editor was very often glad to have them because they made such good copy. Sometimes, it is true, he wrote to dissuade an angry author if he thought publication might be specially damaging to him. A good example involved Sir Osbert Sitwell, upset by a review of his third volume of autobiography, *Great Morning*. He wrote a heartfelt protest for publication. "From my point of view," Kingsley replied on 19th May 1948, "the letter is good copy and I am happy to print it. I hope you will not take offence, however, if I say that I think authors make a mistake if they write to complain of what any honest critic says about their work. After all it is the critic's job, and my experience is that in the eyes of the public authors lose dignity when they show that their feelings are hurt by adverse criticism." Sir Osbert awkwardly bowed to this. "I expect your advice is good," he wrote the next day. "You are—or so it has struck me when I meet you—a wise man. But you've misunderstood my motives. I wasn't hurt: how could I be, with so much incense in the air? . . . I've never been afraid of 'losing my dignity': and I don't believe you've ever been afraid of losing yours. And I must point out that I don't agree that answering back injures one—I have done so all my life when I feel inclined. . . . PS. I notice how, in explaining my own feelings, I've quite forgotten to say how very much I appreciate the friendliness which prompted your letter. For of course, as you say, my letter was good copy, and you show yourself willing to sacrifice it."

And yet this was what Kingsley wrote to Keynes, and was restrained from publishing only by the fact that an editor can't really publish letters to himself:

6.12.32

Dear Maynard,

It is sometimes best to say what one feels right away, and I hope you will forgive this note.

It seems ungracious to complain about your very flattering review [*sic*: but there had been one or two nice bits] especially when you are horribly busy and did it at my special request.[1] What troubles me is this. If you had attacked the opinions that

[1] Which can but be described as "asking for it"?

I think came through pretty clearly, though not dogmatically, I should not have minded in the least. Nor should I mind, though I should be sorry, if you said my stuff was bad. But you have given the one impression which I feel to be unfair. The suggestion is that the book is written by a superficial observer who hates everything but is courteous enough to give Russia the benefit of doubts and be nice to it. I think to apologise for Russia is the silliest attitude, and I tried to avoid it. . . . Is it true or not true that the Russian system provides a complete answer to the problem of unemployment? However, the thing I hate about your review, and the thing which makes me hate printing it[1] as it stands, is that it reads as if you thought my stuff bosh and just wanted to avoid saying so because I am editor of the paper.

These are my reactions, and I thought it best to explain them right away. If you had slanged the book I would have been content, but I did try to do a serious job and it does offer a challenge, not a bit of polite eyewash.

If Kingsley had a reply from Keynes, he does not seem to have kept it. Perhaps it was too wounding. But if his own letter had come in from some other affronted author during the forties or fifties, how he would have grinned as he passed it for publication! And, to be fair, he would grin now to realise how his own anger had been so hurriedly dressed up as dignified sorrow.

Since the death of Maynard Keynes the *New Statesman*'s board of directors has never had another member remotely like him. For all that Kingsley has loyally said about him, editing the paper must have been the easier for his departure. Kingsley had not followed all the vacillations that swayed the political thinking of Maynard Keynes, as of every intelligent man, in that bewildering decade. "Madmen in authority who hear voices in the air," Keynes once said, "are usually the slaves of some defunct economist."[2] And Kingsley did not live to see the letter about Keynes that Professor A. L. Goodhart sent to *The Times* on 28th March 1972. This described an evening with him in a Lisbon Casino in 1941, when Keynes (using a system) consistently lost while Professor Goodhart (trusting to luck) consistently won:

[1] But he *did* print it, on 10 December 1932.

[2] Quoted by Lord Balogh in the *Guardian*, 16 November 1970.

When we left, Keynes explained that a player's success depended more on intuition than on intelligence. He gave as an illustration his own reputation as an astute business man because he had made staggering profits both for King's College, Cambridge, and for himself by investing in the shares of a Chicago traction company. For no particular reason he sold these holdings two weeks before the stock market collapsed in the autumn panic of 1929. If he had not done so the College would have been in serious financial difficulties and he would have been wiped out. It was not reason but chance that made him choose the crucial date. The fact that he was an economist, he said, was irrelevant.

In 1931 Leonard Woolf was a great stay and comfort to Kingsley—and in that year even wrote a good deal of his London Diary, as Kingsley acknowledges on page 10 of *Editor*. Both Keynes and Woolf had been known to him since 1919, when both were old enough to be his father: but at the start of his editorship Woolf was the more benevolent, and since he was not then on the Board of Directors it was perhaps possible to consult him freely, privately and less guardedly. His warm friendship, to say nothing of his vitriolic quarrels, with Kingsley went on over so many years that he must now come into this story repeatedly. I shall not therefore say more about him at this point than is necessary to recall two episodes as illustrative of the two men's relationship. In the forties and fifties Leonard Woolf, who had had much editorial experience, would frequently act as *New Statesman* editor when Kingsley was away. (In fact, Kingsley was reluctant to entrust the job to anyone else though in the late fifties Woolf did it with increasing unwillingness—he was now in his mid-seventies and living permanently in the country.) In 1954, after an absence abroad of three or four weeks, Kingsley was much disturbed at the tenor of some of the articles the paper had been publishing. At the week-end he went over to Leonard's cottage to make his protest, and did it at some length. Leonard, who was now living alone, heard him in a watchful silence which, to a man less excited than Kingsley was at that moment, might well have seemed ominous. Then he said his piece. He was 74, he began. He found the daily travelling from Rodmell to London arduous, the proof-reading filled his evenings, he was held up in his work on a collection of Virginia's letters, he was not particularly well and he was very tired. He had foolishly supposed that Kingsley was coming over to convey some kind of thanks for the stewardship that had enabled him to get away for a month, and he had found Kingsley's outburst almost past belief. Kingsley was so taken aback that, rather to Leonard's dismay, he burst into tears and then apologised humbly. . . . "It is more blessed to apologise," Leonard Woolf wrote uneasily to him a few days later, "than it is to be apologised to"; and another quarrel was over.

I thought that Leonard Woolf was one of the most comprehensively civilised men I had ever met, and this may have been because he seemed the truest personification of selfhood, the inviolably private man. ("There is no place for pity or humanity," he wrote, "in a society in which human beings are not regarded as individual human beings but as impersonal classified pegs in a rigidly organised society.")[1] I know that from the time of the Nuremberg rallies he thought he could foresee that the mass mind, the vast jelly-mass of ignorance and cruelty, would eventually take over; and despite his long life of political dedication, by the time I knew him, with his frail body and his perpetually trembling hands, he was a bewildered aesthete involved in a protracted leave-taking from a world he never made. I greatly envied Kingsley their close association. Accordingly the second of these stories puzzled me all the more. It was a month or two later, and I met Kingsley by chance near Charing Cross. He had just been playing chess with Leonard Woolf. "I very much doubt if I shall ever speak to that man again," he said. "It's really most extraordinary. I simply *cannot* understand him, nor do I understand why I should be expected to tolerate his rudeness." They spent the following week-end together as they so often did. I do not, in my turn, understand these ferocious short-lived enmities between highly intelligent men who are really close and mutually dependent friends, and I find them difficult to write about. One can, I suppose, merely report them as they came to light.

Noel Brailsford when I knew him was a very short, stocky, slow-moving old man with a quizzical but shy manner, a great

[1] *The Journey Not the Arrival Matters*, Hogarth Press, 1969, p. 19.

fund of stories about Greece, the Balkans, the USSR, Germany, Ireland and India, and a sense of humour that was inadequately represented by his slow, tentative smile. He was the international Socialist *par excellence*. For Kingsley he could do no wrong—"the best journalist and leader-writer I have ever known"; and Kingsley, as I have said, was under the constant necessity of defending him against the withering abuse of Keynes, for whom he could do no right. In the twenties, after being chief leader-writer on *The Nation*, he had edited *The New Leader*, the weekly journal of the Independent Labour Party, and there his regular contributors had included Shaw, Wells, E. M. Forster and Bertrand Russell. *The New Leader* gave Labour politics a cultural stimulus that was certainly comparable with that of the *New Statesman*. He had been leader-writer for the *Manchester Guardian* (long before Kingsley's time), the *Morning Leader*, *Tribune*, the *Daily News*, and the *Daily Herald*. His internationalism never got in the way of his support for oppressed or threatened nations, for if you wanted internationalism you had to have self-governing nations to co-operate with each other. So he had fought with the Greek Army against the Turks in 1897 (later describing his experiences in a novel),[1] and supported the Russian Revolution of 1905. In the latter connection he had helped to develop the Common Law of conspiracy, always obligingly sensitive to development, by unlawfully agreeing to allow another man to adopt his name in obtaining a passport for Russia. They were both prosecuted, and *R.* v. *Brailsford* remains a leading case in the *Law Reports*,[2] where it is narrated in a less spirited version than the one he once gave to Kingsley and me over lunch.

C. E. M. Joad, to my generation a born teacher, the man who gave shape to moral philosophy and made it accessible to all but the very learned, was a much loved friend whom Kingsley thought disreputable. (He gives his reasons in *Editor*, pp. 135–9.) In the forties and fifties Joad was a prolific contributor to every corner of the *New Statesman*, being one of those unaccountable writers who cannot produce a dull paragraph if they try. He makes appearances elsewhere in this book, but his

[1] *The Broom of the War God*, 1898.

[2] *1905 Law Reports*, King's Bench, Vol. 2, p. 730.

significance in this chapter (as I see it) is that Kingsley once told me he sometimes found himself consciously trying to write like Joad. I remember thinking that Joad might as suitably try to write like him, but that Joad himself had told me at a dinner of the Whitefriars Club that *his* ambition was to write like Bernard Shaw. It was obvious, however, that there was something in Joad that Kingsley found intrinsically attractive, and I supposed it was the quality of his mind. Certainly he was thrown slightly off balance, as a good humanist, when Joad (now virtually on his deathbed) published *The Recovery of Belief*.[1] The keynote of this was Joad's abhorrence of cruelty, his feeling for suffering humanity, a renewed perception of design in the Universe, and a readiness to accept the efficacy of prayer. Among Kingsley's papers, seemingly assembled while he was writing his book *Editor* in 1967, is a scribbled extract from *The Recovery of Belief* which turns out to be from its very last page:

> If you try, however unsuccessfully, to do what is right and pray regularly for assistance, you are assisted—not perhaps directly in the way you expected and which you at the time would have thought most helpful but, it may be, in some other way by a strengthening of character or by a tranquillising of the spirit which, on looking back afterwards, you realise to have been the best thing that could have happened to you.

And Kingsley, writing at about the same time of Beatrice Webb's lifelong belief in prayer ("she was more interested in religion than in any other topic"), recorded[2] that

> prayer was not to her a petition, but a consecration of purpose and a purifying of motive. She believed, *I think rightly*, that in discarding contemplative prayer as one of the superstitions of religion, her rationalist friends had lost an important technique of the good life.

One supposes that the words "I think rightly" (the italics are mine) were a somewhat wistful interpolation.

Dr Harry Roberts, Kingsley once said, was the "goodest" man he had ever known. Not a "great" man, but saved from greatness only by his eccentricity (of which Kingsley gives a

[1] Faber & Faber, London, 1952. [2] *Editor*, p. 80.

racy account in *Editor*, pages 139–48). He was a man upon whom the study of medicine and, perhaps, the experience of working as a young man in a teaching hospital like St Mary's, Whitechapel, had almost the effect of a Marxist conversion. Kingsley, once he had got his cottage at Dunmow, could be lured from it at week-ends only by an invitation to Harry Roberts's house at Liss in Hampshire. Roberts was a tremendous character; and in all his contexts—as medical practitioner among the East End poor, prolific journalist, botanist, philosopher, and in the Robert Owen-type working communities of people he established—he was a common denominator of affection. He liked to recall that his family, who were then farming in Somerset, had selected as his first school "Miss Edney's Academy for Young Ladies" and that it was the only one of his schools at which he had never won a prize. He wrote books about "the troubled mind" and euthanasia and abortion, about *The Sayings of Jesus* and *The Philosophy of Jesus*; and compiled *A National Policy for Labour*. So far as I know, he was the only *New Statesman* contributor whom Kingsley allowed to write regularly—or indeed at all—for *The Spectator*.

He affords an opportunity, which should not be shirked, to demonstrate that Kingsley as a reporter could be careless about facts which got in the way of what he saw as a colourful picture. In his book *Editor* (p. 143) he describes Harry Roberts's house in Hampshire as "a jolly wooden affair" in a clearing "three hundred steps below the road and otherwise unapproachable". Everything in the house except what Roberts made or grew himself "he had carried down the 300 steps on his shoulders". In fact the house was not a jolly wooden affair but a well-constructed brick-built house put up by the best local builder available. Nor was it "unapproachable except by the 300 steps". There was an access road, used by delivery vans, the postman, etc., and a bridle path for horses. The steps were a short cut for walkers. When this was pointed out to him "too late for last-minute corrections", he told his informant with cheerful resignation that "it is for ever historically on record, whatever anyone else may say on any first-hand evidence whatsoever, that Oakshott Hanger is made of wood. So is history made! I will correct it if there is a second edition."

A couple of years before his death in 1946, Roberts rather fell out with Kingsley, and with Raymond Mortimer at the same time, and got near to making them fall out with each other. Kingsley had sent him a book to review (having first consulted Raymond Mortimer as literary editor) and told him on the telephone that he could have 1,000 words. When the review came in it proved to be one of those "reviews" that say nothing about the book but present the reviewer's opinions on its subject. Raymond Mortimer sent it back, asking Roberts to cut it to 400 words *and* be so good as to say what the book was about. The end-product of all this never appeared, and Harry Roberts felt hurt and forsaken. The episode ended no friendship, but it ended one of the longest associations that any contributor had had with the paper, and any notion that a close friend of Kingsley's could wean him from his ruthless policy of putting the paper first.

And by 1934 Kingsley was in dire need of good friends. It was probably the most troubled year of his life. Olga had finally broken with him, his mother had just died after a long illness (and he was intensely fond of his mother), and he himself was in poor health. Keynes wrote on 15th February to the deputy chairman of the Board (Edward Whitley) that Kingsley had "severe rheumatic neuritis", together with dyspepsia, and needed a month's holiday abroad, for which the Directors ought to vote him £100. But Kingsley had also had, since boyhood, two chronic complaints which were always aggravated by overwork. One was a proneness to severe migraine and the other was Ménière's Disease, which he probably inherited from his father—a form of "auditory vertigo", with dizziness, noises in the ear, and violent nausea. Eventually he became almost deaf in the right ear, and began to accumulate hearing aids which he declared were useless and certainly never brought to the office. When you went into his room to tell him something, he always peered into the trees outside the window on his right as he listened. I believe very few people guessed that this was due, not to any sudden interest in the trees but to the need to present his good ear to the speaker. He certainly had attacks of migraine all the time I knew him, and kept a couch in his office so that he could lie down when necessary. (On Monday mornings, at the editorial conferences, three of the planning pundits would sit side by side on this couch.) Above all, he wanted at that time to leave the *New Statesman* because he needed a long rest, a quieter life, and a job where there was no Keynes to breathe down his neck.

And as if the fates were disposed to help him, it was at this point that he was offered the chair of International Relations at Aberystwyth (University of Wales). It is obvious from his manuscript diaries that if this offer had come four years earlier, the *New Statesman* would never have seen him. It was exactly what he wanted to do. It was a well-paid job. It would involve only one course of about four lectures a year, and for the rest of the time the Professor was expected to travel. There would be plenty of time for writing, certainly far more than a weekly editor gets, and there would be the refreshing contact, in the "teaching situation" which he loved, with a constantly renewed flow of youthful challenge and enquiry. He was given six months in which to make up his mind, and it would have been a great kindness to him if it could have been six days. (As it turned out, he had over twelve months of uncertainty; for when he refused the professorship the University nevertheless held the post open in the hope that he would change his mind.) His indecision was agonising, for the rise of Fascism in Britain seemed to him to be setting the scene for civil war, no less; and he saw that the *New Statesman*'s role was going to be a vital one.

On 5th May 1934 he began another diary: "I have made up my mind, tho' I expect I shall fail as usual, to write a diary again. I do not know how long we have before the Fascist Revolution, or in what form it is coming. . . . Graham Hutton told me that Vallance is talking about machine guns, and prophesying the Revolution before two years are out. . . . I think the Labour Party quite hopeless. I wonder how clearly Citrine and Bevin see things, and whether in the event they are to be made officers of the Corporate State or to be turned out? They will make their peace, I think, and so will most of the Labour Party. . . . What am *I* to do? Obviously go on telling as much of the truth as I can for as long as I can. In the final emergency, the *NS & N* being what it has been under me, I imagine I am marked down for beating up. Anyway the chances of death for me are large, I take it. The chances of continuing agitation after the regime has come are small. What then? Russia or the USA? Ireland en route? But I do not see how people will get away from this country unless they go before they have any right to, and while fighting back is at all possible. No convenient frontier to slip across. The real point is not what I and my friends do when the crisis comes, but what to do now. I want to think it out. Say I have another 12 months. . . . What is the best way of spending them?"

Few people, I believe, were taking Mosley and his Blackshirts quite so seriously as this, and even Kingsley was confiding his misgivings mainly to a private diary. He was working out, on paper, whether he should stay "in the firing line" or seize the Aberystwyth chance of getting back into the academic world. On 29th September 1934 his diary shows him still undecided:

> Some things are quite clear. Labour will play for safety and therefore sell the working classes—it can't help it—and by playing for safety it may produce Fascism more certainly. Fascism will not come until Labour is in retreat, so I suppose we are safe until after the return of a Labour Government, which, thank God, will not be next time, I think. . . . I see no way of stopping Fascism in this country now. Not even the *NS & N*, which is now booming, can stop it.
>
> Shall I run to Aberystwyth? Will it be much good? I shan't be able to keep out of the Fascist fight shall I? I give us one more year of National government, then two or three years' more "Conservative-National" Government, then a short Labour Government, then Fascism. Seven years more to live! Very optimistic, because there will be street fighting, etc. long before that. . . . I will work and live really hard these remaining years, and do nothing I do not really want to do. I will publish the books I've not finished. And I will live bravely and conquer the funk that I feel in my bones.

And in March 1935:

> I have often found decisions difficult, but only once—ten years ago—difficult in this absurd way. . . . There is no real difficulty except the horror that will come over me whatever job I take.

Now if this horror were purely personal, no more than the common pathological symptom of a castration complex, it would not be worth while writing about. It might appear as a footnote in someone's textbook of psychoanalysis. The odd part to me is that I doubt if I am really a coward. I'm desperately afraid, but I'm not nowadays incapable of tackling and standing up to a dangerous situation if it comes. Unfortunately I am paralysed beforehand by the anticipated horror, and by my fear that I shall prove a coward. I do all my screaming first, like the Queen in *Alice*; and this screaming incapacitates me. Am I a good journalist?

Why should I not go? I shall not really get any books written at the NS. I am not really happy at the NS because I find making up my mind about existing politics very difficult. I am not really a natural journalist. I always said I would not remain a journalist, and now is my opportunity for going. I can always do journalism from academe. . . . But I might regret the NS very much? As a fact, yes. But the other will haunt my imagination as a wonderful opportunity lost. Can I take up this weekly burden again? [He had just returned from holiday.] Is it really a burden or a joy? Can I let down 20,000 readers? God, I'm defeated! The real question, I'm sure, is whether I can run away from the Communist dilemma.

It was eighteen months later, 7th September 1936, that Keynes wrote to him:

I'd gladly have had you move into the Aberystwyth project if I'd realised you were still considering it seriously. But as I said on Sunday, personally I hope very much you won't take it. Your subject is one which is best done *not* academically, and is dingy in strictly academic circles. So the only point is to get leisure for writing a large book. But is a large book so much to be preferred to the daily task of persuasion?

It was the "daily task of persuasion" which, in the end, pulled the more strongly. But in later years Kingsley would sometimes refer, with mock messianic gravity, to his long period of temptation in the wilderness.

Chapter 12

THROUGH THE THIRTIES TO WAR

WITH SOME ATTENTION to relevant events and personal relationships, we have now seen Kingsley Martin settled (which is not really the word) in his editorial chair. To continue with a documented account of his next 40 years' public life would be possible, but it might take another 40 years to complete and no one would read it. Uniquely well-supplied with information about the successive crises of the Thirties, he committed all through them the socially valuable indiscretion of thinking aloud, saying one week what seemed to him right and seemed tentatively or miserably right to a great number of us, and saying the next week why it had sometimes turned out to be so wrong. This he did with a puritanical and almost obtuse courage, with only rare lapses (and bad ones) into an ungracious and obstinate refusal to admit himself wrong when he knew he was. No one has better described what the *New Statesman* of the thirties meant to its more impressionable readers than Michael Ayrton, who in December 1966 was making a portrait drawing of Kingsley and wrote him a letter which amounted to an artist's rationale:

> In 1936 I was 15 and an art student. I was already deeply concerned with political issues and strongly committed to the left, as were many of my slightly older contemporaries. The Spanish War was of course crucial to us, but we were increasingly doubtful of the political potency of our liberal and cautiously left-of-centre elders. On the other hand, as the war progressed, we were some of us confused by what seemed to be the almost deliberately inadequate role being played by the USSR in the general fight against Fascism. We did not at that time recognise the nature of Stalinism, nor did we recognise either the size or the power of Russia, nor her deliberate isolation; but as political animals we felt, as I realised some years later, much the same about USSR as we felt—being art students—about Picasso. Both, we believed,

were bastions of the *avant garde*, to be accepted and supported regardless, little knowing how inconsequential our acceptance and our support must have seemed to either power. What we did not believe was what we read in the daily papers. . . . That was where the *New Statesman* came in. We did not believe it to be necessarily accurate, nor did we feel it invariably to be forceful enough for us in its advocacy, but we did believe that it was not actually lying, and this made it rare indeed.

I must, however, confine myself here to a few representative episodes which may illustrate an exceptionally involved editorial responsibility. First, it may be fair to say that Kingsley's own subsequent view of the thirties would have run something like this (it is in fact compiled from scribbles in the pages of numerous tattered little diaries): "Where we went wrong was in assuming that economics would turn out more powerful than nationalism. I couldn't bring myself to write publicly about the coming end of parliamentary democracy, about machine guns in the streets, about the forthcoming death or imprisonment or exile of so many people like myself, about my expectation in 1934 that we all had about seven years to live. It would have been mistaken for 'revolutionary defeatism', and besides it would have been bad for the paper. But I was worried that a great many people saw the 'National' Governments under MacDonald, Baldwin and Chamberlain as the English substitute for Fascism. Great Britain, they thought, had once again contrived, according to her tradition of compromise and commonsense, to meet the financial crisis without violence or panic.

"If Labour's most popular figures could be induced to join a Government of confidence, tariffs and economy, if the electorate could be persuaded by propaganda alone to wipe out the Socialist party at the polls, clearly British capitalism was safe, not only from Communism but from black or brown-shirted hooligans. The small votes at bye-elections showed that there was widespread scepticism about the political system, not only among Fascists and Communists but among all those whose interest in the antiquated procedures of Parliament was not actually a vested interest. This scepticism was the best possible soil for Fascism." (Kingsley believed, to the end of his life, that

Britain would sooner or later turn to some "controlled" kind of dictatorship, and would discover too late that the "control" had withered like an umbilical cord. It was one of the reasons why he supported the Monarchy, which he saw in most other respects as an absurdity. The Monarchy was among the slender hopes, which we could not afford to abolish, of preserving democracy.) "The generation of the 1930s," he would have said, "had never seen the Party system functioning, it knew nothing of the dramatic appeal of the great Parliamentary struggles over Ireland, land taxes and the House of Lords. So it was only the *middle* class which might provide the revolutionary element in society; and the middle class, instead of disappearing as the Marxists said it would, was constantly growing in numbers and importance. Capitalism, as we saw it in the thirties, was morally and economically shocking to everyone who didn't do very well out of it. There was a wicked disproportion between production and feasible consumption: and methods of bridging the gap were being invented almost weekly by currency reformers. There were too many of these to get a hearing. One or other of them may have been right, but we shall never know because they obliged the status quo enthusiasts (and the Fascists) by discrediting each other.

"As for the Trade Unions, their suspicion of the 'intellectual', though always present, had not prevented middle-class men leading the Party which has always depended on Trade Union funds for its existence: but for Labour to turn the Socialist appeal into a mild and compromising affair was to frighten its friends rather than its opponents. Without an intelligent proposal for parliamentary reform the Labour Party hadn't the smallest chance of convincing anyone outside its regular membership that it could accomplish the scientific reorganisation of industry which it was pledged to carry out. It was useless to advocate the nationalisation of the banking system" (later he would perhaps have included the nationalisation of anything) "without a clear statement of what it wanted to do with that system. It seemed to me that Social Democracy must fail in Great Britain as it had failed in Germany."

The League of Nations had failed to prevent or contain Japan's attack on China, Italy's on Abyssinia, the Franco–

Mussolini–Hitler attack on "Spain" (if that was what you could call the explosive mix-up of revolutionaries, counter-revolutionaries, Trotskyites and Government forces trying to destroy Franco and each other at the same time). The first was too remote to stir Labour to action. The second split the Party, hopelessly, on the question of intervention (some leading British newspapers maintaining that Mussolini was at last bringing civilisation to the Ethiopians, for whom he would build roads and publish dependable railway time-tables). But the third, the ferocious Spanish Civil War, was the point at which the *New Statesman* was almost able to rally the left solidly to the cause of anti-Fascism. To Kingsley, who at that time over-simplified the Spanish war as most people did, it was the centre of hope and the nadir of despair, the last occasion, until the eve of Munich, when Britain and France could have ceased withdrawing before the threat of the dictators and found themselves, in so doing, in alliance with the Soviet Union; when Hitler could have been stopped without war. Or, if it had led to general war, when the circumstances would have been more favourable to the democracies than those which confronted them in 1939 over Poland.

On all those issues Kingsley canvassed the views of anyone and everyone he judged worth listening to; making that judgment, usually, with a speed that could be obvious and disconcerting to the speaker. (A thousand times I have seen his face "turn to stone" as some speaker lost his attention; but it was nearly always because the speaker was a pretentious bore, gratified at having Kingsley to himself and all set to make an impression. Any simple man, with however little command of language, could hold Kingsley's attention if he had something to say that was genuinely felt.) In *Nash's Magazine* of 10th April 1937, John Gunther[1] described to his mainly American readership a typical session in the drawing room at 16 Great James Street:

> In the evening F. Louis and all of us to Kingsley Martin's. Hutton was there, Fred Kuh,[2] Zilliacus of the League Secretariat,

[1] The American author and columnist.
[2] The United Press Correspondent.

> Ted Acheson, Dorothy Woodman (who first opened up the arms traffic story with her pamphlet *The Secret International*), John Strachey. Kingsley's tactics on these evenings are admirable. He keeps conversation going by asking guests questions in turn. It is a little like a seminar. Everybody speaks his mind: Kingsley controls, canalises, superintends the discussion, keeping superfluous issues out and making everyone stick to an arguable point. Kingsley looked haggard with overwork but his paper, the *New Statesman*, is very far from being haggard.

It was at about this time that Kingsley, to say nothing of the *New Statesman* and its public, sustained the considerable impact of meeting Dick Crossman. Dick was a Fellow of New College, Oxford, expounding Aristotelian and Platonic Philosophy in well-filled lecture rooms, and also writing a weekly column in *The Spectator*. He had come under wide notice with a series of radio programmes called *Plato Lives Again*. He seems to have filled in any Oxford time left over by reading (which he does at three times the human speed); exploring poetry with Wystan Auden, Christopher Isherwood and Cecil Day Lewis; playing rugger and being an Oxford City Councillor. Now although Kingsley was an assiduous gamekeeper in the control of his own editorial brood, he was a resourceful and shameless poacher when the necessity, as he saw it, arose. It arose over Dick Crossman, whose enticement away from *The Spectator* began at the suggestion of G. D. H. Cole, with the offer of a book to review; an editorial gambit which combines the qualities of the angler's fly and the litmus paper.

Dick began writing regularly for the *New Statesman* in 1936. The following year he left New College, intending to "go into the BBC", but what attracted him instead to the *New Statesman* was presumably the prestige and the opportunity to write. It could hardly have been the money, for Kingsley paid him a "retainer" of £250. He succeeded Michael Foot, whose *New Statesman* retainer, whether or not it was in any way comparable, would have been unlikely to help him in resisting Beaverbrook's offer of a leader-writer's job at the *Evening Standard*. Within the wide limits of Labour Party thinking, Dick Crossman could hardly have been more sharply opposed, ideologically, to Kingsley. He had been persuaded by Hugh

Dalton and Ernest Bevin of the need to convince Socialists that they *must* accept rearmament in order to defeat the Nazis. He had spent a year in Germany—New College had given him his Fellowship before he had taken his degree, and then sent him away for a year to get a bit older (he was 22) and prepare himself for life as a Don. He went to Frankfurt and Berlin, got caught up in German politics, and married (briefly) a girl who was courier for Willi Münzenberg, the brilliant working-class editor of the two Communist newspapers and compiler of *The Brown Book of the Hitler Terror*.[1] A close association with Münzenberg enabled him to study the German Communist strategy, which aimed at overthrowing the Social Democrats by combining with the Nazis, who were then to be destroyed in their turn. Finally Münzenberg offered him a Moscow appointment "on the side of the future"; and when Dick convinced him that he was going back to lecture at New College, he said "Oxford is collapsing—there will be bread riots before you get back", but gave him a 20-mark note because (he said) the pound would be worthless. Münzenberg went to Moscow and in due course was murdered by Stalin's agents. Dick had concluded that the German Communist Party was completely bogus—unlike Arthur Koestler, who had been a member at that time and thought it sincere but completely misguided.[2]

But when he joined the *New Statesman* he found that Kingsley accepted the German Communists' line, which by that time was that they had *never* had a pact with the Nazis and were the leaders of the anti-Fascist movement, the Popular Front, and the campaign for anti-Franco intervention in Spain. The Communist theory was that the Nazis were the lackeys of High Capitalism in its decadent phase, and Hitler merely a weak agent of German big business. At that time it still seemed to many British Socialists that Communism, as distinct (in some way) from Stalinism, was the hope of Europe. But even if you were not disposed to accept this, or wanted to inform yourself better before rejecting it, the mere fact that you were enquiring, or frequenting the people who could inform you, was enough to brand you as a Communist or as a fellow-traveller. Kingsley,

[1] Gollancz, London, 1936.
[2] See *The Invisible Writing*, London, 1954.

as he remarks in *Editor*,[1] had "got to know Otto Katz, a Czech Communist who worked with Willi Münzenberg", and whom Kingsley describes as "a fanatical and ruthless Commissar". (He later changed his name to André Simon.) Otto Katz was a great friend of Dorothy Woodman's and she saw herself as wrestling with Dick Crossman for the mind of the man who was editing the *New Statesman*; Dick's attitude being that the Nazi movement was a *mass* movement, that the German people were behind Hitler, that the German Communists by conniving with the Nazis had demonstrated their utter futility, that there wasn't the smallest chance of a Communist revolution in Germany, that "you can only beat the Nazis by *war*". Laski, Cole, Aylmer Vallance, and others close to the editorial ear thought this was wrong. But Dick was by this time on the editorial staff, sub-editing articles from Laski and the former deputy editor G. D. H. Cole (both of whom he thought insufferably dull), and ruthlessly, almost gaily, disregarding the ensuing trouble which Kingsley smoothed over with a skill that developed week by week. Usually he had first got through a minor row with Dick himself over some last minute change at the printers in a leading article which Dick had persuaded him to accept. This situation continued until 1940, when Crossman went off to the Enemy Propaganda Division of the Ministry of Information, but it was resumed as soon as he came back.

In 1940 Dick Crossman and Kingsley had collaborated, under the pseudonym of "Scipio", in writing a small book called *A Thousand Million Allies If You Choose*. Its message was that the only way to win the war was to join a European Socialist revolution to fight Hitler. It was warmly welcomed by all those members of exiled socialist governments who were then in England as refugees, and it gave the *New Statesman* a central position among them, as among the resistance movements in the occupied countries. And yet Kingsley, at that time, with the other half of his mind, believed that the war could *not* be won at all: the fact that the Communists were not fighting undermined the righteousness of the Allied Cause, and the whole conflict was, as all others had been, a wicked capitalist war. In this he was probably more influenced than he ever

[1] P. 217.

admitted by D. N. Pritt[1] and Alexander Werth, with whom he had long been friendly. Even two years later (10th April 1942) Harold Nicolson was noting in his famous Diaries: "Lunch with Kingsley Martin. He thinks that unless we have Socialism immediately we shall lose the war. He is worried by the bad morale of the Army."[2]

It was however in the late thirties that there evolved in Kingsley's mind a gradual and in the end unshakable conviction that Dick Crossman was essentially a politician and that his future was not in journalism. This was to have an effect on the relationship of the two men in the post-war years which was of the utmost importance to them both. We will return to it; pausing now merely to note that it was at about this time that the club-story was put around that Kingsley always looked as though he were on his way to Clarkson's to hire a crown of thorns. You can always find, if you turn back far enough in the newspaper gossip columns, that this kind of label has been attached to a succession of public figures. The crown of thorns one was commonly attached to Mr Asquith, and in 1967 was transferred by Claud Cockburn to Ramsay MacDonald.[3]

Kingsley at times reacted too strongly against the "policy" danger of over-involvement in party politics, and it brought him an important private letter from Clement Attlee on 9th May 1937, so badly typed as to show that Mr Attlee felt it necessary to do it himself. The following is an extract:

> A colleague in the House made the following remark to me last week which is perhaps worth passing on with some comment. He said "Why does the *New Statesman*, which professes to stand for democracy against Fascism, hardly mention Parliament and never the Parliamentary Labour Party?" I think there is substance in this. The *Statesman* gives less attention to Parliamentary proceedings than does the *Spectator*, while the Parliamentary Labour Party does not seem to exist at all. I think this is a pity, as your paper goes out pretty widely. For instance, when I was in

[1] MP for Hammersmith, President of the Society for Cultural Relations with USSR, and a prolific author of pro-Soviet books and articles for over fifty years.

[2] *Harold Nicolson: Diaries and Letters, 1939–45*, p. 221.

[3] Claud Cockburn, *I Claud*, Penguin Books, 1967, p. 142.

> India I generally found it on the tables of the more intelligent civil servants and Indians. These readers would gather that the only Socialist activities are those of the Communists and perhaps the Left Book Club, and one or two of the intelligentsia. . . . You will never find the name of a Labour speaker mentioned in the paper. Yet if we want to oust the other side, it is important that the public should know of the existence of Labour men in the House. . . . Excuse this grouse. If you run your eye over the files for the last few months you will I think admit that there is some justification. I think it would be a pity if the NS got so highbrow that it entirely ignored the existence of Parliamentary institutions.

Kingsley thought this, too. Although a quick glance through the paper for 1937 does not fully support the criticism, he decided to revive the institution of a regular Parliamentary correspondent. Of these there has now been a distinguished succession, sometimes MPs, sometimes not, but their political allegiances have been surprisingly varied and, as a rule, their tenures of office brief.[1] Most of them would say, I believe, that having appointed them he left them to write almost what they liked, and he had critics who maintained that this was because he was simply not interested in politics or Parliament. It is probably an absurd over-statement containing the usual grain of truth, but what did interest him about the political machine was the fairly innocuous cloak-and-dagger arrangement by which editors like himself exchanged confidences with civil servants from the Foreign Office and other Ministries. His somewhat detached contemplation of the Labour Party's affairs is illustrated by the episode of Dick Crossman's *New Statesman* article on the annual conference at Southport in 1939, one of the peaks, or troughs, in the Labour Party's history.

By that time the "Popular Front" campaign had been running for four years. It began as a "United Front", a proposed collaboration of all Left Wing political parties throughout Europe against Fascism; and it had the disadvantage for many people, Dick Crossman included, of being the brain-child of the

[1] Alan Watkins, the present incumbent, has been writing the *Spotlight on Politics* for six years and is still carrying his bat, having survived a number of confident appeals; which is a record.

Communist International in 1935. In this country it dropped the idea of a class struggle and became a movement for uniting dissidents of all kinds, Labour, Liberal and "Independent" (i.e. disenchanted Tory), in opposition to the huge, supine and impregnable "National" government of Neville Chamberlain. The Labour Party hated the idea. The proper course, it said, was to bring the Liberals and independents into the Labour camp and make an election victory certain, not to dilute Socialist principles by compromising with Liberals and Independents. Sir Stafford Cripps, who was a member of the National Executive of the Labour Party, was a Popular Front man. He presented to the Executive a plan for "a positive policy of peace by collective action" (though there was nothing in it about re-arming to enforce the policy) with Russia, France, the USA and other democratic countries. When the Executive rejected it, he circulated it as his own private proposal to all local Labour parties. He was then sacked from the Party. Herbert Morrison promptly got a letter from Beatrice Webb upbraiding the National Executive for its "much advertised" expulsion of her nephew Stafford—"I am quite aware of his defects". It weakened the Party for coming elections. Even Mosley wasn't expelled, she pointed out—he "wandered into the wilderness". Lloyd George and his supporting pro-Boers were not expelled from the Liberal Party. Gladstone was not sacked for his sudden *volte face* in 1895 about Irish Home Rule. As if by way of an answer to Mrs Webb the Party then expelled Aneurin Bevan, G. R. Strauss and Sir Charles Trevelyan for sympathising with Cripps. The 1939 Southport Convention upheld all this, George Brown telling them on behalf of the Transport and General Workers Union that they didn't need Cripps's money, this fellow who kept on telling them they ought to be grateful that he gave his services free. Dick Crossman was there for the *New Statesman*, and reported these events in a signed article under the title "Labour Lays a Ghost". "This article, I should have thought now," he told me, "would raise consternation in *New Statesman* readers—the mere fact that it should be published at all. Although it was very critical of George Brown and said the whole proceedings were nauseating, it also said that Cripps was utterly irresponsible, that his

Popular Front agitation was a hopeless failure, and that he was a hypocrite. . . . Looking back, I'm quite sure that I myself as Editor would not have published it. I might have said: 'You can write a letter like this, but I'm not using that as an article'." Kingsley had an essential frivolity, a week-by-week appetite for the startling, but he was also as bitterly disenchanted with the Labour Party as it was, *en bloc*, resentful about him, and the paper he was editing. At that time he and Cole and Laski were deeply disturbed about what they saw as the total failure of democratic government.

The heavy seas thus thrashing the front half of the paper in the thirties were contained by a dam which left the literary half comparatively calm. This had been gratefully inherited by Kingsley's literary editor, Raymond Mortimer, who had found, when he took over, that the tradition had been established and maintained by Clifford Sharp and Desmond MacCarthy. Raymond Mortimer was fortunately more interested in the arts than in politics, a state of mind which enabled him to hold Kingsley and Dick Crossman in equally high esteem while suppressing an occasional longing to bang their heads together. He had been introduced to the *New Statesman* by Francis Birrell in 1922, when Desmond MacCarthy gave him some novels to review. The paper was then about ten years old and was adding a non-political readership to its original public of faithful Fabians. When he succeeded David Garnett as literary editor in 1931 he had been doing the job for a six-months' period because Garnett wanted to write a book. At the end of the six months Kingsley didn't want Garnett to come back, and Mortimer, who was a friend of Garnett's, accordingly felt on apppointment rather like a cuckoo in the nest. He had been a regular contributor all through the difficult final period of Clifford Sharp's spasmodic and turbulent editorship; but then in 1931 there began an extraordinary partnership with Kingsley Martin which he looks back on with infinite pleasure. "He always gave me the longest rope possible and was incredibly patient. I always asked him who should review any book on a political subject, but otherwise I didn't care a damn what the political opinions of critics were. We had an occasional show-down. I once accepted a rather whimsical little article by Gerald Brenan, who writes so well about Spain. Kingsley said it was 'silly' and refused to publish it. We had an argument. Eventually we decided to call in a referee, and chose Desmond MacCarthy, who supported Kingsley and that was the end of it. And once, by making a frightful scene, I did persuade him to leave out an article he'd got in print—it was an attack on General de Gaulle and was already on the page. I threatened to resign if it went in. All the German broadcasts to France, all the newspapers in France, were saying the English had seen through de Gaulle, who was nothing but a Fascist and so on. I thought the damage would be absolutely horrible. It's the only occasion I can remember getting into a rage with Kingsley."

Raymond Mortimer, a lifelong Francophile, had left the *New Statesman* at the beginning of the war to work in the French section of the Ministry of Information. He was unwell there, and glad to get back after a year. By then his literary editorship, though not his long friendship with Kingsley, was in its last two or three years. "Kingsley was very much the son of a dissenting parson," he told me, "and he revolted against religion. I came from a pleasure-loving home—I was brought up on golf courses and racecourses and so on, and I revolted against *that*. We both bore the marks of these different childhoods, and I suppose could hardly have been more different as men." They never in fact became out-of-office friends—"we were two human beings of entirely different kinds. I am really, I suppose, an aesthete (though I hate the word), and I don't think he had much feeling of that kind. He *wanted* to like pictures and music and so on, but . . ."

The "independence" of the literary half, although it was something considerably short of autonomy, was not a new principle introduced by Kingsley, and so much has been written about his unique wisdom in this regard that this should probably be made plain. Clifford Sharp, although he took a greater interest than Kingsley did in music, art and letters, left that half of the paper entirely to Desmond MacCarthy—who, if he took any interest in the front half, probably disapproved of it. In Kingsley's time the independence of the back half had two main bastions. One was the aesthetic barrier, the closed door of what successive literary editors saw as Kingsley's cheerful philistinism; the other was that Raymond Mortimer was too busy, and aloof from party politics, to do more than storm into Kingsley's room on selected occasions and say "Look here, we can't *possibly* have this sort of thing". And he was busy because, in his half of the paper for most of the fifteen years of his literary editorship, he virtually "ran his own show". He set and judged many of the week-end competitions himself under a series of pseudonyms, wrote countless unsigned notices about books and plays and operas and art exhibitions, and wrote the signed critical essays for which he became famous. His output was prodigious, his quality seldom flagged, and he was always afterwards surprised that his successors wrote so little. "He was the sort of literary editor," wrote Kingsley in *Editor* (p. 7), "with whom I scarcely ever wanted to interfere." "He was the sort of editor," said Raymond to me, "who has real flair; he was absolutely dazzling." It goes far to explain why, for those fifteen years at least, the *New Statesman* was never the "pantomime horse" that it was so often alleged to be. It was rather, if one is to accept that kind of metaphor, a bicycle made for two; on which the man at the back, who never flagged in his genuine pedalling, worked too hard to realise whether the man in front worked or not.

Geographically these two were well placed for popping into each other's offices, for they were next to each other on the same floor, with windows looking out over Lincoln's Inn Fields. They did a great deal of this, but it was rarely that they lunched together, either tête-a-tête or with others. But in Raymond Mortimer's office throughout that time and for some years afterwards there worked that quiet, elusive and enchantingly inventive writer G. W. Stonier; whose work seemed to some of us like a specially lucid kind of modern verse pushed into conventionally-shaped *New Statesman* paragraphs. He always looked like Adolphe Menjou, though in fact he described himself as "one of the world's non-actors" and would never attempt to broadcast either by radio or television. In Clifford Sharp's time, there were Press days on which Sharp was drunk and Desmond MacCarthy, lunching with some interesting companion, had totally forgotten the time. On those days George Stonier was *de facto* editor, and put many an issue to bed unaided. Publication day in the thirties was Friday. In its relaxed atmosphere there was usually a lunch party at the Holborn Restaurant to which, as a rule, Kingsley and Stonier both came: and to the best of my knowledge this was the only regular occasion when the "front and back" halves of the paper were represented together at a weekly lunch meeting. Their lunch-time contacts inhabited different worlds. (The old Holborn Restaurant was rather a splendid place, but this weekly lunch-gossip was usually held in what was called the Long Bar, with everyone sitting on high stools and having sausage-and-mash.) After the war G. W. Stonier became film critic, for which role he rechristened himself William Whitebait; no one quite knew why, though when he began setting week-end competitions as Willy Tadpole I extracted from him the explanation that he rather liked fishy names (a visit to the London Zoo produced an ingenious *New Statesman* poem about sea-horses). "He never seemed to belong to the world in which the rest of us lived," wrote Kingsley in *Editor* (page 7), "and the time came when he turned his back on this civilisation and took a Land-Rover into the wilds of Africa." Actually his wife took it, with George as navigator. She drove from Cairo to the Cape and they settled eventually in Rhodesia. He was a gentle creature who would, nevertheless, sometimes write withering book reviews. He is one of the older "Statesmen" to whom, in the estimation of most people who know the paper's history—and certainly in Kingsley's—much of its early success was due.

Towards the end of the thirties, however, that success was becoming a commercial matter. The paper had increased its circulation from 14,000 (in 1931) to 30,000, and was making a profit. This was a development which involved—perhaps the better word is embroiled—Kingsley Martin with the managerial side of his *New Statesman* in a way that he had neither foreseen nor wanted, though he came to regard the paper's success with considerable pride. In particular, it saw the beginning of a long feud with John Roberts, the managing director, which was of such importance to Kingsley's peace of mind—it led him several times to the verge of resignation from the editorship, and he once said that it was the cause of a serious breakdown in his health—that it merits a chapter to itself. But if we are to observe some sort of chronological pattern we should first consider the major political crisis in Kingsley's career: his attitude to the Munich "settlement" with Hitler and to the outbreak of the war which that made inevitable.

Chapter 13

WAR AND TRUTH

"AMONG THE CALAMITIES of war," said Samuel Johnson, and a thousand other aphorists have said it since, "may be justly numbered the diminution of the love of truth by the falsehoods which interest dictates and credulity encourages." It was the theme of Kingsley's Cambridge Fellowship thesis, of three of his books, of many broadcasts and of countless articles. In particular, he would always ask, was there anything you could call public opinion? How was it formed? How could you find out what it was?

In the mid-thirties he met Tom Harrisson, co-founder with Charles Madge of "Mass Observation", the social survey organisation whose "unscientific" methods the social historians still deprecate while they rifle its archives for information.[1] Mass Observation ("the science of ourselves") was then an unfamiliar process, marshalling voluntary observers all over England to assemble sociological data, and publishing reports whose value Kingsley was among the first to recognise. Tom Harrisson regarded him as one of the promoters of Mass Observation: and indeed in the late thirties, when so many believed—and Kingsley did not—that *vox populi*, if only you could hear it, would be universally against war, he was ready to publish almost anything that the Madge and Harrisson field-workers could find out. What specially interested him just then was that during the abdication crisis of 1936 everyone knew the story before a single word about it had appeared in a British newspaper. Mass Observation discovered then that the predominant public emotion was not the agonised royalist disenchantment discovered by the newspapers, but great excitement plus a certain amount of gilt-edged eroticism; and for the first time it recorded in print what the people *thought*

[1] The Mass Observation archive is now at Sussex University, where Tom Harrisson is again running it after twenty years' absence in Borneo.

they had heard each other saying, as distinct from what their newspapers told them they had said.

The kind of press and public reception usually accorded to a new project like this is to hit it, smartly and experimentally, on the head. Mass Observation was assailed on all sides as "gimmicky" and amateur and even sinister. But Kingsley was intensely, perhaps uncritically, interested in it—that is to say in its results rather than its techniques; and he may well have been readier even than its authors to accept and quote some of its earlier findings without sufficient thought as to what the techniques might be. A good example, perhaps, is the contrasting of public and private opinion about Chamberlain's war-time leadership, quoted in Angus Calder's *The People's War* (page 61):[1]

> Approval for Chamberlain's premiership in the opinion polls, which had been running at an average of 60 per cent before the war, had increased now to an average of nearly 70 per cent. This was "public" opinion. But private opinion was disillusioned, and Mass Observation noted that there was steadily less and less applause for the Prime Minister from cinema audiences when he appeared on the newsreels.

Mass Observation itself would often set little store by such a finding, which might get detached from its source and gain credence by repetition. (How do you measure and compare quantities of cinema applause for Prime Ministers? You use an "audiometer", which measures not only applause but even blood pressures, heart beats, and breathing rates.) The general findings were of course a useful antidote to official pap. And yet when Mass Observation's services were engaged by Mr Alfred Duff Cooper, the Minister of Information, there was a press campaign against it of quite unexpected fury (with a rallying cry about "Cooper's Snoopers"); partly because the press wanted to get rid of Duff Cooper and any stick was good enough to beat him with, but mainly because Mass Observation was seen as a potential danger to the edifice of half-truths by which the political, commercial and advertising structures are sustained. But the real trouble was that neither Duff Cooper

[1] Pantheon Books, New York, 1969. Published in Britain by Cape, 1969.

Kingsley's cottage, The Old Stag at Little Easton—Kingsley on porch

Kingsley with members of the *New Statesman* managerial staff, 1941

“Mr Park”

nor his predecessors would allow the public to know what the MOI was up to, or what methods it was using. So the "leak" about the use of Mass Observation was a Fleet Street festival. Kingsley fostered the new system of social enquiry by every means he could think of. And he put Tom Harrisson in touch with wealthy potential backers like Lord Simon of Wythenshawe, and published in his London Diary and elsewhere Mass Observation "exclusives", especially during the war, which made people say "wherever does he go for his information?"

On the other hand, by some standards he could be over-discriminatory in the kind of information that he would use. In 1937 he delighted his enemies by refusing to publish a review by George Orwell of Franz Borkenau's book *The Spanish Cockpit.* It was a decision that displayed the front and back halves of the paper as being not exactly out of harmony but playing the same music in close harmony and by accident; and Orwell's version of it is given in detail in Sonia Orwell's collected edition of her husband's papers.[1] He had been fighting in Spain with the Anarchists and the POUM.[2] He had seen the latter brutally suppressed by its friends and allies the Spanish Communists (though they were all supposed to be fighting Franco and his "nationalist" revolutionaries), its members imprisoned without trial, tortured and executed. He believed then, as is so obvious now, that the strict "non-intervention" of the British, American and French governments, a craven and suicidal policy as it turned out, had forced the Spanish Government into dependence on the USSR, split its supporters into mutually hostile factions, and in fact nourished the whole network of fratricidal treachery and double-dealing that weakened and destroyed the anti-Franco forces. Orwell totally disagreed with Maynard Keynes, who had rejected, in a letter to Kingsley dated 9th August 1937, any suggestion that Spain was being let down by the democracies. "I am not a bit sure," wrote Keynes, "that not making her territory the seat of a general European war is 'letting her down'." It depended on whether the Fascist powers were "intending to use the negotiations as a way of getting out

[1] *The Collected Essays, Journalism, and Letters of George Orwell,* Vol. I, Secker & Warburg, 1968.

[2] Partido Obrero de Unificacion Marxista.

without too much loss of face, or whether the plot is really something quite different, not yet disclosed. Being an optimist, I am still hopeful that it may end in the division of Spain geographically into two States." Historians still dispute whether the provision of arms, supplies and "technicians" by Britain, France and America would have unified the anti-Franco forces or encouraged them to decimate each other with deadlier enthusiasm. The doubt existed at the time, and (it must be said) was not an encouragement to "intervention" of the sort that provides war materials.

But Orwell was wounded in the fighting, and as soon as he got out of Spain in 1937 he telegraphed from France to Kingsley Martin and sold him an article about the course of the civil war. "When they saw my article was on the suppression of the POUM," he wrote to Rayner Heppenstall on 31st July 1937, "they said they couldn't print it. To sugar the pill they sent me to review a very good book which appeared recently, *The Spanish Cockpit*, which blows the gaff pretty well on what has been happening. But once again, when they saw my review they couldn't print it, as it was 'against editorial policy'.[1] They actually offered to pay for the review all the same—practically hush-money." (If that was hush money, a good many of us have been hushed by the *New Statesman*, usually making the simpler assumption that we hadn't this time delivered the goods and yet the paper didn't want to lose us.)

Orwell was learning from a number of sources that "one must not tell the truth about what was happening in Spain, and the part played by the Communist Party, because to do so would be to prejudice public opinion against the Spanish Government and so aid Franco." And this, in fact, whether one

[1] And in fact, since Orwell had already reviewed the same book in *Time and Tide*, this is something he might have known. Moreover, Raymond Mortimer told him, in a letter dated 9 February 1938, that he had used the review "merely to express his own opinions and present facts which he thought should be known". He had had a separate letter from Kingsley saying that the review was against "political" policy—not "editorial" policy, though the difference may seem elusive. And in the end the book was reviewed by V. S. Pritchett (4 September 1937) who *did* say what it was about and that it "stood head and shoulders over anything yet published" about the war in Spain.

likes it or not, was precisely Kingsley's position. Orwell, however, felt that the only way to help the people imprisoned without trial in Spain, ill-treated in the jails, libelled in the press, groomed (as it were) for assassination, was to denounce the pro-Communist censorship. It infuriated him to find that the *New Statesman*, in effect though not in intention, supported it. He announced that he would never write for the *New Statesman* again, and the resolution actually lasted two years: after which he did many more book reviews. But he never forgave Kingsley. "He hated Kingsley for that," Malcolm Muggeridge told me. "I was lunching with him in one of those Greek restaurants in Percy Street and he said 'Would you mind changing places with me?' I said 'OK, but why?' And he said 'When you've moved round you'll find you are looking at Kingsley Martin: *I* can't bear to look at him.'[1] But Kingsley never withdrew from the position he took up over those articles —I rather admired him for it in a way," continued Malcolm. "He said, and this is significant of the way he ran the paper, 'They were brilliant articles, and they were true, but they would have damaged the Republicans'. In this sort of thing he was like Gollancz, who turned down Orwell's *Animal Farm* because it would damage our relations with the USSR. I said to Gollancz in a television interview: 'You turned down one of the few books of our time which are really works of genius—from a publishing point of view is that rather a heavy thing to have on your mind?' And he said 'From a publishing point of view it was a great error, but I still think it was right'."

Certainly Kingsley was given many opportunities to admit that he was wrong about the Orwell articles. In a broadcast interview on Canadian radio (again with Malcolm Muggeridge) in 1965 he said:

> I find that, looking back, I *minded* more about losing the war in Spain than about anything else that ever happened in my life. . . . If the Republicans had won, the situation would have been vastly different. After the destruction of the League, and the end of Collective Security over Abyssinia, we confronted the only occasion when Russia could have been allied with the West.

[1] Muggeridge later told this story in his autobiography, *Chronicles of Wasted Time*, Collins, p. 15.

We should automatically have become allies of Russia—not politically aligned of course (I had no use at all for Stalin)—but it would have meant that Hitler would have known from the outset that he faced a war on two fronts.[1] It would have been *so* much easier than waiting until Hitler invaded Russia. Of course, Spain would not have been a Communist satellite country; but all the small European countries were against Franco, to say nothing of public feeling in U.S.A., Britain and Russia. There would have been some kind of consortium, some sort of Popular Front government.

As an editor, Kingsley said, "one had the job of separating truth from propaganda. To me, this was THE war, the war with Germany, the war against the Fascists and Mussolini and the Vatican. You had to avoid being untruthful so far as you could, but your picture of the world is unavoidably one-sided in such a war. From the beginning I was unashamedly a partisan."

The whole press was open to propaganda on the other side, it was almost entirely in the hands of anti-Republican propaganda. Both sides behaved with abominable cruelty; but I had to make my decision on general public grounds *to the end that one side might win rather than the other side.* I happened to like Orwell very much, and I would never have thought I wouldn't want to publish anything he wrote. But let me remind you: we didn't have *Homage to Catalonia* to publish—nothing balanced like that. We had two or three articles of violent anti-Negrin propaganda—and of course anti-Communist too. I would no more have thought of publishing *them* than of publishing an article by Goebbels during the war against Germany. . . . In the Spanish Civil War I was very much alone, fighting the republicans' battle in a very lonely way; and I didn't see it as my function to play the other side's game.

So Kingsley himself, by this time, would tell lies, or suppress the truth, if the cause were grave enough. And who would not? He constantly explained that "Communism means lying and cheating in peace time, in the way that we all resort to in war

[1] Kingsley never abandoned this backward-looking belief, despite all the efforts of Dick Crossman and others to demonstrate that it was politically naïve.

time—the Communists don't see this as wrong because they are fighting a war *all the time*". This perfectly logical view (which British Communists, at all events, do not accept) must at some point encounter the difficulty that war is no longer easily distinguishable from what used to be called peace. When does the good side start—and when does it stop—telling lies?

I have used the episode of the Orwell articles to illustrate Kingsley's honest capitulation, once religion had gone, once pacifism had gone, to the demands of expedience in the interests of human survival. But I suppose it should be left to any interested reader to choose for himself from the available explanations the one that seems most likely to account for Kingsley's decision:

1. The first Orwell piece was, in his view, pro-enemy propaganda even though true.
2. The second one, the book review, wasn't really a review of the book.
3. Both of them attacked the Republican government on atrocity grounds; and although Kingsley had small doubt as to the truth of them, he was editing the only weekly paper of its kind that was not supporting Franco, and he thought Orwell had plenty of room in those that were.

A study of Orwell's collected writings shows that he, at any rate, never ceased to hold that suppression of the truth (in which he would include the refusal to publish an article) was indistinguishable from lying. He disapproved of the P.O.U.M., but when he said in a letter to Frank Jellinek in 1938 that "there had been far too much fuss about the P.O.U.M. business" and that it could "prejudice people against the Spanish republic"[1] he was concerned that a relatively minor dispute could distract attention from the appalling world significance of the war in Spain. It may even be true that, in the words of one of his reproachful correspondents, Kingsley's refusal to publish remained for many people a decision that was "largely instrumental in misleading a whole generation of socialists into a false assessment of the real nature of Soviet despotism". As with his

[1] *Editor*, p. 215.

attitude to the Munich Settlement the following year, it is a controversy over which argument will continue; it was a "choice of the soul".

By the end of 1937 Kingsley had concluded that the Socialist government in Spain could not survive, that the opportunity of crushing it was being used by Hitler and Mussolini (and watched by Stalin) as a rehearsal for the bigger war to come, and that democracy throughout the world was doomed. He had been in Spain at the same time as Lillian Hellman and Ernest Hemingway, who were making a film. Lillian Hellman also "knew it was defeat" (she told me); "I knew what was going to happen and I'm sure Kingsley did too—it was such a mess, everyone on the same side was quarrelling. I knew they wouldn't get any aid from America." Kingsley came back in a state of desperate incredulity that men were going to be such fools as to destroy the entire world they had built. He has often been attacked for his pessimism about international affairs, but in the thirties and forties it served a salutary purpose among all the fatuity of the prevailing optimism; and only once (so far as I can find) did he sound Byron's "hideous note"—

> Of all the horrid, hideous notes of woe,
> Sadder than owl songs or the midnight blast,
> Is that portentous phrase "I told you so".

This was in a letter to Keynes on 25th May 1940, written from Dublin (Kingsley had gone to see De Valera in the hope of finding out why Irish newspapers were backing the Nazis):

> You may recall that you were annoyed with me early in the war because I said that the small neutrals would fall into Germany and we should find ourselves in a desperate position. If my pessimism, of which I am much ashamed, were not so often right, I might have cured myself of it. But it has been, blast it, incredibly right, and reinforced every week since 1931. Occasionally, as over Norway, I have conquered it and written optimistically—and been wrong with a more depressing effect on morale than when I am gloomy. . . . Personally I would rather fight to any bitter end, because I and my kind are on a proscribed list for execution; but that is a bad reason for condemning hundreds of thousands of people to death who have not so much to lose. That of course is

not a matter for public discussion. . . . I doubt if gaol is the right remedy for people like me [Keynes had angrily said that pessimists like him ought to be in prison].[1]

Two or three months after I had first met him, he dined at the Savile with an old Cambridge friend, Professor Otakar Vočadlo of the University of Prague, who was then lecturing at Kings College, London. "Ota," he said, "we shan't live long." He lived another 32 years, and Professor Vočadlo is still lecturing in Czechoslovakia despite war-time experiences which, as a direct consequence of the Munich Settlement, included four years in German concentration camps. (I must return to him.) But I came to know that Kingsley reserved his worst despair for those, like myself, who treated him with some deference and forbore to argue. Among those who did not was Aylmer Vallance, who had come to the *New Statesman* as assistant editor in 1936 when he lost the editorship of the *News Chronicle*, and whose part in Kingsley's story may, at the expense of another twist in chronology, conveniently be outlined here.

Aylmer Vallance, at the *New Statesman* office, always seemed to me like a ship's pilot who has forgotten to go ashore and is quietly supposing that some new kind of relationship with the Captain will work itself out during the long voyage ahead. The impression was heightened by the fact that his pointed beard made him look like C. J. Cutcliffe Hyne's *Captain Kettle*, and indeed he was known in the office as "the Admiral". (Kingsley says in *Editor* that he was like the sea captain in *Under Milk Wood*.) He was a most attractive character, a brilliant journalist who would frequently belie his appearance of detachment and bored *savoir faire* by devoting an hour or so to the patient instruction of some fledgling writer. He had crammed so many adventures into his life that the capacity for real excitement, which had long forsaken him, was a source of amusement to him (and an opportunity for leg-pulling) when he found it in others. In this, Kingsley was his prime victim. And there was something about this process, now that Kingsley was on the way to becoming a Father Figure himself, that could be distressing to any onlooker who felt called upon, as an adolescent

[1] See *Editor*, p. 270, *et seq.*

son might, to conceal and protect what he felt to be his father's innocence.

For example, during a critical period in the Ethiopian War in 1935, Lady Rhondda invited Kingsley and Graham Hutton to lunch with Bernard Shaw, having first incited Shaw to pull Kingsley's leg about Mussolini's "civilising mission". (I rely upon Graham Hutton for the details.) Shaw had been reading the *New Statesman*. "My dear man, you can't possibly believe what you're writing in this paper of yours. This man Mussolini knows what he's doing, he's bringing light and civilisation to these barbarians." Kingsley hammered his knees in exasperation. "Shaw, this is monstrous! Are you really talking about civilisation? The Ethiopians have a civilisation *thousands* of years old." Shaw said, "And would it be the civilisation that's taught them to cut off their prisoners' genitalia? What kind of civilisation will you call *that*?" At length the lunch party broke up with Kingsley in almost speechless distress. As he walked back to the *New Statesman* with Hutton he clutched his hair at the sides and said, "Graham, to think of such a man coming to *that* in his old age!"

Kingsley discovered that if he confided to Aylmer his fears about "the international situation", Aylmer would immediately outdo him in terrifying prophecy. Later when the war came, and Aylmer was a Lieutenant-Colonel in the Intelligence Department of the War Office, Aylmer's competitive prophecies (particularly concerning new "secret weapons" about to be unleashed by the Nazis) took on added authority in Kingsley's sight, so that even he didn't want to hear any more. "The government *think* we may be able to carry on," Aylmer would say, stroking his beard, "even when London is a heap of smoking ruins." Kingsley would ask him whether they should be making plans to move the paper out of London? He believed that Aylmer was extremely well informed on military matters, providing him with providential and secret lines to the Military Intelligence Department, though the rest of the staff told each other Aylmer's job was so secret that he didn't know what it was himself. It seems likely enough that he was playing a fairly devious game, using the *New Statesman* with the knowledge of the Intelligence Department to plant useful items of pro-allied propaganda, but also planting, under cover of the two-way prestige this gave him, "fellow-travelling" material about war-theatres like Yugoslavia. This was a source of constant friction; and the commonly-heard accusation in the 1940's that the *New Statesman* was a fellow-travelling paper was due not merely to Kingsley's ambivalence about Russia, but also to Aylmer's stealthy insistence on putting in, deliberately too late for censorship or amendment, extreme statements about Eastern Europe.

One of his last-minute leaders, which got the innocent Kingsley into trouble with Keynes and the rest of the Board, was in fact slipped in while Leonard Woolf was editing for a few days, and there was a tremendous row which Aylmer, as usual, imperturbably survived.[1] He was probably a born "double agent", skilled in so timing his *coups de main* that nothing could be done to correct them and they would usually be *just* capable of some dubiously disarming explanation. While he was editing the *News Chronicle* he had so manipulated that solidly Liberal paper during the run-up to the 1935 General Election as to bring it out on the side of the Labour Party. This infuriated the Cadbury proprietors to such an extent that they sought at once a face-saving reason for sacking him, which he shortly afterwards provided by way of a brief saturnalia discovered *in flagrante* in the editorial office.

I suppose Aylmer's most attractive story describes his own appointment to the Intelligence Corps during the first World War. In 1914 at Balliol College he went to a farewell party for an undergraduate who was in the Yeomanry and was being called to the Colours. The farewells reached such an emotional pitch that they all got on the train to Taunton, where the Yeoman was to report. The drinking continued, and the next morning they all woke up to find that they had enlisted in the Somerset Light Infantry. Aylmer was sent to India, commissioned, and then transferred to the Intelligence Corps. He seemed to accept this story himself, rather liked it, and could not be faulted under the closest questioning.

By the early fifties he was on rather bad terms with Kingsley,

[1] The story is fully told in the fifth volume of Leonard Woolf's autobiography, *The Journey not the Arrival Matters*, Hogarth Press, 1969.

who had lent him money to sustain him through the growing complication of his domestic life; and Kingsley was finally treating him, indeed, with an overt contempt in the presence of other people which was rather embarrassing to witness. In 1955 a long and painful illness ended an eventful life in which he had charmed and helped a host of friends and colleagues. A good way to evoke his memory would be to recall that almost everyone who knew him reacts now to the mention of his name with a thoughtful and affectionate grin. But it would not be Kingsley's reaction.

Before leaving these pre-war years I should record that it was in 1937 that Kingsley went to stay with Herbert Agar (then back in Kentucky editing the *Louisville Courier*); had an interview with President Roosevelt; and went on to Mexico City to see Trotsky, who was living, heavily guarded, in a beautiful borrowed villa and writing *The Crimes of Stalin*. Trotsky, he thought, was a dramatist playing his own title roles, but he was "charming and friendly . . . and pleased to talk because he regarded the *New Statesman* as one of the few honest and genuinely radical papers".[1] They discussed the iniquitous purges and "trials" going on in Moscow, the faked evidence and the "confessions"; but to judge from Kingsley's notes they do not seem to have fully discussed the likelihood that the confessions were obtained, and not repudiated in Court, because any man who failed to "confess" or withdrew his confession in public would be condemning his family or some other hostages to death or to life imprisonment. When I talked to him about this, years later, Kingsley had come to accept that it was not really necessary to seek further for an explanation of most of the abject performances which have since become so familiar a feature of "people's justice".

The Phoney War, or sitzkrieg, brought none of the relief or exhilaration which so often blankets other emotions at the start of a "just war". Perhaps a just war is one in which, having retreated backwards to an escape-proof corner and emptied out all your pockets on the way, you prepare to hit out because it seems that the alternative is death. Whatever exhilaration

[1] *Editor*, p. 232.

might then possess you is unlikely to last if your enemy just stands and waits for you to start hitting. It was, said Kingsley in *Editor* (page 265), "a miserable period. It is commonly presented as a time of preparation and rearmament during which everyone publicly assumed that fighting would soon begin in earnest; but in fact many people still thought Britain might keep out." And indeed nearly everyone did.

They thought there would be a patched-up peace as soon as Poland was over-run, and mention is made below of some of the evidence coming into Kingsley's possession that such an arrangement was being sought on many sides. But in that interval, from 3rd September 1939 until 9th April 1940 (when the Nazis invaded Norway and Denmark), there was some time for reflection; and in it Kingsley produced a short essay, so far as I know unpublished, on discovering that his theme of "Never Again" had been taken up by an extreme group of Tories. From the millions of words he wrote in his 50 years of journalism, nothing more characteristic could be found for inclusion in his biography.

"For ten years or more after the last war," he wrote, "any speaker with a resonant voice could win applause from almost any British audience by saying 'Never Again'. Those applauding included Pacifists who meant that they would never fight anyone again, Right-wingers who particularly intended never again to fight the Germans, Left-wingers who thought they would never again fight their working class comrades, and League of Nations supporters who would never again shed blood except in a cause certified at Geneva to be *bona fide* police work. . . . The cry of 'Never Again', the most potent of all political slogans in Britain between 1919 and 1935, has now been snaffled by a particular group of imperial thinkers who apparently believe there will never be another war if Germany is sufficiently hard hit after this one.

"I recall the mood of 'squeezing Germany till the pips squeak', and the contradictions and follies that followed over reparations and the rest of it during the subsequent years. I recall that then the 'smash Germany for ever' school fought a drawn battle with pro-League opinion, and that the net result of the confused conflict was the worst of both possible worlds. While this issue was being contested on the official platforms, a far more fundamental argument was to be overheard in every place where two or three students or factory workers were gathered together. All very well to say 'Never Again', but what were the real causes of war; how prevent them having the same effect next time?

"If two or more dogs are fighting, how would you answer the question why are they fighting? I suggest that there are four answers, each of them true on its own level and each of them, if taken alone, leading to a different form of action. The indignant owner of the gentler dog will point, quite correctly, to the aggressive character of the German mongrel which started the row. A bystander will point out, again correctly, that if the dogs had been kept under proper control there would have been no fight. A third spectator will say that there was only one bone and several dogs, and if there had been plenty of bones, carefully distributed, the dogs would not have quarrelled because they would have been too busy eating. At which a cynical student of canine nature will remark that dogs fight anyway sooner or later, because it is their nature to do so.

"The analogy will serve. One nation at an expanding moment of its history starts a particular war: that is the argument for regarding Germany as the sole delinquent, just as it was the argument for regarding France as incorrigibly oppressive in the 17th and 18th centuries, for denouncing Spaniards as enemies of the human race in the 16th century, Americans as the most rapacious of Herrenvolk in the 19th century, and the British as insatiable in their lust for conquest (if you were among coloured people in any backward area) at any time between Clive and Cecil Rhodes. Secondly, if there were an international political authority, to which all nations paid respect, the anarchy of sovereign states could be curbed and an international police force take the place of private armies. Thirdly, the principal cause of war in our time is economic rivalry. . . . How impossible it is to imagine that smashing Germany and big armaments make an appropriate policy for a body that calls itself the Never Again Association. Suppose that every German is killed: will the Never Again Association then feel so safe that they will propose complete disarmament? On the contrary, remove Germany from the map and immediately one hears, in the loud silence that follows, voices discussing the relative potentialities of the USA and the USSR, the bitter strife of American and British business, the fear of a mighty Chinese nationalism when Japan, like Germany, is destroyed. . . ."

On 6th October 1939 he had said in a letter to Maynard Keynes that he had been talking to Cabinet Ministers about Britain's war aims—which, he thought, were not at that time sufficiently definable for publication:

> India may well be the most important thing on the map soon—I find that Home agrees about its importance—but I see little hope of any satisfactory compromise. . . . If there is civil disobedience, concentration camps again, and so on, the results in USA will be very serious. Also it will help USSR. Result of recent talk with Cabinet Ministers is that if one section of the Cabinet gets its way we shall soon cease fighting Hitler and join with Germany against Stalin—if the Reichswehr can be persuaded to do so. But I think the odds are against this party winning.

He then went through a period of wretched indecision; and in this he was much influenced by Lloyd George, whom he visited frequently in his home at Churt and who was strongly in favour of a patched-up peace with Hitler.[1] There was an unbreakable military deadlock in the West, Lloyd George constantly reminded him, and more was to be gained by a compromise peace than by a long and unprecedentedly destructive war. The old Welsh Wizard saw himself as once more the country's probable saviour; believed that the country would call upon him when Chamberlain had betrayed us by his bungling ignorance and Churchill by his chauvinism; but insisted that the peace talks must not begin until a German attempt at invasion had been beaten off. This attempt would be a deliberately half-hearted affair, Lloyd George and Hitler jointly arranging its weight and timing by negotiation through the neutrals. And the

[1] Kingsley tells the story in Chapter 14 of *Editor*, which he heads "Lloyd George and the Policy of Despair".

old man was immensely encouraged in all this by a deluge of letters from private citizens (there are, it seems, twelve box-fulls of them in his collected papers, labelled "Compromise Peace"). He also had the qualified support of Capt. B. H. Liddell Hart, the military historian and tactician, and of a Peace Aims Group led by George Lansbury, Malcolm Macmillan, Sydney Silverman, Reginald (later Lord) Sorenson and Richard Stokes. There were of course countless other rumours of peace plans in the making, but most of them were the products of enemy propaganda.

The details of many were made available on 1st January 1971 when, under the 30-year rule, the British Government's records for 1940 were open to public inspection for the first time, and "the sinister trance of the twilight war" could be studied in detail. Apart from those records, there was a strong body of opinion which took Joseph Kennedy's line: the only country to gain from the war would be Russia, and anyway the British would lose. The German Foreign Ministry documents in the Foreign Office Library include Ribbentrop's long report at the end of his Ambassadorship (1938) urging Hitler to get on with his projects for Austria, Czechoslovakia and Danzig as quickly as possible before British rearmament was formidable. He said: "It is conceivable that there are in the British Government men (my experience and observation make me doubt whether Chamberlain and Halifax are among them) who even today believe in the possibility of an amicable arrangement with Germany." But the only names he mentioned were Monsell, Londonderry, Edward VIII, the Astor Group and *The Times*, Rennell, Lothian, Allen of Hurtwood, Arnold and Noel-Buxton. There was an offer of mediation from Queen Wilhelmina and King Leopold. The Society of Friends was in touch with German sources. And there was a visit to occupied Holland in 1940 by the Archbishop of York, Dr William Temple, to confer with the leaders of all Protestant churches in Europe; as to the results of which Temple's biographer is a little shy.

To most of these Kingsley felt himself to be duly alerted by his many contacts in the field of psychological warfare; while as to his beliefs about the war and its purpose and outcome, the gradual discrediting of Lloyd George and of the Peace Aims

Group left him with no more than a weakly recurrent belief that somehow, for some reason, this war for survival would end in the preservation of the Western democracies, however temporary that preservation might be. His acceptance of the idea that this would take a long time dates from a letter he wrote to Liddell Hart on 11th October 1940, which shows how his attitude had hardened. The *New Statesman* had just been bombed out of its offices at Great Turnstile, and he was writing from the printer's office (the Cornwall Press) in Blackfriars:

> If you and Lloyd George, who are the only people talking about a possible compromise peace whom one can at all respect, believe that such a peace is possible, I wish you would let me know how you envisage it, what sort of terms you would offer, and so forth. Unless you do that, I feel that it is mischievous to discuss it. As you know, my own inclinations would be in favour of any compromise that did not mean a renewal of war or a return to the psychology of 1938. . . . This of course must not be confused with a quite different thesis that I have always maintained, that we ought to lay down conditions under which we would stop fighting, and tell the world what our aims are. It is absurd to fight without war objectives. . . . It is unfair merely to go on urging the desirability of stopping the war at the proper moment, if you give no idea of that moment or of how the war can be stopped without putting Hitler in Whitehall. Things might of course become different if, as some of the experts seem to hope, a defence against the night bomber is fully worked out in the next few weeks.

If it had been known that a defence against the night bomber was never going to be worked out, everyone's reasoning would presumably have been different but it would still have been wrong: for the officially expected rate of civilian casualties from enemy bombing was at least 40,000 deaths a day (and plastic coffins for them were being turned out by the hundred thousand in the early months of 1940). The estimates—so many deaths per ton of bombs—had been based on the experience of Barcelona in the Spanish Civil War, Shanghai in the Sino-Japanese war, and London in the first World War. They were wildly wrong. Moreover mass bombing in all theatres of war, terrible as it was, achieved only the toughening of resistance, and Kingsley, conscious of the process (as his war-time London Diary shows), shared in it and gradually stiffened. He was, however, seldom out of difficulty until he had reluctantly accepted the Churchill objective of a German "unconditional surrender". (He never accepted this publicly, and indeed attacked it consistently in his Diary; mainly, I think, because he felt that *someone* should be expressing the "voice of sanity".) Even then he had powerfully persuasive friends like the Communist D. N. Pritt and fellow-travellers like Zilliacus and Alexander Werth, who saw it all as a "wicked capitalist war" and induced in him frequent moods of defeatism and guilt, deepened by horror at the massive and mindless cruelties now being perpetrated in all parts of the world.

As late as 17th May 1941, in a leading article, he implied that America should put up peace terms on the lines that Germany would merely withdraw from the occupied countries. This was precisely what the Germans, who knew even by this time that they couldn't win, were then stealthily advocating in the captive Paris newspapers; and on 17th June he had a furious letter from Lady Rhondda, owner-editor of *Time and Tide*, who "disliked to see an organ of the standing of the *New Statesman* even appearing to be the British medium through which the current version of negotiated peace proposals was published in this country". Naturally in September 1940, when Hitler presented the Allies with his famous "Last Appeal to Reason", Kingsley was racked by indecision, as his *New Statesman* colleagues well knew. "The Polish and Czech problems are settled," said Hitler in effect; "all Europe is now pacified and the danger of Communism removed. What are we fighting for?"

A party of friends discussed this in C. E. M. Joad's house at Hampstead—Kingsley and Frank Hardie among them. "I hope to God we shall agree to stop it all," said Joad. Kingsley admitted that he didn't quite see what was to be gained by further bloodshed. And then, characteristically, he suddenly said: "I'll ring up Philip Noel-Baker." The others then heard one side of a telephone conversation, a monosyllabic side. "Kingsley put the receiver down," Frank Hardie told me, "and he said 'Well, that is really most preposterous. Philip says *of course* we must go on with the war. He says the object should be to restore freedom to Poland, for one thing. We shall *never* be able to do that? I don't see how we can possibly win.' Then there was a long pause. And then quite suddenly: 'But perhaps he's right after all!' "

Of Kingsley's editorial campaigns over the next four years, once he had decided against a stop-the-war movement, there is no space here to write: of the prolonged agitation for the opening of a "Second Front" in Europe, for the release of harmless alien refugees detained under Defence Regulation 18B, for adequate public air raid shelters, for the housing of bombed-out people, for the support of resistance movements in the Nazi-occupied countries, for encouraging Indian self-government (in the last two of these Dorothy played a growing and vigorous part). All of them are on record in the files of the *New Statesman*; and it has to be admitted that without a prolonged course of reading in them no one could truly assess their editor's position in the war, or his likely influence on the public and private attitudes of others. I must however return to the private man.

His name was on the list of the famous 3,000 whom the Nazis would have arrested and, quite probably, killed once "these islands" (as Churchill used to call Great Britain) were occupied. He himself was in no doubt that they would liquidate him, whether or not the alleged list was authentic; and its authenticity was established, so far as he was concerned, in September 1945 when the Allies entered Berlin and the list was discovered. "This list," tartly commented Collin Brooks, the editor of the Right-wing weekly *Truth*, whose name seems not to have been included and who was not one of Kingsley's more fervent admirers, "is one further proof of the fatuity of German espionage. Its compilers, while recognising that Conservative cabinet ministers must be regarded as enemies, appear to have cherished the ordinary German delusion that the only other opposition would come from Jews and Left-wing intellectuals."[1] As Kingsley records in *Editor*, page 279:

> invasion was taken for granted and occupation seemed likely. . . . One of the leading American journalists in this country called

[1] *Truth*, 21 September 1945.

> on me one day to discuss how I could best escape death by torture; and an MP. . . . had a better idea—he told me he planned in case of occupation to get lost as a cloth-capped worker in some factory, where he was not known. Harold Nicolson arranged with his wife Vita Sackville-West to escape "torture and humiliation" by procuring a poison pill from a friendly doctor. In reviewing his book Rebecca West remarks that most of us had taken similar precautions. Personally I carried some morphia tablets, with the rather vague idea that they might come in handy in an extremity.

But he doubted whether he or anyone else would have committed suicide "when it came to the point". I have little doubt that many of them would, and that although he wouldn't the time would have come when he wished he had. Twenty years after the war some of Kingsley's friends, to say nothing of those who were not his friends, were finding cause for merriment in the recollection of his fears at that time. They may have forgotten, they may not even have known, how utterly defenceless we were in 1940; how many intellectuals had died, or were still to die, as skeletons in Hitler's extermination camps; how the Government were planning to move to Canada and carry on the war from there; how our own factories, airfields and railways (and therefore our cities and villages) would then have been bombed by both British and American planes from North Africa and Greenland. But there is possibly a note of wry comedy in Kingsley's belief that he was the more vulnerable because (he seems to have thought) he looked like a Jew.

It was this that led him, at the height of the invasion threat, to ask Walter Hudd, the drama producer and actor-manager, for advice about "make-up" adjustments or, if need be, plastic surgery for his nose. Walter Hudd had been organising for some years a scheme for helping refugees from Germany. He assured Kingsley that he did not look Jewish and that, even if he did, a disguised appearance would not long conceal him from the Gestapo. Kingsley was, beyond doubt, a frightened man; but he had good reason to be frightened and lacked the disingenuousness to pretend that he was not. In some of those who knew him (and were perhaps themselves in no danger) this has provoked ridicule. To others, it was a side of his nature that involved him in living his life publicly and vicariously for everybody. And these, he would have been amused to know, felt rather protective about him. I have dealt with these matters out of sequence because they give depth to the story of his personal crisis at the time of the Munich Settlement in 1938. This was probably the emotional and spiritual climax of his career; and it convinced him, as a historian turned journalist, that he could never have become a politician and turned statesman.

"Some strong souls," said Critic in the London Diary on 8th October 1938, "were always convinced that Mr Chamberlain would fix up something with Hitler; and they even regard the arrival of the invitation to Munich during Mr Chamberlain's speech as a brilliant piece of stage management." Well, we know now that the "strong souls" were right about the stage management, though we can differ among ourselves as to its brilliance. It is clear enough from Sir John Wheeler-Bennett's vivid and appalling book *Munich—Prologue to Tragedy*[1] that the dramatic episode in the crowded House of Commons on 28th September 1938, with Sir John Simon interrupting Chamberlain's long and gloomy speech by handing him Hitler's telegram, was a charade. The telegram was available before Chamberlain got up to speak, let alone before he could send his fulsome reply; and he knew it was. The French prime minister, who had had a similar message, had already replied to it. C. L. Mowat says in *Britain Between the Wars:*[2]

> Bonnet had in fact anticipated Chamberlain in a message which reached Hitler first and outdid Chamberlain's in generosity. Everything was really settled on the afternoon of the 28th: the dramatic interruption of his speech was all but a put-up job.

Presumably the "all-but" means that the French premier was actually off-stage at the time. But the British leading players were all on stage; and this handful of desperate cynics must

[1] Macmillan, London, 1963. Lord Butler recalls in his book *The Art of the Possible* (Hamish Hamilton, 1971) that Wheeler-Bennett also described the Munich Settlement as "inescapable" and that this is "all the more creditable to his historical mastery".

[2] Methuen, London, 1956, p. 616.

have felt, as the thunderous applause broke about their ears, that they were the deadliest illusionists of all time. A *News Review* poster found its way into the *New Statesman*'s "This England" column: HOW CHAMBERLAIN SCARED HITLER.

Nevertheless, balancing the resolutely "stop Hitler" editorials for which Kingsley had been responsible during 1938, there were signed articles that could pave the way for a change of front. (Though it has to be conceded that unless the signature was that of Elizabeth Wiskemann, Alexander Werth, or Dick Crossman they were likely to be intuitive and "from the heart" rather than well-informed.) On 26th March, Kingsley was writing (with "Hitler in Vienna and Barcelona in flames") that

> in this struggle it is the duty of all those who value civilisation and democracy to back with all their might the forces, wherever they may be found, which oppose Fascism.

But in the same issue C. E. M. Joad, taking his cue from the Anschluss between Germany and Austria, went on to discuss Czechoslovakia's coming fate:

> Why all this fuss when the Germans have taken the very step which, before the Nazi revolution, we were prepared to regard as right and proper? The Treaty of Versailles has bedevilled Europe for 20 years: are we to fight another war, resulting in another Versailles, because it has at long last disappeared? Similar considerations apply to the case of Czechoslovakia which my friends wish to make a new *casus belli*. In Czechoslovakia there are 3,000,000 Germans. It is no doubt odd that anybody should desire to be a member of Hitler's Third Reich; but Germans *are* odd, and this, apparently, is what they do desire. Why should we be concerned to resist this desire, or be willing to asphyxiate, burn, mutilate and disembowel hundreds of thousands of human beings whom we have never seen,[1] in order to prevent Germans rejoining those from whom they should never have been separated?

Nor were the *New Statesman*'s vacillations any more violent than those of Maynard Keynes, whom Kingsley quotes so much in his autobiography. The difference was that the paper vacillated in

[1] It was an ominous anticipation of Chamberlain's famous phrase about "a quarrel in a faraway country between people of whom we know nothing".

public. If Kingsley had followed Keynes's line throughout the late thirties the *New Statesman* would have been on the whole an appeasement paper. What he said in the famous issue of 27th August 1938 was that even then it might still be possible

> if the Czechs make an imaginative offer of partnership to the Sudeten Germans, to reconcile them to the existing frontiers. But if Lord Runciman reports that this is impossible, the question of frontier revision, difficult though it is, should at once be tackled. The strategical value of the Bohemian frontier should not be made the occasion of a world war. We should not guarantee the *status quo*.

On 7th September *The Times* said much the same thing—Czechoslovakia might be a safer and more united country if it let the Sudeten German areas go to Germany; and it has always since been said that Geoffrey Dawson, the *Times* Editor, and Barrington-Ward, his Assistant Editor (though the latter was actually on leave at the time and critical of the article when he came back),[1] were much influenced by the "Cliveden Set" and hopeful that Germany would eventually destroy the USSR. Kingsley therefore found himself publicly in uncongenial company. "It was extremely upsetting to my colleagues," he said in an interview 30 years later, "and although it was logical . . . nevertheless at the moment it looked like betrayal." And he described how it happened. "I had got all the rest of the paper done and I was by myself in the office, just before press-time. Those front page notes went, in those days, very late on a Thursday morning. I wrote this down with the tremendous feeling that 'nobody else is saying this and I'm bloody well going to say it'. I actually remember going out of the door with a cold feeling in my heart—I'd said this terrible thing. And it has pursued me ever since that time. Writers simply love saying—every writer on this period says—the *New Statesman* was the first paper that wanted to give up the Czechoslovak frontier. As a matter of fact, *everybody* did."

When he recalled the affair as "extremely upsetting to his colleagues" he may have been even more accurate than he knew. Ritchie Calder had kicked his own radio set across the

[1] *In the Chair: Barrington-Ward of The Times*, Weidenfeld & Nicolson, 1969.

room. Dick Crossman told me: "I didn't even know about it until I saw it in the paper. It was an insane thing to do because he didn't *know* much about these frontiers or what it all meant. . . . It wasn't the Munich issue, it was whether, in the heat of the negotiations, a Left wing paper should suddenly give the Nazi point of view." Elizabeth Wiskemann, the paper's Central European correspondent throughout the thirties, was desolated.[1] Aylmer Vallance, Raymond Mortimer, ("I was very horrified when he came out with that note about Czechoslovakia: I hadn't seen it before or I should have made a scene"), Leonard Woolf, John Roberts, all registered their protests. Alexander Werth wrote to him from the *Manchester Guardian*'s Paris Office:

> I have not the slightest doubt that France *will* go to war in the event of an invasion of Czechoslovakia, and the opposition in the country to such a course will be nil. Flandin and other defeatists don't count, and will count even less after the mobilisation order. To let Germany get away with Czechoslovakia is to hand over the whole of Europe to Fascism. . . . Have you noticed the remarkable reactions in Poland and Rumania and even Jugoslavia in the last week? All saying that if Germany goes to war she will have Europe against her. All are taking an anti-German stand so long as England keeps it up.

Devastating letters came in from readers, the bitterest from Professors Lancelot Hogben and J. D. Bernal. Kingsley published only the politest ones, the longest and most cogently argued being from Professor Vočadlo in Prague (15th October 1938), headed FINIS BOHEMIA? But on the whole, the correspondence pages of the *New Statesman* in the post-Munich weeks would not lead you to suppose that British readers had minded very much. It may well be a consequence of this that, discussing the *New Statesman* episode with some of those who remember it, one encounters surprise that it caused much of a stir. Ivor Montagu, for example, told me that he remembered little of it though he was in close touch with Kingsley and the paper at the time, and though every other detail of the Munich crisis was clear in his exceptionally clear mind. Others say that the *New*

[1] See her book, *The Europe I Saw*, London, 1970.

Statesman note merely gave expression to what millions were thinking, as did the MP who shouted "Thank God for the Prime Minister!" when Chamberlain had staged his dramatically delayed reading of the Hitler telegram. And a Keynes letter assured Kingsley on 4th October 1938 that "the damned thing about the settlement is that from our selfish and short-sighted point of view there is so much to be said for it. Good *may* result from what no wise or good man could have brought himself to accomplish. Vile and dirty work can be beneficial to those who do it—or do you believe in the eternal justice of the world? I don't." Kingsley's anxiety was shared by his father,[1] who wrote to him from Finchley on the evening of the sell-out:

> The whole story of these negotiations is most shameful, and the final ultimatum from Chamberlain to Beneš was one of the meanest and most disgraceful things I ever heard of. The adulation given to this Deliverer is sickening enough, but the culminating disgrace is the hypocrisy and cant (perhaps unconscious) of the Archbishop, which I suppose represents the pious sentiment of our nation. A Service of Thanksgiving to God—a sermon telling us this treaty is an answer to prayer—is enough to drive thoughtful men away from all kinds of faith.

The outcome was that, exactly a month later—8th October 1938—Kingsley's London Diary was saying this:

> We knew from his past utterances that Mr Chamberlain would not champion the Czech cause if he could possibly help it. His views about Czechoslovakia and Eastern Europe were much the same as Hitler's. . . . It was especially the business of those who were known to be the most ardent pacifists to screw up their resolution and assert their readiness to run the risks of a firm stand against aggression. The whole British Press from the extreme Right to the extreme Left was solid at that minute. Hence the general anger when the public found that its resolution, attained at terrific internal cost, was mocked, that we were

[1] The Rev. Basil Martin still exerted an encouraging influence upon Kingsley, though they now saw less of each other. Basil had remarried at the age of seventy-eight. He left the Finchley house when it was bombed early in the war, and went to stay at Chipperfield, Berks, in the house of William Fiske (later Lord Fiske and leader of the Greater London Council). He died there in 1940 at the age of eighty-two.

> not making a stand at all, that the Czechs were to be sacrificed, and probably the last chance of checking Fascism without war allowed to slip by. . . . With the British Fleet mobilised, the French and Russians ready, and Czechoslovakia holding firm, Chamberlain and Daladier went to Munich holding strong cards. But that is assuming there was still an intention to put pressure on Hitler. In fact all that occurred was that the Big Four united to put pressure on the Czechs.

And as to this, when he came to write of it in his autobiography[1] he said: "My self-reproach was bitter. I felt guilty towards my friends in Czechoslovakia, who refused to admit that destruction and occupation and a world war might have been worse than the loss of independence. I also realised that in my excoriating analysis of Chamberlain's behaviour I had really been attacking myself."

But that was 30 years after the event. What he had said privately in a letter to Maynard Keynes on 19th September 1938 was what, presumably, no editor could say contemporaneously and publicly and expect to survive:

> I fear that the sell-out is going to be complete, and thinking it over I believe I was wrong even to discuss the *possibility* of a frontier revision settlement; because under no circumstances shall we get Chamberlain to co-operate with Moscow, without which condition no guarantee is worth more than the present one. I am inclined to think that the result now is worse than a world war. If the Czechs agree to the final terms put up to them. . . . I should not expect Hitler to give them an opportunity of building a new frontier, and I should think that Prague will be another and even worse Vienna before long. If the Czechs refuse, I take it that England and France are simply going to let them down, which will be almost unbearable. Worst of all the [Czech] government may be pushed into trying to accept the Chamberlain terms and be faced with a popular rising, which would be called Bolshevism and suppressed by Hitler.

And in a chapter of the autobiography which he did not live to complete, Kingsley said in a reference to Keynes's death in April 1946 ("probably the most influential man of his age")

[1] *Editor*, p. 256.

that his letters were always powerful but his judgment uncertain. "On the occasion which I made my worst editorial mistake I had followed his advice. We were in the same quagmire. Almost any solution of the German problem seemed better than war. I had made up my mind to face it, if it came, but to try every collective expediency to prevent it. He usually, with lapses, supported Baldwin and even Chamberlain; and even put up a half-hearted support, though an angry one, for Munich. He found it almost impossible, as I did, to 'start a war' in defence of Eastern Europe when some sort of peace was offered to us and we were not necessarily engaged." Kingsley's belated change of heart may have been induced by the letters he received from his old Cambridge friend Professor Vočadlo in Bratislava. In 1938 Otakar Vočadlo was head of the Department of English in the University of Komensky. Kingsley, visiting him in May, had told him that he had better send his children to England, that he still believed the Czechs should have redrawn their frontiers and got rid of their German-speaking population. "The awful thing is," he wrote when he got home, "that we shall not be able to help you materially even if we want to—it will merely be a bombing match in the West as well as in the East, and I doubt if even God knows what will be the result of that. . . . It is so heartbreaking a world now that I hardly like to write anything further to you."

"You were right," wrote Vočadlo on 19th September, "in warning us to distrust Chamberlain."

> I had thought he was just a naïve old fogey and "honest broker". But it seems to me now he is an old fox, ready to lower himself to anything to keep Russia out of Europe and barter our liberty in order to keep the colonies (since he couldn't offer Portugal's) and befriend Hitler. We trusted his words and accepted old Runciman, little thinking the latter was just used as a decoy. Runciman may not be a hypocrite, but his social contacts here (with snobs and Henleinite ex-noblemen) were highly suspicious. . . . The flight to Berchtesgaden was certainly an ingenious gesture—almost Tolstoyan and pathetic on the surface—and it confused the issue wonderfully.

Kingsley contritely asked again whether Vočadlo would now send his sons to England:

No, we don't think of sending the boys to England, though Radoslav was born there and would be entitled to some protection. Frankly I don't think you are much better off than anybody else, with all your inexhaustible resources. If you let us fall, you'll have to pay the penalty sooner or later. If the thing isn't stopped now, there can only follow a period of endless wars. . . . It was a great surprise that the contributor of your weekly is still under the delusion that the present position has anything to do with the minority problem. He (or she) must be a Quaker, whose ignorance of German aims and psychology is past cure. It is mischievous to write as if our frontiers, which have not moved since Charlemagne's time, were to become "the occasion of a world war". The article was enthusiastically commented on in the Nazi press, and indignantly repudiated in German democratic circles. I am awfully sorry, because up to now your paper has been taken very seriously in this country, and much thought of in spite of Joad's misleading article.

All my friends who read your paper turned on me, and I had to construct an explanation that you were away in Ireland and this silly misrepresentation was smuggled in in your absence. I do hope I have guessed right. But from your letter I get an uneasy feeling that you also think a revision of the frontier would help. We must have that out. From now on you can safely cross Germany. If you *were* on their blacklist, you are struck out after August 27. For once you find yourself in agreement with the Astor clique. . . . I enclose a letter to the Editor which I hope you will publish in your paper. Yours *semper idem.*

It was published, as I have said, on 15th October. It was long and reasoned and yet emotional, and is among the most interesting statements available to students of the tragedy it described. The Sudeten Germans, it said, had never wanted union with Germany. They wanted self-government. "The dictatorial decision came upon most of them as a sudden and rather terrifying surprise. . . . The tricks of ignorant and out-of-date imperialists have only succeeded in reproducing another Ulster in the heart of Europe. . . . Lord Runciman would have to spend at least three years in Czechoslovakia to understand the complications of the age-long Czech-German symbiosis." If Britain and France were really afraid of war "they were free to make a generous gesture by offering Germany some of her former colonies. It would have been more honest than buying her off with other people's possessions."

Further letters from Professor Vočadlo expressed his grief and dismay that Britain seemed unlikely even to give financial aid to the penniless refugees from the districts—some of them 100% Czech—which had been occupied by the Nazis. 20th October 1938:

> What does it all mean? *Another* betrayal? First by Chamberlain, then by Henderson in Berlin. And now. . . . We expected our friends of the Opposition to force them to keep their promises, and now we find them on Beaverbrook's isolationist platform. I am just rubbing my eyes. . . . You lend your money to Turkey: why not to us—the victims of your political blunders?[1]

On 15th March 1939 Hitler annexed the whole of Bohemia and Moravia, seized Memel from Lithuania, and tore up his "non-aggression pact" with Poland. Britain and France immediately pledged themselves to support Poland, war was at last seen to be inevitable, and truth was dead.

"What I said was precisely true," Kingsley maintained in his autobiography,[2] "but I said it at the wrong moment, when most English papers which had been clamouring for appeasement had changed their tune. I was carrying out a consistent policy, for I had always held that we should not in any circumstances go to war with Hitler unless we had a military alliance with the Soviet Union. . . . That after all had always been my policy—to tell the truth when most people were silent."

Any unfettered opportunity to tell the truth was not to recur for some years. However, wrote Kingsley in a post-war memo on "Black Propaganda", "the liar's punishment is not to be believed, and on top of that not to know whether to believe himself. That is why scepticism is so widespread after a war, which always involves an orgy of deliberate lying. Common people, realising how far they have been the victims of propaganda, become suspicious of everything they are told, declaring

[1] Another of Vočadlo's letters appears (pp. 303–4) in *A Journal Under the Terror*, by F. L. Lucas, "the wisest and best informed," writes Vočadlo, "of my Cambridge friends".

[2] *Editor*, p. 256.

that you can't believe a word you see in the papers, and that all politicians of all parties are out for themselves. This process has gone so far in Europe that the most qualified observers wonder today on what basis society is ever again to be integrated. Britain is better off than her neighbours, because we maintained our democratic institutions, and kept to a surprising extent the tradition of truthful or at least not actually false news presentation." We had broadcast the truth to the occupied countries in the belief that it was the best way of increasing British influence. But—

> Britain maintained certain radio stations which were disowned altogether by the government, and were used to conduct a brilliant campaign based on entertainment, false news, and deliberately planted rumour. . . . Sooner or later someone who was engaged in this propaganda will write an authoritative book and let the public know the source of many wild rumours and lies which even now confuse the minds of people all over the world.... By spreading lies to undermine the morale of Nazi supporters, "black" propaganda so muddied the wells of truth that many who were opponents of the Nazis became bewildered, while the Nazis were often encouraged rather than demoralised by the lively and entertaining broadcasts aimed at their undoing. . . . I well remember one day finding friends of mine in this hush-hush world who were deeply perplexed about a strange problem. How were they to persuade the British Cabinet not to act on information which had found its way into the secret and authoritative reports, but which my friends the black propagandists had themselves invented a week or two before? . . . It is good fun to sit in a back room and think out ways of deceiving the enemy, but in a world in which communications are universal there is no way of deceiving the enemy which may not also deceive one's friends.

Bertrand Russell wrote in a letter from prison in May 1918: "One sees how our generation is a little mad, because it has allowed itself glimpses of the truth, and the truth is spectral, insane, ghastly. . . . But for my part, I would rather be mad with truth than sane with lies." Kingsley throughout the war was hoping to keep at least temporarily sane with lies.

Chapter 14

THE BOTTLENECK

THIS IS ANOTHER point at which one must turn aside from world events, mass movements, the weekly spasm, and bring forward one or two individuals who were part of Kingsley's professional and daily life. It happened that I first met him in the company of John Roberts, then "business manager" of the paper. They were quite happily conspiring (for reasons that I can't recall though John's natural benevolence may have had much to do with it) to launch me as a journalist. It was July 1937, and I clearly remember that their conversation at lunch took in, at the very least, A. P. Herbert's new divorce reform bill; the "United Front" (the Communists and the ILP were going to transform the Labour movement); the abdication crisis; Guernica; Mosley's extinction by the new Public Order Act; Chamberlain's new "National" government; and me. Knowing neither of them, I supposed them to be on the best of terms and to have these far-ranging conversations at regular intervals. I learned later that the occasion was probably unique.

John Roberts had taken me into Kingsley's room to collect him for lunch, and I shall always remember Kingsley's greeting—eyes twinkling, mouth wide open in what I took for mock astonishment but may, I now think, have been his customary incautious pleasure at meeting new people, and the comment that the place suggested for lunch would be "jolly" (a word he used all his life). He produced some topical *mot* at which we all laughed (John the loudest) while he put his jacket on—which he did, then and always, in a manner that I believe to be unique. He first threw the jacket round his shoulders like a cape, and then manipulated both arms into the sleeves at once. Years later I asked him why he always did this and he was surprised at the implication that there was some other way. Out of curiosity we tried each other's method, failed, and resumed our ordinary lives.

We were joined during the lunch by Ernst Willison, then advertising manager, with whom Kingsley was on terms of very close friendship though, like most other people, he never once spelled the poor man's first name correctly (Willison used to mourn about the Unimportance of being Ernst). He had come to the *New Statesman* in 1926 as advertising manager and, by way of demonstrating their value as an inexhaustible source of revenue, had built up the "Classified Advertising" pages until they attained the status of a national institution, reflecting readers' interests as various as mind-training, Marxism, family planning, holidays in Greece with three total strangers, sauna baths and "Attractive widow, warm, generous, house, car, interested arts . . .". In 1947 he was business manager while John Roberts was managing director. He was a Scot, slightly built, sandy, and impressively deliberate. Like all Scots, he was an engineer and a skilful horticulturist, and like the majority of Scots I've known he was very companionable. Kingsley used to say that merely to exchange greetings as you passed him in an office corridor was to make you feel that the world was a little better; and it happens that this was absolutely true. His main importance to Kingsley, though Kingsley may not have been fully aware of it, was as a catalyst in the endless hostilities with John Roberts.

Roberts was a friend of mine, and of most men, and I owe him much. This enables me to say the more cogently that if I had been in Kingsley's place I should probably have done my best to get rid of him, and, having failed, given up the editorship. I know that Kingsley sometimes had bad dreams about him. And yet, John Roberts and Willison, said Kingsley in *Editor* (page 13)—

> worked with enthusiasm and success to overcome the advertisers' resistance to making use of a Left-Wing journal. *On this matter*, which might so easily have led to the kind of friction that is always supposed to exist between the editor and the manager of a paper, we never quarrelled at all. I did not interfere with the business side of the paper; and John, who must often have cursed our editorial views, refrained from trying to influence my politics.

An extraordinary statement. I suppose he felt it should be made. The phrase I have italicised, which limits the cause of friction to the single area where there was virtually no friction at all, was diplomatically chosen. The friction came to a head immediately after the Munich crisis and Kingsley's weeks of agonising hesitation. "I am going to unload a few thoughts that have been in my mind for some time past," wrote John Roberts to him on 3rd October 1938:

> The internal situation of your side of the paper which existed a week ago very naturally gave me deep concern. I saw an immediate prospect of you either resigning or being forced to take a holiday, leaving the running of the paper in the hands of Lloyd, with perhaps the assistance of Vallance, Crossman, Brailsford or Cole. Lloyd's health made it impossible, in my view, for him to take this responsibility, indeed he plainly told me so; and you yourself would not have felt happy to have handed over the editorship, even temporarily, to any of the others mentioned.
>
> Realising the position, you decided to make a great personal effort to carry on and we all admired you for it. Nevertheless I am hoping that something can be done to avoid the recurrence of such a situation. I have been asking myself what can be done. I see Lloyd and Raymond [Mortimer], and possibly Stonier, working under conditions which are far from happy and, therefore, I am bound to conclude that they cannot under such conditions put their best into the paper. I would be blind if I did not see what is wrong. You must give me the credit of appreciating the terribly difficult conditions under which you have all been working during the past few weeks, but although those conditions have accentuated your troubles, you know as well as I do that things have not been going smoothly for a long time.
>
> The real cause of the trouble is yourself. Largely out of the goodness of your heart you allow yourself to be imposed upon by all sorts of people and their causes. You dash off to various parts of the country to address meetings when you should be, in my opinion, taking advantage of the intervals between getting another issue ready to relax or to have time for quiet thinking. Your manner of living, in short, seriously reacts on some members of your staff and on me. We hear you making the most wild observations and tremble to think what is going into the next issue of the paper. Generally we are relieved to find that what

> actually appears in print is very different from what you have been saying in the early part of the week; but this constant anxiety wears us all down and, I submit, it cannot possibly be for the good of the paper. . . .
>
> I was rather upset a week or so ago when you discussed with others the question of your resignation before discussing it with me. If I had any thought of resigning I would always discuss the matter with you first, as I am doing now. Instead of writing you this letter I might have poured out my thoughts to the Chairman, but this I would never do in loyalty to what I regard as a partnership between you and me. Moreover, it would be an unfriendly act towards you, and you know that this is the last thing that I would have in mind.

I can find no reply to this letter, nor is there proof that it was ever sent. But it is an early and powerful indication of the relationship between the two men. Nevertheless, Roberts was on intermittently tolerable terms with Kingsley until about 1945, and thereafter the fact that they "got on" at all was, to those who knew, miraculous. You can judge the limits of their mental contact from Kingsley's belief that "John must often have cursed our editorial views". Politically he was often to the Left of Kingsley, and any editorial views he cursed would have been cursed too by others in the office. But Kingsley was not alone, among the paper's governing enclave, in his exasperation with Roberts. A sequel to one of the numerous rows, involving Leonard Woolf rather than the editor, was a memo from Woolf to Kingsley in 1945, typical of several he wrote about Roberts:

> If we were in Hungary I would be saying, like Rakosi (who is also 65) that I had come to realise that my mistakes, as a result of the cult of personality and against the laws of Commercialism, were more serious than I had at first thought. I had done great damage to the Paper. If I stayed at my post I would hamper the development of Commercialism. My resignation would then be accepted and the Chairman would praise my "historic merits".
>
> But we are not in Hungary.

John Roberts's father was a metal-worker, and known in the Bermondsey area as a fine craftsman; a mild and friendly person, showing none of the dynamism that John displayed from boyhood. There were eleven children in the family, living in a small tenement which was therefore uncomfortably overcrowded. By the time he was 16 John, who had worked at Eyre & Spottiswoode's from the age of 13, was, in effect, manager of a small publishing firm known as Alston Rivers—which later published the *New Statesman*. His life might then have taken a different turn, for at about that time a local curate who was teaching him Latin got him into a theological college, and there was a definite plan that he should go into the Church. But he came back to help with his brothers and sisters. He was already thoroughly accustomed to taking the lead; and an example of his confident methods may be seen in the fact that he then found a bigger house for the family, made all the financial and other arrangements for the removal, and took a day off from work to settle them in. After one or two job-changes "on the way up", which included a brief participation in an attempt by W. H. Smith & Son to launch themselves as book publishers, he arrived at *The Athenaeum* as deputy manager. He moved on through the business managership of *Public Opinion* to the *New Statesman*, arriving there in February 1914 as, in effect, advertising manager. He was then 23, and very soon after the War began he enlisted voluntarily in the army.

This annoyed Beatrice Webb very much. "If you insist on joining the Army before there is any need for you to do so," she said, "you need not expect to come back here." She was overruled by the other Directors and Roberts was given a £52 annual retainer (which he gave up in 1916 because it bound him to return to a paper that looked unlikely to survive). He fought throughout the war in France, became an infantry sergeant, and collaborated with the poet Martin Armstrong in publishing the famous little magazine *The Wipers Times*.[1]

He came back to the *New Statesman* at the beginning of 1919, just as Kingsley was going up to Cambridge; and the following year he was appointed business manager. The *New Statesman*'s circulation was then about 7,000, the paper was making an annual loss of about £6,000, its backers were still making this good from their own pockets, and Roberts had to convince them not only that better times were coming but that they

[1] Wipers being the British Army's pronunciation of Ypres.

would come because of him. Against considerable odds he did both. By 1928 the paper was actually making a profit. Clifford Sharp, who had also been away in the Forces, had come back about five months after Roberts to resume the editorship, and there ensued an editor-manager relationship which should have been a toughening rehearsal for what was to come in Kingsley's time. In *The New Statesman 1913–1963*, Edward Hyams—who had discussed these early days with John Roberts for the purposes of his book—says[1]

> To Roberts, Sharp was an unfriendly intellectual snob, contemptuous of the business side and unwilling to cooperate with the manager even to the extent of running a special Christmas number which might earn a little money for the company.

John Roberts was in fact peculiarly sensitive to what he saw as intellectual snobbery, though he often gave that name to the rather unhappy *gaucherie* of the scholar and aesthete who is puzzled by some suddenly revealed limitation of his own hothouse world. And in John's contacts with the *New Statesman*'s editorial circle there was much scope for these misunderstandings. He did not, I think, accept his limitations with the equanimity that leads to happiness. Nevertheless he told me often that he found absolutely no snobbery in Kingsley, and indeed there is little doubt, comparing these two, that if there was any of it in the truest sense it was John's.

The turning of the corner in 1928 would probably have been a short-lived development if Sharp had not at that time begun to fade out. He was likely enough to ruin the paper at any moment with some idiotic breach of the laws about defamation and contempt of Court. But he left behind him a legacy of commercial fear about libel damages that did much to shape the John Roberts–Kingsley relationship and maintain that shape until Roberts "retired" in 1957. (I will return to justify the quotation marks.) Kingsley always understood the defamation laws better than John, as you could perceive whenever you heard them arguing about a specific case. When it was proposed in 1954 to publish a *New Statesman* pamphlet attacking Senator McCarthy of Wisconsin and his egregious anti-communist

[1] P. 79.

witch-hunt, Roberts was quite unmoved by Kingsley's argument that "few publications of a political character do not contain some technical libels" and that Senator Benton "had already published a scurrilous attack on McCarthy to force him to take an action but McCarthy, having filed one, withdrew it". Kingsley and Roberts wrote each other enormous letters about this, having reached the point (as they often did) where face-to-face discussion was impossible. The US Senate, said Kingsley in one such letter in May 1954, "has itself published and put on the shelf a dossier of McCarthy's past which makes it quite impossible, in my view, for him to obtain damages here or anywhere else. If we really could induce McCarthy or any of his friends to take action it would be the best thing we ever did and certainly the best for the prestige and sale of the paper".

Many people in America, Roberts countered, supported McCarthy in spite of disliking him and his methods. "That," said Kingsley, "is the reason for attacking him; hundreds of thousands of people in America welcome such attacks because they rightly refuse to be bamboozled by the argument that he is doing a good job and should therefore be left alone. From the libel point of view the case is parallel with that of Hitler, who was also supported by the majority of Germans on exactly the same grounds that appear to have impressed you about McCarthy." This last phrase was certain to prolong the row. Roberts had not said that the majority argument "impressed" him, and he hated McCarthyism as much as anyone. Kingsley, he complained, had wanted to talk to him about the pamphlet on a Thursday morning at the printers, "in the middle of trying to read the last few pages of the paper" . . . and so it went on. In the end Kingsley angrily scrapped the pamphlet and relationships were worse than ever.

I think it is possible, but not certain, that if Kingsley had known John Roberts and his domestic circumstances more intimately he would have been more forbearing and there would have been fewer rows. The circumstances were sad enough. John's second wife Joanna, 20 years younger than he, was already afflicted at the time of their marriage with disseminated sclerosis (and he knew she was but tried not to believe it). She was at first gay, vivacious, attractive and immaculately smart, shared his love of the theatre, books and music (he had a profound love of music), and was his perfect companion. Her father was a master at Charterhouse. In 1946 Kingsley spent a week-end at their house at West Hoathly—it was intended as a pipe-of-peace gesture. John had two-year-old twin boys, and Kingsley, who took a great fancy to them, took an even greater fancy (as well he might) to Joanna. But as her fatal illness developed despite all the "cures" and treatments that John could expensively buy, she became more and more difficult and querulous and needed continuing attention. (Actually she survived John by two or three years.) He often arrived at the office after a sleepless night spent trying to calm her fears and irritability, and having left her at the height of some insoluble and ridiculous quarrel. I shall never know how, in the circumstances, he ever contrived to do any work of any kind.

There were, however, repeated rows with Kingsley about projects for increasing the paper's circulation, or at least for arresting a decline which was setting in during the early fifties. Roberts thought that a reason for the decline was that people were fed up with a paper that depressed them, and he told Kingsley so in a long letter written at home on a Sunday afternoon (17th May 1954):

> They are tired of reading a paper which, justifiably it may be, expresses each week no great hope for the future. We have often joked about our public preferring the sugar to the pill and reading first the Competitions, "This England" and the lighter parts of the paper. As an ordinary reader I can well appreciate this. People I meet have so often said to me that they have given up the paper altogether, or now read it only occasionally, because it depresses them.

There were rows about overseas sales promotion—"Of course it would be very nice," said Roberts, "to have somebody travelling abroad doing sales promotion for us, but have you ever tried it? I have seen the trade people in most of the countries in Europe, and the results, without exception, have been most disappointing. They will undertake to push out specimen copies or leaflets if you will pay them, but the results have always been most miserably ineffective. . . . The way to get readers is to draw them to the newsagents." (Yet at a Board meeting in September that year he was saying that he "had no belief at all in pushing the paper through increased sales on bookstalls". The only scheme he believed in was the "acquaintance subscription" scheme, by which old readers introduced new ones at a short-term bargain-basement price.)

Perhaps above all, Roberts felt defeated by the failure of the "editorial side" to plan new features far enough ahead. "We cannot at short notice set about an advertising campaign with insufficient information." And this at all events was, in Kingsley's time, a fair managerial complaint. He hated "forward planning", articles in series, special issues, even Christmas numbers.

At another time Kingsley wanted to establish a "progressive" Institute of Foreign Affairs, "to do for the *New Statesman* public, and for a wider audience, what Chatham House has long ceased to do". He once came near to starting something of the kind with some unexpected American money, but the project fell through. Then he read in the *Manchester Guardian* what he described as "a violent attack on Chatham House" which revived the idea in his mind. In January 1954 he put it to John Roberts, who said he liked the plan and would look for a suitable building. Five months later Kingsley was writing to him:

> I have not heard more of this, and in view of your many commitments and worries I am not at all critical of you on that account. But I do think you should understand the dilemma in which I am placed. I now feel stymied because, having mentioned it to you, I can scarcely without offence look elsewhere, and I realise that so big a project cannot be undertaken by you in addition to your present burden. This typifies my difficulty.

You have to remember that these two men were sitting daily in the same small building, their offices within hailing distance, and yet writing letters to each other from home. Roberts was outraged at the suggestion that he had gone to sleep over the proposal for an Institute of Foreign Affairs:

> We had *one* talk about this, at which I warmly accepted the idea in principle, saying I was ready to go into the subject more thoroughly any time you were ready. . . . You, however, have never mentioned the subject to me since we had that one and only talk. I think this is a worthwhile idea and if we ever get to the point of deciding to do it, obviously the first move would be to appoint a Director on whose shoulders most of the work of finding suitable premises and organising the thing from the start would fall. That surely is no more than common-sense.

What is equally sure is that if the plan for an Institute of Foreign Affairs had occurred first to Roberts, and he had been as excited about it as Kingsley was, it would have been established within months despite almost any degree of opposition from the Board of Directors. And nothing could illustrate more sharply than this the difference between the two men. To point it up, there is the extraordinary story of Ganymed Press.

This was a German art-reproduction process, commercially ruined by the war, and available afterwards as a business proposition to anyone with the money to set up new premises and the initiative to go and fetch the shattered machinery from its bombed-out home in Hamburg. In 1947 John Roberts persuaded the *New Statesman*'s directors to put up sums of money which in the end amounted to £35,000, fetched the machinery (and some indispensable German technicians) from Hamburg, rented a factory, equipped a small picture gallery next door to the *New Statesman* office, chose the first half-dozen pictures for reproduction (having enlisted the aid of Sir John Rothenstein by way of pre-empting criticism), and Ganymed Press was in business. At last John Roberts had an outlet for a creative side of his personality which had long been starved; and when John was being creative there was a tendency among experienced bystanders to stand well back. He put such thought and careful manœuvring into every step that he felt, or rather he knew, that his must be the last word on the subject. No one, for example, could possibly have any reason for choosing a different picture for reproduction. He absolutely insisted on his choice, because he wanted people "to have the opportunity of loving pictures that were indisputably great works of art". In this he had some of the hearty bulldozing benevolence of a multilateral publishing giant marketing what is called a part-work.

Ganymed Press London Ltd had a hard fight but deservedly won its way to financial independence: its fine reproductions can now be seen all over the world. It never really won its way into the hearts of Kingsley Martin or Leonard Woolf, where it had to compete with some fairly strong feeling about other subsidiary enterprises which Roberts had tucked under the *New Statesman*'s fully extended wing: *Further Education*, the *Journal of Education*, *Turnstile Press* and others. Woolf's feeling may be judged from a letter to Kingsley on 31st May 1956:

> I have come to the conclusion that I had better resign from the Board of the *New Statesman and Nation*. I can spend my time more usefully than at meetings such as that of last Tuesday. I arrived at 2.25 and left at 4.35. For approximately two hours out of the two hours and ten minutes John Roberts poured out a stream of self-congratulatory statements of what he had done and what he intended to do with the *New Statesman*. When after about an hour of this I made my first remark he said to me: "Please, Leonard, allow me to finish what I was saying?" When I persisted the Chairman, Douglas Cole, who always supports Roberts and allows him to go on repeating himself for two hours, began to say that it was not possible to estimate the probable loss [on the *Journal of Education*]; and it was only your intervention on my side which enabled us to discuss even what we did discuss. . . . The meeting ended, as our meetings nearly always end, by the Board agreeing to a proposal by Dick Plummer that a decision be postponed for six months.
>
> The profits of the *New Statesman* have in recent years been used to meet the losses on a third-rate publishing business, the losses on a second-rate educational journal, the losses on reproducing a large number of good, bad and indifferent pictures, and on increasing the emoluments of some employees[1] . . . I am opposed to this policy. I think that the profits on the *New Statesman* should be spent on improving the *New Statesman* and controlled by the Board of Directors. I could of course put this view before the Board, and I have considered doing so. I have reluctantly decided that it would be a pure waste of time. I do not think there is a

[1] For some reason Leonard Woolf was an implacable opponent, at board meetings, of staff salary increases, bonuses and pension schemes.

chance of my getting any real support from the other Directors. Douglas would probably be in the chair, opposed to me, and allowing Roberts to go on talking uninterruptedly.

This powerful little bomb haunted the wings, so to speak, for at least seven months before it was allowed, heavily sand-bagged, to go off. On 4th January 1957 Kingsley wrote to G. D. H. Cole to say that the Directors were having a lunch-time meeting at the Garrick Hotel to decide what to do about it. "From a conversation I had with John Roberts yesterday it looks as if he will make some statement fully accepting that it is the duty of the Managing Director to abide by the Board, and in that case it would be most unwise to begin with a demand for his resignation."

In the end Roberts was virtually bribed into retirement, as a decent alternative to sacking a man who had done so much for the paper, an operation which would have seemed to him—and not only to him—like cutting the dog off the tail. He retired believing himself to be totally indispensable, gradually discovering that he was not, but consoling himself by paying full court now to the Lorelei that had seduced him, Ganymed Press London Ltd. In any case, his position on the *New Statesman* board was by that time much weakened. A Trust had been formed to hold the voting shares and fend off any take-over bidders; John's shares had accordingly passed to the Trust; and Kingsley, having in effect packed the Board with literary men, had during the same period established the convention that discussing editorial matters at a Board meeting was rather like passing betting-slips in church. Kingsley's attitude at this time is to be judged from a letter he composed for Roberts's final education and (perhaps fortunately) never sent:

> You asked me last week to tell you frankly why in my view we are not nowadays in harmony. I found it a very difficult question to answer or to promise to be frank about because it involved so much that was personal and which I fear you will resent. . . . I have differed from you vehemently and continuously about the use that should be made of the paper's profits. I was shocked and alarmed at the time we went up to ninepence, and our circulation dropped, that nothing at all was done on the managerial side to

counteract this downward trend. You may recall—I still have the correspondence—that because I did not like opposing you at the Board I wrote you two long letters about the things I thought wanted doing. You replied rejecting every suggestion. After many months of Board meetings which were incredibly painful to us all, you agreed to do the things which every other similar paper does, and to do some of the publicity which you had objected to as a waste of money. You were angry when I said you had been absorbed in Ganymed and Willison had been failing.[1]

You told me, as a new discovery some months afterwards, that Willison had not been doing the job, and that you would have to put aside thoughts you had had of virtually retiring from the job of managing the paper. You also boasted of the excellent results of doing a few of the things that *all* other members of the Board had thought necessary and which you had refused to do. All this is back history, which is on the record in our correspondence, and in the minutes, and in the memory of all those who are concerned with the welfare of the paper.

Meanwhile we were spending money like water on other projects, which I thought should be spent on pushing the paper all over the world. . . . We spent as much as £35,000 on Ganymed—which at least is a project that is in itself commendable, even if expensive and not the way I should have liked to spend so much cash. You spent 12 or 15 thousand on a very ineffective publishing business[2] and an extremely expensive monthly; and it took years of work, and many sleepless nights, and an expense of spirit such as you cannot imagine, to end these ludicrous activities. This (as it seemed to me and to the Board as a whole) meaningless struggle on your part to be permitted to throw the money we made down the drain did, I admit, remove from me the respect that I had felt in the past for you as the manager who had played so large a part in building the paper's prosperity up to 1945. [Then follows a reference to John's own salary, to a couple of interest-free loans he was enjoying, and—above all—to a claim that he felt entitled to "some share in the capital value of the

[1] Willison was in fact seriously unwell, and it was only now, in his absence, that we realised the peace-making role he had been playing for years. He died in October 1954, and for the next three years I found myself playing, most inadequately, his role as catalyst.

[2] If Turnstile Press was "ineffective" it was largely because John Roberts, having appointed its managerial staff, simply would not leave them alone and yet had no time to do otherwise.

paper".] Why, in Heaven's name? Am I so entitled? I would not know how to put such a case, though I suppose my case would be, to put it mildly, at least as good as yours.

A fitting end to the story (which of course has taken us chronologically astray) is perhaps to be found in a letter Kingsley wrote to Gerald Barry on 3rd December 1954:

> The truth is that John wishes, naturally and reasonably, to be head, as David Low puts it, of a little empire in Great Turnstile; but that sort of ambition involves the choosing of suitable men to run the various satrapies or subsidiaries with a large measure of independence. I don't think John Roberts has the remotest notion of this; so that, in effect, he has become a gigantic bottleneck.

Kingsley probably meant a very large and immovable bottle with a very small neck. But there was one respect in which John Roberts, as a bottleneck, was larger than the bottle he was supposed to control: he was the most open-handed spender I have ever known, even more with his own money than with the profits of the *New Statesman*. One thinks of this when Kingsley, accusing himself of small meannesses, ascribes it to the poverty of his childhood. By comparison, the poverty of John Roberts's childhood was Asiatic.

I knew him for 30 years, and it seemed to me that he never changed in appearance throughout that time: a strongly-built man 6 foot 2 inches tall, with a slight stoop, a loping walk, and a readiness to burst into hunched-up giggling laughter much more often than you might suppose from the story I have had to tell. He was seldom ill, and he died in his sleep on Christmas night, 1967.

Chapter 15

KINGSLEY'S ENGLISH: PRESS AND BROADCASTING

KINGSLEY WAS A man with several different prose styles of his own, a remarkably quick appreciation of attractive or boring styles in others, and an eye for the comic in rhetoric or journalese. He made many little collections of politicians' statements about profound truth, searching enquiry, honestly facing facts (could one dishonestly face a fact, or would the dishonesty consist in turning one's back on it?). "I am interested in the language of politicians," he wrote in the London Diary. "J. H. Thomas always refers to the treaty with Ireland as a 'Solemn Treaty'. Which treaties are not solemn?"

It says much for his exasperation with John Roberts that it could have betrayed him into the bottleneck image, for he had a comic collection of bottlenecks which he had taken up from Lord Conesford, who had begun it in the *Saturday Evening Post* on 13th July 1957. Kingsley was hoping to use all these bottlenecks in an article, and once offered them to me but decided after all that he had earned the right to use them himself. (He never did.) Lord Conesford's collection, all from the daily press, included:

1. Bottlenecks must be ironed out.
2. The economy of the Ruhr is bound to move within a vicious circle of interdependent bottlenecks.
3. One bottleneck which is particularly far-reaching and decisive. . . .

"My collection now includes," wrote Lord Conesford to him on 11th February 1960, "bottlenecks described as human, vital, aggravated, supreme, over-riding and world-wide. I have read the patriotic call 'Man the bottlenecks' and the poetic 'Is a bottleneck approaching?'"

Even on his way to South Africa at the age of sixteen,

Kingsley had written a contemplative little piece about the conventional description of a ship's company as "1,500 souls". "Why souls?" he said. "They've probably got souls, but since they are nearly all seasick wouldn't it be better to call them 1,500 stomachs? It's the over-eating that stamps them as a community. 'It is feared that the S.S. *Bulawayo* has foundered with 1,500 stomachs.' And why 'foundered'? Does it mean sinks or not? I must look it up." It is the earliest instance of his conscious word-mockery that I have found.

He was interested in categorical denials. An MP, described in a *New Statesman* leader as a pacifist, wrote to say that his answer to this was a categorical denial. "If we had called him a dozen things and he thought he was none of them," said Kingsley, "then one categorical denial might be a way of disposing of them all at the same time, as a category." Yet labelling varied in importance in his estimation: if a man painted pictures for sale you could, he thought, call him both an artist and a merchant. For this reason (or so he pretended) he turned down in 1958 a paragraph sent to him for publication by E. M. Forster, which is interesting to read today:

> A correspondent who was at the Royal Academy Banquet on May 11 writes: By far the most striking event of the evening was the speech by the Lord Chancellor, which has not been fully reported even in the *Daily Telegraph*. Having said that painting was almost a pre-requisite for admission to Ministerial rank, and having thus paid it the highest compliment he could, Lord Kilmuir concluded his speech by saying that it was the duty of his Ministry to protect three institutions in particular, and that they were the Crown, Religion, and Business. Since he was addressing an institution devoted to the Arts, I could scarcely believe my ears. Had he not perhaps said "Art"? No, he had said Business. Others heard him say it too. Perhaps he thought he was addressing the Royal Academy of Businesses.

It was seldom that Kingsley—or, I suppose, any editor—would reject a contribution from E. M. Forster, though even Forster came under the lash of the paper's most watchful critic, S. K. Ratcliffe, who wrote enormous letters to Kingsley from America all through the second World War. "How many writers in England are there better than E. M. Forster, or as good?" wrote Ratcliffe on 10th June 1941:

> As careful, or with a finer ear? Yet he has joined the Ittites! Amazing. Now I ask you, and him, with great respect; look at the first column . . ."It is worth it, it is worth . . . it is the tradition." I believe you were the first, in the Diary, to call attention to this odd development, which lately has run riot in certain quarters. The war on the substantive. Let us go back to Macaulay.

Kingsley once told me that the long article on "It" in Fowler's *Modern English Usage* (of which Ratcliffe would clearly have approved) was written because Fowler had nothing more important to occupy his mind. He would have said this only in certain moods; but he does say in *Father Figures* (page 196) that the *New Statesman* when Ratcliffe was a regular contributor—which was under the previous editorship—was "terribly monotonous".

When he had written a London Diary paragraph in which he was well pleased, he had a way of handing it to someone for comment as soon as the proof came back from the printer's (but not before). If you then ventured to show him that it was in some small way ungrammatical he would alter it at once, but he did it as though you had asked him to brush an insect or a crumb off the paper. It was not what he was asking you about and it was not interesting. More often than not the error would survive, because at the end of the day he was using a different set of proofs. I once ventured to remind him that Britannica had only one T, and as he absentmindedly and indulgently changed it he put two Cs. When the London Diary came out (21st September 1940) the two Ts were back again. And there they are to this day.

"I note that small bad slips in grammar are frequently passed," said Ratcliffe in another letter of reproof. "You permit several of your writers to follow the shocking American usage 'One of those that is . . .'." But this was merely one of the blemishes that Kingsley quite deliberately ignored—indeed he seemed almost to adopt them—in the pursuit of liveliness and informality. I myself ventured to show him an example in the proofs of *Editor* (page 159). J. A. Hobson, he had written (nor did he change it),

> was one of those rare persons who was completely unspoilt by the neglect of his contemporaries.

There were (there still are) equally slapdash sentences in the same book, all of which I showed him on the proofs, and all of which survived either because he delayed too long or because he thought I was rather an ass. Here are half-a-dozen of them:

> I had tried my hand at WEA lecturing, which I could have done well if I had had the modesty to realise that imparting knowledge to the ignorant requires at least as much, if not more, solid preparatory work than lecturing to the sophisticated (page 3).

> The ruling Class in this country have various ways of dealing with revolutionaries. Where it cannot buy them its usual method is flattery. But Maxton refused the "aristocratic embrace", so they have found another way (page 55).

> I now doubted whether the Labour Party, as we knew it, would solve the problem of unemployment and social misery and equally sure that Communism was impossible and undesirable in the West (page 66).

> The endless argument about Russia, however, was not all, or even the most memorable, part of one's visit (page 99).

> Photographs of these weapons and a story of Communist hooliganism was to appear in the Press next day (page 157).[1]

> Victor Gollancz was only one of thousands who was outraged by what he felt was a monstrous betrayal which made war inevitable (page 206, on the Nazi-Soviet Pact).

Which is exactly where we came in. As if to show that it was no accident, in 1963 he wrote of Lord Beveridge that he would be "remembered as one of the men who has contributed most to the form of socialism accepted by Britain, though he was no socialist". When *Father Figures* was published he had a letter from an old friend upbraiding him for using what the *New*

[1] A case can be made out for this, but I don't believe it would be Kingsley's case.

Yorker had called "the Omnipotent Whom". On page 100, the letter pointed out, there was a phrase about "the wicked old men whom we felt were responsible for the war". The writer thought it might be the result of careless proof-reading, "but it soon turned up again on page 108, and once more on page 119". But who-for-whom seems now to be regarded as a barren controversy, and Kingsley was always impatient with it though he usually conformed if he caught himself (or was caught) in time.

He liked clear writing and was himself a master of it, in any of his moods and styles. His books fell, I suppose, into three stylistic classes: the donnish, the polemical, and the London Diary type of protest, reminiscence, raillery and "ribbing". Some of them overlapped here and there. The donnishness, and the most careful writing, are to be found in *The Triumph of Lord Palmerston* (1924 and 1963) and even more in *French Liberal Thought in the Eighteenth Century* (1929 and 1955). The polemical, where the quality of the writing yields a little to the excitement, includes *The British Public and the General Strike* (1927), *Low's Russian Sketch-book* (1932), *The Magic of Monarchy* (1937), *Propaganda's Harvest* (1942) and *The Press the Public Wants* (1947). *Harold Laski, A Memoir* (1953) is hard to place because so much of it was written by his collaborator Norman MacKenzie. But his last two books, *Father Figures* (1966) and *Editor* (1968), are pure London Diary: readability, discursiveness, brilliant observation and to hell with grammar if it gets in the way of meaning. The less careful he was syntactically, and in the London Diary he often threw this kind of care to the winds, the more clearly his meaning came through. It was his own special kind of perversity. He had a resolutely lowbrow attitude astonishing in a man whose editorial position made him the high priest of what many people saw as the acme of highbrow publishing. He greatly disliked having foreign words in the paper—or at any rate in the front half. He once insisted that Aylmer Vallance should find an English substitute for *de haut en bas*, which, considering the context (protested Aylmer) was difficult and silly; and although I once convinced him that we had no English equivalent for *agent provocateur* (the phrase, not the man) I did it only by arguing that we were too hypocritical to confer an English name upon a nasty political gambit imported from Russia through France.

As for the back half of the paper, he rather expected some of that to be less intelligible but accepted it with a better grace if it was unintelligible in verse. He once asked if Proust and Brecht could be forgotten for a few weeks (they were being much used at the time for purposes of comparison), but he never went so far as Harold Wallace Ross of the *New Yorker*, who "once tacked an order on the bulletin-board which read: 'Otto Kahn has been mentioned six times recently. There will be no more mentions of him for six months.'"[1]

The *New Statesman*'s editors have had no bulletin-board. But to look through its published verse from 1930 to 1960 is to realise how the agonising complexity of modern poets must have worried Kingsley; though it is quite wrong to say, as has been said by people who worked closely with him, that he had no mind or ear for poetry. If he thought, as Carlyle did, that poetry and religion were a product of the small intestines he did so as a man of feeling. He could still think of poets, with Shelley, as "the unacknowledged legislators of the world"; and he told the Fabian Society in a lecture in 1960 (by which date he had written off Soviet Communism), that "like Plato, who would have no poets in his society, the Soviet Union will allow no disturbing influences". Certainly he once asked me to find for him, because it had touched him and he wanted to quote and remember it, the essay in which A. E. Housman says that

> experience has taught me, when I am shaving of a morning, to keep watch over my thoughts, because if a line of poetry strays into my memory my skin bristles so that the razor ceases to act.

It is probable that Kingsley seldom bristled over *New Statesman* poetry, but he had great trust in his literary men and was usually pleased to publish what had commended itself to them. There were exceptions. Janet Adam Smith, a literary editor in whom his confidence was rightly unshakable, once put in a short poem in Lallans by Sydney Goodsir Smith. Kingsley saw it for the first time when the literary pages had all

[1] James Thurber, *The Years With Ross*, Grosset & Dunlap, New York, 1957, p. 100.

been made up. What was this? Lallans? (Scottish Lowlands vernacular, somebody explained.) He didn't believe it. There was no such thing, the *Shorter Oxford Dictionary* knew it not, this was a practical joke, something that had strayed from the Competition page. He was persuaded, in it went, and resignedly he shared his readers' perplexity.

He may have shared it, too, over a poem of Donald Davie's,[1] which he saw for the first time at the printer's. He took it out, substituting another poem that had been held over. Before she could get it published, Janet had to see him and go through it line by line, parsing and analysing and explaining. "It was rather a good exercise for *me*," she explained to me later: "and when I'd finished he said 'Well, Janet, if you see something in it I suppose it's all right.' He had a deep suspicion that people were trying to impose on him, a suspicion about obscurity for obscurity's sake. I think," she added, "that people *are* often humbugged by this 'instant poetry' for declaiming at Festival Hall—things like that. But there is a period, when one is growing up, when poetry suddenly seems to express a whole world of sensations. It is the poems you read *then* that stick: even if you lose the taste for poetry in general you go on reading them—Shelley and Keats and Swinburne. I don't think Kingsley ever subsequently made the effort to get to grips with poetry." Here is the Donald Davie poem; he himself disapproves of it now and omits it from his collected poems,[2] but he felt that he was then being encouraged to write—and did write—better things. This one appeared on 30th April 1955:

The Ruins of Rome

Stranger in Rome, seeking abroad for Rome,
"The peoples fable and the spoyle of all,"
Confound it, man, the Goth has just gone home.
Between these fountains or against this wall
Th' earth's new giant brood, the American,
Has had his thirty thousand lire broad;

[1] Now Professor of English at Stanford University, California; and in 1964 English Professor and pro-Vice-Chancellor of the University of Essex, where he started the English Dept.

[2] Routledge, London, 1972.

And animal kingdom's promontory man
(For so long thought an isthmus) has explored
His hinterland. Yes, under such a sky,
We need dark glasses to endure the day,
And strength to crumble daylight Rome away.
How literary are we, you and I?
Can we build ruins, walk the seas today
To old Atlantis in its new decay?

Kingsley himself never used the typewriter for writing an article. When he *did* type anything, the machine acquired "a personality and will of its own—unless of course it was an interpreter of his unconscious. Few words were properly spelt, but he corrected his script conscientiously afterwards in his handwriting, which was totally illegible." (I have gratefully adopted that description, word for word, from his own account of Lowes Dickinson's typing, which must have been another bond between them.)[1] But he did write as if to be read aloud, muttered to himself as he wrote, consciously avoided jingles, and was incapable of writing that someone served his apprenticeship to statemanship.

This made it the more surprising that, when he got to the microphone with one of his beautifully composed scripts for broadcasting, he could *never* sound informal. His broadcasting belonged to Savoy Hill days, even Third Programme days, when distinguished writers, academics and politicians just sat down and read to you; and you were so lucky to have such men reading to you that it would have been as indecent to criticise them for dulness of delivery as to criticise George VI for stammering. Accordingly you went to sleep. Lionel Fielden, who was Head of the BBC's General Talks Department in the thirties, worked hard as a talks producer on Kingsley. "He was a *terribly* bad broadcaster," he wrote to me on 11th January 1972. "I did everything I could to help him, but no good. I don't quite know why. Broadcasting is in some ways a horrid liar. Some people have the trick, some haven't. For example I was very fond of Lloyd George, and devoted to Megan. She and I decided that we *must* make a great broadcaster of Lloyd George, and he came willingly to the studios, and we spent

[1] *Father Figures*, p. 119.

hours and days and weeks on him—and NOTHING! He was simply dull without an audience he could see."

Kingsley was better without a script—and received great encouragement from S. K. Ratcliffe, who heard a couple of his "Brains Trust" performances and wrote from America commending them. But within a short time the competition from smoothly eloquent thinkers-aloud for the Brains Trust was formidable and Kingsley faded out, to make only rare reappearances in that kind of programme. Why, he asked Lord Reith?

> I have had several invitations to write or speak about the BBC—at the Cambridge Union for instance. One question that invariably arises when the BBC is under discussion is whether there is a blacklist of persons who, for political or other reasons, are not allowed to broadcast. I have usually warned people against making any such assumption, since it is only too easily made by people who are not asked to broadcast and think they ought to be. . . . During 1931–33 I was asked to broadcast on a number of occasions. I took a great deal of trouble to learn more of the technique from your very capable staff. . . . Only in 1933 I did a series of talks on public opinion and the press which were judged by Broadcasting House to be unusually successful.[1] I received about 3000 letters as a result of these talks, and I was greatly pleased to receive a personal message of encouragement from you. . . . I know that on a number of occasions recently my name has been suggested for talks on subjects of which I have special knowledge, either through my work as a university lecturer or as a Journalist. But these suggestions have always been refused. It has now been rumoured that I am on a blacklist and that the reason is that this paper has given offence. . . . I have heard it freely expressed that the particular cause of offence was an article in a series of frank character sketches which was believed to have given offence to you at the time. I hope it did not give offence, but even if it did I find it difficult to believe that you would yourself allow a personal consideration of this kind to have any effect on policy.

No offence, said Lord Reith, but no discrimination either. (What *could* one say to such a letter?) After a while Kingsley

[1] Some of the scripts are among his papers, and they are as brilliant as anything he wrote.

was broadcasting again, mainly in the Overseas Service of the BBC (as it was then called), and it brought him letters from his growing army of friends in the developing countries of Asia and Africa. But a Brains Trust in 1942 had earned this comment from James Agate in one of his endless gossipy volumes of autobiography:[1]

> 1942. April 26 Sunday. Another Brains Trust. At Didcot. Eckersley, Bill Barrett, Col. White, Gerald Barry, Walter Legge (question-master), Andrade, and Kingsley Martin—a genial, witty, Rabelaisian, non-specious, non-canting fellow wholly unlike the *New Statesman* which he edits.

To be called Rabelaisian by James Agate must have been an accolade of some kind.

Shortly before the 1945 General Election Kingsley was writing to Ellen Wilkinson about the growing and (he thought) decisive importance of broadcasting, and he gave her some good advice:

> Broadcasting is a technique that very few people possess. Everyone is vain about it at first until they discover how difficult it is. The great broadcasters spend their lives preparing and re-writing their scripts. It does not "come natural" and has nothing to do with public speaking. Indeed the good public speakers are seldom good broadcasters. It is voice and matter—above all being concrete and most of all intimate—and every broadcast must be rehearsed until it sounds talked and not read. . . . A bad speech or a poor meeting does not matter much . . . but a bad broadcast will lose hundreds of thousands of votes because the great non-political public will say "That's a dull or pompous or cocky or boring fellow". . . . Do the Labour leaders who are broadcasting know that they cannot, unless they want to commit political suicide, just do a script as if it were a speech and then go and read it? I hope they know this.

Kingsley certainly believed it all, over-stated as much of it is. But, as Herbert Agar told me, he seemed at his best as a speaker when using someone else's words. His own were so familiar to him that he would throw many of them diffidently

[1] James Agate, *Ego 5*, p. 215.

away: another man's—a playwright's or poet's—were not his property and must be accorded more respect. In 1922 Agar directed a Princeton production of Shaw's *The Man of Destiny*, with Kingsley in the big part of Giuseppe Grandi, the loquacious innkeeper. Agar said he was "*astonishingly* good—an amateur performance I shall never forget". He seems to have been no less successful in a number of plays at Cambridge and Manchester. Many years later, Gabriel Pascal delighted him by suggesting that he play the part of the Inquisitor in a film production of *St Joan*. Then Pascal forgot about it.

However, he was essentially a journalist, a snapper-up of news and views as well as a seeker-out of good writers with the same aptitudes. And proud to be a journalist: "According to the traditional account," he told the Fabian Society in 1960, "the word 'Christian' was a term of ridicule which the Christians themselves adopted and turned into a title of respect. Something of the same sort is happening with the word journalist. 'Mere journalism,' we say, meaning that the article or book has no permanent value but is merely the account of a man who earns his living by filling space for so much a line. But H. G. Wells, who was probably the greatest individual influence on the thought of his generation, was proud to call himself a journalist, and certainly no one need be ashamed to belong to a profession which has produced Defoe, Swift, Tom Paine, Delane, Nevinson, Brailsford, Massingham and Bernard Shaw. These were all journalists in the sense that they were thinking when they wrote, not to please a specialist public interested in the refinements of literary style but to obtain the maximum effect in the immediate conditions of society." What James Thurber wrote about Ross and the *New Yorker* would need little changing when applied to Kingsley and the *New Statesman*:

> I might as well admit, right here, that I have done a lot of brooding about the mystery that some literary scholars have wrought out of, to quote one of them, the central paradox of Harold Ross's nature: that is, his magic gift of surrounding himself with some of the best talent in America, despite his own literary and artistic limitations. Without detracting from his greatness as an editor, it must be pointed out that the very nature of his magazine . . . did most of the attracting. Writers and

> artists of the kind Ross was looking for decided that here was a market for their wares, and to say that the head of such an enterprise . . . was the attracting force is to say that the candle, and not the flame, attracts the moths. I think the moths deserve most of the credit for discovering the flame.[1]

One small modification: Kingsley was, sometimes, the flame abducting moths from other people's candles.

[1] *The Years With Ross*, Grosset & Dunlap, 1957, p. 92.

Chapter 16

THE CROWDED FORTIES

IT MAY NOT in any way set Kingsley Martin apart from the rest of us, but the next great crisis in the political thought of this man who had so reluctantly abandoned his opposition to war was the use of the atomic bomb at Hiroshima and Nagasaki on 3rd and 6th August 1945. "Like many other people," he wrote in his London Diary on 11th August, "I knew that there had been a danger of the Germans being the first to get the atomic bomb and that it was going ahead in the United States."

> But that it was ready for use was a very well kept secret. Novelists and playwrights have been writing for years about the moral problem that would confront the inventor or the nation which possessed such a secret weapon. The most prophetic was undoubtedly Harold Nicolson's *Public Faces*. . . . In the Wells fantasy, the *World Set Free*, the crumbling of atoms, once started, cannot be stopped and our cities fall into holes in the earth. Listening to scientists the last few days, it has seemed to me that quite a small mistake in the job of breaking up the atom might start a process which would go on until this world had become a sun. But I see that this is officially regarded as unlikely.

Nevertheless it was what many of us thought at the time, and Kingsley as usual was articulating for us.

E. M. Forster spoke for Kingsley and many like him when he wrote in 1945[1] that "the intellectual, to my mind, is more in touch with humanity than is the confident scientist, who patronises the past, over-simplifies the present, and envisages a future where his leadership will be accepted. Owing to the political needs of the moment, the scientist occupies an abnormal position which he tends to forget. All this separates him from ordinary men and women and unfits him for entering into their feelings. It's high time he came out of his ivory laboratory. We

[1] *The Challenge of Our Time*, BBC Publications, 1945.

want him to plan for our bodies, we don't want him to plan for our minds, and we can't accept so far his assurances that he won't." This was Kingsley's attitude to science throughout his life. He had not often been very ready to "listen to scientists", and indeed science had had a rather poor showing in the *New Statesman* under his editorship by comparison with that of Clifford Sharp. The group who between them eventually got science back into the paper were Mary Adams, then in charge of science broadcasting at Savoy Hill, J. B. S. Haldane, Lancelot Hogben, Hyman Levy, P. M. S. (now Lord) Blackett, J. D. Bernal and (Lord) Ritchie Calder; and even this formidable combination might not have succeeded without the atomic bomb. "For once," Ritchie Calder told him after Hiroshima, "the press cannot be too sensational. This is the biggest discovery ever made." And it was the same man, quoted in the same London Diary as "my friend who understands atoms and such like", whom he reported as telling him that

> the necessary resources for production cannot be found in any existing countries except the US, the USSR and the British Commonwealth, but the time will come when these great powers can, if they will, sell the stuff by the pound, so to speak, to other countries which can use it for power stations and substitute it for coal or indeed any form of energy. . . . It would now be practicable to make plans for visiting the moon and indeed touring the Universe, and no doubt such ancient fantasies would in time be everyday events. But in the near future it would be more useful to develop vast desert areas—the Arctic, the Sahara, the sterile spaces of Australia. Waste land is waste mainly because of the absence of water. There is now nowhere where it will not be possible to reach deep-lying water. This should end the problem of Indian and Asiatic poverty.

There seemed little doubt that it *could* end world poverty, and none that it would be "more useful to develop . . . the Arctic, the Sahara, the sterile spaces of Australia" than to visit the moon. It would seem more useful, when you come to think of it, for Queen Isabella and her nobles to have put up their money for agrarian reform at home instead of for the voyages of Columbus; but nothing, literally nothing, will ever make men put the alleviation of old conditions before the chance of discovering new. Kingsley, having written a leader which showed how the arrival of atomic power had created a new and tiny hierarchy of "top men", deplored in his London Diary the "tone of solemn jubilation" adopted by the BBC news-readers in recounting "the atomic bomb's success in vaporising a Japanese town with a population of 300,000 men, women and children". He rightly doubted whether this chimed with the mood of the public. "Obviously we are all relieved that the Germans didn't drop it on London, but apart from that everyone I've met was plunged into gloom by the news of the invention."

> I find everywhere an increasing moral revulsion. In 1940 we denounced the Nazis because they started indiscriminate bombing, and justified our own bombing on the score that we did not begin the dirty business. Today there can be no doubt that we have begun a new and far more indiscriminate type of warfare.

We had denounced the immorality of strategic bombing while we busily caught up with the Germans and carried strategic bombing one stage further. Then the Germans in their turn became morally indignant and constructed V.1 and V.2. Caught unawares by this new technique we denounced German terrorism and perfected the atomic bomb:

> And so it goes on. I hope Mr Attlee[1] will break away from the Churchill tradition of moral gloating. We should all be relieved if he told us frankly that, once a total war has started, we, like every other nation, are bound to develop and use every form of warfare against men, women and children which damages the enemy more than he damages us. We cannot without hypocrisy blame the enemy if he does the same.

Mr Attlee had been Prime Minister for only a week, with Bevin as his Foreign Secretary. He did not make the pronouncement that Kingsley called for. But a week later the Second World War was over and all its moral problems could be discussed in an atmosphere of precarious survival; an

[1] Clement Attlee had become Prime Minister on 27 July, six days before the bomb was dropped on Hiroshima.

atmosphere, that is to say, which is as inimical to Fabian and Socialist as to capitalist planning. And survival was suddenly seen to be in the hands of the scientists.

Kingsley's private memoranda show that he was aware of an elusive and yet accessible scientific readership. All through the war he was intermittently planning a series, or a monthly column, of technological comment which (as with so many other series) never materialised. The seed was sown as early as Christmas 1937, when the paper ran a "General Knowledge Competition" involving some questions and answers on scientific matters which stung to fury no less a man than Lancelot Hogben, then Professor of Social Biology at London University and a Fellow of the Royal Society. (It was said at the time that no scientist would risk his professional reputation by writing for the non-technical press until he had got his FRS. Hogben had deferred publication of his *Mathematics for the Million*[1] until after he was made a Fellow; but Kingsley told me that, if the Million included him, Hogben need have no scruples—he still couldn't understand mathematics.) Hogben's excoriating Christmas letter, which is worth some detailed attention here because it changed the *New Statesman*'s attitude to science, told Kingsley that "the lesson of the *New Statesman*'s General Knowledge Controversy" was that Kingsley and his paper did not "belong to the Encyclopedists of Eternity—you don't see social culture as something perennially renewing its youth. You are demanding a Liberal culture which is dead. You are no modern Diderot creating a social culture which will live." All this may have had something to do with the rejection of a Hogben article, of which Kingsley had felt constrained to say, "I don't even remember what it was or why it was rejected. I consider articles quite impersonally. It is a question of what happens to fit at the time. . . . It involves no criticism of you or, I suggest, of the paper that a particular article was not included in a particular week's issue." But consider now what that decision led to:

> What Socialism demands primarily [wrote the angry Hogben] is a programme based on awareness of new technological possi-

[1] Allen & Unwin, 1936.

bilities. If the Labour Party in 1923 had come forward with a thorough plan for socialising electrical industry through and through, it would have carried it with Liberal support at the cost of less concessions than those which Blum now makes and the communists applaud. It did not. Why? Because its intellectual leaders did not conceive Socialism in terms of technological expansion, and its Trade Union bosses still less so. . . . The central problem of social spring-cleaning at the moment is how to replace the literary-legal intelligentsia of old school tie socialism by a technical "expertentsia" in tune with the social aspirations of the salaried middle class. . . . The new destructive powers available for war between large nations (as opposed to civil war, in which there is an inescapable limit to material destructiveness) are such that only those in the know can say just what alliance would be profitable and what countries could afford to support or attack us. I don't know. Woolf thinks he does know, because he is too bloody ignorant to understand the requisite data for a rational discussion of all the issues. For instance whether a Franco-Russian-British Alliance is a good thing may depend (*inter alia*) on whether London can be effectively defended. If not it may merely make us a catspaw for Russian foreign policy by forcing Germany to wipe us out quickly and decisively. I don't know. *But I do know that the issue is a technical one, not a legal one.*

Here let me draw your attention to one fact [Hogben continued relentlessly] which seems to have escaped your notice. While the Bloomsbury Bolsheviks and the old-school-tie intellectuals have exhausted their resources of geographical erudition, with total disregard to the principles of aero-construction and the properties of poison gases, only one domestic issue has kept alive the cause of social progress in the House of Commons. John Boyd Orr's work on malnutrition is the work of a group of young scientific workers who realise that modern politics is constructive or not in so far as it is about the impact of growing scientific knowledge on social institutions. . . . Your scientific policy should be to get scientific articles which show how capitalism fails to use new scientific knowledge, and whatever scientific knowledge a Socialist policy could mobilise for the advancement of general well-being. It is your business to show your readers that we have vast new powers for health and prosperity, that monopolistic capitalism is not making use of them for the satisfaction of common needs and that we can only realise them by a policy of creative socialism. We want a British Light Metals Corporation, a British Food Trust, a British Synthetic Resins Corporation, a British Cellulose Derivatives Development Company—socially owned and controlled from their inception—and, as a preliminary, a National Planning Council with first option on all patents at a statutory rate and complete power to use the fruits of all state-subsidised research. You have got to make your readers conscious of the *Frustration of Science Under Capitalism* instead of prostituting and degrading science to the level of crossword puzzles by printing baby-talk about the pets' corner.

But you won't do it, because fundamentally, my dear Kingsley, you and your entourage expect your readers to pick up an elusive reference to the seventh mistress of a 17th Century minor French poet, and refuse to reckon with the fact that hundreds of people who don't give a damn for your French poet or his mistress know much more about a kilowatt, a calorie or a bacteriophage than you do.

It was not a "letter to the Editor", intended for publication: it was in fact headed Personal and Confidential. But it was the kind of letter which Editors do not publish even with their writers' permission. They carry them in their briefcases for months, looking at them uneasily each time there has to be a sorting-out. And this one seems to have had considerable influence on Kingsley's thinking about the nationalising of industries, the best way of harnessing technological development, and what the *New Statesman* ought to be saying about such matters. Hogben had accused him (and it rankled badly) of approaching the problem of socialist transition as a problem of property rights, instead of seeing it as essentially the creation of new social organs to exploit new technical potentials. "The year of my birth (1895)," concluded Hogben, "saw the first vehicle constructed with an internal combustion engine. At that time Fabians were beginning to make themselves felt, and Sir William Harcourt[1] was telling our parents that they were all Socialists."

I want you to imagine just exactly what would have happened if the Fabians had been just strong enough to induce the electorate

[1] Chancellor of the Exchequer in the Gladstone Government, and famous for his remark "We are all Socialists now".

to swallow a bill for nationalising the hansom cab manufacturing industry. Twenty years later the nation would have had two alternatives: (a) to wind up a defunct industry at the expense of the middle class taxpayer, or (b) to prohibit the import of motor cars. Either way it would have been a defeat for Socialism. This example has all the ingredients of failure inherent in the Socialism of the English Fabians and of the German Social Democrats.

Kingsley's answer, sent on 25th January 1938, was strangely muted and inadequate; making no attempt to defend the Fabians, he admitted that "a vulnerable point in his armour" was that "a programme of scientific articles he once thought out had fallen down": this was due to "internal reasons about space and personalities". But "we have had expert articles on the location of industry, on the economic waste under capitalism, on all sorts of aspects of public health by Harry Roberts and others; and we have, I think, had more material, mostly written by Lloyd, on the malnutrition [policies] of Orr and his friends than any other paper."

The war still further restricted what space he would have allotted to scientific matters, but in 1945 Ritchie Calder, released from war service with the Foreign Office, was absorbed into the paper as, in effect, science editor. (He sat in at the Monday editorial conferences which Kingsley, with some reluctance, had at last instituted; and there was a time in the fifties when Kingsley contemplated making him Deputy Editor.) By 1945 he had been a prolific journalist for 20 years and was at that time science editor of the *News Chronicle*. I suppose few journalistic careers have so clearly reflected the universality of science, taken a man to so many parts of the world, or involved him in membership of so many world organisations for the improvement of the human condition through the development of science, and in particular the peaceful uses of atomic energy. And in 1961, when he was appointed Professor of International Relations at Edinburgh University, he had arrived by a totally non-academic route at the precise kind of competency which had so nearly been Kingsley's a quarter of a century earlier. In the forties and fifties Kingsley's influence on Ritchie Calder was profound. "He was the greatest editor I ever worked for, because he was quite ruthless. He would never let me get away with anything through kind-heartedness: he was always very critical. When I came out of the Foreign Office after the war I wrote one article for him of which he said: 'This isn't an article, it's a memorandum—you've been writing officialese for too long.' At that time I would have been prepared to write for any paper but not for any editor. I wanted to write for Kingsley. You could go and argue with him. He was a 'fumigating' character. He would go on and on saying 'I don't understand' and you would get more and more cross with a stupidity that was in fact entirely feigned. To me he was a kind of hero, but he was also a rate-fixer and a charge hand—he not only told you what to do but how to do it. . . . There were two men in the thirties and forties who, from the journalists' point of view, were right at the centre of things—Kingsley Martin and Gerald Barry. No-one has ever told Gerald Barry's story—we tried in vain to get him to do it himself. He and Kingsley were always on the same sort of committees, and they became closer than ever when the *Week-End Review* merged with the *New Statesman;* and yet the only idea that survived from the *Week-End Review* was 'This England'. I was always pestering Kingsley to do what Barry did so well in the *Week-End Review*—the big 'spreads' on nutrition and Mass Observation and so forth. He was always against spreads—he hated them, hated anything which had a continuity or became a series."

Gerald Barry had founded the *Week-End Review* in 1930, the year of Kingsley's arrival at the *New Statesman*; and for the brief four years of its life it was probably the brightest weekly review this country had seen for many years. It could be said to have owed its existence to Lady Houston, the formidable old lady who owned and rigidly controlled the *Saturday Review*. Barry was only 23 when he joined that long-established Liberal weekly as assistant editor in 1921. He became editor three years later and enjoyed a reasonable autonomy until, in 1930, Lady Houston decided that the *Saturday Review* must come out in support of Lord Beaverbrook's "Empire Free Trade" campaign. Having failed to convince her that this was totally crazy, Barry resigned, the editorial staff followed his example, and together they started the *Week-End Review*. This was lighter than the *New Statesman* (certainly in the latter's earlier days), brilliantly written, ideal for the intelligent general reader, unlikely perhaps to appeal much to the politician or the economist but showing considerable interest in the sciences as well as the arts. J. B. Priestley called it "the last stand of the brilliant broadbrows". In 1934 it was suddenly and inexplicably abandoned by its main financial backer, Samuel Courtauld, and the *New Statesman* promptly bought it for £1,000. It is true, as Ritchie Calder says, that its only feature to survive the amalgamation was the national "idiot's mirror" headed "This England", but the *New Statesman* was greatly strengthened by the new association with Sir Gerald Barry, who became a member of its board in 1934.

As for "This England", it was a "straight crib" from H. L. Mencken's "Americana", which was even funnier because Americans, off guard, tend to be funnier anyway. But everyone involved in its compilation, when asked to explain its purpose, has had a slightly different rationalisation for it. Defining it was always a waste of time. One studied it, grinned, sighed or snorted, and turned the page; sometimes a little nearer to an understanding of humanity, sometimes a lot nearer to giving it up in despair. Kingsley saw it as "illustrating peculiar Anglo-Saxon attitudes", and thought that the collections sometimes published as a pamphlet at Christmas time were historically as interesting as *Punch*, and funnier.[1] Here are a few examples from 1957–1960, which Kingsley thought was a vintage "This England" period:

> In view of the great expense and difficulty involved in firing rockets at the moon, I suggest that future attempts should be made when the moon is full. There would be a better chance of hitting this larger target than of hitting the thin crescent at the time of the latest Russian attempt—Letter in *Glasgow Herald*

> A neurotic man who, during periodic fits of depression, takes his false teeth out and jumps on them, is to get half the cost of a new set from Dorset Health Committee "on the grounds of hardship"—*News Chronicle*

[1] *Editor*, p. 11.

My boy-friend is very good-looking, and we get on well except that he is a "square" and I love jazz and jiving. He says I am a case of arrested development, but my measurements are 36, 22, 36. What does he mean?—Letter in *Woman's Day*

You report that Epping Forest authorities want to shoot a white deer because it may spoil the purity of a herd of black ones through inter-breeding. I think it should be left to the deer to decide for themselves what colour they wish their offspring to be—Letter in *Evening Standard*

Every morning for more than 30 years my wife has warmed my bowler hat over the gas ring before I set out for business—Letter in *Star*

Could you please assist me? I am trying to find a book I read some years ago. It was a small paper-backed one written by a lady. In it were given exercises for mental control, one of which was to imagine oneself inside a matchbox—Letter in *Prediction*

Even as I write I am regaled with a Press photograph of the Queen's First Minister pattering about an Indian temple in his socks, his lady wife, likewise unshod, at his side. This may be a good idea or it may not. As no less ardent and eminent a democrat than the late Earl Lloyd-George was moved to say not long before he died: "In my day these people came to me"—*Horse and Hound*

The danger of the Queen Mother's high-heeled shoes catching in the tram-lines outside Sheffield town hall posed a problem for Corporation engineers yesterday. But they soon hit on the solution. They diverted the city's trams for two hours and *laid tarmac across the lines*—*Sunday Dispatch*

It is about time the Hartlepools Arts Association realised its duty to provide some entertaining plays for the local audience. It is not long since "Look Back in Anger" was presented locally. This abusive play, with its half-dressed cast, was not at all suitable for the family audience. Monday night's "Romeo and Juliet" was about an under-age love affair, and included murder and suicide. I am tired of this violence—*Northern Daily Mail*

Play croquet and enjoy it, but do not teach it to children. Let them cut their teeth on football and cricket, or other gentlemanly games, and when they have proved themselves good losers introduce them to croquet, so they can learn to fend for themselves in the cut and thrust of life—Letter in *Daily Telegraph*

Dorothy, in 1954, at Little Easton

Kingsley in 1954

The flat at number 1 Robert Street, Adelpi 1962

If Kingsley had been asked what peculiar Anglo-Saxon attitudes were illustrated here, he would almost certainly have said it was a mistake to be too profound about it all.

An important event in the forties was the arrival of Norman MacKenzie as an assistant editor, the only man (I believe) of whom it can be said that Kingsley appointed him without so much as seeing anything he had written. Since Kingsley was also choosing a colleague who was to be a daily companion for the next 20 years, he did go so far as to ascertain Norman's capacity to play chess (and that he could beat him). There was at least one other respect in which this appointment was unique: Norman MacKenzie was the only person employed on the *New Statesman* staff who had been a member of the Communist Party. He joined the paper in 1943 and remained a Party member for nearly three more years. "To Kingsley's credit," Norman told me, "he hired me as a Communist[1] . . . but I was never once asked by the Party to do anything vis-à-vis the *New Statesman* as an act of Party loyalty. Nor would I have done so. I was a kind of euphoric war-time Communist who thought there was a real chance then to get rid of all the splits bedevilling the Left." He had been invalided from the RAF in 1942, and returned to the London School of Economics (at that time evacuated to Cambridge) to finish his interrupted degree course in political science under Harold Laski. In May 1943 Kingsley went to Cambridge to address the LSE Students Union on the future of Nazi-occupied Poland and its relationship with the USSR. A large number of Polish Army officers were at the LSE doing courses, and Norman had friends among them. During the discussion he made what he later described as a "naïvely utopian" speech calling for an end to all dissension between the "Lublin" group (mainly the Polish Communist Workers Party), Mikolajczyk's Polish Peasant Party, and the Roman Catholics. Kingsley was much impressed. A previous speaker had suggested in effect that the time had come to "abolish" Poland, as an artificial geographical concept and a source of constant war. "He was promptly rebuked," wrote

[1] And he did it at a time when the *New Statesman* was a happy hunting ground for Special Branch men looking for news of communists and fellow-travellers though not, on the whole, finding it there.

Kingsley in his London Diary on 29th May 1943, "by an able and quiet speaker who explained that he was a member of the Communist Party.

> As I listened to him my hopes grew. He had an independent mind. He used none of the Party slogans. He said things that showed he was not always in agreement with the Party line. And yet he was quite unmistakably and sincerely a Communist. I believe there must be many Young Communists like this . . . I think they will welcome freedom from orders which come from a government whose colossal achievements do not include that of understanding the political position in the Western democracies. If such young men can join hands with young Labour enthusiasts, we now for the first time have a chance of a living socialist movement in Britain.

A few days after the meeting Laski said to Norman MacKenzie: "Kingsley Martin wants an assistant. Would you be interested? If so you'd better ring him up." On the following Saturday morning Norman was met at Dunmow Station by his future boss, who "looked like a scoutmaster in long khaki shorts and shirt", and who drove him to the cottage at Little Easton—"a hair-raising drive, with Kingsley looking over his shoulder to talk at me the whole way". They sat in the garden and talked all day. Suddenly Kingsley said: "If you were Stalin, what would you do now?" Norman was seldom at a loss. "Abolish the Comintern,"[1] he said at once. Kingsley said, "Well, Stalin will never do that." On the way back to Dunmow Station they stopped and bought the *Evening News*. Its main banner headline said COMINTERN DISSOLVED. "You saw that before you came!" cried Kingsley. Norman denied it. "Then you're hired," said the delighted editor; and Norman, after a brief holiday, started at the *New Statesman* on 19th July—at a salary of £6 a week.

Thus began a strange, proto-father-and-son relationship, in which Norman's limitless capacity for hard work was much exploited—I would say thoughtlessly rather than mercilessly.

[1] The (third) Communist International, founded in 1919 to rally all Left-wing governments for revolution against capitalism. It was dissolved in May 1943 as a wartime gesture of USSR goodwill to the West.

Kingsley liked and needed people who would disagree with him, but he liked also to have readily available at least *one* such dissident who (he thought) could be slapped down without causing too much trouble. It was often said that he made few mistakes in selecting his aides, but however few they were Norman MacKenzie was not among them.

It is interesting to recall that before the war, when Kingsley had engaged Michael Foot in a similar way, he made one mistake which in 1943 he tried in vain to rectify. Frank Hardie had been asked to help with the sub-editorial work for a few weeks during the 1936 summer holidays, and wanted to know how long the arrangement would be likely to last. "I'll know more clearly in a few weeks' time," Kingsley wrote to him on 21st May 1936. "I'm not sure how long Michael Foot, who has been working here for the past few months, is stopping. He is not on the staff and is not in any case going to be put on it, but he is working here doing some jobs and some writing.

> He's looking for another job and may soon get one. He's a good fellow and not a bad journalist—but not A+. I tried him out on the clear understanding that he would like the experience and that we should not keep him unless he was brilliantly successful.[1] You see, the point is we have no "vacancy"—as I told him—but that if I found God's own journalist, for co-operation over the Diary etc., I should some time or other *make* a vacancy or rather appoint an additional man. I am in fact going on trying until I find such a man—if, which I doubt, he exists!

Eight years afterwards, as he records in *Editor* (page 296), he was trying to persuade Lord Beaverbrook to allow Michael Foot, who had been acting editor of the *Evening Standard* and was now being paid a special retainer to keep him at Lord Beaverbrook's disposal, to "write occasional articles for the *New Statesman*. . . . I put the point to him today and he tells me he is not at liberty to write for any other paper; but there has always

[1] Michael Foot was in fact "filling in" at the *New Statesman* and getting journalistic experience until *Tribune* started up. He did not come to know Kingsley well until the 1960's. He always thought Kingsley was "a political yellow press man, a splendid gossip writer, rather than an acute political commentator—with a 'headline' sense of news and a gift for making it readable".

been a convention that daily paper writers could contribute to weeklies, since weeklies do not in any way compete with their daily contemporaries". The Beaver obviously thought they did, and the answer was an uncompromising (though not wholly unsympathetic) refusal.

This was a difficult time for Kingsley and the *New Statesman.* Various war jobs had deprived him of Crossman, Ritchie Calder, and Aylmer Vallance; G. D. H. Cole and H. N. Brailsford were both unreliable because of ill-health; and the government, far from any willingness to release someone to help out the *New Statesman,* were asking Kingsley to go to Australia on a mission for the Ministry of Information. (He did not go.)

It was Norman MacKenzie who, in 1947, suggested that the *New Statesman* should invite Henry Wallace to Britain and sponsor a series of public meetings, at which Wallace could explain his views on the prevention of an atomic war. Henry Wallace, an Iowa farmer and research worker in plant breeding, had become US Vice-President under Harry Truman; and resigned in September 1946 to pursue an independent policy designed to prevent a head-on collision with Russia. In the letters he then exchanged with Truman, which the *New Statesman* published in full, he spoke of colossal American armaments, the fact that atomic and bacteriological war, however destructive, would mean that a totally Russian Europe would have to be atom-bombed by America, and the certainty that "victory" no longer had any meaning. He denounced with all the inside knowledge of a Vice-President the whole policy of cold war which, in effect, Churchill had sold to the Americans in his speech at Fulton, Missouri, earlier in the year. Wallace accepted the *New Statesman*'s invitation, and in terms of publicity the visit was an enormous success: the interest was world-wide. A large section of the American press was furious, one reason being that Wallace had brought with him a message of goodwill and solidarity from American progressives, whose signatures included those of Elliott Roosevelt, Lillian Hellman, Thomas Mann, Oscar Hammerstein, and many leading trade unionists. Some papers urged that Wallace should be prosecuted for treason; that his passport should be cancelled; and that the Logan Act of 1932, which made it a crime to influence foreign governments against US foreign policy, should be invoked against him. None of this happened, but Wallace's political career was ended. On his return to America he was promptly nobbled by the Communists, tried to start a new Progressive Party, was indelibly and of course inevitably smeared as a Red and quickly went back to farming. (His incursion into *New Statesman* affairs had one consequence that was of importance to myself and to no one else. At a huge party to welcome him, Kingsley was betrayed by a condition of unusual excitement and euphoria into telling me there was a job for me on the staff of the paper. And he remembered it the next morning.)

The war had not altogether stopped Kingsley's travels—he had been three times to America, visited North Africa, Antwerp, Palestine—and San Francisco for the huge 1945 Conference at which the blue-print for a United Nations Organisation was hopefully produced. (He writes much of this in *Editor*, pages 317 to 322.) But once the war was over his wanderlust returned in earnest, beginning with a visit to Germany with a party of British newspaper editors, all wearing hastily-procured British army uniforms. They had to wear these uniforms because they needed somewhere to carry the British Control Commission's "shoulder flashes". In Berlin he met Heinrich Fraenkel, who had gone there to write some articles for the *New Statesman*. (In the early part of the war Fraenkel had been interned in the Isle of Man, as a victim of the imbecile programme by which even the most hapless of Nazi victims were treated as "persons of hostile origin or association". He was released to do some invaluable anti-Nazi propaganda work. Today, under the name of Assiac, he beguiles and challenges *New Statesman* readers who understand chess in addition to playing it.) One Saturday afternoon they were both arrested at revolver-point by a Russian military policeman because Fraenkel had left his identity papers at the hotel and Kingsley wouldn't be parted from him. Several hours were then filled with Ruritanian comedy of a kind that must have taken Kingsley's mind back to *Arms and the Man*, with incipient tragedy just round the corner. In the course of it Kingsley offered the Russian policeman a cigarette from a big silver cigarette case, and after some glaring hesitation the angry and suspicious Russian policeman seized the case and put it in his pocket. Kingsley never saw it again, and Fraenkel records in his vivid account of 1945 Germany[1] (which tells this story in much more detail) that the policeman was very probably shot for stealing it. The episode was widely reported in the Press of the world—for two possible reasons. One (Kingsley's) that the press were always delighted to report him in trouble. The other (Fraenkel's) that the place was swarming with newsmen from everywhere, it was a quiet Saturday afternoon, and there was nothing else to write about. "Of course," wrote Kingsley later, "the incident was treated as a huge joke by the occupying British. I had at that time, not altogether without reason, a pro-Soviet reputation, and the Rothermere papers were so delighted that I became headline news in more than one paper for two days."

Then off went Kingsley to Yugoslavia as a member of a British Parliamentary delegation. An entire volume could be compiled by anyone who could decipher his notes on this visit; his renewed contacts with Tito (whom he and the *New Statesman*, to say nothing of Dorothy Woodman and the Union of Democratic Control, had supported warmly and, some would say, blindly from 1944 onwards); and the violently conflicting letters he received from Tito and Mihailovic supporters. Both sides in Yugoslavia had behaved with such appalling savagery that Kingsley, had he not "supped full of horrors" and become partially immunised in the course of the war, would surely have been hesitant about supporting either. Here he was again in the same predicament as over the Spanish Civil War and the Orwell articles: "Both sides had behaved with abominable cruelty; but I had to make my decision on general public grounds to the end that one side might win rather than the other side." And his mind was made up. In 1968 he had actually begun the writing of a third volume of autobiography with an enthusiastic account of what Tito and the Partisans had done for the "common people" of Yugoslavia and how the liberated Yugoslavs responded in the 1945 "free elections". In this he was greatly influenced by Basil Davidson, who accompanied him on much

[1] *Farewell to Germany*, Bernard Hanison, 1959.

of his Yugoslav journey—and had a first-hand knowledge of the political scene acquired as a member of British Intelligence there.

In 1948 he was in India at the time of Gandhi's assassination. He had had several long conversations with Gandhi since he first met him at the India Round Table Conference in London in 1930. One of their talks in India in 1948 was written down by an Indian princess, Rajkumari, whom he described as "a kindly, sentimental woman who worshipped at Gandhi's feet, and who later became a conspicuously inefficient Minister of Health". India was then at war with Pakistan over Kashmir, and Gandhi considerably shocked him by announcing that, since the technique of non-violence was not in this instance politically possible, he was morally supporting the war against Pakistan. Everyone, it seemed, even the Mahatma Gandhi, supported war when some "greater evil" threatened. On 29th January 1948, the day before Gandhi was assassinated, Kingsley heard him address an audience of eager and reverent Muslims, explaining to them that the India of the future must permit no strife between Hindu and Muslim, and that his own life was on offer, if need be, as a sacrifice in the cause of communal love. When Gandhi was shot in Delhi the next day by a fanatical Hindu, on the way to his daily prayer meeting in the garden of Birla House, Kingsley found himself engulfed in the general wave of alarm, grief, and anxiety that there might ensue an outbreak of massacres like those which had followed partition the year before. Nehru's own life was in obvious danger, since he preached the same gospel of religious and tribal tolerance and resolutely refused any personal bodyguard. And Gandhi's funeral, attended by millions of mourners, might well have seen the beginning of a fresh holocaust. Nehru, from that time, became politically all-powerful, the transfer of authority to the newly independent State was completed; and Kingsley, as his collected correspondence shows, became greatly attached to Nehru as well as to Earl Mountbatten, who was then presiding (at the express invitation of Congress) over the final twelve months of British rule in India.

In the same year there assembled at Wroclaw,[1] in Poland, a

[1] Pronounced Vrots-Wuff, and formerly the German town of Breslau.

World Conference of Intellectuals for Peace, at which 450 people from 40 countries represented the values which they cherished as important and the achievements for which they had earned international respect. Those from the West, at any rate, did not suppose themselves to represent their respective countries. The expenses were borne by the Polish Government. Among the English representatives were Edward Crankshaw, Louis Golding, Richard Hughes, Jack Lindsay, J. D. Bernal, Ritchie Calder, J. B. S. Haldane, Julian Huxley, John Boyd Orr, Kingsley Martin, Herman Ould, Olaf Stapledon, Ivor Montagu, Hewlett Johnson, Felix Topolski, J. M. Richards, Christopher Hill, A. J. P. Taylor, Rutland Boughton and George Weidenfeld. From other countries came Julien Benda, Irene Joliot-Curie, Pablo Picasso, Freda Kirchwey (editor of the New York *Nation*), Ilya Ehrenburg, Alexander Fadeyev and Mikhail Sholokhov. And messages of goodwill came to the Conference from Bernard Shaw, Professor Albert Einstein, Dr Joseph Needham, Desmond MacCarthy and Stephen Spender. A four-day Conference ended with a resolution designed to warn the nations of the danger confronting them, to urge remedies, and in particular to arouse intellectuals to their heavy responsibility. The resolution contained seventeen paragraphs, all in seemingly innocuous language and full of good intent; but there were two which began a storm of controversy which is still likely to break out afresh in any gathering containing two or more Communists, since it called down upon the Communist representatives the charge of hypocrisy:

1. Against the will and desires of the people of all countries, a handful of self-interested men in America and Europe who have inherited fascist ideas of racial superiority and the denial of progress, who have adopted fascist methods of solving all problems by force of arms, are once again making an attempt against the spiritual treasures of the peoples of the world.

2. Realising that modern science has released great new powers which will inevitably be used by mankind, either for good or ill, the Congress protests against the use of science for destruction, and calls upon you to do your utmost to spread knowledge throughout the world and to apply science to the rapid reduction of the poverty, ignorance, ill-health and misery which afflict the

> majority of mankind; and to collaborate in reducing restrictions on the free circulation of persons who serve the cause of peace and progress, and on the free publication of books, results of research, and all scientific and cultural achievements which serve the same ends.

Most of the British Socialists present (including Kingsley but not A. J. P. Taylor, who had eloquently denounced the whole affair as a fake) were persuaded to accept the resolution although they regarded its "verbose jumble of generalisations" as totally unworthy of a gathering of intellectuals; and Kingsley said so in a *New Statesman* article (4th September 1948) headed *Hyenas and Other Reptiles.* He took his title (which the printer queried on the ground that a hyena was not a reptile) from what he called "a brutal oration" by Alexander Fadeyev, the Soviet writer, which had sounded to him like a declaration of war. "Even those who most disapprove of writers like T. S. Eliot, Eugene O'Neill, Dos Passos, Sartre, and André Malraux" he wrote, "felt hot under the collar when Mr Fadeyev said: 'If hyenas could type and jackals could use a fountain pen, they would write such things.'" The resolution, in fact, concealed much political vituperation of the kind that must surely have been foreseen. The Slav states were represented by solid blocs, while the British and American individuals represented nobody and hotly disagreed with each other. But 10,000 people, wrote Kingsley,

> listened breathlessly, with bursts of wild applause, to the Dean of Canterbury. . . . Certainly the Dean preached the gospel of peace on earth and goodwill to men. Certainly the reverent multitude desired sincerely, and with all its heart, the peace he offered. Somewhat inconsistently, however, it is also being taught by other, less angelic voices that peace on earth is only possible under Stalin and that only extermination is good enough for hyenas, jackals and other reptiles.

"Mr Kingsley Martin," retorted *Pravda* in a leading article on 24th September 1948 (and newspapers in the satellite countries dutifully followed suit), "voted in favour of the resolution. Now, in his publication, he is drawing back from the resolution, hiding ill-concealed chagrin behind a shoddy irony. This duplicity is characteristic of the bourgeois British intellectual. Why did Kingsley Martin vote for the resolution? Why is he now, as it were, repudiating it? It is not hard to guess. . . . He did not dare to vote against it at Congress since this would have done considerable damage to his reputation as a liberal journalist. He was giving rein, too, to his anti-American feelings. But then he quailed. He was afraid that he might be suspected—horror of horrors!—of Communist sympathies."

Yet he could have signed, with equal propriety, a resolution at a cannibal congress declaring that eating people is wrong. If there was one episode which, more than any other, finally disenchanted Kingsley about Soviet Communism as an alternative to the capitalist economy, it was I think the Wroclaw Congress in 1948.

Quiet week-ends in the country had been Kingsley's hope when he bought and sparsely furnished the cottage at Little Easton in 1934. But there were still, at the end of the forties, many week-ends when he could not be there; and few that were quiet in the sense that lulls a troubled mind. The editing of a weekly journal of opinion is like painting the Forth Bridge: no sooner has this week's issue come off the presses than the planning of the next must begin, and he often took his week-end problems, forebodings, and perplexities to Little Easton with him. Many times he went alone, for Dorothy was now a world traveller too, and with the end of the war her interests moved further and further East and took her abroad for longer periods. One of his neighbours at Little Easton was Paul Dixey, the well-known underwriter and Chairman of Lloyd's who in the early thirties had taken over H. G. Wells's beautiful house Easton Glebe; and he tells of the worried state of mind in which Kingsley would sometimes walk with him in the quiet Essex lanes. They were not often there during the war (Dixey himself was away in the Royal Artillery), and the cottage had a succession of "evacuated" occupants from London, some of whom complained bitterly about its spartan comforts.

The garden and the fine orchard were always in the expert care of "Mr Park", whose bucolic wisdom rounded off so many pages of London Diary. His real name was Bill Lodge and the village children knew him as Lodgie. Bill's wife was the local "children's friend", with an apron pocket always stocked with sweets; and she had a story to comfort anyone distressed by adult stupidity or indifference. Bill Lodge knew he was the subject of countless Diary paragraphs, Kingsley knew he did, and Bill knew that Kingsley knew. Yet they never made a single reference to it in conversation; nor had they any common ground politically, for Bill was a dyed-in-the-wool Tory, a squire's man.

Laski and John Strachey had houses nearby; so did A. E. Coppard, John Pudney, Lionel Hale, John Armstrong the painter, and Michael Denison and Dulcie Gray. A joint event brought the decade locally to a close—the Dunmow Flitch Trial was revived on 1st October 1949, the first to be held since the outbreak of war, and Kingsley was appointed to officiate as its red-robed judge.[1] There had been 50 applicants, reduced by a preliminary enquiry to four for trial. Escorted to the court by red-uniformed trumpeters and supplied with a jury of six maidens and six bachelors, Kingsley thoroughly enjoyed himself and was made much of in the local papers.

But the occasion had a strange echo. Kingsley had been persuaded to stand for election to the Dunmow Parish Council, and the election in 1949 was to be by ballot for the first time in its history. The total number of votes was about 200, of which Kingsley got 80 (not enough, rather to his relief, to get him in). "To my astonishment," he wrote in *Editor* (p. 129), "a paragraph appeared in the *Daily Express* saying that though Kingsley Martin, editor of the *New Statesman*, might possibly persuade some gullible people to listen to what he had to say in his paper, those who knew him well rated him at his true worthlessnesss. . . .

[1] A piece of bacon, originally a flitch or "side" but now a gammon, is presented to a number of married couples who prove to a local judge and jury, at a trial conducted with much jocosity and homespun wisdom, that they have had no quarrel for a year. It has been the custom since Chaucer's time that "any person from any part of England going to Dunmow, in Essex, and humbly kneeling on two stones at the church door, may claim a gammon of bacon if he can swear that for 12 months and a day he has never had a household brawl or wished himself unmarried" (Brewer's *Dictionary of Phrase and Fable*). Since its revival in the nineteenth century after a long lapse, in its mock-trial setting with witnesses and counsel, it has been "a travesty of the old ceremony".

He had been unable to persuade more than 80 people to vote for him. It appeared almost unchanged I think five times in one or other of the Beaverbrook newspapers." [One of its grateful users was "Cross-Bencher" in the *Sunday Express*.] "Years afterwards, Christiansen, recently retired from editing the *Express*, asked me if I knew why Beaverbrook had given orders that this paragraph should be frequently inserted." Kingsley then mentioned a London Diary paragraph in which he had said that Beaverbrook should not be brought back into the War Cabinet. "Ah," said Christiansen, "that would certainly be enough to explain those paragraphs."

The true story, as established by A. J. P. Taylor while working on his biography of Beaverbrook, is quite different. First, the London Diary paragraph had said that Beaverbrook had been a good minister, and that Churchill would like to get him back, but that of course the orthodox people and the Labour leaders didn't want him. "That," says Alan Taylor, "is exactly what Beaverbrook himself would say. He didn't take offence at all. But there is a letter from Christiansen to Beaverbrook, then in Jamaica, telling him Kingsley Martin had been down to the Cambridge University Labour Club and attacked the British newspaper press. 'So,' says Christiansen, 'I noticed an item that he had only got 80 votes in a local election, and in retaliation I put it in.' Beaverbrook had nothing to do with it. When Christiansen made his excuse to Kingsley he was covering up for himself, because he was the chap who had played the trick. And Beaverbrook, when he heard the story, was absolutely baffled—he had never seen the Dunmow election story in his own paper. He thought it was funny, of course, but he had no connection with it whatsoever."

A Dunmow Conservative voter wrote to Cross-Bencher in protest—and in vain. "Mr Martin is pretty popular here," he said (and Paul Dixey remembers the letter being sent); "and no-one is in the least likely to think he has any axe to grind by standing for the Parish Council! I hear that he is so popular that he has been asked to act as judge in the coming Dunmow Flitch Trial. He is very good fun on the platform as we know from hearing his replies at local brains-trusts. Your attack has for the first time made me wonder whether some of your other personal attacks may not be misinformed too and dictated by some personal malice."

A trifling episode, with nevertheless important implications for history at any level of significance; and a quiet note on which to conclude an account of Kingsley's second stormy decade as editor.

Chapter 17

COLD COMFORT FIFTIES

"THE SITUATION IS too bad to be true," wrote Kingsley in January 1950. "At any rate it is so bad that it has become difficult to tell the truth." But then, in a long unpublished memorandum, he tried to set down the truth as if to see whether it *could* be told. Drastically summarised, this is what he wrote.

The Russian view first. Marxist analysis showed that wars and revolutions would be inevitable until the class struggle was ended and a federation of socialist republics of the world was established. The only instrument for achieving this was the Communist Party founded by Lenin. Its world-wide discipline ensured that its agents everywhere followed the Politburo's directives, the interpretation of which fell on the national Communist leaders. During two "five-year plans" in Russia all improvement in the standard of living had been abandoned because of the obvious danger of war, and the wisdom of this had been proved when the Soviet Union found it possible, with vast lend-lease aid from America, to oppose the far more developed and industrialised military might of Germany. The 1945 Yalta Agreement between Stalin, Roosevelt and Churchill had given the politburo a period of hope that Russia would have time to reconstruct in peace. At some later point in 1945 it had become clear that this was an illusion, that Britain and America were determined to intervene in the sphere of influence allotted at Yalta to the USSR, and that the USSR must gather all the allies available throughout the world.

If the capitalist system continued to break up in Europe, Communism would take its place there: and the victories of the Chinese Communist Parties in the Far East would create a land bloc supported by fifth columns everywhere, strong enough to make it impossible for America to win a war even by dropping bombs on the Soviet Union. And everywhere the underdog would take the Soviet side. The first world war had produced the Russian revolution. The second had greatly extended the Soviet area. The third would hasten the Communist world revolution whether the Russians won it or not.

A bourgeois country like England would not surrender to Communist influence until it had been through sufficient misery to proletarianise its population—it must go through the same process as Germany did between 1917 and 1947. France was already half-way through. America must at all costs be prevented from bolstering up these decaying but still powerful middle class forces in Europe. Therefore Marshall Aid must be refused. [And it was.] The Communists had been unable to prevent General MacArthur from reconstructing Japan as a strategic and economic satellite of America, but they had largely neutralised this by their successes in China.

Then the American view. This was difficult to estimate because America was a babble of voices. But the State Department's policy was dictated by big business executives who knew what they wanted as clearly as their opposite numbers in the Kremlin. They had to pay attention to currents of public opinion, and clothe their real intentions in acceptable ideological phrases. In private conversation (according to Kingsley) they said something like this: "If it had been possible for us to arrange a preventive war, we should have done so in 1945 or 1946. No doubt the Russians know of our discussions with leading scientists on the technical possibilities. It was a misfortune that, having so great a lead in atomic warfare, we could not give Russia a knock-out blow. We were prevented by the political necessity of allowing the G.I.s to come home and the demand of the American people for demobilisation and the change-over from war production to consumer goods. Anyway Russia gave us no *casus belli*, and this President Truman of ours has pledged us to work with Russia in the Security Council of the United Nations. We don't fear Russian bombs—that's merely a convenient popular hysteria which should not be too much discouraged. What we fear is the growth of Communism in this country. We know as well as any Socialists that the era of competitive capitalism is nearly over. We are monopolists and heads of great trusts, not small-time traders and manufacturers.

We are the men with power and we mean to keep it. We are in a position to dominate the entire world and make this the American Century.

"Soviet obstructiveness at UNO, and Soviet disregard for the democratic idea which still holds the American mind, have fortunately enabled us to put over conscription and rearmament more quickly than we had expected. This solves both our economic and military problems. A few people like Henry Wallace will describe us as Fascists, but by that time the Committee on Un-American Activities will have removed everyone with those sentiments from positions of influence, and there are plenty of Americal gaols for those who still make trouble. If not, we can build some more. We have however one difficulty. Since it is technically impossible without a great army and air force, neither of which we now possess, to make war on Russia, Soviet propaganda may in the meantime make dangerous headway in areas which we do not now control.

"Some of our leading business men are in too much of a hurry to destroy the British Empire and capture its markets. That will come in good time. At present we need the British to hold the line for us in the Middle East and to some extent in Europe. Therefore General George Marshall, supported by many idealists who dislike Europe being starved, has done well to put forward his plan for dollar aid in Western Europe. If we can hold the Communists back by supporting clerical Fascism in Italy and Spain and de Gaulle in France, and in the meantime rebuild a Germany which might like its revenge against Russia, we could begin the war in the West in a strategic position at least as good as that in the Middle and Far East."

And what about Britain? There was a heightened sentiment in the British Labour Party that Britain should be the leader of a "social democratic" middle way between the United States and Russia. It found expression in demands for an independent grouping of Western European powers strong enough to resist American pressure, either financial or military, strong enough also to resist Soviet penetration. MPs of all parties tended to accept that Britain was part of Europe and that closer economic unity would not upset the Commonwealth countries. They also accepted the idea of a combined military staff. . . . "As long as

Western Europe is disintegrating, the temptation to push forward with Communist penetration must be overwhelming. If Western workers were offered the alternative, they would prefer Socialism with freedom to Socialism without freedom. War would be less likely if a new economic and power bloc were developed in Western Europe, strong enough to stand up for itself in negotiation with both America and Russia. If that has taken place in the course of the next few years [wrote Kingsley] I should not rule out the hope of a long period of peace." And Communist groups throughout the world might remember, even if Moscow forgot, how the Communist Manifesto of 1848 says that "where the class war is resolved, the result has sometimes been, not the victory of the oppressed over the oppressors, and the reconstruction of society, but the common ruin of both the contending classes".

Kingsley's admission that there might exist this hope of "a long period of peace" did not suppose that there would be no localised, "conventional" wars; it was a cautious readiness to accept that a united Western Europe, acting as a kind of "Irish vote", might defer a worldwide nuclear war by its capacity to tip the balance against an aggressor. It would be the "Third Force" for which Paul-Henri Spaak, the Foreign Minister of the Belgian government-in-exile, had contended as early as 1944, the plan that developed into what we know as the Common Market. But so far as I know Kingsley kept this many-conditioned optimism to himself.

The period when, in his own view, he might most reasonably have been accused of being pro-Soviet was while he still saw the centre of policy as being the prevention of an Anglo-Soviet head-on collision. If the Russians "would only be sensible" in Czechoslovakia, which was essentially Western, and in Poland, which was essentially Catholic; and if the United States would give up the idea that all non-capitalist countries were breeding grounds for aggressive war against the West, then perhaps we might all gradually learn to co-exist. Meanwhile, it seemed to him ridiculous to expect Russia to behave "reasonably" after what she had suffered, with memories going back to the Western invasion of the new Soviet Republic in 1919, to the years of boycott and abuse and the *cordon sanitaire* and the efforts to persuade Hitler to attack the Soviet Union—culminating in the Munich settlement.

For some years he always had the same advice for refugees from Soviet-dominated countries who came to him, as they often did, to ask whether they would be wise to go back home. "If I were in your place," he would say, "I would go back and have a shot at making a successful coalition of Communists and Left Social Democrats." He thought that exilitis was a terrible disease. Those who suffered from it were either deluded into thinking that their homelands would always want them back as leaders in some kind of capacity, or discouraged into settling down, sour, embittered and restless, in the country which had given them asylum. It seemed to him that President Beneš *might* have been right in thinking that Czechoslovakia could act as a bridge between East and West. Kingsley and Dorothy had discussed the possibility with Jan Masaryk in the Czernin Palace only a few months before he was found dead under the window of the very suite where they had dined. Masaryk was then clinging fiercely to the Western democratic idea of Czech civilisation, though he saw that Russian domination of his country was inevitable. "After all," wrote Kingsley in his draft for a third volume of autobiography, "the West had let Czechoslovakia down, and Russia had liberated it from the hated Germans."

He went sometimes to Germany during the 1950's as a guest at what became a well-known annual conference at Königswinter, where British and German politicians met to discuss Germany's problems. The convenor was Frau Lilo Milchsack, whose anti-Nazi husband had owned a fleet of Rhine barges (confiscated of course by the Nazis) and whose home had been occupied by German troops while she and her family kept quiet in the cellar. The Königswinter house where the conference assembled was within sight of the wooded hill where Hitler had first met Chamberlain. There Kingsley met many liberal-minded Germans, and, over glasses of Rhine wine in the evenings, learned what they were thinking. It was a great attraction to him that he always met there a number of British politicians and publicists whom he would never have seen at home. They all regularly discussed the rearmament of Germany, and the

East Germany and the Soviet Union. (The Berlin Wall was not constructed until 1961.) What they did *not* discuss was the horrors of the Nazi regime, the extermination camps, the mad cruelty to the Jews.

Kingsley seems to have been unimpressed by the Social and Christian Democrats, who, he thought, had learned nothing and forgotten nothing—with the outstanding exceptions of Willy Brandt and Dr Adenauer (who was then Federal Chancellor of Western Germany). "Adenauer's deeply lined face," wrote Kingsley after a lunch-hour talk with him, "every now and then melted into a sweet-and-sour smile which looked as though it would crack the parchment. He had as much energy as a man of 40, and only showed his age by remaining very still during the conversation." (He was then 80.) "I began the talk by hoping that the cold weather had not damaged his roses as much as mine, and this turned out to be a good lead-in to a long conversation which his secretaries ended because, they told me, they were hungry and wanted their own lunch. We discussed what became known as the Rapacki Plan (we call it the Gaitskell Plan) for creating a small belt of neutrality in Eastern Europe.[1] He was against it. He said Germany could have no security until there was control of nuclear weapons—and Germany needed some of her own. He also said that in time the Russians would find it impossible to make Communists out of the Germans, and some day reunification would be possible as Russian control in Eastern Europe was eroded. But I came to the conclusion, from this conversation and many others, that West German politicians found it necessary for propaganda reasons to demand the reunification of Germany, and did not even dare to tell the public that they must permanently accept the loss of that territory beyond the Oder-Neisse line. Certainly Adenauer did not want to disturb his new capitalist Western Germany by mixing it up with the

[1] Adam Rapacki, Foreign Minister in Poland, proposed to the UN in October 1957 that a central European zone should be free of nuclear weapons. The zone would include Poland, Czechoslovakia, Eastern and Western Germany. Russia supported the plan, Britain and the USA rejected it—because it did not provide for German reunification and because it would favour the Communist bloc.

German people's relationships with the occupying powers, with Socialist economy of the East. Catholics kept him in power in the West, and he didn't want them diluted by goodness knows how many Protestants, Communists and atheists from across the new frontier. Deep down, all Germans might desire to rebuild Bismarck's frontiers, but it was only a dream for platform use, not the basis of a practical policy."

Kingsley saw, as he pursued the possibilities of a "third force" in the world of great-power politics, that the next cause worth fighting for was the prevention of a Soviet-American clash. Could Britain, with its Welfare State, be the leading nation in a Third Force, with India and other growing countries as followers, refusing to join either bloc? He made this the basis of his world travels, testing the reactions of statesmen and publicists in those many countries where the *New Statesman* now had a secure foothold. As the Third Force dream faded, blotted out by the Korean War, the growing isolation of India and the domination of UN assemblies by the new countries, he nevertheless remained urgently interested in finding out where they all stood in relation to the Cold War, and how the emergent nations could be aided without becoming tools of either America or the USSR.

The Korean War had begun in June 1950. General MacArthur's brilliant campaign as leader of what was euphemistically called a "United Nations force" had been turned into defeat by the sudden intervention of a huge Chinese army. MacArthur was thereupon heavily reinforced and there ensued a to-and-fro succession of bitter offensives. These culminated in MacArthur's widely-publicised proposal that the Chinese Nationalist forces, locked up for years in Taiwan, should now be used to invade the Chinese mainland and destroy the Communist regime before it was too late. For this and a number of other political indiscretions, each representing a new stage in the cultivation of an extraordinary *folie de grandeur* MacArthur was summarily sacked; but the Korean War dragged on until 27th July 1953. Those three years were years of cliff-hanging danger for the peace (and indeed the survival) of the whole world, and today one can but be astonished that the Korean War is so dim a recollection in the minds of so many.[1] It had only been going on for a few months when President Truman declared at a Washington press conference (30th November 1950) that "the forces of the United Nations are in Korea to put down an aggression that threatens not only the whole fabric of the United Nations but all human hopes of peace and justice;" and when a newsman asked him whether the weapons to be used would include the atomic bomb, instead of responding with the horrified denial expected of him he said "there has always been active consideration of its use. I don't want to see it used. It is a terrible weapon." A shock of intense alarm spread throughout the world. The House of Commons was actually debating the Korean War when Truman's words became known. More than 100 MPs of all parties signed a letter of vehement indignation, and the Prime Minister, Clement Attlee, sent an immediate cable of protest to President Truman. For the Conservatives Mr R. A. Butler said: "The British people as a whole wish to be assured, before their fate is decided, that they are helping to decide their own fate." It was Professor Arnold Toynbee who said of American foreign policy, in a spine-chilling parody of the Boston Tea Party slogan: "No annihilation without representation". Attlee announced that he was flying at once to Washington to see Truman. There was a widespread belief in Europe that the Third World War was about to begin; and so far as one could judge by listening to him, no one believed it more hopelessly than Kingsley. "Are there still people," he had just written in his London Diary (10th November 1950) "who believe that Communism would be defeated if the Kremlin were blown up? Have they still not learned the lesson that war, capitalism and Communism have their roots deep in society and human nature? The answer is that we all know these things, and that in our more thoughtful moments we do not need to be told, as H. G. Wells once put it, that 'you can't shoot the square root of minus one'."

Kingsley's relationships with foreign secretaries had usually reflected their dispositions rather than his. At the "victory rally" at Central Hall, Westminster, by which the Labour

[1] Lillian Hellman told me in New York, for example, that in 1970 when she was lecturing about the Korean War no one seemed to know about it and three "adult education" students asked her when it took place.

Party celebrated its triumph in the 1945 Election, there was a preliminary behind-the-platform gathering of 30 or 40 jubilant politicians. As the Labour leaders assembled for mutual felicitation, Ernest Bevin suddenly came in, glared round like a basilisk, and spotted Kingsley. "'Ullo, gloomy," he said very loudly. "I give you about three weeks before you stab us all in the back." By contrast, as Lord Halifax came out of a late night meeting with foreign diplomats he saw Kingsley, shook hands with him warmly, and said in a tired voice, "Hullo, Martin. These meetings at night are no good at all—they spoil your eye for the high birds." Halifax of course knew this was the kind of observation Kingsley would expect from him. (They got on extremely well together; and during the second war Kingsley used to stay with him in Washington, where they groused to each other about Churchill.)

In April 1951 Harold Wilson, President of the Board of Trade, and Nye Bevan, then Minister of Labour, resigned from the Labour Cabinet. Ostensibly this was in protest at the imposition of Health Service charges to meet increasing defence expenditure; but Bevan, who as Minister of Health and Housing had established the National Health Service, providing free medical care for all, had long been out of sympathy with his government's policy of alignment with America and the "containment" of Russia. The "Bevanite group", which then threatened to split the Labour Party in a way that must grievously weaken it, was forced into line the following October at a meeting of the Parliamentary Labour Party which banned all unofficial groups and splinter movements. But what proved to be more immediately important for the *New Statesman* was that John Freeman, then Parliamentary Secretary to the Ministry of Supply, resigned over the same issue. It happened that at this time Kingsley was in some editorial difficulty about "the succession". The men working with him—Aylmer Vallance, H. N. Brailsford, G. D. H. Cole, Dick Crossman, Norman MacKenzie—he judged to be unsuitable for the editorship in one respect or another; and not all of them would have wanted it. At that time the succession was passed down, almost literally, by an editorial laying-on of hands. Among members of the Board there was usually much deliberation about the appointment of a new director, but none at all about the appointment of a deputy editor: that was left to the Editor himself. It was an arrangement that led to some heartburning, and to the difficult confrontations which can result from leaving all the hire-and-fire work in one pair of hands. The experience of Basil Davidson is probably the best illustration.

Basil Davidson before the second World War was on the editorial staff of *The Economist*. During the war he served with the British Army in the Balkans, North Africa, and Italy, and was a lieutenant-colonel by the time he could return to journalism and become Paris correspondent of *The Times* in 1945. Two years later he was its chief foreign leader writer; and in 1949 he became a special correspondent of the *New Statesman*. Kingsley had met him in 1937 when he accepted an article about farming conditions in Northern Italy—Davidson had been learning the language and "looking at Fascism". When Kingsley went with other editors and journalists to Yugoslavia in 1945, he found himself in the same aircraft as Basil Davidson, who was going to report the Tito elections for *The Times*. Davidson, who had fought with Tito's partisans for eighteen months and knew both the country and the language, borrowed a jeep from UNRRA and gave Kingsley a three-day conducted tour which delighted him. Kingsley records in a scribbled diary:

> This was one of the most interesting and moving experiences of my life. As we entered the villages, people would run out crying "Nicola, Nicola!" (Davidson's Partisan name), and after kissing him on the cheek carry us both into their houses, where it was hard without offence to avoid getting drunk on Slivovitza and good old red home-grown wine.

By 1949 Davidson had finally decided that *The Times* and Barrington-Ward (its editor) were politically uncongenial to him. As leader-writer he had walked a tight-rope whenever he had to refer to matters like Britain's massive 1944 invasion of Greece for the purpose of crushing the resistance movement;[1]

[1] There were sharp dissensions in the *New Statesman* office about this, resulting in some confused editorial writing. To quote A. J. P. Taylor's *English History, 1914–1945*: "The British government backed the King of Greece in the name of democracy, though the King's past record was far

and even so the Foreign Office was very angry with him. He unburdened himself to Kingsley, and the idea began to take shape that he might join the *New Statesman* staff. Kingsley was very hesitant because he saw that he would really be appointing his putative successor. He had almost made up his mind in March 1949 during a chance meeting with Davidson in Copenhagen. They then spent a walking holiday in Ross and Sutherland, and finally it was arranged.

Davidson was then (and for three more years) general secretary of the Union of Democratic Control, of which Kingsley was still the Chairman. And there he had distinguished himself in two different but not unconnected capacities: first, as an extremely effective pamphleteer, and secondly as an object of intense disapproval by Dorothy Woodman, who was a member of the Committee. There is little doubt that she sharply counselled Kingsley against his appointment to the *New Statesman* or that he earned her even greater disapproval by being appointed in spite of all that she could do. Kingsley talked to him unreservedly about his becoming deputy editor after a trial period (and indeed it was generally anticipated in the office), though Davidson's private feeling was that he wanted more freedom of opinion than this could afford him; and that he had not left *The Times* in order to trim his sails on the issues that worried him. Particularly he worried about German rearmament and the need to convince the German people that they would not be allowed to regain their international status by exploiting the differences between their victors as they did in 1918. He soon upset G. D. H. Cole with an article exposing the impossibility, as he saw it, of establishing a "Third Force" in France, a middle vote which could curb and control both Right and Left by lending its weight to the party of its temporary

---

from democratic. 60,000 British troops were sent to Greece and defeated the resistance after considerable fighting. Stalin sent no aid to the Communists and made no protest. In England criticism was not so easily silenced. . . . *The Times* followed its usual principle of being strong upon the stronger side." Indeed the only protest came from Roosevelt, who spoke for many in Britain and America in deploring the fact that Allied arms were being used not against Nazis but against Greek patriots who had tried to eject them.

choice. This plan, said Davidson, was a non-starter; and Cole, who had been in dispute with Aylmer Vallance about having the article written at all, told Kingsley it was very doubtful whether anyone who would write so tactless a piece at such a time could possibly make a good deputy editor for the *New Statesman*.

The idea then began to grow, and was subtly fostered by no one quite knew whom, that Davidson was a fellow-traveller, if not worse. Certainly his total determination to oppose German rearmament had taken him on to platforms shared by Communists. Leonard Woolf and David Low both came to regard him as a "red", Dorothy Woodman vigorously supplemented at home what Kingsley heard from them at Great Turnstile, and the Foreign Office allowed it to be understood that, so far as they were concerned, he was now rather more *persona non grata* than he had been at *The Times*. Davidson was soon convinced that this was not how deputy editors were made, but despite Kingsley's suggestion that he "pour some water into his wine" he continued his association with movements which were more pleasing to the Marxist than to the Whitehall concept of a pacified Europe. In 1951 and 1952 he went on a long tour of Africa and sent home a series of articles, never since equalled, about the rise of black nationalism. In reading these articles one needs to recall the "cold war" atmosphere of the time and the fact that it had not proved possible to confine McCarthyism to America. When he got back he found that he had acquired a status of "guilt by association" which, in his view, amounted to condemnation for having the wrong kind of thoughts. And a letter from Kingsley on 5th December 1952, congratulating him on the African trip—"I'm glad this came off and I was proud to publish the articles"—ended:

> I want to make this as little awkward for you as I can. . . . I shall be pleased if you are still available to write for us on special topics, in particular about Africa, but if you have had to hive off to another paper I shall obviously understand. . . . I am sorry that our cooperation has had to be limited in this way. It has not worked out as I once hoped, but there it is and there is no more to be said.

This was the sack; and much more, in Davidson's view, remained to be said. He had been sacked by an editor who had been "proud to publish his articles" and must therefore have been moved by some other consideration which he would not, and never did, disclose.

There was a miserable sequel. Davidson was approached by UNESCO as a possible editor of all its publications, Kingsley gave him a warm reference, and he was appointed. Then the man who had appointed him, the UNESCO Director of Communications, revealed (to Ritchie Calder) that he had been forbidden by the Ministry of Education, *ex post facto*, to employ Basil Davidson at all. Why? Because he was a fellow-traveller. The Ministry defined a fellow-traveller as (1) a member of the Communist Party who kept his membership secret, (2) a would-be member whom the Party didn't want, or (3) a writer who was consistently quoted by Moscow. The first two did not apply to Basil Davidson, who had neither been a member nor wanted to; but, said the Ministry of Education when Ritchie Calder enquired, he was always being quoted by Moscow. That, said Ritchie, was because he was colonial correspondent of the *New Statesman* and very quotable. The Ministry protested that he had "never written anything critical of the Soviet Union". Kingsley declined to publish this extraordinary story, so did a number of other editors, and the episode was closed. Davidson, it is satisfactory to record, then became successively (and successfully) special correspondent to the *Daily Herald*, leader writer to the *Daily Mirror*, and a prolific author of books on the history and modern politics of Africa. He also became a skeleton in Kingsley's cupboard.

Kingsley was precipitating other staff changes at about the same time. The *New Statesman* lost in 1950 the best and wittiest of all political poets when Mrs Hugh Miller, who signed her weekly satirical rhymes "Sagittarius" and was known to everyone as "Sag", decided that 20 years of this was enough. Kingsley turned down a poem about Sir Stafford Cripps which he thought might offend the religious: it was, he told her, "brilliant but blasphemous". Since he was an atheist and she was not, she found this puzzling; and linking it with one or two other recent rejections she decided that on many subjects her opinions were no longer those of the *New Statesman* and that she must go. She had views to express and found no satisfaction in "an endless prospect of producing light verse about nothing". Kingsley had said to her "My dear, you're getting dull." He almost certainly meant "Pep it up a little", but she decided it meant more. It ended a long working association, but did not impair a close friendship. In the 1930's she and her husband (Hugh Miller, the actor) had lived a few doors away from Kingsley in Great James Street, and during the war they were again neighbours (and shared the same air raid shelter) in Buckingham Street, Adelphi. She wrote for years as "Mercutio" in the *Manchester Guardian*, as "Roger Service" in *Tribune*, as "Fiddlestick" in *Time and Tide*, and as "Scorpio" in the *Daily Herald*. She has, incidentally, a recollection of Kingsley which I have heard from others who knew him well: "It was an odd characteristic—he tended to pursue those who disliked him, and he could be rather cruelly indifferent, sometimes, to those who would seek his company unbidden."

Alexander Werth, the paper's Paris correspondent, departed soon afterwards with much greater reluctance. The paper could no longer afford, Kingsley had told him, to maintain regular correspondents in foreign capitals, and anyway France was much overweighted in the *New Statesman*. "You're *not* maintaining me," Werth wrote from Paris; "you pay less than half my maintenance . . . and I have often suggested going to any place you like as a 'special'—we talked of Germany and India, etc. You will realise, of course, that having worked continuously for years on the N.S. there can be no question of my getting a job on any 'conformist' paper—and what paper other than the N.S. is not conformist? I have really put all my eggs in the N.S. basket—quite as much as you have."

But the major change was the arrival of John Freeman. Kingsley had twice tried to interest him in joining the *New Statesman*, encouraged perhaps by the belief that he was not altogether happy in the Government. Finally, as the crisis about increased Health Service charges drew nearer, they lunched together and discussed the proposal in detail. "You understand, I know," wrote John Freeman to him in a provisional acceptance the next day, "that while I feel increasingly reluctant to remain in the government in present circumstances, I feel very much inhibited as to the manner of my going. I realise that this 'acceptance in principle' of your proposal does little to help you solve your immediate practical difficulties," but "I should like you to know that it is a carefully weighed decision and indicates a real belief that we might work together permanently, happily and fruitfully." On 23rd May 1951 he wrote a firm acceptance from a holiday address in Nice, and added: "I would ask you to have two things in mind. First, that you will really try—having regard to your judgement of my capacity—to find me a proper, reasonably secure and reasonably remunerative job in the NS and N; secondly that you will exercise some care and patience in teaching me the rudiments of the job, which is new to me, and not lose patience if I show some initial clumsiness and ignorance. If you are a friend and ally, as I'm sure you will be, during the difficult early months, I'm sure I shan't regret taking now the decision I've taken even though, on the face of it, it's financial lunacy!"

It was within a few months that John Freeman was *de facto* editing the paper in Kingsley's more and more frequent absences abroad. For the first three years he had the steady, "unflappable" support of Aylmer Vallance who, in emergencies, had a rare capacity to suggest quick decisions. Aylmer did this with a confidence that always made the decisions look quite unchallengeable; so they were seldom challenged. The confidence would have been likely to infect almost anyone, but John Freeman was already equipped with clear-sightedness and an experience of authority. Accordingly, anyone who worked in that office under Freeman was soon aware of a relaxed atmosphere. There is always excitement on such a paper, but it was becoming rather indecent to show it.

"Kingsley was one of the formative influences in my life," John Freeman told me. "And one of the things to remember about him is that, for all his 'good causes' and so on, he was a very crafty and skilful old journalist, he knew all the tricks of the trade and could teach them. I find constantly, in writing or in making other people write, that I am embodying Kingsley's rules into my own work. But he hated work, all other forms of work except writing, which he loved. It was however one of his characteristics as a journalist that he had remarkably little regard for facts. Not that he didn't want to take account of them—he would not quote anything he believed to be untrue: but he was capable of forming opinions on an extremely sketchy notion of the facts. And yet I am in no doubt that he was one of the greatest journalists of his day. I don't know how you judge such a man, but if the test is how you succeed in colouring the ideas of a number of people by your own views, I don't know whom one could find, since the first world war, to equal him."

Kingsley's longed-for travels took him to all the countries where the *New Statesman* had become one of the text books of colonial liberation; and (to the disgust of his right-wing critics at home) he was given a liberator's welcome in many of them. The newspapers of the new republics fêted him in lyrical leading articles, of which the following may be selected from a great number as typical—it comes from the *Ghana Evening News* of 7th November 1953:

> When Ghana shall have been free, when the tricolour of our brave new Negro democracy shall have been unfurled on this side of the Atlantic, when our patriots and martyrs shall have been remembered and naked statues raised to our heroes, grandsires and architects of Pan Africa, we shall solemnly pay tribute to our dear friends overseas, who by their daring humanitarian efforts laboured unceasingly to bring the rectitude of our cause into prominent focus. One such man is in our midst today, a stout-hearted anti-imperialist and Defender of the Rights of Man; and unto him we extend the singular honour of welcoming him in the language formerly exclusive to visits by dignitaries of British Imperialism and Downing Street proconsuls—YEN WURU KINGSLEY MARTIN, AKWABAOO!

There is much more of this; of "the Common Man's bloodless revolution, political emancipation, economic determinism, social security, the conquest of illiteracy, abundance for all. . . . We are aware," concluded the *Ghana Evening News*, "from your productions, and those of Asa Briggs and Basil Davidson, your forerunners, that you are as alive to these facts as ourselves. Your visit raises the prestige of the Socialist movement in this country. Ambassador of goodwill, Yen Wura Kingsley Martin, Akwabaoo!"

It may have seemed heady stuff, but for years the *New Statesman* itself had been heady stuff in the emergent countries. On a long tour of Asia in 1955—Andhra, New Delhi, Rangoon, Tokyo, Hong Kong, Peking, Colombo—Kingsley did what he could to foster the right atmosphere for the forthcoming Afro-Asian Conference at Bandung in Indonesia, the first inter-continental conference of African and Asian peoples. All the countries represented were those where he and his paper were known and welcomed: Afghanistan, Cambodia, Ceylon, China, Egypt (which wants to be called the United Arab Republic), Ethiopia, Ghana, India, Indonesia, Iraq, Japan, Jordan, Laos, Lebanon, Liberia, Libya, Nepal, Pakistan, Persia, the Philippines, Saudi Arabia, Sudan, Syria, Thailand, Turkey, North and South Viet-Nam, Yemen. It is a list that shows how comfortably Kingsley outdid Marco Polo. Archbishop Makarios was there as an observer from Cyprus, a Negro Senator from America, a Pan African from the African National Congress. "The importance of the Bandung Conference is that it is going to happen," said Kingsley to a Press Conference in Colombo in 1955. "It is a demonstration to the Western powers that many countries of Asia and Africa, which were long thought of as colonies, are now capable of independent action. This importance will remain whether it produces any immediate results or not." The Conference sidestepped some sharp differences between the pro-Western and pro-Communist blocs, agreeing upon economic and cultural cooperation and self-determination, and upon opposition to colonialism—including French rule in Morocco and Tunisia, and Dutch in New Guinea. Its endorsement of the UN Declaration on Human Rights did not have the approval of the Chinese; nor did Kingsley after he had returned to England and written two articles exposing Chinese brain-washing techniques.

His private diary for 1955 describes an interview with a Minister in Peking (he had failed to get an introduction to Chou En-lai himself). "After several unsatisfactory exchanges I decided that this was a polite Chinese way of refusing to answer my questions. I therefore thanked the Minister and said we had perhaps gone as far as we could go? Was the interview finished then, he asked? I was embarrassed and rose. I felt an atmosphere of restraint. I thanked the Minister warmly and departed without any formal goodbye to the experts, who had said not a word. I had learned nothing at all. My questions had not been answered. After I left, I realised with the help of my interpreter, who had also been present and said nothing, that I had left just at the beginning. The Minister had been willing to impart information at this point, but my interpreter had not been clear. I had in fact behaved like an impatient, insensitive, bungling Westerner in the face of extreme courtesy from the Chinese. My head was bowed to the ground with shame; and at subsequent interviews I made sure of [not] making my departure before the thing had begun."

But he and Dorothy Woodman had stood well with the Chinese during and since the long war with Japan, and had been welcomed in China as chairman and secretary of the Union of Democratic Control and chief sponsors of the wartime China Campaign Committee. Kingsley did not live to see the great rift between China and the USSR or the astonishing rapprochement with Washington, but in the year before his death he was saying that "the Chinese, if they are left alone, are the great hope of the world". And by "left alone" he meant given recognition that they were no one's "natural allies"—certainly not Russia's or India's. They believed the middle kingdom, as they called themselves, to be the only civilised society. They were wrong but it was important, and would one day become vital, that they should go on believing themselves to be right. However, if the future lay with China's 800 millions, they were not to have (and did not need) Kingsley's help in working it out: his interest in China waned rather more than Dorothy's as other less formidable "democracies" engaged his attention. His former esteem for the Chinese had not really survived the universal disgust at their invasion and occupation of Tibet in October 1950. And a few years later he and Dorothy took only a brief interest in the formation of the Society for Anglo-Chinese Understanding, formed in 1963 by a group of people well known to him, including Professor

Joseph Needham, Dr Joan Robinson and Mrs Mary Adams. But it seems highly probable that his interest in China would, if he were living today, be rekindled by the disappearance of Mao Tse-tung's personality cult, the decline of the Little Red Book, the end of the struggle for power, the emergence of Chou En-lai as leader and the admission of Red China to the United Nations. Among the Western journalists now getting into China with the assurance of a welcome, Kingsley would surely and frequently be found.

In one continent, which he visited (for the second time) in 1958, he was not accorded a liberator's welcome, certainly not a hero's; and that was Australia. He had been invited to deliver the Dyason Lectures for the Australian Institute of International Affairs. As reprinted in pamphlet form these are brilliant lectures, full of encapsulated and dogmatic wisdom straight from "Critic" of the London Diary, classic simplifications from teacher:

> The Russian illusions stem from Marx's strongly misguided and very unprophetic remark that "the worker has no nation" . . . a natural enough remark to make in the days when the workers were starving while the capitalists were making great profits.
>
> Perhaps capitalism may still collapse from its own inner contradictions. I don't know. All we can say today is that each time capitalism has been seen to be on the edge of another great slump since the war, this has been avoided.
>
> Nasser has moved towards the Communist powers because of our folly. It would seem obvious to me that the right policy for the West would be to back Arab nationalism . . . towards using the vast profits of oil development to raise the standard of life throughout the Middle East.
>
> The unhappy story of Kashmir has long been bedevilled by the Indian fear that Pakistan will become a satellite of the United States.
>
> In 1947 the British were wise enough to understand that the Burmese nationalist movement was powerful. They gave Burma independence. If they hadn't, Burmese nationalism would have been captured by the communists as the Vietnamese nationalist movement was. Then the British would have fought a similar and hopeless war.

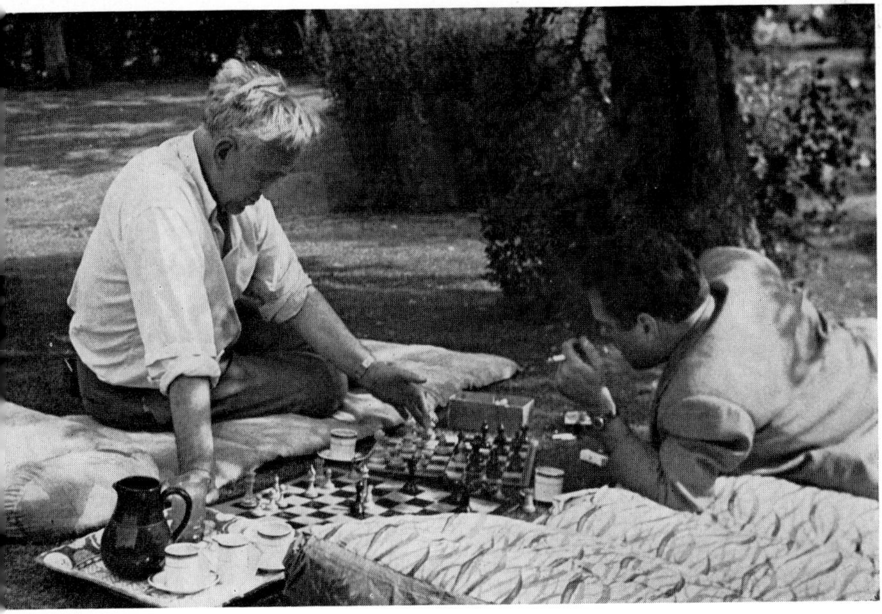

A game with Arthur Wang, the American publisher, Little Easton, 1954

With Ninka Copley in Venice, 1965

Kingsley by Michael Ayrton, 1966

Everywhere in South East Asia you see *Time* Magazine and other American papers given almost free through the generosity of the State Department. It is supposed that American propaganda counteracts the communist propaganda literature equally conspicuous on Asian bookstalls. . . . The advertisements only rub in the lesson that the capitalists of the world have an unfair advantage over the rest of mankind.

There is once again a call for the proletariat of the world to unite—but the proletariat now consists of the coloured and still poverty-stricken Asian and African workers, not the comparatively prosperous workers of the United States, Britain and Australia.

Suppose that at some point the choice is actually between going to war on behalf of the West Berliners or leaving them to their fate, what would the Western Powers do? . . . Does it not seem certain that an isolated West Berlin, 150 miles inside Communist-controlled Germany, will in time be absorbed within the Soviet orbit?

There are no little cosy arks and islands where prosperous people can escape world events. The white races no longer possess that technical superiority which has enabled them to dominate. Sooner or later there will have to be integration between the white and coloured races.

In Australia there has never been a long-lived socialist magazine, and accordingly at some of Kingsley's well-attended meetings probably one person in every four was a press representative. The result was an enormous press coverage and a spate of correspondence which showed that, as usual, he had pulled no punches. (As Dyason lecturer he had followed a formidable precedent set by Bertrand Russell and Sir Julian Huxley.) Australians seem to remember his lectures as frequently inaudible, discursive chats rather than carefully prepared addresses, with some name-dropping of the kind typified by "my good friend Nehru". (But it should be said that if Kingsley dropped names, they were those of people he usually knew well, and Nehru was a close friend for many years.) Kingsley, as ever, was a great success at the parties that followed his lectures, where everyone found him charming, relaxed and receptive. To judge from the itinerary of his tour it must have been a gruelling four weeks. The Australian newspapers called him "the most peripatetic editor in the world"; and Australians saw to it that, while he was in their charge, he lived the part.

By 1955 he had (unconsciously, no doubt) allowed it to become gradually apparent that he was no longer effectively editing the paper. It would not be far from the truth to say that John Freeman, Norman MacKenzie and Paul Johnson were running it while he was contributing the London Diary. Indeed he was not often going to the printer's to "put the paper to bed", and he occasionally read an article for the very first time when it had actually been published. If he did telephone to the printer's with a late amendment to one of the unsigned articles, the incorrigible Aylmer Vallance, sitting at the receiving end in the noisy room at the printer's, would be observed to be "shadow writing" with his pen-point three inches from the paper. Kingsley would never notice, Aylmer said, that the amendment had not been made. If he did he seldom said anything.

During the immensely dangerous Suez Crisis in 1956 he had been like a man caught in the crossfire between two armies in a place where it was dangerous even to lie down. The paper had regarded the Suez Canal as an international and therefore a United Nations interest. When President Nasser seized it in defiance of the world and Anthony Eden was obviously taking the country into war I met Kingsley, one morning in August, on the stairs at the *New Statesman* office, going up them two at a time with an ashen face and no time even to say "Good morning". The evening before, he had been on the platform at the Central Hall, Westminster, where A. J. P. Taylor had told a mass meeting that "this is the Boer War all over again, this is Hitler's attack on Poland. We've got to stand up. If what the British Government is doing now is justified, Hitler was entitled to attack Poland because of German interests. All you chaps who sneered at the Germans for not resisting Hitler—come on, it's your turn! We must get going on war resistance, and we haven't got many hours." Kingsley bustled into his office and rang bells. "Tear out that leader!" he said to a group of colleagues accustomed to these dramatic changes. "We are going to fight." (British families were already being air-lifted from the Suez Canal Zone, and diplomatic double-dealing was preparing the way for the biggest British military fiasco since Gallipoli. The Anglo-French bombing of Egyptian airfields did not come until the end of October and the adventure was over by 7th November, with UN troops taking over to keep the peace.)

Even for the purposes of his London Diary Kingsley would often spend a long time looking at what he had written in past volumes of the paper for some inspiration that the current news seemed unable to provide. On the home front his time was largely given to the Campaign for Nuclear Disarmament; the movements for the abolition of the death penalty and flogging; the reform of the laws about homosexuality; an oddly-motivated absorption in the campaign against "horror comics"; the emotionally charged problem of "factory farming"; and (here he wrote with all his old pungency, wit and fury) the long battle with the Law Officers about the prosecution of "obscene" books which ended in the passing of the Obscene Publications Act 1957. Of these, obviously, the supremely important issue was CND. In 1957 Aneurin Bevan, precariously restored to favour (and to office as Treasurer) in the Labour Party, vehemently supported Hugh Gaitskell in crushing a Party motion that Britain should renounce, unilaterally, the use of nuclear and hydrogen bombs. To do that, he said, would be to send any British Foreign Secretary naked into the conference chamber. The rank and file of the Party, no less than the intellectuals, were horrified. J. B. Priestley, in particular, saw the need to reverse this decision as soon as possible and that it could be done only by a popular movement. He told John Freeman he would write a long signed article by way of setting it in train; and Freeman, who was (as so often) acting editor during one of Kingsley's trips abroad, readily agreed although he was himself in sympathy with Nye Bevan and the Party's decision. This article, called "Britain and the Nuclear Bombs", appeared on 22nd February 1957. It led to an enormous correspondence, and was the starting point of the Campaign for Nuclear Disarmament, the story of which is well told by

Christopher Driver in *The Disarmers*.[1] (A rather more intimate and subjective account, which nevertheless carries greater conviction, is given in Canon Collins's autobiography *Faith Under Fire*:[2] the CND part of this book was the product of a close collaboration between Canon Collins and Kingsley.)

"But I still think," J. B. Priestley told me, "that Kingsley came back to a rather ambivalent attitude about it. He was not quite with us and not quite against us, although he turned up for meetings." The first meeting took place in Kingsley's flat at number 1 Robert Street. J. B. Priestley was there with his wife Jacquetta Hawkes, Bertrand Russell, Lord Blackett, Denis Healey and Professor George Kennan, who had come over from Princeton University to deliver his famous Reith Lectures on "Russia, the Atom and the West". "Kingsley always seemed to me to be dodging in and out of this," said J. B. Priestley. "I don't merely mean that he didn't often join the marches: I myself never marched a yard—I did all my marching in the first World War. He wasn't wholly with us. John Freeman of course was against us, but editorially he behaved superbly." It was John Freeman's view that Kingsley was having "a half-baked love affair" with CND, presenting an appearance of enthusiasm at its committee meetings and of ambivalence in the *New Statesman* office. "I think there are basically two kinds of journalist," John Freeman told me; "one that wants to expound a situation, and one that wants to *redress* a situation and doesn't care much about the facts—he wants to preach sermons. Kingsley was a preacher. While he was absolutely certain about his tenets and what he wanted to say, he wrote like an angel. I think if there was a decline in his writing it was at least as much due to the decline in his certainty as to any decline in his power to concentrate."

Kingsley's editorial henchmen were not in fact with him on nuclear disarmament; but one perennially disturbing thinker, Dick Crossman, was about to leave them, in circumstances that must now he told. While Kingsley was in Japan he had had a letter from John Freeman dated 23rd February 1955 which said:

[1] Hodder & Stoughton, London, 1964.
[2] Leslie Frewin, London, 1966.

> Dick has greatly startled us all by thinking very carefully through the British defence problems and coming to the conclusion that probably the Labour Party ought to support the British manufacture of the H-bomb, though the policy which accompanies it should be different from the present policy. His logic is impressive but I find the conclusion unacceptable; and anyway a *volte face* which cannot be offered to our readers as the *New Statesman* line without a lot more thought and preparation.

Accordingly the article did not appear as an editorial, but bore the signatures of Dick Crossman and George (later Lord) Wigg, who had helped him with it; and an editorial in the same issue made it plain that although the paper accepted some of the reasoning it did not at that stage approve the main conclusion. For Britain to go into business as an H-bomb manufacturer was a totally different question from the later controversy about refusing to renounce its use, which must involve Britain's withdrawal from NATO. Here Kingsley's editorial colleagues were solidly against him: they thought that to abandon NATO would be idiotic, and there is evidence that in discussing it they sometimes shook him severely. The full story of the CND's adventures is told elsewhere, but Kingsley's main reasons for supporting it, as evidenced by his private notes, were that the current disarmament Conference, like all its predecessors, was hopelessly bogged down; that the stalemate might be broken if Britain came out with a declaration that she was about to abandon nuclear weapons; and that ordinary people throughout the country felt themselves excluded from power, thwarted in their idealism, and horrified by the seeming indifference of the authorities to what the scientific experts had just revealed. But he was certain that nothing would happen unless the CND could persuade the leadership of the Labour Party to pledge itself to non-nuclear policy when it came into office. Accordingly at an early meeting of the CND committee he urged that their sole business was to convert Hugh Gaitskell to their point of view; and Bertrand Russell expressed total agreement. In this of course the Campaign never succeeded; indeed its leaders heard Gaitskell say in 1960, at the Labour Party Conference at Scarborough, that he would "fight, and fight, and fight again" to reverse a Party decision against the bomb and to "bring back sanity and honesty and dignity so that our movement with its great past may retain its glory and its greatness". Shortly afterwards Kingsley and Dorothy gave a party at their Robert Street flat. They usually invited the leader of the Labour Party to their gatherings but hardly expected Gaitskell to come. He did come; and when Dorothy, entering the crowded room with a tray of quasi-Oriental comestibles, saw him arriving she muttered to those near her: "Here comes the Traitor."

The ensuing conflict about ends and means, the formation of the "activist" group which called itself the Committee of 100, and the bitter quarrel between the two factions which gradually robbed both of effective popular support, are all now recorded history. Kingsley always felt that Canon Collins of St Paul's, CND's Chairman, had been let down by the movement, though that is not the view taken by Canon Collins himself. Among the minor "ifs" of history is what the *New Statesman*'s attitude to CND might have been if Dick Crossman had still been there in 1957.

To savour this, one must go back again to 1954. Dick Crossman had felt very strongly that the *New Statesman* should support the Bevanites, whose dislike for heavy expenditure on armaments seemed to offer a chance to unite the entire body of political dissent in this country. They were not to know that Bevan would later change direction, but in any event Kingsley was implacably determined not to give the paper any factional label, and he was not fond of Bevan. (Bevan was even less fond of him and of his paper: and Kingsley used to say that Bevan's famous declaration that Britain had "the most prostituted press in the world" was the opinion of a man who had never read anything more steeped in harlotry than the *Anglo-Welsh Review*.) In 1955 Crossman, who had been writing a political column in the *Sunday Pictorial*, was asked by Hugh Cudlipp to go on to the *Daily Mirror*, write a three-times-a-week "Lippmann" column on a four-year contract, and make it a whole time occupation. He felt he could not decide this without settling the whole question of his future with the *New Statesman*. On the *Daily Mirror* he could continue his political career. On the *New Statesman* he must, sooner or later, give it up; and

Kingsley would certainly require him to give it up if he appointed him deputy editor. Moreover the *Mirror* was offering him £4,000 a year and the *New Statesman* was paying him rather less than £1,000. Nevertheless he told Kingsley: "I'm perfectly content to stay with you if you will just say that my title is deputy editor and that when you retire I shall have a chance with the Board. I have only one ambition in life and that is to be editor of this paper."

"But you're a politician," said Kingsley.

"I'm prepared to give up being an MP if I become editor. And if I can't have this assurance I shall take the *Mirror*'s offer."

"You're putting a pistol to my head, then?"

"I simply want you to be fair to me."

Kingsley took two days to think it over. It can have been known to very few people at the time, but he was seriously thinking of retiring. He wanted to write some books, and he had discussed it with his old friend J. W. Robertson Scott, former Editor of *The Countryman*, who was then, at the age of 88, writing his autobiography.[1] On 20th December 1954 the old man sent him a long and remarkable letter which concluded:

> One does not like, as their biographer, colleague and friend, to think of the latter days of Stead, Cook, Spender, Massingham and some of the rest. They felt *lost* without their pulpits, had nowhere to go, and had some miserable hours despite honourable jobs they got for themselves, like Cook's 39 Quartos of Ruskin and Spender's series of books.
>
> One is always fearful and sorrowful when one has any hint of an Editor friend giving up his chair. Ernest Parke's wisdom always comes into my mind: "Let the other fellow resign". The books that resigned editors will have freedom and time to write will bring a certain satisfaction, and exert a certain influence; but just where has one all the influence and satisfaction that may be had in the right kind of editorial chair, if one is young enough and well enough? Do the men who have resigned *never* regret doing so? At 57 you seem to be, in my "88 eyes", quite young. What cannot you do at Great Turnstile? If you keep fit, you

[1] "*We*" *and Me*, W. H. Allen, London, 1956.

have years of first-class editing in you and *then* the opportunity of writing ripe books. . . . The NS is unique and you have made it so. You are at the top of the tree, and have such advantages as journeys abroad with all expenses paid. Away from it, neither House of Parliament attracts you. What else is there? To be one of the 3,000 retired "Sirs"—there are several utterly undistinguished in my mind? What is there in that? Like Spender, I *did* take the C.H., as rarer and with a better sound (after a day and a night's doubts). Grown people are past all this titled nonsense.

Kingsley might almost have written it himself: so much of it was precisely what he wanted to believe. And in this frame of mind the problem of who should succeed him had to be faced with resolution. He wanted John Freeman. After the two-days' interval he saw Dick Crossman again.

"There can be no question," he said. "I've thought about it and I would never trust you to put the *New Statesman* first in your politics."

"I've told you—I'd give them up."

"I don't believe it—you're a politician, and John Freeman isn't. He's really given up politics to live for the *New Statesman*."

"I knew you brought him in for that purpose, Kingsley—to get rid of me."

But there was no more to be said, and Dick Crossman left for the *Daily Mirror*. "We really treated each other," he told me, "as if we were citing each other for divorce. I had no farewell party. I left the office in utter disgrace. And I don't think I saw him or spoke to him after that for four or five years. I didn't want to. I thought he'd behaved abominably and that he was very stupid. I know John Roberts thought so—the people who said good-bye to me were the managerial side: they were very sorry this decision had been taken—it was unnecessary and taken with acerbity."

With Dick Crossman's departure went all likelihood that the Cold War might, instead of focusing the paper's attention on nuclear bombs and NATO, be used to foster what Crossman called "competitive Socialisms". He thought the Cold War could be used to stimulate people. If you could persuade the Americans to embark on development work in the Third

World, you could turn the Cold War to good account by encouraging beneficent competition. He was a pragmatist; and took the view that the Cold War was a chance to *direct* American funds, not only to Europe but to the new democratic countries. No man is indispensable, but Kingsley clearly felt that Dick Crossman, if only he could have been weaned from active political life, would have come closer to it than anyone who had helped him run the *New Statesman*. Among his papers there is a galley-proof of the obituary notice in which, with the ghastly anticipation necessitated by week-to-week readiness, he himself had written in 1963 about a man who was long to survive him. In many years of close association with Dick Crossman, he wrote, he had been constantly reminded of Lord Keynes:

> Crossman argued with the same ruthless and passionate logic. He had, like Keynes, an exasperating and disarming fluidity of mind which enabled him without embarrassment to reach the conclusion one day that he had decisively refuted the day before. If you wished to change his mind, it was a mistake to argue: it was easily done by inserting a different premise in the machine.... He would have been a peerless Q.C., and his ability to present any side of every question would have been pre-eminently successful if the New College don and brilliant extra-mural lecturer at Oxford had become a professor of philosophy and politics. Old students of his still talk with something akin to awe about the series of lectures which were published in his *Plato 1937*. . . . He was more than anyone else responsible for the *New Statesman* view that we had "two enemies, Communism and anti-Communism"; and he conceived of *The God That Failed*—a book he created and edited—not as anti-Communist propaganda but as an opportunity for thinkers who had been Communists genuinely to explain why they had been taken in and what the results of the mistaken adventure had been. . . . He led the left rebellion against the Attlee Government's foreign policy. He and Bevin first clashed over the 1946 Anglo-American Commission on Palestine. Bevin had promised to carry it into effect if the report was unanimous. Dick worked with concentrated zeal to make it so, and was brushed aside disdainfully by both Bevin and Attlee. . . . Later he was the unofficial secretary of the Bevanites, who were smashed by the cannier Gaitskell. If Nye had lived, this

group might have transformed English politics, because it was the only one of many left rebellions within the Labour Party that could not be dismissed as tainted with Communism.

But Crossman had been lost, John Freeman was the heir apparent; Kingsley was more tired than he admitted to anyone, there were books to be written. And there was the growing happiness of "Sunday painting", in which he had found not only relaxation but a fresh view, an almost startling view because it widened suddenly, of the world of aesthetics; and a sense of lyrical intuition. He claimed no skill, his paintings were agreeable; and for perhaps ten years of his life, from 1955 onwards, he was doing something that involved sitting still, neither talking nor listening, but thinking and being. In the late fifties, when John Berger was giving him lessons, he got so absorbed that he would start painting in the early morning, forget the time, and rush at last to the office still wearing an artist's smock with paint all over it. ("Kingsley!" his secretary would exclaim. "You've not come through the streets like that *again*? And there are three people waiting to see you.") In the none-too-happy years of his retirement, painting was an incomparable solace.

And above all there was the prospect of unlimited foreign travel, with all expenses paid out of the profits which he, more than anyone, had helped to build up in 30 years. Although no longer editor, he could justify the expense as a kind of Walter Lippmann, sending home long dispatches which were sure of publication. It was not to be.

Chapter 18

RETIREMENT

WHEN A MAN has been editing a journal like the *New Statesman* for 25 years—a prodigious achievement—there will be no lack of candid friends to suggest ideal moments for his retirement. Perhaps if there was an "ideal moment" it was in 1957 on the occasion of the famous *New Statesman* correspondence between Bertrand Russell, Khrushchev, and John Foster Dulles, the US Secretary of State. J. B. Priestley's "ban the bomb" article in February, and the intense CND activity to which it gave rise, led Bertrand Russell to write in November "An Open Letter to Eisenhower and Khrushchev". It was long and eloquently persuasive, urging the two leaders to abandon every attempt to spread their conflicting creeds "by force of arms", which meant by the use of nuclear attack. A month later Norman MacKenzie, opening the morning's mail at the *New Statesman* office, found a letter in Russian from the Soviet Embassy, enclosing a long translated article headed "Nikita Khrushchev Replies to Bertrand Russell". He took it in to Kingsley, who was very busy, thought the whole matter was not a suitable one for practical joking, and put the letter aside, dismissively. Even when his incredulity had been nursed into half-accepting the incredible, he made Norman telephone the Soviet Embassy to make quite sure that the *New Statesman* had truly pulled off this unprecedented scoop without really trying. Khrushchev's letter of about 3,000 words accepted everything that Lord Russell had said, and added: "It is not necessary that either side should abandon belief in its own creed; it is only necessary that it should abandon the attempt to spread its creed by force of arms." There was no reply from Eisenhower; but two months later, in February 1958, there came a letter from the US Secretary of State. It said that the Soviet Communist Party had never repudiated the use of force rather than law as a means of spreading its creed, and reminded Khrushchev that the Red Army had just been brutally crushing a revolt of the non-believers in Hungary. It seems likely enough that the State Department, reading extracts from this *New Statesman* correspondence in the press of the entire world, had felt itself stung into some kind of response. But it was a good moment for the editor who had raised his paper to such a status; perhaps his supreme moment. He had entered the fray himself with a personal letter to Khrushchev which showed him to be still in good preaching form:

> No sane person [he wrote] could disagree with the main drift of your reply to Bertrand Russell. Only madmen, faced with the kind of warfare that now threatens us all with destruction, would reject peaceful competition as an alternative to war or wish to maintain the nuclear tests and all the infernal business of modern armaments. Since your letter was published the NATO conference has decided to dole out nuclear weapons to other States, including Western Germany, and to set up rocket bases in this island. Nor are any of us oblivious to the appalling danger of American planes circling the air with deadly cargoes of H-bombs. . . .
>
> You must begin by understanding that in the West it is now quite untrue that the workers have nothing to lose but their chains. . . . They cherish not only the improvement in their standard of living but also their Western concept of liberty. . . . Those of us who were most opposed to Britain's ludicrous attempt to revive the old imperialist methods in Suez were the same people who were critical of the Soviet Union in Hungary. . . . Western observers in Hungary [at the time of the 1957 revolution], including old-type Communists and pro-Soviet journalists, were outraged by what they saw. What worried them was that Communism had no respect for the workers' aspirations for national or individual freedom. . . . I remember, as we all do here, the speech that you made about Stalin after the Twentieth Congress.[1] It was you yourself who denounced the "knock on the door at 3 a.m." which was a feature of all that was hated most in Stalin's Russia. . . . Your famous visit to Belgrade, when you admitted Russia's errors in trying to ride rough-shod over Yugoslavia, gave us great hope—which was disappointed in Hungary. . . .

[1] This, incidentally, was the starting-point of the Soviet quarrel with China which changed the whole concept of the Cold War.

> There is no difficulty here in persuading people that we ought to get rid of the H-bomb. But it is difficult to remove from people's minds the terror of Communist advance as long as Communism means not the liberation which it claims but an even more ruthless denial of liberty to ordinary working-class people than imperialism has meant. You are mistaken if you think that people like Aneurin Bevan, who talk about retaining the H-bomb as a bargaining weapon, are the dupes of capitalist propaganda.

Retirement was now much in his mind, and yet, though he had never wanted power, he still loved his position of undoubted influence; which, as Robertson Scott had reminded him three years before, could be a source of unique satisfaction and was largely the product of his own abilities. On holiday in Sicily ("Taormina, the most beautiful place I've ever known") he wrote in his diary:

> I remember Richards at the Heretics[1] reading a paper which began by asking what you would do with a friend who you knew would die within a few hours. He decided the right thing was to read him Hamlet—or, to summarise the point, to give him the best aesthetic experience you could in the time available. Well, my guess is that the third World War started some time ago, and that for many months or even years we may go on having the same kind of experience we've had in the last year: appalling wars like that in Korea while we are comparatively immune from danger. Orwell depicts this as becoming—after a dose of atomic war—the regular thing in a world divided into three blocs, none of which can conquer the others but none of which wants to stop the desultory war and the cross-alliancing that goes on because war prevents people from questioning the necessity for sacrifice. If I'm at all right, I'd like to write a diary of the last year or two of my life, and perhaps of the kind of life in Britain that we know.

In 1959 John Freeman interviewed, in the highly successful BBC television series called *Face to Face*, a succession of interesting public men and women who subjected themselves to a new kind of questioning. It extracted from the subject himself, by public examination, the kind of information you would seek

[1] The Heretics Society in Cambridge, founded by C. K. Ogden. Kingsley mentions this address by I. A. Richards in *Father Figures*, p. 108.

from other sources if you were writing a "candid profile" for a newspaper. The difference was that the people interviewed were willing victims. The programmes were immensely popular in many parts of the world. Because of them, and because of his appearances as narrator and "link-man" in a variety of other programmes, John Freeman in 1960 was awarded the title of "television personality of the year" (an award made at that time by the Guild of Television Producers and Directors, and later by the Society of Film and Television Arts). He was accordingly receiving at this time offers of a kind which, if money was all that mattered, would wean most men away from the deputy editorship of the *New Statesman*. But there were other considerations equally important to him.

He never had the umbilical feeling for the paper that Kingsley had. It was not his child: it was a job that was eminently worth doing as long as one wanted to do it, and he would not have stayed much longer as Kingsley's Number 2. In that capacity he was in fact better off financially than at any time before or (I believe) since, because of the total freedom to do as he liked and earn what he could. But by the middle of 1960 he believed that the *New Statesman* was heading for disaster, since Kingsley by that time seemed to him incapable of taking coherent decisions and yet quite capable, in an extremely destructive way, of interfering with the machine that was carrying on underneath him and, in fact, running the paper. Early in 1959 Kingsley had asked him if he should leave—and, if he did leave, whether Freeman would step into his shoes. Freeman said no, because at that time the editorial waters were navigable and he was comfortable. Asked the same question six months later he said he thought Kingsley should leave. "I then said I should find it difficult to stay," John Freeman told me, "unless he made way fairly soon. And this was partly to avoid the pain of having to tell him I thought he was no longer up to it and was beginning to destroy what he had created. I never had intended myself to stay there long. And with the awful example of Kingsley before me I had formed a very clear impression, which others obviously didn't share, that the *New Statesman* ought to be edited by a relatively young man. The task that I set myself, on becoming editor, was to tidy things up, modernise the paper a bit, and then hand over to someone else who should preferably be a generation younger.... I did think that what had been a marvellous operation until the middle fifties had sadly deteriorated, and that what was now needed was a short incumbency by a non-genius to see if a certain amount of order could be put back into it."

Kingsley formally retired in December 1960 and was appointed "editorial director" for twelve months; a phrase and a device which, however commonly called in aid to comfort departing editors, should have had ominous overtones in the case of a paper whose editors had been traditionally free from "direction" by anyone whatsoever. He had many letters from people who didn't want him to retire. They expressed alarm, astonishment, dismay, good wishes, and (from older readers) what Wordsworth called "the unimaginable touch of time". Kingsley Martin retiring! As might be expected, the irrepressible A. J. P. Taylor crowned all these messages:

> The end of an era! It is most distressing to think that the *New Statesman* may now follow a consistent line two weeks running.

He simply could not accept retirement. He asked where his office was to be, and was allotted, with some embarrassment, a small room used in those emergencies when someone not on the staff has a last-minute article to write and dislikes writing in pubs. He later described this, fairly enough, as "a cubby-hole at the end of a passage". He began to turn up at the Monday morning editorial conferences; and this was quite unexpected. To the acute embarrassment of John Freeman's personal secretary, he took to making last-minute changes in leading articles she had typed. One of his oldest friends, Professor W. A. Robson, remembers as "the attitude of a super egoist" his announcement that after his retirement his name "would appear even more frequently in future issues". It may well be that it was only to a less sophisticated majority of his readers that he had become a personification of his paper. For others he was now displaying, as Professor Robson said, Lawrence of Arabia's "genius for stepping back into the limelight".

To John Freeman it was "a difficult problem to displace a

person like Kingsley, because there's a lot of politics in it as well as judgment about the quality of his work. And Kingsley was quite right," said Freeman, "in perceiving that I judged, immediately I took over, that painful as it was he really had to be got out of the paper completely. Then, once he was out, he could be brought back again on an *ad hoc* basis when he had something to contribute. But it would have been impossible to let him sit in his own chair and fill a page every week, after this tremendous effort on his part and everybody else's to effect his retirement. It is true that I looked with a jaundiced eye, not so much on what he contributed (though I did that in one or two cases) as on his continuing to occupy half the editorial chair—this really was not possible. The paper had to be given a new look, even if the look was less good. This is after all the small change of 'succession', and Kingsley couldn't face it."

Fortunately he left a considered statement of his own feelings about all this, in the form of a chapter for the projected Volume III of his memoirs. It was written in 1968, when he was a very sick man and had only a few months to live. Its relevance at this point will excuse the departure from strict sequence in telling the story, as will the opportunity to let Kingsley tell it himself in context. The following extract from it omits, in the main, the passages which in my own diffident judgment fell below the standard of cogency by which he would have wished to be remembered:

> In writing this chapter of my life I should explain that I have taken more than the usual care not to overstate or dramatise, well aware how great those temptations are for a man as incurably self-centred and sloppy-minded as I am. . . . I write not only in self-explanation but also because events since I resigned from the editorship of the paper which was so much associated with my name have led to much misunderstanding.
>
> Those who have read these pages so far will realise that, while I suffer from an acute sense of failure in many ways, and plead guilty to grave errors of judgement as editor, I do broadly feel proud of having turned the paper of a sect into one of world reputation and influence. The one thing I do value about myself is that I have made the paper trusted by many people as an

organ which can be relied upon not to neglect the truth, and to champion those at home and abroad who struggle for freedom and enough to eat. I was very mindful of this reputation when I resigned, and I believed in doing so that I was doing the best thing for the paper by giving myself the freedom to continue to work for the same causes. I add that I still believe I was right to do so, and I believe the traditions of the paper are being maintained since my resignation.

I had worked for nine years with John Freeman as [my] second-in-command. We had not always been in agreement, but he was a stickler for loyalty, as well as one of the most efficient people I've known. There had always been an understanding between us that I should prefer him to anyone else as my successor; and it bothered me a little that I might continue for so many years that he might repent of his devotion. I managed with his help to do what no editor could normally expect to do—that is, write a Diary into which I put my heart, and which I was determined always to keep gay and fresh, as well as often writing other articles and keeping a pretty shrewd eye on all else that went into the paper. John lent himself to this position of second fiddle in a way that was entirely admirable.

One of the essentials for such a combination was that I should travel abroad once or twice a year for considerable periods. I could not possibly have maintained a fresh outlook for the editorship and the Diary over so many years otherwise. The reports I did from foreign countries were considered by many people to be my best work, and to contribute materially not only to the prestige of the paper but also to the paper's main purpose of trying to modify the imperialism of Britain and to help people in India, Kenya, Ghana, etc. to understand that they had friends in England. While I was away on these jaunts, John held the fort for me, loyally interpreting the policy about which we were in agreement.

In 1959 I felt that a change had come. First, I was tired, and becoming doubtful of my capacity to say anything that was fresh and useful about the cold war or other issues which were all-important. I realised that there was a danger that I might be like other editors who cling to their positions while members of the staff on lower rungs of the ladder regard them as unnecessary obstructions. Secondly, I felt it was unfair to John, when he was often making decisions and increasingly running the machinery of the paper, to keep all the credit to myself. Also I realised that he had built for himself a great national reputation as a broadcaster and that I should be lucky if he remained content for long in a subordinate position. I asked him in the Spring of that year whether he was content, and he replied that he was content to be my assistant for as many years as I cared to remain editor. As the year went on, however, I began to doubt whether this could remain true. We were not so good a team as we had been, because owing to the change of printers to Wycombe,[1] and my own tiredness, I was leaving an increasing amount of work to him, while he was becoming more deeply and personally involved in "Face to Face". Projects I outlined to him were not carried out: I lazily left them to him and he was very naturally too preoccupied to remember and set them on foot.[2]

I therefore again put to him whether he did not think I ought to leave the editorial job to him; and got the pleased answer that he no longer felt as he had done six months before. He had had six important jobs offered him, which he had refused because he wanted to be editor before anything else.[3] In fact he could not any longer say what he had said in the Spring. He would not be able always to refuse other offers. I felt that this fully clarified the situation. I could not begin with a new editor, I could not do all the jobs I used to do 30 years before, and if there was to be someone to take over from me, who else than the man I had worked with and trusted for so long? I therefore resigned the editorship at the end of 1960, agreeing to act as editorial director for the next year with the special job of building the paper up abroad. . . .

At [John's] request I went first to Cuba and other parts of Latin America, and did my best. A most disturbing event happened, which turned my world topsy-turvey. After leaving Cuba I learned that an American raid was reported; and since I had

[1] The printing was transferred in 1959 from Cornwall Press, Blackfriars, to Merrett & Hatcher Ltd, High Wycombe.

[2] The reason why these projects were not carried out, says John Freeman, is that they were "projects best forgotten".

[3] "The point was," John Freeman told me, "not that I wanted to edit the paper above everything else—though perhaps I did—but that in the intervening six months I had come to the conclusion that his continued retention of the editorial chair had become seriously damaging to the paper. I saw no purpose in continuing, at some sacrifice to myself, to buttress a position which I felt I could no longer support. It seems that he never quite got the point, and this may have been why he felt so resentful afterwards."

believed (correctly as it turned out) that an American intervention was likely, I sent a wire reporting the alarm that this story had occasioned and suggesting that it might be a precursor of something larger. To my astonishment when I saw the New Statesman in the United States I found that a scrap—a few inches—of my report, leaving out the whole point of my prophetic message, was in the paper with my name attached.[1] I also sent an article containing descriptive matter about Cuba that I knew I should not want to include in my political articles. This was not printed. To my vigorous and distressed protest about the emasculated cable John replied with an apology which left me utterly bewildered—it gave no explanation of the sort of editorial misconduct which neither he nor I would ever have committed when we were running the paper together. To this day I have no notion what possessed him to make or permit so gross a breach of the most elementary rules of professional journalism. As to not using my article, that was of course within his rights and he explained that he thought it unwise to print an article that might interfere with my subsequent survey. This also troubled me because it was surely a matter in which I was the best person to judge, and I was not an inexperienced reporter who would be expected to write articles if they were not likely to be used.

During the rest of my year as "editorial director" I wrote constantly and I think up to my standard. In Cairo I cabled a long interview with Nasser, explaining, according to the usual journalist's habit, after my signature that I had gone to the expense of the cable because it was an unusual interview given in an informal and relaxed atmosphere. To my horror, this private note to the

[1] It may be useful to recall that a sudden and ill-prepared invasion of Cuba was carried out by a group of Cuban exiles trained in Florida by officers of the American CIA; and was a disastrous failure, immensely strengthening the position of the Marxist Castro and his finance minister Che Guevara. The CIA knew that Russian rockets were in Cuba and that ten launching pads were being built for Russian ballistic missiles with a range of 2,000 miles. Current feeling divided the American War Council into "hawks" (led by Dean Acheson) and "doves" (led by Robert Kennedy). The President's policy was to "play it cool", and if possible preserve total secrecy until the Russians had been diplomatically manœuvred into withdrawal.

The hawks urged that the American Air Force should bomb Cuba at once, or at the least that Cuban ports should be blockaded against Soviet supply ships. The victory of the doves may, I suppose, be attributed to the human instinct for survival.

Editor was inserted in the text of the interview, so that I was made to boast of having had a unique and domestic talk such as no other journalist had ever been granted. I could do nothing to put this right, and had to bear the shame of it as best I could. In answer to my protest John again apologised handsomely, but gave no explanation. Members of the Board to whom I mentioned that my cable had been altered at once said they had been astonished at this uncharacteristic and silly boast. A friend who had had several far more important private interviews with Nasser complained vehemently to me about my lying presumption. I have been ashamed to write or speak to my friends in Egypt who had helped to arrange the interview.[1]

This, however, is to step ahead of the more serious matter which made me gravely concerned about John's attitude to me in the future. While [I was] in Washington he rang me to ask me on a particular week to write "very short or not at all". I agreed of course; but wrote asking why, with the whole paper to choose from, he had thought it worth while to spend the money on a long distance phone call rather than shorten some other contribution. This was perhaps touchy of me, but I explained in my letter that my real worry was my doubt about the part he wanted me to play on the paper in future. I said that I had conceived of my role as that of a sort of Lippmann figure, writing signed pieces from time to time; and that occasionally I should write the Diary when he was not doing it himself. I begged him to be candid about this, as I was much depressed about my future. . . . The difficulty was to explain why I was not writing it [the London Diary] to people who had supposed that it was a considerable asset to the paper. The impression was given either that I was not willing to do the Diary, or that John had no further use for me in this feature of the paper that I had made peculiarly my own. . . . When I asked John if he would like me to go to India for the paper he was enthusiastic. He said truly that it is a particularly good moment to do a thorough report on India. I am therefore about to pay my sixth visit there, and hope to stay long enough to write something really solid and important. I am grateful to

[1] John Freeman has this recollection: "By one of those idiotic accidents which happen when the paper is going to press, and to which I was not privy at all at the time, a 'service message' at the end of one of his cables got left on it and was published. And we all had appalling red faces the next day." *Quaere*: was it a unique interview or not, "such as no other journalist had ever been granted"?

> John for this opportunity. I leave however with a heavy heart; for thinking over this unhappy year—the most unhappy since I reached sexual maturity—I realise that on my return I must carve a new career for myself in which the *New Statesman* will play a minor part. It is because that is so difficult to explain to the many people who now ask me with surprise whether I have broken my association with the paper which has been my life, that I have written this account of my disillusion. I make no comment on this. I record the facts, and beg those who had regarded me as a valuable interpreter to look elsewhere for my writing. I do not yet know where that will be, but clearly it must be in some journal of opinion. I am still no more than the age when many do their best writing. I have published two books since my retirement, and may publish others; but the habit of current comment is too strong inside me to resist it.

It reveals something about his state of mind that, having begun this rationale as if for a chapter in a book about the past, and sustained it thus for two-thirds of the way, he slips into the present tense to discuss his imminent departure for India in 1968, and his worried contemplation of his own future in journalism. I showed it to John Freeman, who was not altogether surprised at its tone and burden:

> It was a painful and difficult experience, in which I sought to hurt him as little as I possibly could, but in which I was absolutely determined that I would finish this job, and "do it clean", before asking anybody else to take over from me. That was a hard decision, and some people may well hold it against me; but it had to be done and I did it as little woundingly as I could. My impression had been, though the dating of this document doesn't support me, that he had in the end come to terms with it, and had realised that it was better for him to be right out of it. But I see now that it must have rankled with him to the end. This does surprise me, for though I had a very strained relation with him for some time after he left, it was my impression that all was intimate and friendly by the time when this passage was written. I didn't see him very often then, because I was abroad for most of his last years. But whenever I came to England I used to go and see him, and we had conversations of the greatest intimacy and apparent friendliness, in which he revealed to me for the first time

> some of the more intimate matters in your book. . . . It may be that on some days he felt genuinely affectionate and on other days remembered past bitterness.

To return to the quieter scene of his domestic life, he had moved to new quarters both in town and country during the John Freeman period. He left Little Easton in 1954, when Leonard Woolf told him of a vacant cottage high up on the Sussex Downs at Rodmell. The week-end journey to Little Easton had been taking longer and longer, as the development of Harlow New Town added to the volume of road traffic. The village itself was no longer quiet. He was sometimes alone at the cottage because Dorothy was now travelling widely, and he had begun to fear sudden attacks of illness (particularly his lifelong affliction of "Menière's Disease") while he was alone in a house—this had happened at least once at Little Easton. And, crowning calamity, Bill Lodge ("Mr Park") had sadly told him that the time had come when he must give up working in the garden.

During those 20 years Kingsley had brought to the little village—especially since the war—some exciting visitors. People like Arthur Koestler, Paul Robeson, Ernst Toller, and Jomo Kenyatta had been down there as Kingsley's guests. The little pub next door, the old "Stag", was in fact a new Stag because the original pub was now occupied by Kingsley; and its bar was often enlivened by bright-robed Africans or dapper Indians and Chinese, who consumed soft drinks and were ready to believe that Kingsley was able to teach them how to play darts. It would sometimes happen that while this was going on Dorothy, a hemisphere distant, was staying with someone like the King of Nepal.

Kingsley was a companionable man; no man for solitary walks, and prone to melancholy if alone for more than an hour. Yet although he was the soul of hospitality he had, once the war was over, felt his way rather carefully back to the "open house" atmosphere which had prevailed at Great James Street and overflowed to Little Easton at weekends. "The experience of war-time evacuation," he wrote in a diary, has made everyone cautious about sharing homes—there has never been a kitchen large enough for two women. There were two schoolteachers who came to our cottage and soon left because they had expected the cooking and housework to be done for them. There were 17 soldiers who lived there during six weeks of bitter frost. They used up all the wood and broke the stove, but were wonderfully grateful for any small additions to their comfort that we could make. Several of them were afterwards killed in the fighting before Dunkirk. One day the wife of a Sergeant-Major came to stay. She complained that there were no wardrobes in which to hang her clothes. She had, she explained, several boxes of them and they must be properly treated. We pointed out that all the walls in our bedrooms sloped from floor to ceiling and there was nowhere to put wardrobes even for ourselves. She said it wasn't what she was used to and left the next day. Many other people used the cottage, including an officer and his wife on a week's honeymoon. Summing it up I should say that having people as visitors works very well if the hostess gives up all her time to them.

"Hill-Top", at Rodmell, had few of the attractions of The Old Stag; a small and featureless modern house with, however, a splendid open view across the Downs to Newhaven, and within easy walking distance of an attractive little village whose main street bears a sign pointing "To The Shop". The keeper of that buried-away little shop, possibly the tiniest supermarket in the country, had a long friendship with Kingsley Martin and Dorothy (of whom she was specially fond), with Leonard and Virginia Woolf, and with a great number of people to whom those names were significant. Kingsley loved village communities, and could, if need be, conjure one up if it seemed not to be aware of itself already.

This he did in the Adelphi district of London, where he lived from 1944 until 1963, first at 14 Buckingham Street and then at number 1 Robert Street. The former was a tall eighteenth-century building divided into chambers: its predecessor, first occupied by Charles Sackville, Sixth Earl of Dorset, was blown up by the military when it caught fire in 1684 and there seemed no other way of preventing the fire from spreading: to the great disgust of Samuel Pepys, who lived next door, who had witnessed the Great Fire of London, and who considered himself more damaged by the explosion than he would have been by the fire. It was nearly burned down again in the 1830's, when its occupants included William Etty the painter and Sir Humphry Davy the scientist (and this time the man next door was Charles Dickens, who describes the flat in *David Copperfield*). Thereafter a long succession of artists and writers lived at number 14, represented in 1936 by Aylmer Vallance, who handed it over to Kingsley in 1944.

And it was Kingsley who, in his London Diary, took up from Pepys and Dickens the chronicle of what he himself christened Charing Cross Village. If the Adelphi district really had a village "feeling" it was the product of common adversity—first the war and the sharing of air-raid shelters, and then the dwindling proportion of residents as against landlords, lawyers, advertisers, merchants, travel agents, oil tycoons, builders. By 1958 number 14 was completely occupied by Montague Meyer Ltd, the timber importers (whose economic adviser was the Rt. Hon. Harold Wilson); and it is now the home of the still vigorously developing Consumers' Association in which Kingsley took a great interest—"I could almost become involved as a new comrade," he said. But he had left in 1956 to rent a beautiful flat on the second floor at number 1 Robert Street—still in "Charing Cross Village" and still overlooking the river. In his written diaries Kingsley describes it as "shabby splendour".

"We had held on to 14 Buckingham street as long as we could," he wrote in the draft for his next book, "partly because the address now meant so much to so many people of many countries.

> We moved at last into No. 1 Robert Street, the one remaining Adam building[1] which belonged to the original Adelphi pattern. . . . It had for a time been used as a hotel. Many of its splendid flats—among the first, I think, built in London—had been cut up and ruined. But the second floor of No. 1, where we lived, still had its lovely little round hall, its Adam ceilings and fireplaces; and its large sitting room was one of the prettiest I ever saw. We lived there, in a peace which has quite deserted the Adelphi now, until 1963, when speculative builders decided to

[1] William Adam himself had lived at No. 1.

pull it down to make way for more profitable office blocks. We set about organising an opposition to this vandalism, but though most of London's best known architects signed a letter to *The Times*[1] protesting against the demolition of any more of Adam's London, we lost our case at a public enquiry and left for a comfortable but less elegant address near Victoria [25 Carlisle Mansions]. The joke was against the vandals. I think that the problem of rebuilding was, as we had told them, very difficult. This part of the Adelphi stands on pillars which raise the street level out of the mud of the Thames. After several attempts a plan was eventually produced for reconstructing the building, but by that time a Labour Government had refused to allow any more offices to take the place of dwellings, and the final result looks as if it will be exactly what I wanted to achieve five years ago—the façade unchanged, with improved flats behind it. I need only add that I hope a lot of people were disappointed with the financial return.

They were. But the "improved flats" have not materialised, Kingsley need not have moved, and the lesson is plain for all those threatened by the wave of modern Goths whom we call "developers" and Kingsley was still calling speculative builders.

[1] *The Times* letter (22 June 1962) bore the signatures, among others, of John Betjeman, C. M. Bowra, Hugh Casson, Kenneth Clark, John Freeman, Osbert Lancaster, Henry Moore, Raymond Mortimer, John Piper, Sir John Rothenstein and Lord Silkin. Two hundred years earlier, the Adam Brothers had organised an "Adelphi Loan" from No. 1 Robert Street, in their campaign to overcome eighteenth-century problems of "planning and developing" the Adelphi, so well described by Fanny Burney. A plaque now bears the names of Robert Adam, Thomas Hood, John Galsworthy, and Sir James Barrie—who used to exchange courtesies with Bernard Shaw from his window across the road.

Chapter 19

"ALL SORTS OF INTERESTING WOMEN..."

In his last decade Kingsley was putting together, in a desultory way, some notes and papers concerning three important aspects of his life, two for eventual publication and the third, I think, not. The first, a collection of the *New Statesman*'s adventures among the laws of libel, is looked at in the next chapter. The second was a résumé of his views about religion, racialism, and the growth of the new Asian and African republics; and the third was a contemplative review of his romantic friendships with women. "When I was young I was afraid of women," he said in a Granada Television interview in August 1968 (which has not yet been broadcast); "and I didn't even fall in love until I was 25. I was very retarded indeed, by my whole upbringing. And when I look back on it I know that all sorts of interesting women fell in love with me that I've given the brush-off. . . . I had a sort of virtue: [but] there's something else that holds you back. It's a lack of assuredness in yourself, a lack of certainty. . . . But I think anything like psychoanalysis is silly."

He was attractive to women. To those who do not understand what attracts women, this was a source of some perplexity. Was it his appearance? I think he was alternately proud and worried about his appearance. In 1957, I received a long letter from Caryl Chessman, then under sentence of death in San Quentin Prison, California, for kidnapping. It was about the problem of capital punishment; and surprisingly objective it was, since Chessman seemed to know only too well that the authorities intended, sooner or later, to kill him. (It took them twelve years to do this, during which Chessman wrote and published two books about the prospect before him.) Kingsley was very distressed when I showed him this letter, and we published an article about it. I also showed him Chessman's photograph and mentioned that some of us thought it was rather like himself as a younger man. He looked at it long and, I thought, compulsively: so long that I began to fidget. At length he returned it to me without a word. I have always remembered it as one of his more eloquent silences. I think he was in one of his periods of satisfaction about his appearance, and the Chessman comparison upset him. He had an actor's awareness of himself, and an actor's feeling about exits and entrances. "I remember a party," said Frank Hardie, "at which he made some very pithy and witty remark (I was so used to them) and then said instantly 'And now I must go'; and with a wide gesture of his arms he made his way through the party—and out. Well, why not? It's a great thing to know when to go, and you might as well leave on a good line as do it in the confused way that most of us do."

At the top of the stairs in the Savile Club, as you go into the dining room, there is a huge wall-mirror. When you followed him up the stairs on the way to lunch you could see him using this mirror to settle his features in what he must have supposed to be the best arrangement for the occasion. I could never decide whether this was vanity or controlled apprehension, but since he was to me rather a great man I always found it endearing; and I never knew whether it meant that he really thought himself good-looking or was making the best of a bad job. Many women, however, thought him good-looking and had certainly told him they did.

Among those who did not, the woman whom he had known from Cambridge days as Verity was beyond any doubt "the love of his life". Until his break with Olga they met very seldom; but they resumed their special relationship in the thirties, and during the war they shared the same kind of London life and friends.

It is quite obvious that Dorothy Woodman never filled such a place, neatly though she and Kingsley supplemented each other's lives, both domestically and politically. They came to understand each other perfectly, and with a tolerance which, it may be, is sometimes more easily achieved without marriage. The tolerance on Dorothy's part had its maximum opportunity when Kingsley, in his fifties, began a prolonged and ecstatically romantic love affair with a girl he called Nikki.

He met Nikki in a delayed aircraft at Colombo Airport in 1951. She was sitting immediately behind him and they got into conversation. The woman sitting next to her suggested that they might like to sit together, and she was right. "I suppose it was nothing more or less than a pick-up," Nikki told me. He was then 54 and she was in her thirties. She was, and is, extremely attractive and quick-witted. They talked for hours, and when they got to Cairo they both discovered, without undue dismay, that they had insufficient money to complete their journey to England. They stayed in Cairo for the night, and began an association which lasted, a source of continual happiness for him, until his death eighteen years later. In England she introduced him to her husband, a well-to-do industrialist who had never heard of him ("who's Kingsley Martin?") but knew of the existence of something called the *New Statesman*. He thenceforth tolerated an association which a less busy and preoccupied man might have found insupportable; and she stayed with Kingsley many times. She visited him often at Robert Street, at Carlisle Mansions, and at Rodmell, and was always welcomed by Dorothy, who told her repeatedly that she was "good for Kingsley". Whenever he was going abroad he would ask Nikki to go with him, and she always went; not at first at the expense of Kingsley or the *New Statesman*—or of her husband—but by getting her wealthy parents in New York to cable her the money. In 1959 her husband died. Then her father died in America and, in consequence of a family quarrel in which she was not involved, she was disinherited and her brother became the main, if not the sole, beneficiary under their father's will. The association with Kingsley nevertheless continued, through many trips to India, Egypt, the Far East, and the Mediterranean countries. It is abundantly plain from Kingsley's letters to her that she was not the pursuer, though she was deeply in love with him: they are exactly the letters of a highly literate adolescent who finds himself bewilderingly, obsessively, and poetically in love for the first time. In 1968 she remarried and settled abroad, but still retained Kingsley's close friendship and indeed his love, with her new husband's full knowledge and approval.

When Kingsley died in Cairo in February 1969 it had been

his intention to call on her, on his way home, to discuss the inclusion of this story in the third volume of his memoirs—as to which, she had always been reluctant but had at last agreed. Since the stroke in 1963 he had grown weaker and slower, and had become intermittently dependent on her in a way that would move almost anyone to sympathy and concern. From then onwards he saw her abroad two or three times a year, though she came to England more often—and visited him in hospital when he was ill. But he seemed to expect a letter from her almost daily, writing anguished and ill-typed letters of reproach when they did not come. For example on 19th July 1967:

> My dear even now you do not answer my very plain question. You ask how I am and what I am doing. I've just finished the new book[1] and sent it to the publishers, and I've got a multitude of articles to write. In health I go up and down, and Dorothy, perhaps rightly, asks me each day I'm down if I've yet heard from you, because she thinks it's worry about you and never getting a proper answer from you that accounts for my bad days. She may be more than half right. Why in Heaven's name, if you still love me, do you not say right out that you want me to come out again, and when (I suggest October); and where you think I should stay? Or do you not want me to come out, for some reason? Why do you not answer?
>
> Too bad to bully you when you're ill, but I'm going round the bend trying to find a reason for your evasions.
>
> Love none the less my dear,
>
> Kingsley.

Dorothy's approval of Nikki was unmistakable, and is expressed in letters between the two women. Kingsley wrote from Carlisle Mansions in an undated letter:

> Dorothy had many happy love affairs when she was younger, and I come across her ex-lovers often and always happily. It's hard for her to grow elderly and stout, and lose her attractive looks. But I find people still fall in love with her—men and women. She has been wonderfully generous to us; and as long as I go on loving her, as I shall do, she is happy about us. I posted

[1] *Editor.*

a letter to you from her, which I expect you had and which you may have answered. She minds about your *friendship*, and wants to share our love.

On 5th May 1968 he wrote a letter which was specially revealing about his state of mind in the last few months of his life:

I want to know whether you have been married and whether you are ever coming over here at all. On my side I have to report that I am in generally good health, with bad days thrown in; that my book has been on the whole well reviewed—I'll send you the NS with Crossman's article in it; that I am beginning on Volume III and expect to live for another two years or till it's finished, but that I pray I do not live to get dependent or senile; that if you hear that I've killed myself it will not be for any reason except that I think I've done all I can and, having finished, I drop out. At the moment there seems much to do. Race has become the dominant issue here as in the U.S. It's horrible beyond belief that this is so, and in so far as I can I'll spend the rest of my life fighting this horror. (My book will work in with this.)

And finally—14th November 1968—he told her of the last serious development of his illness:

I've got a new complaint which makes me unsure of going away to stay with anyone. As you know from experience, and from my Hospital Diary,[1] I have had odd bouts of sickness—most appallingly embarrassing and unpleasant. Now I've had a bad aching tummy for three days. It's an odd trouble—both the sickness and the ache are due to "pockets" in the colon—I've forgotten what they are called.[2] It is not as I first thought Cancer or serious, but an X-ray shows clearly what it is and I don't think it will be cured. The doctor says I should go away and risk its coming back. It gives no warning. Obviously I must only go where my hosts will not be too upset. I have a drug to take if it begins, but I shall not know beforehand, damn it. However, be a pet and decide not to keep me away because it may happen again!

In fact, he never saw her again. In the same letter he had said, "We shall not go to India as I thought we might, but—would

[1] *New Statesman*, 21 December 1968. [2] It was diverticulitis.

you believe it?—we might go to Cairo to stay with the Indian Ambassador, who is a great friend of ours."[1]

Nikki's place in his story is established and important, for she brought him considerable peace of mind as well as the recurring torment of separation—the latter mainly in his declining years, when he was ill and often lonely. It was not an "infatuation" in the strict sense of the word, since that is a state of besotted fatuity: it was an outpouring of erotic tenderness not unusual (though often ridiculed and condemned) in a man approaching old age.

One wonders if Kingsley, at these happy times, ever recalled what he had written 40 years earlier in reviewing the Marquis of Zetland's edition of *The Letters of Disraeli to Lady Bradford and Lady Chesterfield*:[2]

> He was a great letter writer [wrote Kingsley] and though we have not the replies to his letters the story is plain enough. It was Lady Bradford who was really his "dear darling"; it was on her account mainly that he scribbled notes on scraps of paper, using his top hat as a rest, in the long dreary parliamentary sittings. It was her moods, her reasonable embarrassments (for she was a married woman and no romantic), and her frequent displays of coldness which drove him to impassioned outpourings of which few men would have been capable though 50 years his junior.

It is best, in this context, to allow that inversely prophetic passage to speak for itself.

When he said that "all sorts of interesting women" fell in love with him he did not speak as a womaniser. Certainly many women sought his company and then found themselves to be scintillating, for he was a companionable man, with the attractive capacity (rare in the well-informed and not always exercised by him) to give his whole attention to what a companion was saying, even if he then crushed it. It seems likely that his early difficulties with sex had impaired his judgment

[1] Apa Pant, later Indian High Commissioner in London and now Indian Ambassador to Rome.

[2] Ernest Benn, London, 1929. Reviewed by Kingsley Martin in the *Listener* of 13 November 1929.

about women, to the extent that any woman who was not treating him with perceptible coolness would seem to be throwing herself at him. Men who knew him well in the forties and fifties do not believe that women fell in love with him, though many women certainly liked him, liked talking to him, teasing him and being seen in public with him.

But there was one tragi-comic episode in which he was certainly the quarry, and the woman in pursuit brought him to the very verge of breakdown. Her story is worth telling because, as a person seriously but not dangerously deranged, she may have been "acting out" unconsciously and defencelessly the feelings of the more inhibited "interesting women". Luckily it can be told in Kingsley's own words: the following, headed 'Persecution', is from the unfinished draft for his third book of autobiography:

"Miss X was middle-aged, white-haired, bespectacled and goggle-eyed. I first met her by mistake. In the early post-war years, I was speaking at a meeting for International Help for Children. I shook hands, as one does, with people one recognises after the meeting. For the moment I mistook her for another white-haired lady I knew, and expressed my pleasure at seeing her there. To my surprise she walked with me to my car and asked if she could accompany me. I told her I was only driving to my garage near Charing Cross. She hopped in all the same; and it was eight years from that day before I ceased to see her.

"It seemed that she had only one object, which was to go to bed with me. Her custom was to wait outside my flat or office and ask me in a gentle voice if I would spend the night with her. At first, I treated her with the courtesy one naturally shows to someone who is slightly dotty. When I became rude, and complained of her persecution, Dorothy thought I was being unkind. She changed her mind one sunny day, I recall, when Miss X was sitting on the kerbstone in Robert Street sketching my flat while she waited for me—she was rather good at pen-and-ink drawing. Dorothy, returning from shopping, approached her with a bag of peaches. She refused to take one, and said: 'It's not peaches I want to share with you.' Dorothy then ceased to regard me as unsympathetic.

"At this point I must explain my difficulty. What does a

man do when an apparently respectable elderly female pursues him relentlessly and peaceably? I tried asking the policemen we passed on the road if they would not stop her pursuing me. The usual answer was: 'Is she your missis?'; and when I explained that I had but a short acquaintance with her, [the policeman] would ask her what she wanted. She always replied in the sweetest of tones that she only wanted a word with me. When I turned and walked away she followed me again. She was remarkably fleet of foot. Sometimes in my exasperation I would run to an Underground station. I never succeeded in throwing her off, though once in her anxiety to catch me she was dangerously caught in the door when the train was starting. I recall a day when she caught me five times, outside my flat and my office, my club, and at meetings at which I was speaking. Once when I was addressing a meeting in Manchester I was astonished to see her sitting in the front row waiting for me. She wrote later to tell me she had hitch-hiked all the way. She had very little money, and often picked up the fruit which lies about near the stalls in Covent Garden Market.

"I tried pretending anger and shouted furious insults at her. She would blanch for a moment and then beam at me as though I had paid her compliments. She was Scandinavian; and I approached her Embassy, who knew all about her. They explained that she had a small pension from a patron of the arts in her home town, and that she might lose it or be deported if for some reason she got into trouble with the police. Thereupon I consulted solicitors. They all agreed that there was one remedy open to me and, as far as they knew, only one. I could take her to court and charge her with molesting me—which, technically no doubt, she was doing. Just imagine that! The *Express* and the *Evening Standard* at that period were ragging me on all possible occasions. What a jolly bit of fun it would be for them if I had to give evidence in court asking for protection from an elderly lady who expressed a desire to service me!

"Clearly I had to find other means of defence: I arranged for friends to walk home with me from the office every evening, and I had to write to various organisations for whom I was at that time speaking, and explain that I could only address their meetings if they provided me with a bodyguard. For months

M

on end I would leave the platform after meetings with a group of organisers keeping Miss X at a distance. But she never gave up, and she never made a disturbance which would have justified the police in interfering. I know it sounds funny, and there were times when I would laugh at it; but in truth I must admit it ceased to be a joke. She would pop out at me from behind trees or street corners, and on one occasion in Holborn she made a bid to kiss me. I became frightened—not of Miss X, but of my own reactions. I pushed her away with some violence and realised that if she had slipped on the pavement or fallen and been run over I should have been accused of molesting her, or even of manslaughter."

I should here interrupt Kingsley's own narrative, because it was at this point that I myself tried to set the law quietly in motion in a way that had not been suggested to him. As the law then stood she could have been arrested as a "wandering lunatic" and detained three days for medical examination; but since it was quite obvious that she was not "certifiable" it would have been an inhuman course to take. Moreover she had three times been persuaded to have short-term treatment in psychiatric hospitals—once by Kingsley's old friend Dr Joan Malleson—with absolutely no result. I had frequently been one of the people to walk home with him in the evenings, forming a kind of *cordon sanitaire* that must have looked specially discouraging to Miss X (as I suppose I had better go on calling her, though I know her name and the women's hostel where she lived). Alternatively, if Kingsley was leaving the office some time before I wanted to stop work, I would go down to the street and "detain her in conversation" while Kingsley got away. (At least, that is how he thought she was being detained, but in fact I used to hold her tightly until he was safe. He would have been beside himself with anxiety if he had known this, for she might have screamed, attracted the police, and got the whole thing into the papers.) She came to know me by name, and regarded me without enthusiasm. I was prepared, if need be, to appear in Court as the reluctant swain who had ill-used her. Greater love hath no man. But I persuaded Kingsley to come with me to see the Magistrates' Clerk at Bow Street, after Court hours, and apply for a summons calling upon Miss X to "show cause why she should not be bound over to keep the peace and be of good behaviour", a condition of the recognisance to be that she should stop following Kingsley around and accosting him. The Clerk was most unco-operative, I remember, sitting at his desk with his back to us and ostentatiously occupied with other matters. He said at first (and he was quite wrong) that the Court had no power to make such an order until Miss X had committed some offence, preferably an assault. Kingsley was horrified. She had technically assaulted him often enough, he said, but he thought the whole purpose of this discussion was to avoid bringing any kind of charge, with its inevitable publicity. At the mere mention of avoiding publicity, the learned Clerk gave way on the question of power to bind over and switched to the impossibility of keeping it out of the papers, whatever the nature of the proceedings. I think he was wrong again, but Kingsley had had enough. As we walked back to the office he upbraided me roundly and bitterly for the defects of the British magisterial system and the inadequacy of the Commission of the Peace. He then suddenly realised that he had once discussed this very possibility, five years before, with Mr Attlee, who had been telling him about some embarrassing experiences of his own with lunatics, "including one who sent periodical parcels of waste paper". Let Kingsley now conclude his own account:

"At this desperate juncture I found a way out. I was lunching with Monckton[1] and told him my tale of woe. Had the law no sensible remedy for me? Yes, he said, there was a little-known procedure which might serve my purpose. If it had been used by anyone else, and I had commented on it in the paper without an intimate knowledge of the facts, I might easily have said something highly derogatory about a *lettre de cachet* or the Star Chamber. Miss X could be instructed to cease molesting me, it seemed, in the strictest privacy. The procedure would be eased by the fact that for several years she had been writing me letters, well-phrased, long, and amorous. I remember only one of them; in which she said that so sure was she of my company on the following night that she had put on her

[1] Sir Walter (later Lord) Monckton, Q.C., then Paymaster-General and a former Solicitor-General.

'pretties'. By making a précis and giving quotes from these letters, a case was easily established; and another prominent Q.C. presented my case before a Judge in Chambers. Miss X was enjoined not to molest me in future. I am glad to say that the story stops there, because if Miss X had disobeyed and continued the persecution, I should still have had no remedy except to report the matter to the police and to have made my case in open court. In fact, I presume the Embassy came to my rescue. I have not heard or seen anything of Miss X from that day to this" (and he was writing in 1968).

It seems just a story now, and by 1968 he could probably think of it calmly; but at the time it was a nightmare to him. He has omitted some of the more grotesque episodes: he sometimes found, for example, on going to draw the curtains at night in his cottages at both Little Easton and Rodmell, that she was staring at him from the dark outside. After the incident in Holborn, touched on so lightly in his own account, he was in a state of such frenzy that I saw for the first time the stark possibility that, finding the law unable or unwilling to give him the smallest help, he would eventually kill her. It was for this reason that I got him to come to Bow Street and try to get her quietly "bound over"; but if I had told the Clerk what was in my own mind, there would have been a sudden discovery that you *can* bind over a person who hasn't yet done anything wrong, and the summons would have been issued against Kingsley himself as a potential homicide whom the law must restrain. Looking back on the story, I think I may have been spurred to more dynamic action than mere sympathy and escort duty by the fact that Miss X had suddenly started besetting my own house at Blackheath, more to my wife's amusement than to mine. I never for an instant saw the whole affair as a joke; but if it was, this was the point at which the laughing had to stop.

But even if, among the women he failed to "brush off", he played the part of Bunthorne for something like 40 years, there came a time when he was pathetically dependent on women (always attractive ones) and not at all disposed to escape. He had a succession of outstanding secretaries and research assistants, both at the office and for private literary work at home, whom he clearly chose for their femininity as well as their efficiency. He had a way of saying to them, "All secretaries fall in love with their bosses, do you know that?"; but they did not, though he flirted harmlessly with them all. It is fair to say that his first private secretary at the *New Statesman*, Eleanor Robertson, had been there ten years when he arrived and that he therefore didn't choose her; but he always said she was the best secretary he ever had. The one kind of secretary he could never stand, and got rid of with delegated ruthlessness, was the kind which fusses and brings flowers for the boss's desk.

To one woman, however, who was neither secretary nor Katisha he devoted much of his time in his last few years. This was Ninka Copley, at that time the wife of that fine actor Peter Copley. She had met Kingsley in 1960 in connection with the Committee for Nuclear Disarmament. The Copleys lived then at Brighton, and Kingsley wanted her help in 1963 in the preparation of the CND part of his autobiography (a part which in fact he never wrote). He was spending much time—not only weekends—at Rodmell, only a few miles away. It was early in 1964 that he had his first coronary thrombosis, and he was from that time increasingly dependent on friends who were able to visit him either at Rodmell or at Carlisle Mansions, among these being the Copleys and their daughter Fanny. He was distressed when their marriage came to an end; he retained a warm regard for them both, and came almost to regard himself as acting *in loco parentis* to Fanny, at that time twelve years old. In 1965, when Ninka herself was needing rest and recuperation, it was suggested both by her husband and by Dorothy that she should take Kingsley to Venice for a few weeks. Kingsley's acceptance of the plan was the less hesitant because she was an exceptionally attractive and vivacious companion: he liked what he always called a "cosy relationship" with women, but the cosiness had much to do with their being pretty ones.

When she called to collect him by taxi on the morning of their departure from Carlisle Mansions, he said to her with the utmost gravity, "Now my dear Ninka, you do realise that if we are to go to Venice together, for the sake of the photographers and pressmen at the airport I shall have to pretend you are my nurse?" She said she didn't mind so long as she could have a uniform. But at the airport there were no photographers to record their departure, no pressmen to see them off and report Kingsley's latest adventure in newsworthiness. When her marriage broke up, for reasons quite unconnected with Kingsley, he nevertheless went through a period of acute anxiety, assuring her (to her great surprise and affectionate amusement) that "in no circumstances can I ever leave Dorothy". Once he had been convinced that this was not on the agenda, she was able to see him often during the remaining years of his illness; and he confided to her much of his past life, present misgivings, and increasingly confused plans for the future. She appreciated the still vital quality of his mind, his zest for enjoyment, his wry humour, and his devotion to friends, and accepted his frequently insensitive tactlessness and his didacticism. But she was not one of the "interesting women who fell in love with him", nor indeed did she think him physically attractive. What she shared with the other women was his capacity for attentive listening, readily available for her when she had serious troubles (and a serious illness) of her own. He heard the story of her troubles the more readily because, he told her, she wasn't always crying about them. Like Wilde, he saw weeping as "the refuge of the plain woman and the ruin of pretty ones". And thus he found distraction in a relationship which he, at any rate, would not have recognised as avuncular.

And thus he chose his companions and amanuenses with a discrimination which made it an agreeable experience for any biographer to interview them. "It is always interesting," said John Morley, "in the case of a great man, to know how he affected the women of his acquaintance." It would still be interesting if Kingsley had been an ordinary man. But his emotional relationships with all the women in his life except Verity, whom he never ceased to love, and Dorothy, who gave him security, were terminable from the outset.

Chapter 20

DEFAMATION

IN THE EARLY thirties, if you went into a music shop for a working man's recording of the *Kreuzer* or the *Spring Sonata*, you would get one with a plum label, it would be by Arthur Catterall and William Murdoch, and for most people it would be marvellous value. But not for W. J. Turner, then music critic of the *New Statesman*, who in August 1932 went on behalf of the paper to hear Arthur Catterall play the Tchaikowsky Violin Concerto. He thoroughly disapproved of the performance, and accounted for its failure to reach Turner standards by saying: "Nobody has ever claimed that Mr Catterall was a soloist of extraordinary ability." Although in fact this claim was commonly made for Mr Catterall, he might not have minded Mr Turner's having missed it if the notice had not gone on to attack his general ability, competence and sincerity, and even to accuse him of deceit and affectation. (It takes a *New Statesman* music critic to find deceit in a Tchaikowsky performance.) W. J. Turner, Kingsley Martin and the *New Statesman* duly received writs for libel. And if this was not Kingsley's first editorial brush with the law of defamation, it is the earliest one of which any record survives in his papers.

There was the usual exchange of solicitors' letters, putting into the usual costive language the hurt done to Mr Catterall's feelings, the disavowals, the draft apologies and the rest. And after many weeks the paper published its apology over Mr W. J. Turner's signature:

> The criticism made by me on 27 August of Mr Arthur Catterall was intended to apply solely to his performance of the Tchaikowsky Violin Concerto on the particular evening in question. It was incorrect of me to say that nobody has ever claimed that Mr Catterall was a soloist of extraordinary ability. If certain phrases can be considered as criticism of his general ability, competence or sincerity, or accuse him of deceit or affectation,

> I unreservedly withdraw them with apologies to Mr Catterall, as that was not my intended suggestion.

Catterall, still burning, was very reluctant to accept this; but his solicitors persuaded him, as all good solicitors do if they can, to do so and keep out of Court, the *New Statesman* paying the legal costs he had incurred. (Did you ever hear of a musician whose reputation was enhanced by getting a jury to say it was untrue that he couldn't play or sing?) Kingsley seems to have been amused rather than worried; and once the lawyers had bowed themselves out he wrote privately to Arthur Catterall what must have been a mollifying letter (no copy of it survives). For Catterall replied on 3rd November in a letter headed PRIVATE:

> It was *very* good of you to write, and I was glad to know your own opinion of the criticism of me by W. J. Turner. The whole subject of musical criticism is a difficult one, and I think something ought to be done about it. Perhaps some day I may have the pleasure of meeting you and having a chat about it.

There was a recurrent feeling at the office that "something ought to be done" about W. J. Turner, and an editorial tendency to regard him as mainly a poet (he was a very distinguished poet), not sufficiently knowledgeable about music, and inclined to run particular heroes of his own among composers, of whom Tchaikowsky was not one. All the same, there are many who will remember his music notices with the sharpest nostalgia that the *New Statesman* of the thirties can evoke. He came from Melbourne, which exports musicians (and where both his parents were outstanding pianists). He loved and hated among the composers with engaging candour. The trouble came when he gave rein to his loves and hates among the performers—Arthur Catterall was not the only one he upset. Perhaps all that needed to be done was to cut him down from 2,000 words a week to 600, but they were spacious days and you could—he could—go on for two columns about the right way to play a single phrase in a sonata. When at last he was supplanted by Desmond Shawe-Taylor in 1940, paper-rationing was having a salutary effect on weekly criticism of all kinds.

Perversely, of course, we all wanted Shawe-Taylor to have more space.

Kingsley came to know a great deal about the law of libel. His office bookshelf contained the best text-books on the subject and he knew his way about in them. But he would seldom admit to understanding it, and he liked to tell you that he had spent his editorial life waiting to meet a one-armed lawyer because the lawyers he knew always said "on the one hand this, on the other hand that". He recognised that in this country, almost alone among European countries, the libel laws were a branch of the entertainment industry, with a glorious Dan Leno kind of past, an inexhaustible literature for the hack writer to draw upon in lean times, and a rich vein of gold to be worked by sensitive victims so long as trial by jury survived. And he thought that British newspaper-readers would never allow the libel laws to be effectively changed unless Parliament restored something like public flogging, or at least bear-baiting, to take their place.

He was at the same time one of the few editors I have known (Gerald Barry was another) who wanted more protection for the small man against wealthy newspapers; and no lawyer convinced him, though several tried, that in the Legal Aid and Advice Act of 1949 Parliament was justified in withholding legal aid from deserving litigants in libel actions. His private papers contain instances of humble citizens victimised by the law as it then stood—and still stands—not only because they could not afford to sue but also because they could not afford to defend themselves when frightened vested interests shut their mouths by serving writs on them. The one thing he could never understand was how it could come about that a successful defendant in a libel suit was so often grievously out of pocket although he had been "awarded his costs in the action". He had intended to write a long chapter about all this in his next book, the burden of which would have been that if a journal was to be usefully critical it must always run the risk of libel and that an editor worth his salt must in the end rely on his own judgment. In relation to politicians, whom he thought the touchiest of all, he believed it to be legally safe to say that a Chancellor of the Exchequer had mis-spent millions of pounds but not that he ought to get his hair cut; a comparison which he used repeatedly in public lectures. The *New Statesman*'s legal advisers (and libel insurance underwriters) no doubt tensed slightly when they began reading a London Diary paragraph opening "I hear that . . ." or "A friend tells me . . .".

He soon came to know that lawyers habitually draft letters for publishers and newspapers to send off as "all their own work" in reply to libel claims, in the hope that a complainant may be mollified or silenced without bringing lawyers perceptibly into the picture. He knew, nonetheless, that every editor receives solicitors' letters which threaten libel actions without the smallest intention of following them up, to see if they will produce any money for a client who hasn't much of a case. His collected examples of these are sometimes so laughable that the opportunity to retell them here is a great temptation. It must be resisted, lest their leading characters might see in them the chance to send in more lawyers' letters, pursuing the hope of reward on the ground that it is defamatory to imply that they would send in lawyers' letters in the hope of reward.

However, Kingsley knew a genuine complaint of hurt feelings from an impudent try-on. In 1933 the *New Statesman* said that Graham Seton, the writer of so many good army stories, was about to become the editor of a Nazi periodical. There was absolutely no truth in it; and the angry author, whatever he thought about Hitler ("my views are my own, whether you like them or not"), wrote on 29th August to say so, apparently without going to a solicitor. "It is either a deliberate falsehood," he said, "or you have published it without taking the ordinary editorial precaution of making an enquiry. Moreover, although with a sneer you pass me by as a 'writer of military thrillers', a wide and well-informed public opinion has been good enough to recognise me as someone different from that." Kingsley looked into it, found that he had been given wrong information about the defamed author (whose real name was Graham Seton Hutchison), and published a paragraph saying so. The author was completely won over:

> I take the earliest opportunity to write to you and thank you for the notice which appeared in your issue of 23 September. You

have phrased this in such way that there can be no further room for misunderstanding; but beyond this I note with particular pleasure that you have seen fit to add a sentence in which, as it appears in your columns, no man could do other than take some pride. For this I am grateful. Our views may be as divergent as the poles, though as one of your readers I do not think so. You would find, I believe, in my books "Footslogger", "Warrior", and "Meteor", which are not "military thrillers" and are the only ones published in my own name, many expressions of view coincident with the policy of your own paper.

But more than once Kingsley had the mortification of publishing an apology and paying compensation to soothe the outraged virtue of someone who then went to prison for having done precisely what the *New Statesman* had alleged. Sometimes an undue trustfulness about a new contributor ("who ought to know better", as Kingsley would always complain) would land him in trouble. In 1941 he decided that Robert Lynd, whose inimitable essays were signed "Y.Y." and no one knew why, must appear fortnightly instead of weekly. This was partly because it was war-time and the *New Statesman* was severely rationed for paper, but mainly because Kingsley was anxious to use some articles that James Bridie wanted to send him from Ireland. So Robert Lynd was gently demoted. "I am writing to ask you something very difficult," Kingsley told him. "We are now as you know hard up against it in the matter of space, and Beaverbrook doesn't look like giving us any more paper.[1] I want to know whether you could write as Y.Y. every other week instead of every week. I know that doing the weekly article is a habit, and that I am asking a lot; but it would certainly help me very much indeed if you could manage it.... A few weeks ago when we had rather more space I printed a delightful article by James Bridie about Ireland. He offers me others, and I shall have to refuse them purely on the grounds of space, unless I can have a week when Bridie takes the place of Y.Y." The number of weeks when Bridie took the place of Y.Y. was limited by a swift development. The delightful

[1] Lord Beaverbrook was then Minister of Supply; and was credited with the view that a good way to conserve paper would be to close down all the weeklies, as distinct from the dailies, for the duration of the war.

article about Ireland produced a libel writ from an angry Dublin publican which led the paper into endless trouble. But Robert Lynd, to the general joy, came back every week and stayed with the paper until the end of the war; when Kingsley, incredibly it seemed to many people, dropped him on the ground that he was getting "dull". It was perhaps the one major casting error of his editorial life, and it is within my knowledge that he was regretting it within a few months. Robert Lynd, who died four years later, was—and is—irreplaceable.

The following year (1942) Kingsley himself was thinking of having a go at *Reynold's News*. "Why shouldn't I for a change take an action, instead of having one taken against me?" he asked the firm's solicitors. Sir Alfred Watson, a Liberal who for 20 years was first managing and then editing the *Westminster Gazette*, was at that time editorial director of a weekly paper called *Great Britain and the East* and political adviser to the India-Burma Association. He had written in his weekly an article about the India League, describing it as a subversive organisation which ought to be suppressed and alleging that its funds and support came from "sentimentalists", including the *New Statesman*—which he described as "one of its props". This was reprinted in *Reynolds's News* on 4th July 1942. Kingsley was very angry. "We have in fact no connection of any sort with the India League," he wrote to the firm's solicitors; "we have never supported it, and although sometimes we have agreed with its policy, more often we have not. The India League itself has complained that we are hostile to it. . . . I think we can insist on a pretty full withdrawal from Sir Alfred Watson, from *Great Britain and the East*, and from the India-Burma Association." I can find no trace of the withdrawal, but I do not believe for a moment that Kingsley would have sued for libel, in this instance or any other. He never lacked for opportunities.

Strange to relate, a month or two later he found himself co-defendant with *Reynolds's News* in an action by Austin Hopkinson, MP for the Mossley division of Lancashire. The *New Statesman* had reproduced in "This England" an observation alleged by *Reynolds's News* to have been made at a public meeting by Hopkinson, who complained that the report was materially wrong and exposed him to ridicule. To fight this action, noted Kingsley at the time, "would mean to collect various reporters and witnesses whom *Reynolds* say they can mobilise, to contradict other members of the audience who will take Hopkinson's view. I gather, though I haven't talked to *Reynolds* myself, that they haven't got a shorthand note." As he had no interest in attacking Hopkinson and no principles were at stake, the *New Statesman* apologised. "I meant to keep in step with *Reynolds* in the matter," noted Kingsley, "but found our lawyers could not agree. It seems to me the kind of libel action against which it is almost impossible completely to safeguard oneself."

Even while this was going on, the *New Statesman* was in much worse trouble about one of those London Diary "I hear . . ." paragraphs. On 25th April 1942 Kingsley had published a Diary Note about Captain Bernard Acworth—beginning, incidentally, with one of those characteristic outrages on syntax which he seemed to reserve for the London Diary:

> As one Independent candidate supporting another, I hear that the Hon. Leonard Cripps attended Captain Bernard Acworth's inaugural meeting at Putney, spoke of Acworth's foresight, and called him "a recognised naval strategist". A friend sends me some examples of Acworth's foresight. In his *The Navies of Today and Tomorrow* (p. 160) he argued that Hong Kong was the base to defend and not Singapore, because of "the complete immunity from attack of Singapore, for the defence of which a few guns and troops were sufficient".[1] At a lecture in London in 1933, as reported in *The Naval and Military Record*, "he expressed his pleasure that we had so few aeroplanes"; and in his book we read "The Terror of the Air . . . is the obscene child of propaganda by oil and aircraft interests". *The Naval and Military Record* in 1933 reported that "his chief platform planks are that the Navy should return to coal firing, battleships should be reduced to 12,000 tons and 17 knots, destroyers should be abolished and flying is all wrong—at any rate in relation to sea power."

[1] Singapore was in fact surrendered to the Japanese on 15 February, having proved hopelessly vulnerable to a land attack which had been deemed impossible.

All this was in due course held by the Court to be fair comment. "A man who expounds views on matters of public interest of such a character," said Mr Justice Stable,[1] "must expect that newspapers and others who hold different views will subject him to criticism. I don't think the statements made by the defendants in the first four paragraphs exceeded the bounds of fair comment. On the contrary I think the defendants might have expressed themselves much more strongly than they did, without rendering themselves liable to an action for libel."

But the references to Singapore and the futility of air power were followed by another "I hear" paragraph:

> I hear that during the Putney election Captain Acworth admitted that he was once a member of "The Link",[2] and has argued about his friend Admiral Sir Barry Domvile having a raw deal in being detained under 18B.[3] His election slogan is "God, King and Country".

This cost the *New Statesman* £300 and costs. It meant, in Mr Justice Stable's view (for there was no jury) that Captain Acworth was "a humbug, who was presenting himself to the electors as a patriot whereas he was, in fact, a man who if not engaged in subversive activities himself was associated with those who were." He had taken no part in "The Link", never went to its meetings and paid it only 2/6d.; and at his election meeting he had attacked 18B detentions in general, not Sir Barry Domvile's in particular. It was "a grave attack on Captain Acworth's sincerity, patriotism and loyalty", but "the result of the action will be completely to vindicate him if not

[1] *The Times*, 5 October 1943.

[2] "The Link" was an Anglo-German fellowship organisation, founded some years before the war in the genuine hope of preserving peace, and Admiral Sir Barry Domvile, a former Chief of Naval Intelligence, had been its Chairman.

[3] Defence Regulation 18B empowered the Home Secretary to imprison anyone he thought likely to endanger the safety of the realm. Many of those imprisoned, including "Link" members, were completely harmless; and although France and Norway had shown the danger of giving the apparently harmless the benefit of the doubt, the *New Statesman* had waged a great campaign about "panic" internments under 18B.

necessarily as a naval critic, at least as an honest man". So he got only £300: a jury might have given him £3,000.

The interesting thing is that Acworth had wanted only a published "correction" and 40 guineas towards his legal costs. Kingsley for some reason was prepared to pay the 40 guineas, but he utterly refused to publish the "correction", although the *New Statesman*'s solicitors reminded him that "any libel is worth settling for £42, especially if it is doubtful whether the plaintiff can pay the costs if he loses". Kingsley was furious about the result and was dissuaded with difficulty from adding mightily to the costs by storming off to the Court of Appeal, which in those days very seldom overturned a libel verdict.

The importance of the Bernard Acworth case in Kingsley's career is plain from a letter he wrote on 5th October to Edward Whitley, the Chairman of the *New Statesman* board:

> No doubt you have seen the report in *The Times* and elsewhere and will have realised that we came down rather heavily. I am upset about it, because I have always prided myself on not getting into Court on an action (this is the first time in my 12 years on the paper . . .). I should have apologised and got out of the action very cheaply at an early stage had I not been advised by a very sober Counsel that the case was as water-tight from our point of view as any case could be. This judgment has since been corroborated by two other KC's. We suffered from the worst of luck. Our solicitor, whom I was going to suggest changing in any case and whom we only had because he is the Insurance solicitor, has been very ill and was in bed when the action came on. Our Counsel, Slade,[1] was found to be out of the country on Government work two days before the action. We went to Pritt because he had all the facts at his finger ends, since he is fighting Acworth in his next libel action. The choice proved most unfortunate, for though Pritt dealt brilliantly with the first (factual) part of the case, he introduced a great deal of highly prejudicial matter at the end which clearly further alienated the Judge. . . . I was also unhappy because I believed that if I had been put into the witness box I could have given a reasonable interpretation of the words, which would have influenced the Judge's mind. It was decided at the last minute not to call me. I believe Pritt thought the case

[1] Later Mr Justice Slade.

was won and that it was unnecessary to run the risk of another cross-examination.

Running at the same time was a complicated correspondence with solicitors about yet another libel action—Kingsley refers to it briefly in *Editor*, page 19: and this was one which indeed might have cost the paper a fortune. Kingsley himself, at an early and desperate stage of the negotiations, said in a characteristic letter to Keynes that "we have got into what is probably the worst libel action in history". It arose from a bald and confident statement, in a contributed article attacking two women journalists of whom the *New Statesman* disapproved, that they were one and the same person. This statement had seemed to Kingsley so inherently unlikely in the circumstances that he had gone to quite extraordinary lengths to have the allegation verified. It was totally verified, to the satisfaction even of the solicitors; and it was totally wrong. "You may have noticed," wrote Kingsley to Edward Whitley on 22nd October 1943, "the most grovelling apology in the paper this week to two ladies." And the apology had to be accompanied by payments of £100 to one lady and £750 to the other. However, it was kept out of Court, where it would have done the paper's reputation considerable damage, cost a lot more, and perhaps made the unfortunate Kingsley begin to lose his confidence.

This he never seriously did. He faltered sometimes, and there could perhaps be no better example of "editorial nerves" than his refusal in 1944 to print a Sagittarius poem about Ivor Novello. He sent this to the paper's solicitors, who replied that "the introductory words will allow the poem to be construed as libel". Here it is:

IMMORTELLES

[Really, I am engaged on important
war work for morale—Ivor Novello.]

Morale! what crimes are covered by that name,
What word so overworked and so abused!
What wishful thinking shows behind the claim,
What vapid entertainment is excused
When ageless idols in their corny roles
Dare lay that flattering unction to their souls!

The O so *passé* musical romance
Does not excite the pulses of the nation
Via melodies of Austria and France
(Now theatres of bloody occupation).
No matter how the valse-theme may be plugged
The audience is not inspired but drugged.

Morale is not appreciably aided
By contributions of the wartime stage,
All trumpery, irrelevant or jaded—
A damned disgrace to this, or any, age,
Where we must view through our nostalgic tears,
Old darlings dancing down the lilac years.

Whatever aids our national resilience,
Whatever gives us confidence to "take it"
Amusements offered to our war-worn millions,
Far from sustaining morale, almost shake it;
Our confidence, so far as one can judge it,
Is equally affected by the Budget.

But normally his confidence sustained him through many libel scares, big and small, in the course of the next fifteen years; and he needed it most of all in an extraordinary case occurring—or rather beginning—in 1959, with which I must round off this very small selection, mainly from his earlier days because to rake up more recent libel stories is inevitably to bang the rake riskily against toes still sore. The case dragged on well into his retirement years, but it was he who maintained the necessary editorial contacts with the solicitors throughout.

In 1957 he went to Portugal with Gerald Gardiner, QC,[1] who on behalf of "Justice", the British Section of the International Commission of Jurists, was attending the trial of 50 students at Oporto, believed to have been tortured while awaiting trial. The PIDE[2] (the Portuguese political police) were acquiring an international reputation as torture experts, and two of their prisoners had just died in unexplained circumstances. At about that time the *New Statesman* had carried a number of articles sharply critical of Dr Salazar's regime. Few

[1] At that time a member (and later Chairman) of the *New Statesman* board; and from 1964 to 1970 Lord Chancellor.

[1] Polizie Internationale Defenso Estado.

English editors thought it right to be beastly to the Portuguese, though Portugal's status as "Britain's oldest ally" rested mainly on the none-too-solid foundation that in 1294 the two countries had concluded a commercial treaty, that in the fifteenth century Portuguese and British mariners had contrived to plant their national flags in other people's countries without fighting each other, and that Charles II had married Catherine of Braganza. In the second World War the Portuguese allowed the British and Americans to establish an airbase in the Azores, which would probably have been forcibly occupied if they had refused.

Then in 1958 General Humberto Delgado, whom I remember seeing in Kingsley's office gesticulating in the way that makes European politics look so much more vivid, had the hardihood to offer himself to the Portuguese as a better Presidential Candidate than one of Dr Salazar's yes-men nominees. By getting 25 per cent of the votes he established two propositions. The first was that it would be better for him to go and live in Brazil. The second was that the Portuguese constitution must be amended. Since then the President has been appointed indirectly, by an electoral college which kept Salazar in office until his death in 1970. And a few years after his impudent candidature, Delgado was murdered by political opponents in Portugal. In June 1959 there appeared a *New Statesman* leader about a forthcoming visit to Portugal by Princess Margaret, and its title was "What the Princess Won't See". It described the extremely reactionary policies of the Portuguese Government and the use of torture against prisoners (invariably described as Communists) in Portuguese gaols; and it named three senior police executives as having inflicted the torture.

In October 1959 the *New Statesman* received from London solicitors acting for the three Portuguese police officers a letter threatening libel proceedings. The usual legal preliminaries creaked into action, but no claim was pursued, and Kingsley was beginning to hope that the matter might die. Then in December General Delgado came to England from Brazil and wrote an article for the *New Statesman* which had the effect of speeding things up. The Portuguese Government, which may have supposed that the *New Statesman* had been bluffed into defeat, seems to have been stung to action by the reappearance of Delgado, and instructed its London solicitors to issue writs against the paper for "a really infamous" libel.

It was considered by lawyers to be a case in which, owing to the extreme difficulty of supporting a "plea of justification" by the calling of witnesses (some of the tortured prisoners had escaped but were living untraceably in Latin America and elsewhere), the *New Statesman* might well be ordered to pay damages as high as £50,000 apart from costs, and those might be considerably higher. I have seldom seen Kingsley so worried. His belief was that the Portuguese Government would exploit the case in every possible way to ruin the paper and put it out of business. It seemed certain that they would seek to show that the whole of the evidence reflected a Communist plot to overthrow the Government of "our oldest ally".

Meanwhile there came to public knowledge a petition sent by a group of 40 prominent Portuguese Catholics to Dr Salazar, protesting about the brutal methods used by the PIDE—"methods that no sound human conscience can tolerate and that the Christian spirit must necessarily repudiate". This had been sent to Salazar on 18th April 1959, copies going to Catholic Bishops in Portugal and throughout the world with the request that the whole thing be kept secret until Dr Salazar's reply was known. The document gave details of the most unspeakable tortures used on political prisoners by the PIDE. When Salazar had allowed a month to go by without any response, stencilled copies were distributed in Portugal and shortly afterwards published abroad. In August 1959 all the signatories were rounded up and interrogated at PIDE headquarters, all confirming that they had signed the petition and some admitting that they had helped to make it known. Later they were all prosecuted. The Archbishop of Oporto (the second priest of Portugal) who was one of the signatories, went on a visit to the Vatican, was not allowed to return, and now lives in Spain awaiting a change of government.

The *New Statesman*'s lawyers were in no doubt that this obviously expensive litigation was not being sustained by three Portuguese policemen: the plaintiff was the Portuguese

Government on their behalf. The suggestion was put to the other side that the Law Courts in the Strand were not the proper forum to try such an issue. There should be an independent enquiry, in some neutral country like Switzerland; and then if the *New Statesman*'s criticisms proved to have been unfounded they would be unreservedly withdrawn, with apologies and amidst the utmost publicity. If they were sustained, then it would be hoped that the torturing would stop. The Portuguese Government lawyer took this suggestion to Lisbon and presented it to the Deputy Prime Minister (Dr Salazar being too ill and infirm to be seen). On his return he said: "This matter has been carefully considered. There has been far too much criticism of the Portuguese regime, and it is totally unwarranted. *They are determined to smash the New Statesman.* They will not agree to your proposal under any circumstances."

So the long business began of assembling evidence against the torturers. The *New Statesman*'s solicitor arranged to go to Lisbon and find some Democratic Liberal lawyers who, to his knowledge, had defended political prisoners in the Portuguese Courts. The day before his departure he had a telephone message from one of the *New Statesman*'s informers in the case, at that time in Stockholm, saying: "The PIDE know all about you and what you are going to try and do. It will be better for you if you don't go." In Lisbon the next day he found that the lawyer he was seeking had been concerned in cases involving the three police officers who were suing the *New Statesman*. After much investigation it was possible to say, in the *New Statesman*'s answer to the writ, that evidence was available not merely about the tortures described in the article but about many similar acts against other prisoners—seventeen other torture cases were listed, and four murders. Edward Hyams[1] flew to Portugal and with the aid of the underground Communist Party traced two lots of PIDE victims, many of them lawyers, who had broken out of prisons in Lisbon and Oporto. Having arranged to see them all in more leisurely and suitable circumstances, Hyams returned to report, and then spent a longer time in Portugal under the friendly cover of a commission from another paper to write (as a horticultural expert)

[1] Author of *The New Statesman 1913–1963*.

about Portuguese gardens. He did in fact meet all his contacts in big Portuguese gardens, and obtained from them a number of valuable affidavits.

Then Paul Johnson went to Latin America, and in Brazil—which at that time was not known to have gone in for torture itself and was behaving hospitably to the victims of political police in Europe—got some damning evidence in signed statements from exiled torturees. Further similar statements were obtained from Portuguese exiles working in Paris; and from these and the three leading Opposition lawyers in Portugal it was ascertained that the Salazar Government, which had maintained concentration camps in the thirties even before the Germans did (there was a particularly grim one in the Cape Verde Islands), had sent police and prison officers to pre-war Germany for training courses in the use of torture on recalcitrant prisoners.

Meanwhile nothing was heard from the Portuguese Government, or the three PIDE men, about the libel action; and after about five years, having elaborated their plea of "justification" and then left it to the Plaintiffs to make the running, the *New Statesman*'s lawyers applied to the High Court to have the action dismissed "for want of prosecution". This is always a difficult and dangerous step. It can have the effect of reactivating inert litigation to the detriment of the applicants. But it was successful. Judgment was given in favour of the *New Statesman*, with costs; and then there arose the problem of recovering the costs—they amounted by this time to about £3,000.

The Portuguese Government's London lawyers were not very forthcoming about the costs. They were acting, they now said, for three poor foreign policemen, who couldn't afford to pay and were anyway outside the jurisdiction, so that an order for costs would not be enforceable. But it was not the poor foreign policemen who had insisted that the libel action must be relentlessly pursued with a view to destroying the *New Statesman*. The party responsible for the costs was the Government of Portugal, which had wrongly charged the *New Statesman* with defamation under circumstances making the preparation of a defence almost impossibly difficult. That defence had now been prepared, it was clearly unassailable, and the Portuguese

Government was not merely liable but had tacitly admitted that it was. The *New Statesman* through its lawyers then embarked on the process known as leaving no stone unturned. The Foreign Office was urged to take up the issue, if necessary to the point of suspending diplomatic relations. Dossiers were prepared for the United Nations, for the International Court of Justice at The Hague, for every kind of organisation which might be able to wring the money out of our oldest ally. Suddenly in 1964, out of the blue, there arrived a cheque in full settlement.

A number of developments subsequent to the High Court judgment may have helped to precipitate this decision, which of course (like the money) was that of the Portuguese Government. Among them was the fact that an *ad hoc* committee, including the Portuguese opposition lawyers who had helped the *New Statesman* during the investigations, were going to arrange for a meeting of all the possible and available victims of Portuguese atrocity, with tape recorders and newspaper men present, so that a full record could be prepared. Dr Salazar's Portugal had avoided all this unsavoury publicity.

Instead there had been a long article in the *Daily Telegraph* on 9th August 1963, by Lord Russell of Liverpool, entitled *Portugal's Political Prisoners*. It "described the results of a personal investigation, the evidence of which refutes recent allegations about ill-treatment made in irresponsible quarters". The Portuguese Government, said Lord Russell, had been "most anxious to get some impartial and objective observer to enquire into these prison conditions, and the allegations of the torture and ill-treatment of those serving prison sentences for offences against the State. . . . Last March it was suggested to me that I should undertake such an investigation, and I agreed to do this on condition that I would be given a completely free hand, and would have access to all the Portuguese prisons where such offenders were held in custody while awaiting trial and after sentence, and have every opportunity of talking to the prisoners." Lord Russell actually watched some healthy-looking prisoners being questioned by the PIDE in light airy rooms and noticed that they were not being tortured.

However, his article was the subject of a libel claim by

Amnesty International and one of its leading officials; and this was "settled" on terms which included publication by the *Daily Telegraph*, on 10th February 1964, of an agreed article written by Lord Gardiner, of comparable length and in the same conspicuous position as Lord Russell's on the leader-page. In it Lord Gardiner said he was

> quite certain that the Portuguese authorities have tortured political prisoners, that Lord Russell of Liverpool is mistaken in attributing the charge to irresponsible writers influenced by their political views, and that such practices have continued since his visit. . . . I have myself applied, before writing this article, to the Portuguese Government for the same facilities as he was given but have been refused them. I regret this all the more because, of course, I have been able to interview many political prisoners whereas I believe Lord Russell saw only those still in prison.

Lord Gardiner then reviewed at some length the collected and sworn evidence of torture, and observed that Portugal was "part of Christian Europe, a partner in the Anglo-Portuguese Alliance, and a member of NATO"; he also recalled that its "elections" allowed only Government candidates, that its Press was subjected to rigid daily censorship, its police empowered to imprison without trial, its members of political minorities tried (if they were tried at all) before special political courts which admitted "confessions" obtained under torture, and its people forbidden to form even a United Nations Association. And he ended:

> Whatever assistance the Salazar Government may have given the Allies during the war, on 3 May 1945, when Hitler died, the flags on all Government buildings in Dr Salazar's Portugal flew at half mast.

It was Norman Douglas who said that justice is too good for some people and not good enough for the rest. But for none of them is it often thus attainable through the English law of defamation.

Chapter 21

OLD MEN REMEMBER

FOR THE LAST six years of his life, ailing, slowing down but fighting all the time, he was mainly in his large and rather gloomy flat at 25 Carlisle Mansions, Victoria; overshadowed by the tower of the Roman Catholic Cathedral, of which he used to say: "Of course, it would be praised if it had happened to be a chimney." There were many stairs up to his flat, and no lift. From the middle of 1967 onwards, if you went up these stairs with him for a talk and a drink, he would drop heavily into a chair and gesture in silence to where the drinks were kept: he couldn't speak for a time. Carlisle Mansions is an enormous complex of elderly flats, solidly built at a time when domestic servants abounded. (You needed a tall pair of steps to change an electric light bulb in a ceiling pendant; and Kingsley possessed no pair of steps.) Neither the building nor the neighbourhood seemed, after Robert Street, "right" for him. Nor could even he conjure up a village atmosphere between Victoria Station, the Army and Navy Stores, Caxton Hall and the Black and White Minstrel Show. He sorely missed the Players' Theatre at Charing Cross, a "theatre club" (at first a transparent device for dodging the Lord Chamberlain's censorship) which came to specialise in "old-time music-hall"; and at which he had always joined vociferously in the laughter and groans provoked by the hard-working Chairman with his gavel and his elephantine bonhomie. Now there was not so much of that. But Kingsley and Dorothy became well known and well liked in the small shops and restaurants around the Vauxhall Bridge Road. And they were only a few yards from Victoria Station where they took train for Rodmell at week-ends.

He had a mountain of letters about his retirement, and a distinguished collection they are, from the four corners. I cannot withstand the temptation to quote, from among them all, tributes from two readers who, so far as I am aware, were totally unknown to him or to any of us. What they said would be likely to mean more to Kingsley than all the encomiums of the famous. The first was from a woman:

> Now that you are leaving your famous editorial chair, I want to thank you very sincerely for all the pleasure and enlightenment you have given me over the years—for I have been a reader as long as you have been Editor. For a long time you were our family mentor; we valued your ideas and convictions so much, always courageous and thoughtful and right. And I am extremely grateful for all the information, help, interesting articles and reviews on every page of the journal, by the splendid staff you had around you. . . . I am now an old woman, and can do nothing but talk (and think); so please forgive this intrusive letter and do not trouble to acknowledge. I just wanted you to know, as I hope you do, your value to so many.

The second was from a man teaching in a Perthshire school:

> The *New Statesman and Nation* has been my Bible. I have come to regard it as the one place where I could find, almost infallibly, the things being said that in a civilised world must be said by somebody. It wasn't merely a question of Socialism. It was a question of your magazine always standing up and shouting out for common sense and common humanity. I have come to judge people and their capacity for responsiveness by sorting them into *New Statesman* types or—as we say in Scotland with an almost audible curl of the lip—*Glasgow Herald* types. . . . Even in Scotland my writer friends, much though they long for a good review in *The Scotsman*, long even more for the accolade of a notice in the *Statesman*. . . . May I thank you for what you have done for my generation, the people who grew up in the thirties and who, whatever their political stance today, owe their intellectual and political awareness to the *New Statesman* and particularly to that most fascinating person, "Critic".

Dorothy was now, at Kingsley's insistence, increasingly living her own busy professional life as a research student and reporter of the Far East, and particularly of Burma. Throughout the fifties she had been much more absorbed in China and Indonesia. She would sometimes say that when she and Kingsley went East together, it was he whom the Indians and Pakistanis loved and greeted; so that she was glad to move on to China, Burma and Indonesia, where she was the better known. Her oriental allegiances took some strains during those years. She was friendly with both U Nu, the intermittent Premier of Burma, and General Ne Win, the man who alternated with him until 1962, when, tiring of the ballot-box, he turned him out by military force.[1]

It was frequently said of Dorothy that she became romantically—and even sentimentally—obsessed with the people of the Far East; but a study of her papers and books suggests, on the contrary, a scholar's approach to a vast problem of social justice and political emancipation. She relegated the romanticism and the "never-the-twain-shall-meet" to the world of Kipling and his *Ballad of East and West*, a different and politically inept view of a shrinking world. The full story of the part she played in the development of the new Asiatic countries would require a volume to itself; and would contain a variety of episodes at least as unusual as the following story about the Indonesian Government's seizure of the Royal Dutch Trading Fleet (the KPM).

[1] Either of these remarkable men might have been able to enlist the totally one-sided support of any Left-wing enthusiast less well-informed on Burmese affairs than Dorothy Woodman. U Nu was a Socialist, a devout Buddhist, a teacher, and founder of the Anti-Fascist People's Freedom League. When Burma became independent in 1948 he was the first Prime Minister, remained in office for eight and a half years, and then began his struggle for power against Ne Win, who finally ousted him by a military coup in 1962 and is still in office as virtual dictator, harried all the time by guerrilla forces directed by U Nu from exile in Thailand. U Nu told *The Times* on 28 December 1971 that "Ne Win and his military clique have plundered Burma. The last of the nation's gold reserves were sold in London very recently for private gain." On behalf of Ne Win, a very sick man when this book was being written, that story has always been strenuously denied. Dorothy somehow continued to be on good terms with both these contenders for power, and may well have inclined them both towards conduct rather more moderate than their angry rivalry would have prompted. If so, she saved a considerable number of Burmese lives. Beyond doubt the two men had a high regard for her; and Madame Ne Win in particular, herself a cultivated, poised, cosmopolitan and shrewdly perceptive woman, regarded Dorothy Woodman as one of the founders of modern Burma.

In 1958 the underwriters at Lloyds were faced with a tremendous claim on the London market. It amounted to about £10,000,000, and depended on the fulfilment of a clause in a contract insuring the Dutch merchant fleet. The Japanese had of course seized these ships during the war in Indonesia, and they were now, after a stormy and bloodstained decade of "political resettlement", at the disposal of the new Government, headed by Dr Sukarno. The underwriters were to be fully liable unless the Indonesian Government released the ships within four months. Although Lloyds had a good relationship with the new re-insurance body set up in Djakarta when the Japanese had left, this proved unable to bring much influence to bear. Paul Dixey was then a deputy chairman of Lloyds—and a neighbour of Kingsley's at Little Easton.[1] At week-ends he had met, in the company of Kingsley and Dorothy, some of the leading Indonesian politicians; and he found Dorothy sympathetic when she heard his account of the underwriters' dilemma. "She could have refused to help in any way," said Roy Merrett, one of the involved underwriters. "She could have said: 'Why should I, with my Socialist views, put myself out to assist the capitalist City of London in this venture?' She did nothing of the kind. She knew all the Nationalist leaders from the earliest days of the Indonesian Republic, though by 1958, when our delegation went out there to take up her introductions, they had lost some of their authority. Dr Sukarno[2] of course was still President, but I wasn't able to meet him until the thing was all over. But there was Mr Sabandrio, who had been the first Indonesian Ambassador to London, and his wife, who was in the Ministry of Health—both very close friends of Dorothy's. There was Madame Santoso in the Cabinet Office—of whom it was said that if she was against you, you stood little chance of succeeding in anything. Of course the man who eventually had to give the word for the release of the ships, once the Cabinet had agreed

[1] See p. 298.

[2] Ahmed Sukarno, President of the Republic of Indonesia: imprisoned three times by the Dutch when the country was the Dutch East Indies; appointed by the Japanese President of the Java Central Council; and first President, from 1945 onwards, of the new Indonesian Republic.

to it in principle, was Ahmed Sukarno, the President. He gave it, and the vessels put to sea—just one week before the period of four months was up."

Socialist or not, Dorothy would not be unmindful, in her concern for Indonesia, that there might be value in securing the interest of some well-to-do City men in the fortunes of that emerging country. It is a country of immense natural resources, and it lacks the ready money to develop them. At the same time the continuing, indeed the intensifying, interest of Dorothy and Kingsley in the Afro-Asian countries was assuming a character now separating them somewhat from the *New Statesman*. For ten or fifteen years there had been a feeling among the editorial staff, and it was especially the view of Paul Johnson, editor since 1965, that Kingsley was uncritically sympathetic to new political regimes which were sometimes sustained by horrifying cruelty. Paul Johnson likened it to the attitude of the old Social Democrats, to whom it seemed that the working classes, because they had been persecuted and exploited for so long, had somehow acquired a greater collective moral strength than any other class. If they could be put into power, they would behave in a significantly better manner than anyone had been seen to do before. In a curious way this also applied to religion. Kingsley, said his critics, felt that religion West of Suez was wicked or at best stupid, and that East of Suez it somehow became intellectually worthy of respect. "He would put up with all kinds of nonsense from Hindus and Buddhists," Paul Johnson would say, "which he would never tolerate from Protestant or Catholic Christians. East of Suez, somehow or other God was Left wing, and once you got West of Suez he was a right-wing reactionary. This was very deep in Kingsley's whole credo."

Paul Johnson was not alone in thinking that Kingsley and the paper misled readers about Far Eastern regimes, and for Paul this was particularly true about Indonesia. He saw the Sukarno regime as a horrible tyranny. "Yet for years," he said, "it was presented by Kingsley and Dorothy, but particularly Dorothy, as a great and noble democratic experiment. When I finally got to Indonesia I was horrified by what I found there." It should be said, in fairness to Kingsley and Dorothy, that they made no protest about the article in which Paul presented his findings, and both thought there was probably a good deal of truth in his criticisms.

An anti-imperialist guilt complex undoubtedly coloured Kingsley's attitude to the Afro-Asian leaders when he met them in person. It was sometimes an embarrassment to see his propitiatory behaviour, amounting almost to sycophancy, in the presence of men like Pandit Nehru and Jomo Kenyatta. It was a black law student who told me, with permissible exaggeration, that the one unquestioned passport to Kingsley's office was a black face; and this was the complaint of an African deploring that the *New Statesman* was hearing too much about the wrong side of the black side.

Kingsley's friendship for the Afro-Asian peoples was not entirely uncritical, however. He would say of some newly installed President or Prime Minister, who in the past might have been frequently seen at Great Turnstile, or by the villagers at Little Easton or Rodmell, "Of course he's a bloody-fingered murderer and some might say a thief as well, but what else do you think has shaped Western diplomacy in the past?" It was a terminological concession: Western diplomacy had always said *coup d'État* and frontier revision.

Anti-colonialism had played a big part in Kingsley's life, especially when it became an exciting reality after the second world war; but I am certain that in his last few years, having observed the ferocity and hate with which some of the emancipated peoples were killing and torturing each other, he had slightly modified the anger with which he once used words like imperialism and British Empire. He could never quite take the view sometimes found among educated black men, and typified in an article written in 1972 by Davidson Nicol, High Commissioner in London for Sierra Leone:[1]

> In my opinion, in spite of its human imperfections, the former British Empire has brought the concept of universal justice for the weak and oppressed closer to reality for more millions of human beings than any secular institution that the world has ever known.

[1] *The Listener*, 24 February 1972.

But whatever view he might have taken, and whatever his ambiguities as between one black school and another, the black people among his immense circle of friends took him as the man we all knew and some of us loved. He could not offend them. When Tom Driberg got married in 1951 and had his wedding reception on the Terrace at the House of Commons, Kingsley was among the guests. So was Seretse Khama, heir apparent to the chieftainship of what was then British Bechuanaland and is now the self-governing Republic of Botswana; and so was his English wife Ruth Williams, the daughter of a retired British Army officer. Seretse Khama's marriage had taken place in 1948 at a London Register Office because the Bishop of London, under pressure from the Colonial Office, had ordered that any question of a church wedding must be at least postponed; and there had been a great deal of fuss in the papers, as though this Balliol rugger blue, handsome and gifted by any standards, was staging a real-life abstract from *Othello* and *Beauty and the Beast*. When Tom Driberg introduced Kingsley to Ruth (now Lady) Khama, Kingsley said delightedly: "Ah, you're the nigger in the woodpile, aren't you?" At which monumental clanger it was the surrounding black men who roared with laughter and the white ones who grinned wanly and turned away.

Writing regularly in the late sixties for *The Illustrated Weekly of India* (where his "London Letter" could still, on occasion, rival the best weekly diaries in the world) he gave rein to his fears about racial prejudice in Britain and the coming role of the immigrant population as scapegoats in a fascist revival:

> Extreme groups of right-wing Tories,[1] many of whom are in fact, if not nominally, fascists, some even being apologists for the Nazi regime, see an opportunity of creating a fascist movement in this country in which coloured people would be regarded in much the same way as the Jews were in Germany. . . . The situation is in many ways favourable to those who desire an authoritarian regime. Many people resent the loss of Empire and feel that Britain is nationally humiliated. . . . There is an apathy, indeed one might say contempt, for all the political parties, a

[1] He may have meant the so-called National Front, which is a little hard on the Right-wing Tories.

> situation presenting an opportunity to a new class of demagogues. . . . There is considerable unemployment, readily attributable by thoughtless persons to coloured people taking the jobs of Englishmen.[1]

In a long memorandum which he circulated to some of his colleagues in July 1968, he said he expected the race issue to dominate British politics for years (though he profoundly hoped he was wrong), and proposed the formation of a consortium of newspaper publishers to settle an agreed policy. In particular he was concerned about proposals that immigrants be subjected to special directives as to where they must live. "What happens to the notion of an integrated society," he wanted to know, "if you can give orders to whole blocs of citizens and move them from place to place, and how do you provide them with work in the new places? . . . I think people who feel as we do ought to have some conference with the people who work at the racial problem. Can any consensus policy be reached in which the *New Statesman*, *The Guardian*, *Times*, *Tribune*, *Observer*, *Sunday Times*, *Daily Mirror*—even the *News of the World*—could agree? Maybe the best way would be for the *New Statesman* to take a lead?"

This proposal was not adopted. Already, indeed, there were scores of groups and societies concerned with racial integration, plus an articulate body of Asiatic immigrants who pleaded that what they wanted was not so much integration as the right to be let alone. Kingsley would not have been able, in any event, to carry editorial policy to the point, which he himself had now reached, of urging that all immigration should (for the time being at least) be stopped. This had led him into some sad quarrels with old friends, at a time when what he needed was a tranquil mind, some passive conversation and a little chess. It had started two years before when, to his great distress, he quarrelled with Vicky, the cartoonist, for whom he (like everyone else) cherished a warm affection.

Vicky[2] was born (as a Hungarian citizen) in Berlin. He

[1] Kingsley Martin, "The Colour Problem", *The Illustrated Weekly of India*, 12 May 1968.

[2] Victor Weisz, cartoonist for the *Evening Standard*, *New Statesman*, *News Chronicle*, and *Daily Mirror*.

left there, already an established political cartoonist, in 1935. As a teenager he had seen the bestial cruelties inflicted by the Nazis upon Jewish and other racial minorities in Germany. For him the ultimate crime was the persecution of innocent people for belonging to the wrong race or creed; any proposal that reminded him of it was simply not bearable. In fact the world became too horrifying for Vicky, who took his own life in 1966 and was said to have considered himself a "failure". By this he meant, I do believe, that the wit and poignancy and the savage irony of his superb cartoons had seemed to him, over the years, to change nothing. People nodded, smiled, even passed the paper round for others to read or smile at; and then nothing. (Do the best of cartoonists ever change anything? Does the most brilliant war reporting ever change anything?) Vicky drew for the *New Statesman* under Kingsley for twelve years, beginning in 1954; and he did it for a fee that hardly paid his taxi fares. Every Monday midday, when this shy little man peeped round the edge of the editorial door, and then came in with the assortment of huge drawings from which the week's cartoon would be selected, was for Kingsley a high spot of the week. Whatever was happening at that moment, everything stopped for Vicky, who stood back watching with childish anxiety as his drawings were compared. Not even the sourest misanthrope could have helped loving Vicky. To quarrel with him was some kind of achievement; and Kingsley did it only by adopting, with whatever reluctance and in face of anxious opposition from some of his colleagues, the view that unrestrained immigration from the Commonwealth would create a serious race problem in Britain and thus erect platforms for racist demagogues. He genuinely feared that it would come to serve, in Britain, the same purpose as the Jews had served in Nazi Germany.

Racialism and nationalism, Kingsley had long ago decided, were founded on superstition. They might just possibly have been prevented, or beneficently canalised, by the Christian church. In the thirteenth century, he used to point out, all Europe was of one faith. Thereafter the proliferation of Protestant sects hastened the destruction of Christianity as a unifying force, and there began the deadly business of killing, burning and torturing people for going to the wrong church or for believing that the sun went round the earth. If one may judge from the letters and memoranda he had collected and arranged, it looks as though Kingsley would have given much space in his projected third volume to Humanism and Ethics. Long though he had forsaken all religious belief he retained to the end of his life a religious temperament. Like Albert Camus he rejected both Christianity and Marxism, ending his life still searching for a third faith better than either. In a BBC radio talk in 1953[1] he had said:

> I believe in the supreme virtue of exploring. I believe in finding out. Even if I don't succeed, I still believe in the value of the search. The goal is better human relationships and more human happiness. Pursuing this adventure, I find myself in a goodly company of men and women both alive and dead; our friendships are cemented by failure and frustration, but our search is now and again rewarded by the occasional creation of some new beauty of form or the perception of some new aspect of truth. One hears it go "click" like the latch of a door when one finds the right key. It is this click of friendship, of knowledge, and of art in which I believe.

He wrote countless articles about Humanism without once saying more clearly than that what Humanist ethics meant to him. With his studies of Voltaire and the Encyclopedists he had imbibed the hope that, as religious belief declined, so would human intolerance, hatred, torture, massacre, and armour-plated apathy. When the measureless cruelties of the second World War convinced him that this was not going to happen, he could say no more, wretchedly, than that one must "enquire".

Among the assumptions that had died in the post-war cultural crisis of the Western world, said Dr George Steiner in 1971,[2] was the assumption that knowledge and humanism lead to humane social conduct. "Men who administered the 'final solution' in Eastern Europe were avid connoisseurs, and in some instances performers, of Bach and Mozart," said Dr

[1] "This I Believe", 19 March 1953.
[2] T. S. Eliot BBC Memorial Lecture, *The Times*, 3 April 1971.

Steiner. Kingsley nevertheless held that the pursuit of good must still be worth while, because he believed that there *could* be found a sufficient well of goodness within man himself —"I can see no reason whatever, and no advantage whatever, in making out a God". As an old man he saw no evidence to disprove what seemed to him the probability that all forms of life were the product of pure chance, through unpredictable mutation and Darwinian selection; therefore one could not accept any system, religious or other, that assumed a master plan of creation. But he had what seemed to some of his intimates a rigidly earthbound concept of "chance". Might there be an "advantage in making out a God" if one looked at "chance" as a tremendous conception involving a God whose design *must* eventually prevail, on the principle that a succession of monkeys and typewriters must eventually produce the works of Shakespeare? I once heard him brush aside that familiar theme as comic, pseudo-Shavian and irritating.

His dismissal of "design" as having any place in the Universe was not always confident, and sometimes transcendentalism would, like something almost cheerful, insist on breaking in. For example when he was in America for the 1945 San Francisco Conference he went with Bob Boothby to see the Colorado Grand Canyon. Looking down into it he said he "rather *felt* there must be a creative intelligence", and they had a long discussion about it, which continued during their train journey and convinced Bob Boothby that Kingsley had a fundamentally religious temperament. (Incidentally he had wanted to take mules and go down into the Canyon, but his companion thought this would spoil all the magic. Kingsley always preferred descending mountains and running down slopes to climbing them; and the preference was imaginatively traced by some of his familiars to the fact that his undergraduate friend Joseph Fryer had fallen to his death in the Austrian Alps while they were on holiday together in 1921.)[1]

A fascinating *New Statesman* correspondence touched off on 3rd April 1943 by Mr R. A. Edwards, the Rector of Dartington, had never strayed far from Kingsley's conscious memory. He

[1] See *Father Figures*, pp. 109–10.

had kept a great number of the letters and clearly intended to draw copiously upon them in his next book.

The Rector's letter, Kingsley decided, offered a serious challenge to the *New Statesman* way of thinking:

> In our agnosticism he sees a spiritual emptiness making way for a totalitarian state and the submergence of the individual with whose full development both he and I are concerned. I, on the other hand, see at some removes behind his friendly criticism the shadow of authoritarian clericalism, the return to established ignorance and sanctified superstition. If he foresees the guillotine, I smell faggots. . . . When the rector suggests that in some way we should gain security against Fascism by a revival of Christian theology in the schools, I can only stand astonished. Where in Europe during the period of Fascist growth has orthodox Christianity in the schools proved a bulwark against the corruption of youth?[1]

The correspondence shows that, in the view of a persuasive minority, this was not an answer to the Rector of Dartington, whose article appeared under the heading "An Open Letter". It told Kingsley that there must be some reason why the agnostic *New Statesman* was always "on the right side", and that it was worth looking for:

> In the Spanish Civil War you supported the Republicans; but you did not do it because you liked the Republicans, or had family connections with them, or because you considered them models of what a political party should be, or even, I think, because you thought they would govern Spain in an exemplary manner and give it everything that so long-suffering a country ought to have. You did it just because you thundering well thought it was right to do it. . . . A glance through almost any issue finds you energetically championing a cause not because of its expedience in the circumstances of the moment, or for any of the lamentable reasons that draw the politicians to its support, but because it conforms with your absolute idea of what is right. . . . That is an essentially religious attitude, and indeed I have often thought of you as our leading religious newspaper.

[1] Kingsley Martin, "Ethics Without Religion", *New Statesman*, 3 April 1943.

> What worries me about it is that, so far as I can make out, you haven't the smallest idea of why you believe in your good cause. What is the absolute principle to which you refer before you choose your side? . . . As a matter of historical fact you are the inheritor of a view of life that has come to you through Christianity, and I should not be at all surprised to learn that you, like the great majority of English left wing thinkers, came to your social problems from a religious background. The causes you uphold depend upon that view of life; the virtues you approve are religious virtues, and ultimately they depend upon a belief in God.

And the gist of this, and of other letters from the crowd who joined in, was that while people like Kingsley were all right—"you can't get the Christianity out of your skin"—a subsequent generation had been taught the virtues minus the religion. "They are the prey of any specious philosopher who sets up a graven image of pragmatic efficiency."

Kingsley published a letter from his sister Peggy (Margaret Barclay),[1] a child psychotherapist who was at that time running a progressive school in Epsom. "Man is in dire need of spiritual anchorage," she wrote, "a faith whereby he may test his actions and plan his life. At the same time we are unable to believe in a personal Deity or to accept the theology of the Christian churches." (In fact, she later joined the Roman Catholic Church herself, a shock to Kingsley which for some time he found totally inexpressible. However, when he recovered he wrote her a very nice and understanding letter.) "Probably our acceptance of the Sermon on the Mount as a way of life is sufficient for us who have had a religious upbringing," Peggy continued, "but what of our children?"

> To many people of my generation the New Psychology came as a glorious release. No longer did we have to put a moral value on anything. Children were not good or bad; they were either free or inhibited. All one had to do, as an educator, was to provide the right environment for growth, allow scope for free expression; and the child would grow up a rational, happy being, able to get the best out of life as a balanced individual and give his best to

[1] *New Statesman and Nation*, 22 May 1943.

> society as a mature citizen. Many progressive schools are now coming to the standpoint that this simply does not work. . . . When my five-year-old daughter says to me "Is God Jesus' father?" and I try to explain as simply as I can the nature of God to me, she is not a little puzzled. A father is something she can understand; and the idea of an all-powerful, loving Father is a comforting one in a world where one's own father is in the army and the sirens shriek in the night. Is one to deny one's children this because one's own intellect will not admit it, or is one to teach orthodox Christianity not believing it fully, in the hope that the child will grow up to challenge what he has been taught? Or is there, perhaps, a third course open to us, whereby the coming generation may have a religion embracing the "absolute" without theological trappings which many of us cannot accept?

There is one anonymous letter on which Kingsley has scribbled: "Is this really to be taken seriously?" It concludes:

> Let us suppose this civilisation fails to use its freedom to carry out the wishes of God. Then there will be another civilisation, and it may not be on this planet or in our galaxy. If that fails there will be others. There may be myriads. Chance is not on our side: it is on God's, and for him chance is an eventual and cosmic certainty.

And his old friend Lionel Fielden wrote, from retirement in Italy:

> I am not a Catholic: I don't think I am a Protestant, but I certainly as an average human being do *hope* there may be, in the Universe, a power somewhat nobler and more intelligent than the appalling freaks who "govern" us. . . . If you argue that miracles are impossible because the scientists say so then you also must logically and finally assert yourself as a disbeliever in Christianity. Perhaps you are right. Perhaps all the churchgoings and the funerals and the baptisms are mumbo-jumbo—very well, say so! But the odd thing is that, when it pleases you, you do in fact appeal to "Christian principles". Can you have your cake and eat it?

People who, in his last few months, talked to Kingsley with the intimacy of old friends found that he was very frightened of death. He simply could not come to terms with it, and would sometimes talk of it obsessively. Unusual perhaps, in a convinced Humanist, but it became touchingly usual in Kingsley. And it is interesting to compare what he said about the ceremonies that followed the deaths of three of his closest friends—Gerald Barry, David Low, Maynard Keynes. For Gerald Barry there was a memorial service in St Paul's Cathedral. On the way out, as people moved slowly through the smaller West doors by which their progress is confined to a seemly shuffle, Kingsley was heard saying loudly "How *can* people believe in such utter nonsense?" Among those who believed in the nonsense, no one seems to have told him. . . . For David Low there was a memorial meeting at Friends' House, Euston Road, which Kingsley in his address as the principal speaker quaintly called "an unconsecrated place". He said approvingly that "Our friend David was an agnostic and would have thought it humbug to have a church service". But most interesting and revealing of all was what he had said in his London Diary[1] about the Westminster Abbey Memorial Service for Maynard Keynes the "staunch rationalist". I reproduce it in full:

> I suppose only a minute percentage of those present actually accepted in any simple sense[2] the doctrines and beliefs embodied in the words of the hymns and prayers in which they joined. Certainly Keynes, a staunch rationalist, would not have done so. And yet none of us would have been willing to forego the service or felt inclined to criticise the words. They were singularly well chosen. They were all familiar. And it was because they were familiar that they meant much, so much more than their superficial content. Rationalism has argued the Church out of existence, yet not dethroned it, mainly I think because although men no longer believe in the Judaic God whom they evoke, they do demand on the great occasions of life—birth, marriage, death and festival—a ceremony to satisfy their emotions and to celebrate the occasion in community. Tradition cannot be invented, nor can consciously devised ceremonial take the place of words whose associations are so much more important than their surface meanings. Witness the pathetic efforts of Positivism to substitute intelligent hero-worship for the traditional mythology of

[1] 11 May 1946.

[2] A phrase that went unexplained.

> Christianity. Take the items at the Keynes Memorial Service: "The King of Love my Shepherd is . . .". What astonishing assumptions that hymn implies! And yet imagine trying to write one that would say as much even to people who do not believe in one of them! The same may be said for the Psalm "Lord who shall dwell in thy tabernacle?", for the hymn "O God our help in ages past", and for the apt and lovely collect "O God the physician of men and nations, the restorer of the years that have been destroyed. . . ." There are fewer reservations to make about "Let us now praise famous men", about Walford Davies's exquisite anthem "God be in my head" or about Blake's "Jerusalem". A memorial to Keynes could not end better than with the words "I will not cease from mental fight . . .".

Those were not the thoughts of a man who had told himself, glancing at the clock at midday on a Wednesday, "I suppose I'd better do a paragraph about Maynard's memorial service." And they require no analysis at my hands, or anybody's.

Among his mass of papers there are two letters, separated by 33 years, which mark his Odyssey from failure to achievement. The first is one that he wrote to Maynard Keynes on 24th April 1933 and the second is one he received from Dr G. P. Gooch on 28th February 1966. "I am extremely grateful," he wrote to Keynes, "for your frank, friendly and abusive letter." (I have searched in vain for the letter, but the description fits almost any in his Keynes collection.) "As to defeatism, you are perfectly right: it's corroding, harmful and cumulative. I've tried to keep it out of the paper but it's in the whole atmosphere:

> I am bitterly disappointed with my failure to give the paper a more constructive and crusading meaning.

And the letter from G. P. Gooch, who died four months before Kingsley at the age of 95 and had edited the *Contemporary Review* for 50 years, said this:

> You have fulfilled yourself as I have had the good fortune to do, and I feel that that is the greatest happiness that any human being can achieve.

It was signed, in enormous handwriting, "George Gooch, 92".

What had Kingsley wanted to achieve, what recognition would have seemed fitting to a man of whom, in any week, a quarter of a million *New Statesman* readers could say *si monumentum requiris, circumspice*? He didn't, at any rate, want the Knighthood offered to him by Harold Wilson in May 1965. "I much appreciate your kindness in proposing that I should become a Knight", he wrote to the Prime Minister:

> I hope you will not take it amiss if I do not accept. I should hate to be a Knight. And if I were one, I should not even have the satisfaction of being able to do a better job for the Party or for any other cause I have at heart. It would merely look as if I were permanently on the shelf, whereas I have in fact recovered my health and am full of beans.

In fact he thought the offer of a Knighthood was rather a mean way of "paying him off". A Knighthood gave you no influence, it bracketed you with the Civil Servants who were automatically given Knighthoods at a certain point. It was (he said in a television interview in 1968) the Government's way of saying: "Well, you've been on our side and we want to recognise you, and here's to hell with you." And he added: "I was rather offended by this, honestly. I'm simply amazed at people wanting to be Knights. It's quite different from being knighted for some particular service, like Gerald Barry who was knighted for the extremely and wonderfully successful production of the Festival of Britain; that's an honour given for a particular reason. But this was just out of the blue. To accept it I thought would be ridiculous."

At that time he would have rather liked a life peerage, as is implied in his phrase about Knighthood's not even offering "the satisfaction of being able to do a better job for the party". He had discussed with Leonard Woolf what he would do if he were offered a peerage, and Woolf had told him that socialists who took peerages were contemptible. But on 1st May 1963 he wrote to Woolf:

> When I was asked not long ago whether I would be a life peer if requested, I took your view and emphatically said I would not. But I do not necessarily feel contempt for people who do accept. And

when Barbara Wootton, for whom neither of us feels contempt, accepted,[1] it occurred to me that she might be right and you might be wrong. Does that seem to you impossible?

A number of peers would have liked him in the House of Lords, where he was well known and had many friends. Strings, in fact, were pulled, an aspect of the Honours Lists that always amused him. (There is in his papers a typed memo about a conversation in 1952 with Clement Attlee, then Leader of the Opposition. It records that Harold J. Laski, according to Attlee, "did not romance for personal advantage, but did it to amuse." Laski had obviously been saying that he had declined a peerage, but Kingsley's note says: "C. fills out information about H.J.'s peerage by saying not only that he did not offer H.J. a job and a peerage, but that H.J. wrote asking for it, and that he refused.") However, Kingsley thought that in his own case it had all been left rather late, and in the course of 1968 and his failing health the idea lost all its attraction for him. It had never attracted Dorothy, who could not have shared his title without marrying him and for whom, I suppose, a title would have been the last reason on earth, at least ostensibly, for marrying anyone.

One unfulfilled ambition formed the subject of an article written (but not I think published) in 1968. It was called "The Book I have Not Yet Written". "A journalist needs to be more alive than other people," he wrote, "but he can never be alive enough to create anything. One could count good books written by journalists on the fingers of one hand, and even then they have written them either before they became journalists or after they had retired.[2] If you write for the day, you may have many unfilled hours, plenty of time as they say for your own writing. But the tempo of your mind, haunted by the next job and conditioned by the habit of writing for immediate consumption, means that nothing you write will be either recollected or created in tranquillity. I had written a couple of substantial books before journalism swallowed me up at the

[1] In 1958.

[2] It would have been nice to argue this with him, having first looked up, say, fifty of the famous authors and playwrights who were journalists for many years before becoming "creative" writers.

age of 33." He went on to say how the praise bestowed by the historians on his *Triumph of Lord Palmerston* had turned his head, so that he "foolishly" imagined he could "write any number of books which would throw fresh light on some aspect of Victorian thought. . . . I had managed this book in nine months; why not a library of important books about the Victorian period every two years or so?" In the Crimean War,

> events were decided not by the facts but by the image of them created by a popular Minister and by the Press. I hoped in the book I did not write but always intended to write, to show that historians have often been led astray by analysing documents and discussing the motives of statesmen. . . . You might find that the Chartist March had little to do with the Chartists and much to do with French events in the same year; and that the excitement about the Reform Bill was less due to Francis Place or other Benthamites, or even William IV, than to a hangover from the French Revolution of 1789. In short, my book, if I had ever written it, would have ended History as we know it and compelled all the historians to begin work again.

In Chapter 1 of this book I mentioned some of the roles he had once wishfully foreseen for himself: history don, philosopher, national newspaper editor, actor, "television personality", etc. Less specifically, he had two heroes—a great contemporary and a figure from the classical past, Shaw and Socrates. In a draft for his next book he wrote:

> I would rather have lived Bernard Shaw's life, I think, than that of any man I've ever met. He has had, always, such infinite gusto, such tremendous vitality, and he lived most of his life in a period when it was possible to believe that the job of exposing hypocrisy and upsetting convention was clearing the way for a world in which there would be less hypocrisy and more true morality.
>
> The key to Shaw is to understand that he is a religious genius; intensely moral, a Puritan who admires John Bunyan more than Shakespeare and whose Socialism is part of his religion.

And at the end of a long recorded interview for Granada Television in 1968, he said this:

> I believe it's possible to build up a society which, by tradition and habit, is good and in which the people are happy. To my mind the only sensible reason for believing in God is that you believe in the brotherhood of man. If people behaved like brothers we would be happier. I could go through all the ethics of Christ in that way, showing that they had a practical, realistic basis. . . . And it isn't only Christ. The man I admire more still in history is Socrates. Socrates is my favourite figure, my Christ figure if you like. He could honestly explain why people should love one another.

As Janet Adam Smith once said, religion in Kingsley's life played the same kind of part as the monarchy—it was a nagging interest. And he always allowed that, for others, it might sometimes be better than psychoanalysis, which he had come to regard with cynical amusement. (He once told me that at the end of a three months' course of analysis he had found that it was the analyst who was feeling better, while he himself felt a bit worse.)

In his last few years his loneliness and dependency, though not surprising in so gregarious a man, were pathetic. Old friends who made a point of calling on him regularly at Carlisle Mansions found him more often than not alone: Dorothy was at the India Office Library newly installed in Blackfriars Road, she was at a meeting, she was abroad, she was staying with friends in the country in order to write, rejoining Kingsley at Rodmell for week-ends. The specially welcome friends were those who could play chess—Vicky, Ben Hooberman (a director of the paper), A. J. P. Taylor (who often got him out to the Savile Club for an evening meal and some good talk). I have a letter from Verity's daughter—Verity came to see him sometimes and was still, at the end of the day, the woman who securely held his more romantic devotion. Her daughter did not know of her mother's real relationship with him until after his death, but had known him for years. "I saw Kingsley seldom," she wrote, "and then mainly after his retirement, when he was an old man."

> I was still a student. Once I invited him to my college and we sat talking in the Common Room for a long time—far longer than

> I expected. I was taken aback; because I still expected that his personality would have some force. It didn't. He seemed lost, rejected and in need of company. He gave the impression that he had failed in life. Although he didn't say so directly, of course, somehow he conveyed it by the way he kept admitting uncertainty. He seemed not to know what he thought or where he stood. He would sigh and look in a sort of guilty way out of the corners of his eyes. I felt sad. And yet somehow he couldn't conceal his basic open-mindedness (though I got the impression that he regarded this as rather sinful at his age). He didn't pretend to know about anything that he did not know about[1]—my work, for example; and he listened without interrupting. I felt it was this lack of pretence that made it possible for him to have friends regardless of their age. He made one feel, too, that his own knowledge and great experience in a world I knew nothing about were no barrier to our friendship and understanding.
>
> Once after his illness he took me out to dinner before we spent the evening together. He was "out of things", and seemed to look forward to our evening with an almost childish excitement. When it came to the meal he scrutinised the menu and said "How about scampi?"; and when I responded enthusiastically he muttered: "They seem rather expensive—I think we'll have soup." At the end, I almost wanted to pay for the meal myself! But somehow this didn't spoil the occasion; Kingsley seemed oblivious to his unusual behaviour—and oblivious to the food too.

Behind that "I think we'll have soup" lay an incurable failure to recognise that little girls and even nieces grow up. (Verity's daughter was by this time in her mid-twenties.) Boys grew up, but less interestingly. When Kingsley wrote to his nieces they remained permanently at about eight years old, but the presents he brought them from his foreign travels showed more signs (probably under Dorothy's guidance) of keeping pace with events. One of his nieces, Mrs Brigit Morton, wrote to me:

> I was a very shy child and "Uncle King" would just about paralyse me. He had no idea how to get to know me. . . . We

[1] This was one of his sterling characteristics: I never heard him make the smallest pretence to knowledge for which he had no backing. I have heard distinguished academics say, by no means unkindly, that he was "essentially not a scholar". But he had scholarship's two greatest *desiderata*: respect for knowledge in others and a Socratic love of enquiry.

> several times had holidays with him at the cottage in Dunmow, but I don't think he noticed I was there. He gave a wonderful party at his flat in Buckingham Street to watch the fireworks celebrating V.E. Day, but he was usually too involved with his work to bother much with the family. . . . When he was getting older and frail I was able to cope with him, answer him back and tease him, which of course he liked.

Yet, given a chance, he could make contact. To another niece, Mrs Gillian Parsons, he was a "glamorous uncle", treating a child as a mature individual, asking for her opinions and ideas; and nonetheless providing Christmas highlights in the way of family visits to the Players' Theatre—where the compère would greet Dorothy with "Not that old fur again, dear?" or some such provocation, Kingsley and Dorothy shouting back some hurriedly improvised abuse, to the delicious embarrassment of the children. "Kingsley was really a very warm and affectionate person, and because he was famous perhaps we failed to realise how much he wanted our affection in return. Perhaps if we had shown our appreciation . . . he would not have been so easily hurt and offended, which became even more apparent after he retired from the *New Statesman*."

But if he now seemed sensitive, rather lonely, and sometimes sad, he could also be courageous and resilient. Sometimes in those last months, when people asked if he was feeling better, he almost shouted "Me? I'm in rude health!", exerting what must have been a huge effort to be cheerful and make the best of himself. On his 70th birthday he and Dorothy gave a party at Carlisle Mansions—"to mark this melancholy event", as he wrote on the invitation cards. Surrounded by old friends from the world of the *New Statesman* (and sitting most of the time) he was as happy as I have ever seen him; and I hope I have not understated his capacity for infectious happiness. Dorothy said the next morning that it would "do him good to have a 70th birthday party once a month".

The shadows were lengthening. In the autumn of 1968 he had delivered a course of lectures at the University of Sussex, which was conveniently accessible from his Rodmell cottage. Both he and Dorothy were acutely apprehensive about these lectures, and his typewritten notes and scribblings show that, whatever may have been thought about their delivery, they were meticulously prepared. They were, alas, badly delivered and not well attended; for he was a sick man, addressing a predominantly student audience about dead institutions like the League of Nations and the forgotten personalities who had shaped them. It was at the end of the last of these lectures that he collapsed and was taken to hospital by ambulance—to the annoyance of Dorothy, who was reading in the University library and felt that she should have been told earlier what was going on. It proved not to be another coronary thrombosis, and he was about again in a few days. But it was in fact the "new complaint" to which he had referred in his letter to Nikki[1] and which attacked without warning. It was plain that he was not well enough to make the trip to India which he had been eagerly planning for some months; and the substituted stay in Cairo, where he was also to do some lecturing, set the scene for his death.

He was staying with Apa Pant, the Indian Ambassador to Egypt, and on 10th February 1969 he had a slight stroke (his second). He was taken to the Anglo-American Hospital and for a few days seemed to be recovering. "It will be fine if I don't lose my speech," he whispered to Dorothy. But on Sunday 16th February he had a further heart attack and died at 9 p.m. without recovering consciousness.

"I gave him all I could, and he gave me what I needed most, love AND independence," wrote Dorothy in a poignantly revealing letter to Verity.

> We did not have secrets. I've loved others, and always we were frank; and several times the three of us have had moments of such harmony that could only come of complete trust and frankness. For me, there is only one shadow, and I've often wanted to say it but never had any chance. Perhaps women can't communicate, though I think we could have done. The shadow is your sorrow. I have felt it, I feel it, and I shall always have the kind of love for you that I felt when we met years ago. But my life is to wander now in fields where you have never wandered. Kingsley has been reborn in me—any Buddhist understands this

[1] P. 350.

extraordinary phenomenon. I am a pagan. I do not believe in any supernatural existence. I gave Kingsley's body to Arab doctors, as I would have given it to Israel, Mexican, Negro or American doctors, for medical research as he and I wanted. But he is with me all the time, and I have a blissful new release of energy to do his work as well as my own as well as I can. This phenomenon I believe to be the result of months of agony which I did not share with anyone. And then I found strength in myself, and he was here with me.

I do not mourn him. He would not have been able to speak properly, nor to walk, nor to write. He *dreaded* helplessness above all. One day he asked me where it would be less difficult to find his body—in London or at Hilltop.[1] He was feeling very ill, dreading another stroke (1st December), and clearly meant to end life himself if he were made helpless. Great courage, great common sense; and how true to his humanism. . . . You were Cambridge to him, and he never ceased to look back with anguish and love on those days. . . . We had no secrets, though details were of no importance and not even discussed. Nor should they be. . . . Sometimes, especially on the Downs, we used to say to each other "How *can* we have found such happiness?" And after 32 years that happiness was still miraculously extending every day, though Kingsley was a very, very sick man. Life was a great struggle for him for the past five years. . . . You and I are lucky to have loved him.

Yours always, Dorothy.

She survived him by only nineteen months. She returned from a week-end at Rodmell with some young Burmese friends on Tuesday, 29th September 1970, and almost as soon as she had climbed the many stairs to the flat at Carlisle Mansions she collapsed and died. If one hesitates to use the "broken heart" imagery, it can safely be said that the mainspring of her life had gone. She had much work to do in furtherance of their joint ideals, but her health had broken up and she did well to finish her *magnum opus*, *Himalayan Frontiers*. When she wrote to me on 21st September 1970, authorising me to attempt this biography (while gently reaffirming that she could "never talk to anyone about the extraordinary happiness Kingsley and I shared during those 32 years"), she spoke of her own "illness

[1] The name of the Rodmell cottage.

and a heart attack" and said, "I'm terribly sorry this didn't arise when I was still in the blooming health I have always had before in my life."

Kingsley liked to recall Dean Inge's version of the Longfellow *Psalm of Life*:

> Lives of great men all remind us
> As we all their pages turn
> That we too may leave behind us
> Letters that we ought to burn.

He left unburned the thousands of letters and the barely legible diaries from which this book has been made. And this is the point at which to stop. The great advantage of writing history in the form of posthumous biography is that, unlike even the worst of historians, you know what happened in the end. For me, the process has called up the figure and presence of Kingsley Martin as vividly as if he now stood at my study door, in his shirtsleeves, saying impatiently in his Wednesday voice: "But what on *earth* are you writing—you've been 20 minutes?" His arm is outstretched towards me, his fingers are snapping, his heavy-lidded eyes have gone unusually circular—with agitation and astonishment. I seem to hand him the manuscript, which he almost snatches. But as soon as it is in his hand his face softens. Even without looking at it he nods at me several times with a wide and tight-lipped grin, looking again rather like Mr Punch; and he goes away. I wish he had not gone away.

INDEX

INDEX

by

Evelyn M. Edwards